British & European

BIRDS

in colour

British & European
BIRDS
in colour

text by Bertel Bruun

paintings by Arthur Singer

consultant editor Bruce Campbell

Paul Hamlyn
London·New York·Sydney·Toronto

The author and artist are grateful for the help and advice they have received from many ornithologists and would particularly like to thank Dean Amadon, Oliver L. Austin Jr., Jeffrey Boswall, John Bull, Erik Hansen, Max E. Hodge, Charles O'Brien, Allan O'Connell, Niels O. Preuss, Chandler S. Robbins, Ole Schelde, Peter Scott, José A. Valverde, Charles Vaurie, Sven Wahlberg, Herbert S. Zim and, of course, Bruce Campbell, whose detailed knowledge has been a great contribution to the book and who has assisted and advised most valuably in its preparation. The American Museum of Natural History supplied most of the skins for the artist.

This book is dedicated to our patient and understanding wives, Bobbie and Judy.

Published by
THE HAMLYN PUBLISHING GROUP LIMITED
LONDON/NEW YORK/SYDNEY/TORONTO
Hamlyn House, Feltham, Middlesex, England

© 1969 Golden Pleasure Books Limited
SBN 600 00456 2

Printed in Italy by Officine Grafiche A. Mondadori, Verona

Foreword

Birds know no frontiers, but it has taken birdwatchers some years to follow their example. Today a knowledge of European bird life is essential for the well-informed British or North American ornithologist; and some idea of its wealth and beauty adds enormously to the interest of exploring Britain or the Continent for anyone who simply enjoys looking at wild places and wild life.

Compared with the tropical profusion of South America and Africa, Europe has relatively few birds; but they are the best known and most studied in the world and, because of the great influence of man on their environment, their future poses some of the acutest problems of conservation. How many, for example, of the birds of prey depicted in this book will our children's children be able to see, free-flying over the hills and forests?

I know it is the hope of both author and artist that this book will do something to make public opinion more aware of the urgent need to save one category of Europe's treasures, as worthy of preservation as her great buildings and works of art. This sense of urgency has driven Bertel Bruun's pen and Arthur Singer's brush.

Bertel has travelled widely from his native Denmark to make first-hand observations on the majority of the species about which he writes with such authority; and Arthur has been equally devoted. I know from personal experience that on the job he is impervious to the worst the British climate can produce in the way of weather.

Their book is the most comprehensive to appear in English on the birds of Europe, for it even includes species recorded only in the USSR; and all vagrants and accidentals are listed. Five hundred and sixteen birds are described and portrayed in a way that will help to identify them in the field. In addition there is a spectacular series of habitat studies, which alone make the book worth possessing; so it is both a work of easy reference and something to enjoy permanently.

Bruce Campbell

Contents

Introduction

Birds have always attracted man by their variety, beauty and charm. The birds of Europe, though for the most part they do not have the exotic plumage and strange characteristics of their tropical cousins, are attractive, numerous and, in many cases, fascinating. In this book we describe and illustrate them, taking pains always to place them in the context of the avifauna of the whole world.

The illustrations show every species breeding or occurring regularly in Europe. Most birds which are less frequent visitors are also depicted. The captions to the illustrations give the common English name, the scientific name, total length, abundance, habitat and the characteristics important in the identification of each species. At the end of each caption, the status of the species in Great Britain and Ireland is given in abbreviated form: R means resident, S summer visitor, W winter visitor, P passage visitor, and V vagrant. On the illustrations, ♂ means male, ♀ means female, imm. means immature, and juv. means juvenile.

The text describes the orders, families and species of European birds, their life and behaviour, migration, food and general characteristics. Accidentals are listed on page 296. Distribution is given in the form of range maps beginning on page 298 for each species occurring regularly in Europe.

The boundaries of Europe are, from a zoogeographical point of view, artificial and dissatisfactory. Europe is part of the Palearctic region, which encompasses Europe, Africa north of the Sahara, and Asia north of the Himalayas. In the north and west the oceans form a natural boundary for Europe as well as for the Palearctic region. But it is interesting to note that a large part of the Greenland avifauna is of Palearctic origin, as is shown by the many species of Greenland birds migrating to or through Europe each year.

In the south the Mediterranean forms the boundary of Europe but the Sahara forms that of the Palearctic region. As would be expected, all the Mediterranean countries share a large number of species. The Sahara, the Mediterranean and the large mountain chains of southern Europe, which all run from west to east, form an effective barrier which has prevented the influx into Europe of tropical families. (By way of contrast, in North America the barriers run north-south and the fauna contains many tropical elements.) Further east the Caucasus forms a fairly natural southern boundary for Europe.

Most ill-defined is the eastern limit set for our continent, the Ural River and Mountains. These features form no natural barrier at all and the fauna and flora of Asia flow unhindered into Europe, indicating the true nature of our continent: that of a peninsula of the much larger Asiatic land-mass.

The climate of Europe varies from the arctic climate of the islands in the Arctic Sea, through the tundra of the northernmost part of the continent, the vast temperate zone stretching south, to the subtropical climate of the Mediterranean countries. The temperate zone is divided into two large areas with rather different climates: the coastal climate of westernmost Europe with rather warm winters and cool, wet summers; and the continental climate of central and eastern Europe with very cold winters and hot, dry summers. Europe is the only continent besides Antarctica which does not include tropical regions, and this particularly accounts for the rather poor variety in our avifauna.

The natural distribution of vegetation in Europe has been greatly altered by many factors. The map shows the vegetation zones as they would have been without man's influence. The great belt of deciduous (broadleaf) forest has been turned into a vast agricultural steppe. The slopes of the Mediterranean countries are in many places bare, erosion having destroyed large tracts where man and goats through the centuries have ruined the protective vegetation. But the distribution of the natural vegetation is still reflected in the distribution of many of our birds.

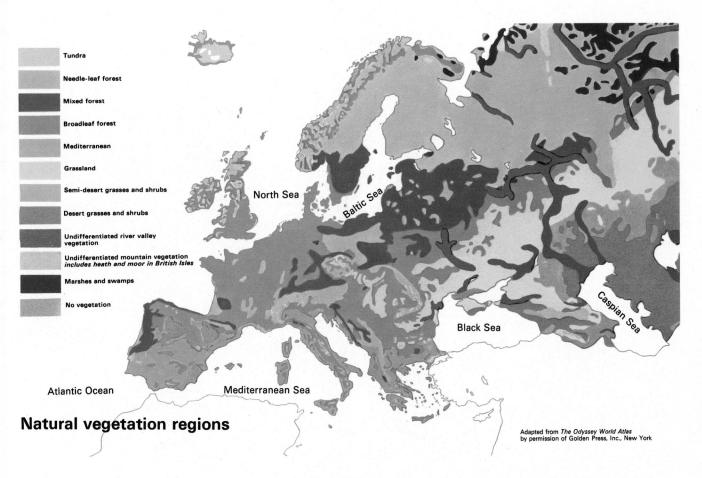

Tundra

Needle-leaf forest

Mixed forest

Broadleaf forest

Mediterranean

Grassland

Semi-desert grasses and shrubs

Desert grasses and shrubs

Undifferentiated river valley vegetation

Undifferentiated mountain vegetation includes heath and moor in British Isles

Marshes and swamps

No vegetation

North Sea

Baltic Sea

Caspian Sea

Black Sea

Atlantic Ocean

Mediterranean Sea

Natural vegetation regions

Adapted from *The Odyssey World Atlas* by permission of Golden Press, Inc., New York

The glacial periods, during which northern Europe was covered by an enormous ice-cap, had a profound influence on the fauna and flora. As the ice started to retreat after the last Ice Age more than 20,000 years ago, plants and animals penetrated northward and westward. This spread has not yet stopped; many birds are still extending their range towards the northwest, a development which has probably been accelerated by the amelioration of the climate in the first half of this century.

The birds of Europe are probably better studied and their life-histories better known than those of any other continent. On the other hand we still have very much to learn, and the continual changes caused by the vagaries of climate and even more by the influence of man, demand constant alertness and intensification of the study of our birds. The latest danger to our already impoverished avifauna is the widespread use of insecticides. We hope this can be checked before it is too late. To do this and to prevent future disasters a strong conservation policy is essential.

Divers

order *Gaviiformes*, family *Gaviidae*

Opposite Great Northern Divers

BLACK-THROATED DIVER *Gavia arctica* L 25" W 47"
Common. Breeds on deep lakes, usually in secluded places in mountains or tundras. In winter along sea-shores, sometimes in small, loose flocks with Red-throated Diver. In summer, black throat and light grey crown are diagnostic. In winter, back is grey with scaly white spots visible only at close range. Bill thin and straight, proportionately more slender than Great Northern's. In flight told from Red-throated by shorter up-stroke of wings. Call on breeding grounds is low wailing cry; in flight utters rapid quack like Red-throated Diver's.
RW

RED-THROATED DIVER *Gavia stellata* L 22" W 44"
Common in breeding range on fresh and salt water; winters mainly along the coast, often in company with Black-throated Divers. Often migrates in small flocks. Much slimmer than Black-throated Diver and thin, light-coloured bill slightly more upturned. Habitually holds head and bill pointing slightly upward. In summer, red throat diagnostic. Winter colour is lighter than Black-throated Diver, with tiny white spots on back. Usual call a rapid quacking.
RWP

There are only four species of divers, all indigenous to the northern part of the northern hemisphere and all occurring in Europe. They form a homogeneous group of expert diving birds, in many ways perfectly adapted to a life in and on the water. Their bodies are long and streamlined with powerful webbed feet set far back. Their specific gravity is closer to that of water than the specific gravity of most other birds, the majority of which have pneumatic (air-filled) bones. This makes it possible for the divers to submerge slowly without attracting attention. Under water they exhibit an elegance and speed unsurpassed by any birds except perhaps the penguins, and they constitute a formidable enemy to the small fish they pursue. The long pointed bill is the expert tool with which they grasp the unfortunate prey. Their specialization for a life in the water is, like all specialization, bought at a price. Elegant as the divers are in their native element, on land they are correspondingly clumsy and helpless. They can only push themselves along slowly and laboriously, and they avoid this undignified mode of locomotion (and the attendant danger) except when nesting.

Their nests are crude depressions in the low vegetation by the edge of a lake, pool or stream. It is at nesting time, in the bright nights of the north, that their yodel-like wails echo through the hills. The young which emerge from the two brown eggs immediately take to the water where they are to spend most of their lives. While they are small, they are fed by their parents, who may do most of their fishing on salt water nearby, and they often ride on the back of one of the adult

Black-throated Diver   winter   summer

Red-throated Diver   winter   summer

birds, finding protection and comfort among the warm feathers and down.

When the young are fully grown, the family leaves the inland lake and heads south to the winter quarters, which are usually offshore. The adults now lose their colourful summer plumage with the bright speckled backs and strongly marked necks and attain their winter plumage which is battleship-grey or dark above, white below.

Even though their wings are short and pointed, divers are good flyers, able to maintain a considerable speed once they are airborne. To rise from the water they are obliged to patter along the surface for varying distances depending on the wind direction and velocity, and they cannot take off from land. The flight silhouette is characteristic with the long neck stretched out, the head held lower than the body.

The two smaller species, the Black-throated and the Red-throated, are quite common in winter along the coasts of western Europe and in larger ice-free lakes and rivers. The Great Northern Diver is scarce except off the British coasts and the very similar White-billed Diver is very rare; both are found almost exclusively along the Atlantic coast. The Black-

GREAT NORTHERN DIVER *Gavia immer* L 30″ W 58″
Rare except on breeding grounds on inland lakes in Iceland. Otherwise along seashores. Although varying in size, it is considerably larger than Red-throated and Black-throated Divers, with a proportionately much heavier, straight bill. Colours in winter resemble those of Black-throated Diver. In summer all-black head and back with bands of white spots are characteristic. Flight heavy, almost goose-like. Calls in breeding season include loud wail and yodelling; quacks in flight like other divers.   W

Great Northern Diver   winter

summer

White-billed Diver   winter

summer

WHITE-BILLED DIVER *Gavia adamsii* L 30″ W 60″
Rare along seashores. The largest diver, almost identical to Great Northern but with light-coloured, slightly upturned bill. In summer plumage, head is slightly darker and white spots on back slightly larger and fewer than Great Northern Diver's. Both species have similar calls.
V

throated Diver shows an interesting pattern of migration. In autumn the birds nesting in northern Russia fly south along the large interior rivers to the wintering grounds in south-eastern Europe, but in spring, when the rivers of Russia are still covered with ice, they travel north along the western streams to reach the Baltic. There they change course to reach their breeding grounds via the Baltic Sea and the vast circle of their migration terminates on one of the thousands of lakes in the Russian taiga.

Grebes
order *Podicipediformes*, family *Podicipedidae*

The grebes resemble the divers in many respects, but in spite of this superficial similarity, the two families are not closely related; they illustrate parallel evolution in an adjustment to similar conditions in and on the water.

Grebes have lobed feet—flaps of strong skin on either side of each toe—rather than the webbed feet of the divers and most other swimming birds. In Europe this peculiar anatomical feature is shared only with the phalaropes and the coots. There are eighteen species of grebes, five of which breed in Europe. They are medium-sized birds with long, slender necks and very short tails. All are expert divers. Almost exclusively found in freshwater lakes and ponds in summer, most resort to saltwater bays and lagoons in winter. The bulk of their food is made up of aquatic insects, with a good proportion of fish. In pursuit of their prey they are able to stay under water for up to one minute but usually take less time to catch it.

GREAT CRESTED GREBE *Podiceps cristatus* L 18″ Common in lakes and sheltered bays with reed cover. In winter also along shores. Sometimes breeds colonially; often encountered in small flocks in winter. Largest of our grebes, best told by long, straight neck. In winter loses prominent ear tufts and can be confused with Red-necked Grebe, but notice greyer back, longer neck, longer pink bill. The mutual display includes diving for waterweed and standing breast to breast on the water.
R

courtship display

winter   **Great Crested Grebe**   summer

winter   **Red-necked Grebe**   summer

RED-NECKED GREBE *Podiceps grisegena* L 17″ W 32″ Common in marshy lakes and ponds; in winter mainly on salt water, scarce on inland water. In summer unmistakable. In winter, can be confused with Great Crested, but notice shorter neck, shorter black and yellow bill. Dark wing always has two white patches, like Great Crested Grebe, but forward patch (shoulder) much less pronounced. Sharp call note: 'kell-kell'; squealing note in breeding season.
W

In breeding plumage most grebes are adorned with tufts and have brightly coloured heads and necks. Their display is picturesque and in spring they are a great attraction for the observer of behaviour who watches them performing graceful bows and inclinations to each other on the open water. The Great Crested Grebe in particular has evolved a display which has become almost a symbol of springtime. The mates approach each other, their necks stretched low over the water; when they meet they raise their bodies to a vertical position, breasts touching and tufts magnificently displayed. Many other less spectacular ceremonies are performed, making the watching of these birds a thrilling experience.

Both male and female build the nest, which usually floats freely on the water, anchored only to a few stems. The three to six eggs are white when laid, but soon become tinged with brown from the wet, rotting nest material. Like many other birds, grebes cover their eggs when leaving the nest. Although this serves a practical purpose in hiding and protecting the eggs, the behaviour is purely instinctive. The striped young spend much of their first month of life riding on the backs of the parents. As one parent submerges, the chicks stay afloat and immediately head for the other parent, crawling up on to the drier and safer position of its back.

Horned or Slavonian Grebe

winter

summer

winter

summer

Black-necked Grebe

HORNED OR SLAVONIAN GREBE *Podiceps auritus* L 14″ W 23″. Uncommon. In summer almost exclusively found in inland lakes; in winter on sheltered sea coasts, scarce inland. In summer unmistakable. In winter told from Black-necked by pure white front and neck, and straight bill. Seems heavier than Black-necked Grebe. Rippling trill in breeding season. RWP

BLACK-NECKED GREBE *Podiceps caspicus* L 12″ W 23″ Sometimes common in lakes with heavily reed-fringed shores where it nests in colonies. In winter found along seashores and in larger ice-free lakes. In summer plumage, black neck diagnostic. In winter similar to Slavonian Grebe, but has greyer neck and slim, slightly upturned bill. At a distance, straighter neck helpful as field mark. Usually forms small flocks in winter, while Slavonian is seen singly. Rippling call and other notes in breeding season. RWP

LITTLE GREBE *Podiceps ruficollis* L 10″ Common in lakes with dense vegetation. In winter also found along rivers, in harbours and other sheltered places, singly or in small parties. Very elusive. Rather uniform brownish plumage characteristic in all seasons. Takes to the wing more readily than other grebes. No wing patch. In spring utters characteristic, far-reaching, whickering trill. RW

By late autumn the chicks have lost their downy plumage and attained the plain winter plumage with dark grey upper side and white underside characteristic of the adults. By this time they are able to fly, but grebes are even more reluctant to take to the air than divers. The flight silhouette is similar to a diver's but most species show a fairly distinct wing-band.

The Great Crested Grebe is the largest of the European grebes and has a preference for large lakes with plenty of open water. Normally solitary, it forms large colonies in some countries. The Red-necked, which is a little smaller and more heavily built, prefers more secluded places for nesting. The Eared or Black-necked Grebe usually nests in colonies while the Slavonian or Horned Grebe may be social or solitary. The Slavonian and Black-necked Grebes are similar in size and are difficult to tell apart in winter. The Little Grebe or Dabchick is the pygmy of the family. It is a discreet shade of brown and lives secretively among the dense vegetation of ponds and lakes. It has a distinct, trilling call very different from the variety of shrill wails and yells characteristic of its larger relatives.

Little Grebe

winter

summer

imm.

partly submerged

Tubenoses
order *Procellariiformes*

This order of highly pelagic birds is divided into four families: albatrosses, storm petrels, shearwaters and diving petrels. Although tubenoses are found primarily in the southern hemisphere, representatives of all but the diving petrels can be encountered off European shores. Only one albatross, the Black-browed, occurs almost regularly. The order's name reflects the unique characteristic of the order: the nostrils extend on top of the bill through two horny tubes. The function

imm.

Black-browed Albatross

BLACK-BROWED ALBATROSS *Diomedea mela-nophris* L 31″ W 7′ Very rare, but the most likely of the albatross species to be met in Europe. Enormous size is distinctive. General coloration of adult shared with even rarer Yellow-nosed and Grey-headed Albatrosses, but yellow bill and dark streak through the eye are diagnostic features of this species. Immatures have dark grey crowns and blackish bills. Most often encountered in the summer months. ⱽ

and benefit of this arrangement are not fully understood, but it is believed that the oil secreted in the stomach reaches the bill via the nostrils. This then makes the oil available for the bird to waterproof its feathers. The secretion of this stomach oil, which can be regurgitated, is another characteristic shared by all members of the order. Combined with half-digested food, it serves as a nutrient for the single young, and in some species it is used as a defence mechanism. The Fulmar is able to aim and eject foul-smelling oil a distance of several feet, which is quite repulsive to human and other predators. Even the chick inside the egg is able to spit oil through the pipped shell.

Tubenoses are exclusively oceanic in habit; they are true and unchallenged masters of the air. By far the largest part of their life is spent aloft, some even sleeping on the wing. They all take advantage of the wind currents found among the waves. Albatrosses and shearwaters are capable of covering long distances without a wing-beat, just tilting and wheeling to take full advantage of the momentum they gain among the endless succession of waves. The storm petrels, on the other hand, flutter in bat-like fashion a few inches above the surface.

Tubenoses only come to land to nest. They all nest colonially, some of the colonies being of enormous size. They all lay a single egg, the smaller species in burrows, the larger ones in the open. On the breeding grounds most of the smaller species are nocturnal, while the larger ones are diurnal.

The young of most species have an extraordinarily long fledging period and in many cases they are abandoned by the parents for the latter part of it. Having a large amount of fat deposited subcutaneously, the young are able to survive this period of starvation and even fulfil the development of their powerful wings. One night, when ready, they will make their way to the sea and take flight over the vast expanse of the ocean.

Among seafaring men many legends have evolved around these little known inhabitants of the oceans and the appearance of the birds close to the ship has been taken as an ill omen of storms to come.

Albatrosses
order *Procellariiformes*, family *Diomedeidae*

These giant tubenoses, unsurpassed masters of the ocean winds, are primarily confined to the southern hemisphere. The calm stretches across the Equator form an almost insurmountable barrier and only under favourable wind conditions are individuals able to cross to the North Atlantic, so dependent are they on strong winds for their gliding flight. The species which most commonly crosses to our parts of the ocean is the Black-browed Albatross. One of these stragglers associated itself with the Gannets nesting on the Faeroe Islands and remained with them in their annual cycle of breeding, migration and wintering for thirty-four years, from 1860 to 1894, when it was shot. To the Faeroese it was 'Sula konungur' or 'King of Gannets'. In 1967 another appeared among the Gannets on the Bass Rock off the east coast of Scotland.

FULMAR *Fulmarus glacialis* L 18" W 42" A large gull-like tubenose. In its light colour phase (the most numerous) it can be told from gulls by the stiff flight, the habit of flapping and gliding, the heavy head and neck, the shorter tail, and, at close range, by the tubular nostrils. Dark phase birds are paler than Sooty Shearwaters, have shorter wings and a broader tail. Fulmars follow ships, often over long distances. When swimming, the bird floats high on the water.   RS

dark phase

Fulmar

light phase

light phase

20

Shearwaters

order *Procellariiformes,* family *Procellariidae*

Although inferior in aerial performance to the albatrosses, the shearwaters too are remarkable for their sustained flight, and among the fifty-three species in the world are found some of the greatest travellers on earth. Only six species occur off the European coasts and only three, Manx Shearwater, Cory's Shearwater and the Fulmar, are found nesting on our shores. Excepting the Fulmar, they form a rather homogeneous group. The wings are long and held stiffly outstretched, lacking the angle of the gull wing. Most are dark above, light below. The wing-beats are fast, but they are able to cover great distances with the help only of the air currents formed above the waves. They are so dependent on the wind that the occurrence of complete calm can have disastrous effects, as the birds are 'grounded' until it begins to blow again.

Sooty and Great Shearwaters breed in the southern hemisphere, the Sooty having a wide range, while the Great nests exclusively on the Tristan da Cunha group of islands in the South Atlantic. In the southern autumn (our spring) they move north through almost the whole length of the Atlantic Ocean, large concentrations being met with as far north as Greenland. The Cape Pigeon, common in the southern seas, is only a rare straggler to our shores.

Shearwaters live on small fish, squids and plankton which they pick up on or near the surface. They sometimes dive, but never deeply. The Great Shearwater is known also to follow whales, probably taking advantage of the turmoil in the surface waters

MANX SHEARWATER *Puffinus puffinus* L 14″ W 32″ Most common and numerous European shearwater. Completely dark upper side and light underside and small size distinguish it from the larger shearwaters. A subspecies with darker underside and less distinctive contrast is found in the Mediterranean. Flight rapid, tilting from side to side. Does not follow ships but gathers in large 'rafts' on sea. Nests in colonies along shores. SP

LITTLE SHEARWATER *Procellaria baroli* L 11″ Very rare visitor to European coasts north to Denmark, particularly in late spring. Closely resembles Manx Shearwater but has more white in front of eye, and some have dark under tail-coverts. Flight very rapid, with fluttering wing-beats between short spells of gliding. If direct comparison with Manx is possible, smaller size should be evident. V

west Mediterranean subspecies

Manx

Manx Shearwater

baroli subspecies

boydi subspecies

Little Shearwater

GREAT SHEARWATER *Puffinus gravis* L 19″ W 45″
A large, fairly common Atlantic shearwater, breeding November to April in the Tristan da Cunha Islands. Black cap and white on tail are pronounced. In May and June migrates north to the western Atlantic and in October and November south through eastern Atlantic. Told from Cory's by distinctive black cap bordered with white.   S

produced by these large mammals. Some, like the Fulmar, take refuse from trawlers and other boats, thus becoming habitual followers of ships. The importance of the feeding habit is clearly demonstrated in the case of the Fulmar. During the last century, when whaling was at its peak in the North Atlantic, large flocks of Fulmars fed on the refuse discarded from the whaling ships. As this once-thriving industry declined, trawling had an enormous upswing. This method of fishing, practised over a much larger area, made an increasing amount of offal

Great Shearwater

Cory's Shearwater

CORY'S SHEARWATER *Procellaria diomedea* L 19″ W 44″ Breeds in Mediterranean and north African islands, occurring from August to November in the North Atlantic. Largest of the Atlantic shearwaters. Some may have white upper tail-feathers resembling Great Shearwater, but always lacks the black-capped appearance. Flight slower, more albatross-like than that of other shearwaters. The only Atlantic shearwater to soar. Does not follow ships but trails schools of whales and dolphins.   P

available for the Fulmars. With explosive rapidity the Fulmar spread from its Arctic homeland over the northern North Atlantic. Thus St. Kilda of the Hebrides was the only British colony until 1877, while today the Fulmar is found in large numbers along almost the entire British and Irish coastline wherever suitable nesting places are available.

Like other tubenoses, shearwaters come to land only when it is time for nesting. Manx and Cory's both nest in burrows, while the Fulmar prefers ledges on open cliffs. The first two species are nocturnal in their habits on the breeding grounds. As dusk approaches thousands of Manx Shearwaters assemble on the water off the colony, busying themselves preening and washing. A couple of hours after sunset they fly to the nesting holes, either to relieve their incubating mates, or to feed the hungry chicks in the dark but sheltered burrows.

The fledging period of the young is long, varying from forty-eight days in the Fulmar to about eighty days in Cory's Shearwater. In the last part of the fledging period, usually for

SOOTY SHEARWATER *Puffinus griseus* L 16″ W 43″ Less numerous than Great Shearwater; occurs in Atlantic from July to February, but most common August to November. More confined to coastal waters than most shearwaters. Easily recognised by large size and uniform brown colour, with lighter stripe on underside of wing. Wing-beats faster than those of Great Shearwater, with which it often occurs.   P

Sooty Shearwater

Cape Pigeon

CAPE PIGEON *Daption capensis* L 14″ Very rare visitor to the Atlantic coast from southern oceans where it is common. Looks and behaves like a heavy shearwater. Contrasting white and dark areas on upper side, especially two round spots on wings, are quite diagnostic.

one to two weeks, the young one is deserted by its parents. It is unable to fly, but is very fat. This is the time when men on the breeding islands collect the young for food. This harvesting led to a great tragedy on the Faeroe Islands in the early 1930s when there was an outbreak of the disease ornithosis among the Fulmars collected for food. This disease also attacks humans, and more than thirty inhabitants of these small islands succumbed before the collecting of Fulmars was stopped and with it the epidemic.

Storm Petrels

order *Procellariiformes*, family *Hydrobatidae*

The name 'petrel' is said to refer to St. Peter who walked on the water. This is an indication of a habit of these birds: they fly a few inches above the grey, constantly moving surface of the ocean with their feet hanging down and paddling, giving the impression of walking upon the rolling surface.

Petrels are small, and they do not have the stiff wings of the other tubenoses. Their flight is fluttering, bat-like, with constant twists and turns but always low enough to protect them from the full impact of the winds blowing a few feet above the crests of the waves. When the direction suddenly changes and the wind blows unobstructed along the troughs between the rollers, petrels have no protection and find themselves at the mercy of the wind they so elegantly mastered before. In such cases they may be driven to shore and sometimes far inland with disastrous results, as they are as helpless on land as land-lubbers at sea.

Petrels live mainly on plankton which they pick neatly from

WILSON'S PETREL *Oceanites oceanicus* L 7″ W 16″
May be seen well out in the Atlantic, particularly from August to December when it is returning to its breeding grounds in the South Atlantic. Dark brown with white rump, light wing patch, long legs, and yellow feet. The tail is rounded. Dances on the surface with wings held high. Will often follow ships in loose flocks. Best told from Storm Petrel by slightly larger size, more square tail, light underside of feet, and slightly lighter upper side of wing; from Leach's Petrel by square tail.   V

Wilson's Petrel

Leach's Petrel

LEACH'S PETREL *Oceanodroma leucorhoa* L 8″ W 19″ Medium-sized, dark, with prominent white rump and grey wing patch. The tail is forked, feet are dark. Leach's is larger than Storm Petrel and is best told from this and from Wilson's Petrel by its forked tail. The flight is butterfly-like, quite different from that of Wilson's. Does not patter like Wilson's and some of the other storm petrels. The bill is noticeably heavier than that of the Storm Petrel. Does not follow ships. Sometimes blown inland after westerly gales.   S

the surface, but they are also able to dive and take larger prey like small fish and crustaceans. They will also take refuse thrown overboard from fishing boats and trawlers.

Of the twenty-two species roaming the seas, only two, the Storm Petrel and Leach's Petrel, nest within our boundaries. Wilson's Petrel is a regular visitor from its southern breeding grounds, and Bulwer's Petrel, which is classified in the *Procellariidae*, a rare straggler from the mid-Atlantic islands. The migration of Wilson's Petrel from its South Atlantic breeding ground is spectacular, not only in its extent but also for the number of birds performing this figure-of-eight traverse of the Atlantic. Wilson's Petrel is believed to be the most numerous bird in the world and certainly has to be reckoned in millions. In the southern autumn they leave their nesting areas, slowly moving north to the Equator along the American coastline where in July they can be counted in thousands from the fishing boats and ships travelling this part of the ocean. By August they have reached the east side of the Atlantic and now start south in a direct line for the islands where they will lay their single eggs and raise their offspring.

The other petrels in the North Atlantic merely spread over a wide span of the sea in the winter, and do not perform any journey comparable in length to that of Wilson's Petrel.

Petrels nest in holes dug into the ground or in crevices in cliffs. In the daytime none are to be seen, but one or two hours after nightfall the colonies are teeming with life, each bird coming in from the sea to relieve its mate in the burrow of its duty on the egg or to feed the starving young. The birds are very noisy at this time as they flutter over the nest holes and their

STORM PETREL *Hydrobates pelagicus* L 6″ W 14″
The most common and widespread of our petrels, also the smallest. The tail is square, distinguishing it from Leach's Petrel. The undersides of the feet are dark, the back and upper side of wings darker than in both Wilson's and Leach's Petrel. The bill is very slim and weak. Flutters above the water like a bat. Follows ships. May be blown inland by storms.   S

Storm Petrel

Bulwer's Petrel

BULWER'S PETREL *Bulweria bulwerii* L 11″ (family *Procellariidae*) A very rare visitor along coasts from breeding grounds on Atlantic isles. Dark upper rump, uniform dark colour diagnostic. Has a rather long, wedge-shaped tail and short pinkish legs. The chin is slightly paler than the rest of the bird.   V

buzzing voices are a pleasant sound, completely unlike the hoarse croaks and wails of the shearwaters. They finally settle in front of the nest and shuffle into the burrow, and by putting one's ear to the ground, one can hear the subdued greetings and conversations as the mates meet in the dark. All our petrels are dark brown, almost black, and except for Bulwer's they all have a distinct white band around the tail, which is forked in Leach's, square in Wilson's and Storm Petrels, and wedge-shaped in Bulwer's. When travelling at sea, these small acrobats are well worth looking for and their elegance is a pleasure to observe.

Pelicans and Their Allies
order *Pelecaniformes*

Opposite White Pelicans and Avocets

Although differing greatly in looks, the six families in this order of water birds have certain anatomical peculiarities in common, justifying the systematic arrangement. From the tern-like tropic-birds roaming the tropical seas in graceful flight, to the clumsy pelicans and sombre-looking cormorants, the *Pelecaniformes* all share the unique structure of the foot. The hind-toe is bent forward and inward and connected with the other toes by webbing. All have a throat pouch, hardly visible

Cormorant

imm.

Continental form

Atlantic form (breeding)

Atlantic adult (non-breeding)

CORMORANT *Phalacrocorax carbo* L 36″ W up to 60″ Common. Usually found along seashores and in larger lakes and lagoons. Rarely very far from land. Distinguished from Shag and Pygmy Cormorant by much larger size, heavier build and white chin. The general colour is bluish black. In breeding plumage the white spot on the thighs is visible. Immatures are told from the other cormorants by the greater extent of white and yellow on underside. Often found in groups. Two subspecies which can be identified in the field occur. The Atlantic form *P.c. carbo*, which breeds on the Atlantic islands, Britain and in Norway, has black neck and nape, while the continental subspecies *P.c. sinensis* has almost pure white neck and nape in breeding plumage. The continental subspecies nests in colonies in trees, bushes, while the Atlantic subspecies prefers rocky cliffs. Like other cormorants it often sits on rocks or poles with half-extended wings. Fly in V-formations or lines. Usually silent, but on breeding grounds various guttural groans and moans can be heard. RSW

in the snake-birds with their long, thin necks, but reaching a grotesque development in the pelicans. Most are primarily found in the tropics and subtropics; but the gannets and the cormorants are more widespread, reaching practically every seashore on earth.

Cormorants
order *Pelecaniformes*, family *Phalacrocoracidae*

This family is cosmopolitan in distribution and only three of its thirty species are indigenous to the European continent. These are the Cormorant, the Shag and the Pygmy Cormorant. The cormorants are large, black water birds with rather long, graduated tails and long, strong beaks, hooked at the tip. Excellent divers, they pursue under water the small fish found in

SHAG *Phalacrocorax aristotelis* L 25″ W 48″ Common, almost exclusively in salt water off rocky cliffs. Smaller than Cormorant, with more uniform blackish-green colour, lacking the white chin and thigh spot (latter only of value in breeding plumage, as is the crest). Bill and head are proportionally smaller than those of the Cormorant. In flight notice head of all cormorants is kept above the horizontal in contrast to the divers which are seen in the same habitat but fly with head held below the horizontal. When swimming and sitting, all cormorants hold the bill tilted slightly upwards. Immatures have light chin and breast but darker belly than immature Cormorants. Nests in colonies on rocky cliffs. Like the Cormorant, a rather silent bird.   R

PYGMY CORMORANT *Phalacrocorax pygmaeus* L 15″ Common. Usually prefers rivers, lagoons and freshwater lakes, often with trees and bushes on shores. Smaller than both other European cormorants, with distinctly thinner and shorter bill. In breeding plumage, head and neck are rich brownish black, body black with greenish iridescence and some white spots not present in other seasons. Immatures distinguished from immature Shag by more extensive light colour on underside, from Cormorant by smaller size. Nests colonially in trees or bushes in swamps, often with different kinds of herons. Told from ducks and grebes found in the same habitat by colour, from coots by long body and tail.

abundance along our shores. The hooked tip of the bill gives them a firm grip on their slippery prey. Having surfaced after a successful dive, they turn the fish round so that it can be swallowed head first, without danger from its spiked fins. While thus manipulating their prey, the cormorants are often harassed by gulls and other parasitic birds, which try to rob them of their meal. Although feeding almost exclusively on fish, cormorants are not in competition with man, as the species of fish eaten are not useful or palatable to us. They do some harm to nets, occasionally becoming entangled in the meshes, but this does not justify the persecution these birds suffer in many places.

The cormorants are predominantly sedentary. In the northern part of their range their winter distribution is directly dependent on conditions at their fishing grounds.

All cormorants breed in colonies, the Shag on rocks and ledges along exposed seashores, the Cormorant also in trees and beside freshwater lakes. The Pygmy Cormorant prefers fresh or brackish water with extensive reed-beds where it builds its nest among dense reeds or in low trees and bushes. Both the Cormorant and the Pygmy Cormorant often breed in mixed colonies with herons and egrets. In continental Europe colonies

Shag breeding

non-breeding

non-breeding

imm.

Pygmy Cormorant breeding

of Cormorants can number more than a thousand nests, but this number is minute compared to the masses congregating off the South American coast, where their guano is systematically utilized as fertilizer.

The two to six eggs are greenish-blue when laid, but are soon discoloured by dirt. When the young feed, they thrust their heads into the throat of the parent bird which regurgitates the contents of its stomach. Rare among birds is the adult Cormorant's habit of carrying water for the young in the throat pouch. When about fifty days old, the brown young leave the nest and join their parents on the fishing grounds offshore.

The texture of Cormorant feathers is rather loose, and to avoid getting soaked, they only spend a short time in the water. They are often seen perched on rocks and posts with wings spread out for drying. In the water they float low and are, like the divers and grebes, able to sink slowly below the surface by changing their specific gravity. Their broad wings give them good support in flight when they move along the shore or riverside in long lines or V-formations, and they are even able to soar.

Gannets

order *Pelecaniformes*, family *Sulidae*

This white, streamlined sea bird has adopted the same feeding habit as the terns. It is well suited for this manner of fishing: its long, pointed wings and long, wedge-shaped tail give it great power and manoeuvrability in flight; the streamlined body offers minimum resistance to air and water; and the strong, pointed bill forms a perfect tool for the task of grasping and

GANNET *Sula bassana* L 36″ W 68″ Common in summer near breeding islands, which are rocky with steep cliffs and used year after year. Winters on the ocean, often visible from shore, especially during strong westerly winds. Note double-ended 'cigar' silhouette. Dark wing-tips and white body identify adult. Immatures best told by size and shape. Feeds by diving from 50′ or more into the water or by swimming under water. In migration, flies just above the water, often in lines. Wing-beats rather stiff, alternately flaps and glides. When fishing it often soars. Brown colour of immature bird gradually disappears by maturity (about three years). Sometimes follows boats, especially off Scottish coasts. Easily told from gulls by characteristic silhouette.   RS

Gannet

adult

intermediate

juv.

holding the comparatively large fish it catches. With alternating flaps and glides the Gannet will examine the surface waters from a height of at least thirty feet. Spotting an unsuspecting fish, it will go into a dive of tremendous speed, hit the water with a splash and with a shallow trajectory, come upon its prey from below. Swallowing it on reaching the surface, the heavy bird immediately takes off again. Often Gannets fish in flocks, congregating over shoals of fish, and there is a continuous diving and splashing as they indulge in the excess of food.

Although there are nine species in this family, only the Gannet is found in the northern North Atlantic, the other members being confined to more southern waters. The Atlantic population consists of about 250,000 birds, of which about three-quarters are found in the European colonies, the largest (on St. Kilda) being between 30,000 and 40,000 nests.

Steep cliffs on rocky islands are the usual sites for the crowded nests, each with a single egg or young one. When the juvenile is about three months old, it is deserted and has to fend for itself. Two weeks later its down has been completely replaced by the dark 'pepper and salt' plumage of the first-winter bird, not to be completely replaced by the flashing white of the adult for three years.

A comparatively large proportion of first-year birds are migratory, working their way south to the African coast in September and October. The older birds only spread out over the vast expanse of the ocean in winter.

Pelicans
order *Pelecaniformes*, family *Pelecanidae*

According to Pliny, the Dalmatian Pelican nested in the western European river deltas; but this is not true today and both this species and the White Pelican are diminishing dangerously in numbers. All six existing species live primarily on fish. The two found in Europe scoop them up in their enormous bills, and at times flocks of pelicans will work together, forming a large circle in which the school of fish is trapped. The pouch of a pelican can hold up to three gallons, making it a perfect tool for fishing in quantity.

Both our species nest colonially in marshes or lagoons. The nest is built of reeds and the one to four eggs are incubated for about a month before the helpless young emerge. At first the young one is fed by the parent bird dripping regurgitated food into its bill. Later, when it grows stronger, it eagerly and aggressively thrusts head and bill deep into the pouch of the adult, until it looks as if the parent is about to swallow its own offspring. After about two months the juvenile can fly and is left to look for its own food.

Pelicans fly like herons, with the head drawn back and the neck in an S-shape. The wings are strong, the wing-beats slow and deliberate, alternating with glides. The heavy bird looks like a flying barrel. Pelicans often fly in lines low over the water, but near their nesting colonies may be seen soaring high up. Not infrequently they mix with cormorants, both for nesting and on the fishing grounds.

WHITE PELICAN *Pelecanus onocrotalus* L 65″ W 100″ A scarce species declining in numbers. In summer found mainly in swamps and marshes, in winter also along coasts, sheltered bays and river deltas. The two European pelicans are difficult to tell apart, but in adults the wing patterns are characteristic: only a little black above, but much black below in White Pelican; much black above, hardly any below in Dalmatian. White Pelican has, in breeding plumage, a rosy tint. Feet flesh-coloured, grey in Dalmatian. Juveniles are brownish and can only be distinguished by pointed end of feathers at edge of upper mandible, as opposed to almost square ending in Dalmatian. When swimming, pelicans float very high. Flight straight, a few deliberate wing strokes interrupted by gliding. Usually fly in lines. Sometimes soar at great height.

DALMATIAN PELICAN *Pelecanus crispus* L 65″ W 100″ Uncommon, nesting in marshes and lakes; in winter often also resorts to sheltered seashores. Distinguished from White Pelican by extent of black on upper wing, and lack of black on under wing, grey (not flesh-coloured) feet and, at very close range, yellow (not red) eyes and curly neck feathers. Immatures similar to White Pelican immatures, but distinguished by square or forked (not pointed) ending of frontal feathers at base of upper mandible. Like White Pelican, social in behaviour.

imm.
White

imm.
Dalmatian

Dalmatian

White

White Pelican

Dalmatian
Pelican

Herons and Their Allies
order *Ciconiiformes*

Of the seven families making up this order, representatives of four frequent our marshes and shores. Ranging in size from medium to large, they are all long-legged, long-necked and long-billed birds. They are well suited to the difficult task of catching fish without swimming and their long toes lend them sufficient support, even on the softest mud-flat. The sexes are similar in plumage. The wings are long and rounded. The three families not represented in Europe each contain only one species. They are the Boatbill, Whalehead and Hammerhead, all named for the peculiar shapes of their bills and heads.

Bittern

BITTERN *Botaurus stellaris* L 30" W 50" Rather common, but very elusive, in large reed-beds. Most active at dusk and night. Sometimes hides by freezing with head and bill pointed upward. Normal gait is crouching. Flight heron-like but low over the reed-beds. Nests singly among reeds. Distinguished from immature Night Heron by larger size, more yellowish-brown colour and lack of white spots on wing coverts and back; from much rarer American Bittern by barred upper side of wings without extensive black, lack of black 'whiskers'. The booming call, often heard at dusk in breeding season, has been compared to blowing in a bottle, or a distant foghorn, and may be heard for up to three miles.   RW

Opposite Grey Herons and Purple Heron

Herons and Bitterns
order *Ciconiiformes*, family *Ardeidae*

In the shallow water of the marsh the heron stands motionless, patiently waiting. Only the bird's eyes reveal that it is awake. Then with lightning speed the long, pointed bill is thrust into the water and its vigil is rewarded. The fish, caught between the dagger-like mandibles, tries desperately to free itself as the heron slowly manoeuvres it around and swallows it head first. The bulging of the thin neck indicates the progress of the fish through the gullet. When it has been swallowed completely, the heron prepares for another long wait.

Of the sixty-two members of this cosmopolitan family, only nine nest in Europe; one, the American Bittern, occurs as a rare straggler from the other side of the Atlantic.

The European representatives fall into two groups, the herons and the bitterns, the Night Heron being intermediate. Herons

33

AMERICAN BITTERN *Botaurus lentiginosus* L 26"
W 45" Very rare visitor to westernmost parts of Europe in
late autumn. Smaller than Bittern, with chestnut crown
and distinctive black 'whisker' marks. On the wing,
blackish flight feathers diagnostic. Like European
Bittern, almost exclusively found in dense reed-beds.
Less crepuscular than Bittern and more often seen
flying.   V

LITTLE BITTERN *Ixobrychus minutus* L 14" W 17"
Common, but very shy and elusive, in dense vegetation
of swamps and banks, with preference for larger reed-
beds. Once seen, easy to identify by size and coloration. In flight, large wing patch of buff contrasting with
black is diagnostic. Sometimes hides by freezing. To
escape danger, runs or climbs rather than flies. Flight
characteristic, with fast wing-beats and long glides,
usually for very short distances low over the reeds. Nests
singly amongst reeds and other dense vegetation, sometimes in bushes. Song is a deep croak repeated con-
tinually day and night.   P

are primarily diurnal in behaviour and are colonial nesters, while
the bitterns are to a large degree nocturnal and nest singly.
In spite of these differences, the anatomical similarities are many.
When flying they withdraw the head, the neck forming an S.
Thus their balance is maintained as, with long and strong wings,
they fly with dignity over marsh and shore.

The Grey Heron is the most widespread representative of the
family in Europe and also the biggest. Its food consists mainly of
fish, but frogs, salamanders, insects and voles are also taken. Not
infrequently a fieldmouse will find its way to the Grey Heron's
stomach. Other herons enjoy much the same diet but the Cattle
Egret has a preference for grasshoppers and other insects caught
on dry ground. Its name comes from its habit of following
cattle, which stir up insects hiding in the grass. In Africa, where
the Cattle Egret is abundant, it will often be seen riding on the
back of elephants and other large animals, descending from its
lofty post only when hunger calls.

Herons, including the Night Heron, nest in colonies; often
several species will nest together, and colonies may include
Cormorants, Spoonbills and Glossy Ibises. These mixed colonies
are usually found in extensive marshes where acres of reeds are
interspersed with an occasional clump of bushes. The nests are
placed in the bushes or among the reeds, the different species
varying somewhat in their choice. In north-western Europe,
where none of its closest relatives breed, the Grey Heron may
nest on sea cliffs and islands, but usually it nests in trees, often of
great height and sometimes close to colonies of Cormorants.

American Bittern

Little Bittern

juv.

adult

juv.

LITTLE EGRET *Egretta garzetta* L 24" W 38" Rather common, nesting colonially in swamps, river deltas and marshes with bushes to give support for the nest. Outside breeding season it can be met with in almost all sorts of shallow water, although it has some preference for salt and brackish marshes. Yellow feet are diagnostic. Distinguished from Cattle Egret and Squacco Heron by more 'heron-like' behaviour. Elongated scapulars (egrets) are only present in summer plumage as is the long crest. Although occasionally met with in flocks, it is less gregarious than the Cattle Egret. The Great White Heron is much larger with different bill and leg coloration and in flight the neck is held in a much more open S than is the case with the Little Egret.   V

GREAT WHITE HERON *Egretta alba* L 35" W 55" Rather scarce. Nests in reed-beds in swamps, deltas and lagoons; outside the breeding season also met with in other types of shallow water. Much larger than any other heron with white plumage. Yellowish bill and blackish legs and feet distinguish it from the much smaller Little Egret. In flight the neck is held in a more open curve and the wing-beats are much slower than is the case with the Little Egret. Like the Little Egret it has elongated scapulars (egrets) in summer plumage.   V

Herons lay three to seven greenish-blue eggs. They often perch in trees, both during the nesting season and when roosting.

The Bittern usually sites the pile of reeds making up its nest in the thickest and most remote part of a marsh. Here the female lays her four to seven olive-brown eggs. The Little Bittern also prefers solitude and builds its nest in similar situations, but occasionally chooses low bushes and trees as a base. Its five or six eggs are white in colour. The Little Bittern rarely flies, preferring to make its way through the jungle of reeds by climbing or hanging on to the stems of reeds and sedges.

Herons and bitterns feed their young by regurgitating the fish and other food caught. After about fifty days the young are ready to fly. They do not leave the nest until they are at least able to flutter along. At first they are very clumsy in flight, but they soon acquire the elegance and dignity of their parents. The

Little Egret

Great White Heron

winter

summer

young of the Little Bittern when only one to two weeks old start climbing the surrounding reeds, exploring every item within reach. At four weeks they can fly.

Young herons are restless creatures. Perhaps because of food shortage in the immediate vicinity of the colony, perhaps for reasons unknown to us, they may move long distances before the actual autumn migration, dispersing, as ringing has shown, hundreds of miles in all directions. In Iceland, where the Grey Heron does not breed, there is an influx each July. Other species sometimes scatter like this much further north than their normal range; for example, the Great White Heron, Little Egret, Squacco, Purple and Night Heron scatter as far as England and other more northern countries. It was erratic movements like these which brought the Cattle Egret across the Atlantic to America in this century, a crossing so successful that the species has not only settled there, but is expanding its range with explosive rapidity.

Below Top to bottom: Great White Heron, Squacco Herons and Little Egrets

SQUACCO HERON *Ardeola ralloides* L 18″ W 34″
Locally common in marshes, lagoons and swamps, where it nests in reeds or trees. Much more buffish in colour and stocky in appearance than other white herons, white wings and tail contrasting greatly with darkish body. In habits, closely related to the Night Heron. Often spends the day perched in the branches of a tree or bush, coming out to feed at dusk. Sociable in nesting and behaviour. Best told from Cattle Egret by bill coloration (red in breeding season, dark greenish outside breeding season) and much darker colours. V

CATTLE EGRET *Ardeola ibis* L 20″ W 37″ Nests mainly in bushes with other herons. Feeds on fields and dry marshes, usually in flocks and sometimes seen in association with cattle. Usually in much drier areas than other herons. Even at a long distance the Cattle Egret can be told from other herons by its white plumage, rather stocky build, characteristic flapping wing-beats and the loose flight formation of the flocks (no lines or V's). At closer range notice colour of bill and legs. Very erratic in its distribution. Can occasionally be met with all over Europe. V

Besides the travels described above, herons and bitterns all migrate to a varying degree, the more sturdy ones like the Grey Heron and the Bittern enduring the coldness of the winter as far north as Denmark and southern Sweden. The other species prefer warmer and more pleasant climates and travel to Africa and southernmost Europe, not returning to the breeding grounds until March. The American Bittern, the North American counterpart of our Bittern, which it resembles closely, sometimes manages to cross the Atlantic to the British Isles.

The Little Egret and the Great White Heron have declined drastically in numbers, mainly due to hunting. They are not eaten, but their beautiful elongated feathers, called 'aigrettes' or 'egrets', present only in the breeding season, are used in millinery. Only rigid protection can restore their numbers and this is at last being realized by governments in the countries concerned.

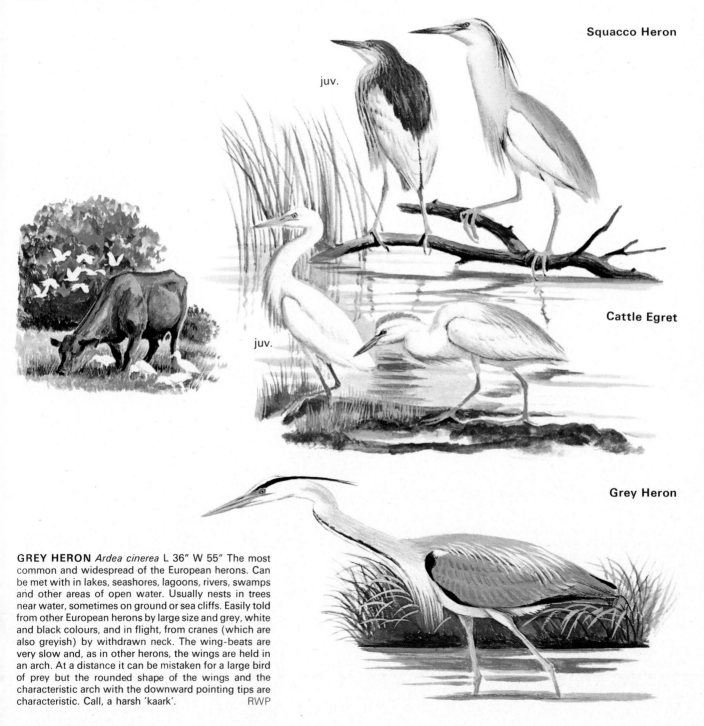

Squacco Heron

juv.

juv.

Cattle Egret

Grey Heron

GREY HERON *Ardea cinerea* L 36″ W 55″ The most common and widespread of the European herons. Can be met with in lakes, seashores, lagoons, rivers, swamps and other areas of open water. Usually nests in trees near water, sometimes on ground or sea cliffs. Easily told from other European herons by large size and grey, white and black colours, and in flight, from cranes (which are also greyish) by withdrawn neck. The wing-beats are very slow and, as in other herons, the wings are held in an arch. At a distance it can be mistaken for a large bird of prey but the rounded shape of the wings and the characteristic arch with the downward pointing tips are characteristic. Call, a harsh 'kaark'. RWP

Storks

order *Ciconiiformes*, family *Ciconiidae*

Familiar to every child, the White Stork is the more common of the two species breeding in Europe. Fifteen other species are found elsewhere in the world. The black and white plumage and the bright red bill and legs of our storks make them unmistakable. The White Stork is almost 'domesticated' and in many places associates closely with man, using his dwellings and protection during its breeding season.

Night Heron

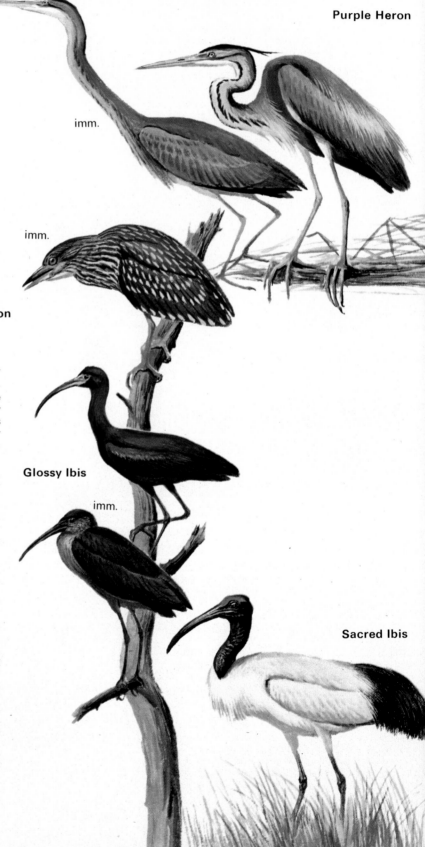

Purple Heron

imm.

imm.

Glossy Ibis

imm.

Sacred Ibis

PURPLE HERON *Ardea purpurea* L 31″ W 45″
Common in marshes and swamps. Prefers denser vegetation than does the Grey Heron. Reddish colours are diagnostic, but at a distance the Grey Heron looks very dark. In flight the neck is held in a more open S than is the case with the Grey Heron. More active than Grey Heron. Very big feet are also characteristic. Nests in colonies, often with other species of herons.   V

NIGHT HERON *Nycticorax nycticorax* L 24″ W 44″
Common in fresh and salt water marshes and swamps. Stockiness and black, grey and white colour pattern easily distinguish the adult bird. Immatures are told from Bittern by large white spots on wing coverts, in flight by faster wing-beats and less yellowish appearance. Night Herons often spend the day roosting in trees or bushes, but can also be seen feeding in the daylight hours, particularly early in the morning and at dusk. Often seen flying in lines. The call is a characteristic 'quock'.   P

GLOSSY IBIS *Plegadis falcinellus* L 22″ W 37″
Uncommon, usually found in marshes and on mud-flats. The curved bill and almost black appearance at a distance are diagnostic. Immatures have light undersides but do not even remotely resemble curlews. Breeds in colonies, usually in reeds, sometimes in trees. The flocks fly in long, undulating lines. In flight ibises hold their necks outstretched. Wing-beats rather fast and wings stiff. Immatures may be encountered outside the breeding range in September–October.   P

SACRED IBIS *Threskiornis aethiopicus* L 26″ Very rare visitor to the Caspian and eastern Black Sea regions from southern breeding grounds. White plumage with black tail and dark neck and head make this bird unmistakable.

The Black Stork, however, avoids contact with man, single pairs nesting in the densest of forests. Storks' nests are huge piles of twigs and branches. The White Stork places its nest on roof-tops, on platforms and cartwheels fixed to poles, on ruins and in trees. In the southern part of Europe it is mainly colonial, a single tree sometimes supporting as many as a dozen nests.

The four white eggs are incubated for about a month by both male and female. The young are fed on frogs, tadpoles, mice and other small animals caught in the marshes and fields

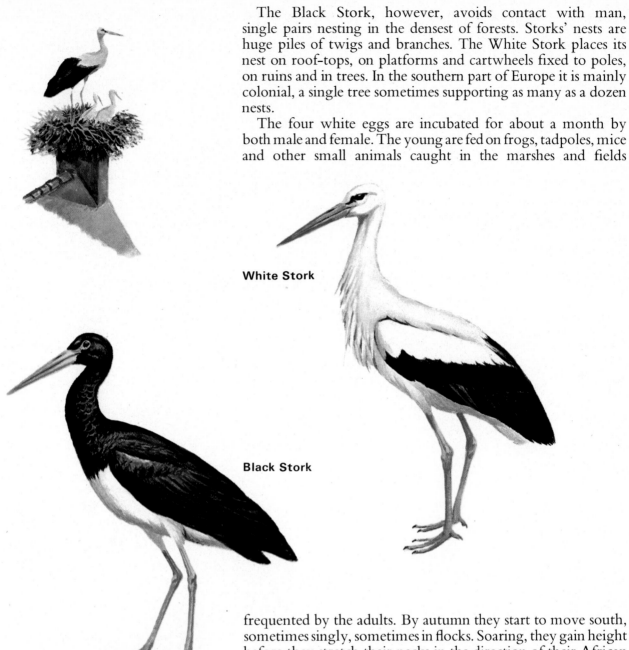

White Stork

Black Stork

WHITE STORK *Ciconia ciconia* L 40″ W 66″ Common, except in the northernmost parts of its range where it is declining in numbers. Prefers marshes, wet meadows and grassy plains. Nests near towns or farms, sometimes in colonies in trees, sometimes on specially erected constructions or on buildings. Usually rather tame and easily approached. Characteristic bird of the open farmland. Easily told from Black Stork by white upper parts. Flies with neck outstretched, sometimes soaring in loose flocks but also migrating in V-formation. Far more numerous than Black Stork. Usually silent, but bill-clattering is a characteristic feature of display. Gait is slow and deliberate.   V

BLACK STORK *Ciconia nigra* L 38″ W 62″ Uncommon. Prefers forests where it often frequents lakes, rivers and marshes surrounded by woods. Easily told from White Stork by glossy black plumage of upper parts. Much more shy and solitary in its behaviour than the White Stork. Nests in forest trees. During migration Black Storks usually fly singly or in small parties. Unlike the White Stork, the Black Stork has various coarse call notes and bill-clattering is less often heard.   V

frequented by the adults. By autumn they start to move south, sometimes singly, sometimes in flocks. Soaring, they gain height before they stretch their necks in the direction of their African winter homes. Two distinct travelling routes are recognized in Europe, the eastern birds flying across the Bosporus, bypassing the Mediterranean via the Middle East, and the western birds migrating over the Iberian peninsula before crossing the Straits of Gibraltar.

Flamingos
order *Ciconiiformes*, family *Phoenicopteridae*

While the Romans enjoyed the tongues of flamingos as a delicacy of the highest order, today we limit ourselves to enjoying the unfortunately all-too-rare sight of these bizarre birds. Of the four species, only one is found in Europe, with only two colonies, one in La Camargue and one in southern Spain. It formerly bred in other parts of Europe, for instance the Volga and Ural river deltas, whence it has now disappeared. Flamingos feed in salt or brackish water by skimming the surface with their decurved bills held upside-down. The two white eggs are laid in a cup-shaped depression on top of the conical heap of mud forming the nest. In autumn large flocks take off from their haunts along the Mediterranean for the lakes of the African interior. Flamingos are occasionally reported from different places in northern Europe but most are probably escapes from zoos or parks.

Ibises and Spoonbills
order *Ciconiiformes,* family *Threskiornithidae*

Two of these twenty-eight medium-sized species breed in Europe. These are the Glossy Ibis with its long, decurved bill and the Spoonbill with its straight, flat bill. While the Glossy Ibis feeds by probing its bill deep into the mud, the Spoonbill obtains its food by sweeping the half-open bill sideways in the surface water. Both nest in large reed-beds, the Glossy Ibis sometimes in low bushes and often in mixed colonies with Herons. Spoonbill colonies are usually separate from those of other species.

The Glossy Ibis is very erratic in its movements, the immature birds spreading over large areas in late summer and autumn before their migration to wintering grounds in tropical Africa. They often move about in flocks, flying in lines or V-formation. The Spoonbill is erratic in its distribution, its Dutch breeding colonies, for example, being several hundred miles from any others. It also migrates to the tropical parts of Africa in the winter.

The Sacred Ibis is a very rare visitor to Caspian and eastern Black Sea regions.

SPOONBILL *Platalea leucorodia* L 34" W 54"
Uncommon and scattered in its distribution. Found in shallow, open water, reedy marshes and lagoons. Nests in colonies in large reed-beds. Sometimes builds in trees and bushes. On the ground distinguished from white herons by the broad and very long bill. In flight the neck is held outstretched. Immature birds have black-tipped wings. Flocks usually fly in lines. The flight is regular with slow gliding and soaring movements.   SW

FLAMINGO *Phoenicopterus ruber* L 48" W 56"
Common within its very restricted range. Single individuals are occasionally met with all over Europe, but may have escaped from collections. Found on mud-flats and banks with shallow water, where usually seen in large flocks. Flies in scattered groups, sometimes in lines. Neck and legs are extremely long, bill thick and hooked. Feeds by skimming surface with bill held upside down. In flight, the long outstretched neck and legs droop slightly. Nests colonially on mud-flats.   ?V

Spoonbill

imm.

Flamingo

Waterfowl
order *Anseriformes*

This order of water-loving birds contains only two families; the screamers of South America, and the ducks, geese and swans of world-wide distribution. The two families share internal anatomical features but outwardly look very different. Only three species of screamers exist, all of which are goose-sized, long-legged marsh birds.

Swans, Geese and Ducks
order *Anseriformes,* family *Anatidae*

The Domestic Duck and Goose are both familiar members of this family and bear witness to the ancient and close relationship between man and waterfowl. The Domestic Duck is a descendant of the Mallard, but was probably not domesticated in the sense that we know it now until the Middle Ages, although it had been held in captivity centuries before. The 'Barn' Goose is a direct descendant of the Greylag Goose and was undoubtedly the first of the waterfowl to become an integral part of the household of man. Frescoes show that the Egyptians had Domestic Geese in 2000 BC. On these frescoes it can be seen that the slim shape of the wild goose had already changed to that of the fat, heavy bird we know today. In China domestication of the Mallard took place about the same time as in Europe, and may even have preceded it; long before this the giant Swan-goose was playing an important role in the domestic economy of the Chinese. In pre-Columbian days the South American Indians had their stocks of Muscovy Ducks, and by the time of Columbus' arrival different colour phases had already evolved.

The members of the family are distinguished by their webbed feet, rather short legs and very characteristic, short, flat bill with rows of small filtering plates along the edges. A thick layer of down covers the body, protected by the regular feathers which form a completely waterproof shell. Waterproofing is effected by the structure of the feathers, while the oil-glands are important in helping the birds to arrange their feathers so that the waterproof texture is maintained. The downy young have functioning oil-glands, enabling them to swim a few days after hatching. Although the oil from the oil-gland helps in maintaining the water-shedding structure of the feathers, experiments have shown that it is not essential for normal life.

Most waterfowl are good fliers, but their wings are small compared with their weight. They fly, therefore, with fast wing-beats (more than 300 per minute in several species), and many have difficulty in becoming airborne, a long and laborious run being necessary to give the heavy bird the required impetus.

They are all excellent swimmers, and when pressed, most are able to dive, even those which usually do not do so. On land they walk with a waddling movement, most pronounced in those species which are habitual divers. The legs are placed rather far to the rear and widely apart, especially in the diving species. This is of great advantage in underwater propulsion, but also accounts for their ungraceful carriage on land.

The family is divided into three subfamilies: the *Anserana-tinae,* which contains only one species, the Australian Magpie-goose; the *Anserinae,* tree ducks (not found in Europe), geese and swans; and the largest of the three, the *Anatinae,* ducks.

These subfamilies are further subdivided, but we shall only consider the European species here.

Three European swans form a homogeneous group of large white birds.

The geese are divided into the genus *Anser* (grey geese) and the genus *Branta*. The Greylag Goose is a typical representative of the genus *Anser,* of which five species breed in Europe (Greylag Goose, Bean Goose, Pink-footed Goose, White-fronted Goose and Lesser White-fronted Goose), while one, the Snow Goose, is a rare straggler from North America.

The genus *Branta* is represented by four species, of which the Brent Goose and the Barnacle Goose are the most common. The Red-breasted Goose is a wanderer from its Siberian haunts, while the Canada Goose has established itself as a breeding bird in some parts of Europe, due to escapes from parks and zoos, where the bird is popular.

More arbitrary (and chosen for reasons of identification and description) is the division of the ducks into four main groups.

The 'dabbling ducks', non-diving ducks of which the Mallard is the best known, are represented by seven native breeding species plus the two shelducks, which resemble them in their non-diving habits, four visitors, two of which are from North America, the other two from Asia, and one introduced species, the magnificent Mandarin Duck, originally a native of the Far Eastern swamps. The Egyptian Goose is a straggler from north Africa, and has also been introduced very locally.

The 'bay ducks' or 'small diving ducks', which prefer inland waters and sheltered coasts, are typically represented by the Tufted Duck. Five of these charming birds are indigenous to Europe. The White-headed Duck is also a small diving duck, but is in many respects an aberrant species. The two goldeneyes and the Harlequin Duck fall between this group and the 'sea ducks', larger diving ducks with a preference for deep water. This group contains five European breeders and two visitors, the Surf Scoter and Steller's Eider. The Eider is probably the best known of the sea ducks.

Finally our three species of merganser, with their long bodies and slender, serrated bills, form a homogeneous group. The Red-breasted Merganser is the most numerous of these elegant birds, which are so well adapted for their life as fishermen.

The habitat preference of the groups is most clearly seen in

MUTE SWAN *Cygnus olor* L 58" W 95" Most numerous and widespread of our swans. Nests along rivers and canals, on shores of small and larger lakes, occasionally in sheltered bays. In winter found on open water, usually in herds, and often along seashores, in sheltered bays. Mute Swans are often kept in a tame or semi-tame condition in parks. When swimming, holds its neck in a graceful S-curve, with bill pointed downwards; secondary wing feathers are often raised. Adult has orange-red bill with black knob. Dull rose bill of immature is black at base. Adult's voice is a low grunt, but cygnets are noisier. Wing-beats of flying birds produce a singing note. Sometimes mixes with other swans. Immatures told from immature Whooper and Bewick's Swans by dirty appearance of the plumage. The so-called Polish Swans are white as cygnets and in immature plumage.   R

Mute Swan

display

imm.

winter, when the sea ducks can be seen along exposed seashores, often quite far out, while lakes, ponds and lagoons shelter the more delicate bay ducks and a number of dabbling ducks. The latter are, however, found in their largest concentrations in swamps and marshes offering plenty of food on or near the surface of the water. The deeper lakes harbour both small diving ducks and mergansers, which are also often found in bays and lagoons where fish are plentiful.

Swans

Swans are the largest of our waterfowl. With their snow-white plumage and long, graceful necks they attract attention and admiration wherever they occur.

In former centuries swans were regarded as prize game, not only in England but also on the Continent, where for instance the Danish king organized great swan hunts at the time of year when these birds were moulting and therefore flightless. In England and many other western European countries, swans were kept in a semi-domesticated state, not for ornament as is the case today, but as a source of food. The English king granted 'royalties' to certain people, allowing them to own and mark swans. The unmarked swans on the River Thames belong to the crown.

This wholesale persecution of Mute Swans caused a disastrous decline in numbers, from which the species has only recovered in this century through vigorous protection. The population of Mute Swans in Britain is now about 20,000 birds.

Three swans, Mute, Whooper and Bewick's, are indigenous to our continent. All have white plumage, the sexes are alike and immature birds have varying shades of grey plumage. The Mute Swan, with its orange-red bill with a black knob above it, is largely a resident bird and only the northernmost elements of the population move south in winter. Most Mute Swans leave the smaller lakes and ponds where they nest to congregate in large flocks on favourite feeding grounds in winter, sometimes associating themselves with wintering flocks of Bewick's as well as Whooper Swans. In these flocks it is quite easy to tell the Mute Swan from its relatives by the S-shaped neck and the more curved back. The threatening posture of the Mute Swan is an exaggeration of these features: with head between its shoulders, and wings raised like sails, the

WHOOPER SWAN *Cygnus cygnus* L 58″ Rather common in winter along coasts and in larger lakes and rivers. Has a greater preference for salt water than Mute Swan. In summer, nests on islands, swamps and lakes of the north. When swimming, neck is held straight and secondary wing feathers are not raised as in Mute Swan. This makes this species and Bewick's Swan easy to distinguish from Mute Swan, even at long range. At closer range, large area of yellow on bill is noticeable. Immatures distinguished from Mute Swans by more uniform grey colour and silhouette, from Bewick's Swans by larger size. Whooper is rather noisy with characteristic deep, bugle-like whooping, which can be heard over long distances.   W

Whooper Swan

imm.

imm.

Bewick's Swan

BEWICK'S SWAN *Cygnus bewickii* L 48" W 80"
Least common of the swans, found in sheltered bays,
lakes and larger rivers in winter; in summer nests on the
Arctic tundra. Like small edition of the Whooper Swan.
Yellow on bill is less extensive. Bill comparatively smaller
than Whooper Swan's, giving the head a more rounded
appearance. Often seen singly or in families, but sometimes in huge flocks probably consisting of whole
populations. Immature is like a small Whooper and there
is no difference in bill coloration. Call is somewhat like
Whooper's but much more musical and pleasant.   WP

fierce-looking beast swims towards its antagonist, pushing itself
forward in violent jerks by using both feet simultaneously.
This display is so frightening that few dare stand their ground to
risk a rough beating with the powerful wings of the enraged
bird. This aggressiveness is most pronounced between the males
or 'cobs' in the breeding season and plays an important role in
the defence of territory. Usually no physical harm is done, but
occasional fights leading to the death of one of the participants
have been recorded.

Paired swans remain together for life as is the case with their
close relatives, the geese.

The Mute Swan's nest is placed among reeds on the shore and
here the female or 'pen' incubates the four to eight bluish-white
eggs for about one month. The cob keeps close by, ready to
defend his home and to take his turn at incubating. After
hatching, the cygnets follow their parents, but these 'ugly
ducklings' take a full two months to attain the power of flight.
The family stays together, often in the company of other
families, until the following breeding season, when the young
are usually driven away to spend the summer with other
immature and non-breeding birds.

Swans live almost exclusively on saltwater and freshwater
plants which they reach by submerging their long necks. To
reach even deeper they sometimes 'up-end' like the dabbling
ducks. Sometimes they are also seen grazing on dry land like
geese, when they are accused of fouling the ground for live-
stock.

The Whooper and Bewick's Swans are both essentially Arctic
in their distribution, and though a few Whoopers have occasionally tried to breed in Scotland and non-breeding birds may
stay all summer, it is only in the winter months that we can
enjoy the honking of these two beautiful birds, adding so much
charm to our snow- and ice-covered landscapes.

Geese

Our geese fall into two groups: the grey geese (genus *Anser*),
comprising Greylag, White-fronted, Lesser White-fronted,
Pink-footed and Bean Goose; and the genus *Branta,* comprising
Brent, Barnacle, Red-breasted and Canada Goose. The Snow
Goose belongs to the first group but this striking bird is only a
rare vagrant from North America where it inhabits the Arctic
areas. The Bar-headed Goose, which has its home in Asia, sometimes ventures west, reaching our continent, but many of those
observed have escaped from parks or zoos.

Canada Goose

CANADA GOOSE *Branta canadensis* L 22–30"
W 50–68" Introduced in many parks. Escapes have
established themselves as breeding birds in Britain as
well as Sweden. In winter Swedish migrants may be met
with in small numbers in most parts of western Europe,
but British birds are more sedentary. Much larger than
any other *Branta* species; black neck and head with
white cheek patch is diagnostic. In behaviour quite
similar to Bean Goose, usually feeding on the ground.
Nests on islands, in lakes and in swamps. Voice is a
hoarse honking, not unlike that of Whooper and Bewick's
Swans.   R

BRENT GOOSE *Branta bernicla* L 24" W 48" Locally
common, mainly along seashores and coastal bays. Very
dark and short-necked. Flight rapid, usually low over the
water, often in flocks strung out in long lines. Sometimes
mixes with grey geese. Two subspecies appear in
Europe: the dark-bellied *B.b. bernicla* breeding in the
Soviet Union, and the light-bellied *B.b. hrota* breeding in
north-east Greenland and Spitzbergen. Sometimes
found together but generally the dark-bellied form is
found in the eastern part of Europe and the light-bellied
form in the western part in winter. Often up-ends when
feeding. Call is a guttural, croaking 'rronk'.   W

BARNACLE GOOSE *Branta leucopsis* L 25" W 56"
Very local. Breeds in mountainous areas of the Arctic and
sometimes Arctic tundras. In winter rarely seen inland,
but prefers wet salt marshes, and tidal areas. Stragglers
sometimes found in flocks of grey geese. Striking pattern
of black and white is diagnostic. Feeding habits are
somewhat intermediate between Brent Goose and the
grey geese. Call is a series of rapid, repeated short barks.
                                                     W

RED-BREASTED GOOSE *Branta ruficollis* L 22"
W 46" Only rare stragglers reach western Europe. In
winter feeds mainly on fields and steppes, near coasts or
swamps. Nests on the Arctic tundra and cliffs. In habits
closely resembles the grey geese and on wintering
grounds it often associates with Lesser White-fronted
Geese. Vagrants are usually mixed in flocks of grey
geese. Small size and striking colour pattern are diagnostic. Call is two-syllabled, staccato, rather high pitched.
                                                     V

light-bellied form

Brent Goose

dark-bellied form

Barnacle Goose

Red-breasted Goose

Geese are large waterfowl, with rather long necks and heavy, strong bills used for cutting and pulling plants. The two sexes are, unlike most of the ducks, of similar plumage and only when they are seen together is the slightly larger size of the male detectable. They are excellent and indefatigable fliers, on migration often covering hundreds of miles without a stop. All, perhaps with the exception of the Canada Goose which has been introduced and now lives in a feral state in Britain, are migratory. Even the Canada Geese living in Sweden migrate in autumn towards the south-west, and ringed birds have been found in Germany.

Migration often takes place at night and may be at great height, so that it is not easily detected. Sometimes whole populations start to move in a few huge flocks, which may comprise thousands of individuals. They attain a considerable speed, sometimes as fast as 50 mph. Their height can also be impressive; Bar-headed Geese have been observed crossing over a Himalayan peak about 20,000 feet above sea-level. Some of the main migratory routes are followed year after year, the goose being a conservative creature; for instance, through the

eastern form

Greylag Goose

western form

Bay of Finland via Lake Ladoga to the breeding grounds along the White Sea and on Novaya Zemlya. This route is used annually by Barnacles and Brents. Similarly, wintering grounds are visited year after year, making them favourable places for the observation of flocks of geese. There are many such places in the British Isles, especially in Scotland, where geese from Iceland and Greenland (Pink-footed, White-footed, Barnacle and Greylag Goose) and some birds from Spitzbergen (Barnacle Goose) are found in tens of thousands. Many Greenland birds also winter in Ireland, while England is visited mainly by birds from Spitzbergen (Brents) and the north Russian tundra and shores (Brent, White-fronted and Bean Goose). Surveys have shown that the population of, for instance, Pink-footed Geese in Britain may be about 50,000. Flocks grazing on favourite fields have been caught in huge nets shot out over the flock with rockets. In this way so many geese have been caught for ringing and subsequently recovered that we now have a good idea of their movements.

The *Branta* species show a greater affinity for seashores than those of *Anser*, but otherwise the habits of the two groups differ mainly in detail. All geese live primarily on vegetable matter. This is cropped from fields and marshes, only the Brent resorting to estuaries where their favourite food, eel-grass, is found. In the 1930s, when the eel-grass disappeared from many areas beacuse of disease, the combination of this and hunting caused a drastic and almost catastrophic decline in the number of Brents and only recently has the species regained some of its former strength.

When spring comes, the geese break up from their winter grounds and one can hear their cackling and honking as they pass through the night sky towards their northern homes. Although still in large flocks, they are already paired. Pairs stay

Below Red-breasted Geese

together for life with a faithfulness rarely found among birds.

On their arrival at the breeding grounds, a favourable spot is chosen for the nest. This is always on the ground or in shallow water and the same nest site may be used year after year. Most geese like to nest in loose colonies, retaining at least some of the social attitude so marked in winter.

The female alone builds the nest and incubates the three to six eggs for about four weeks, but unlike the ducks the male stays close to the nest, warning the female of any approaching danger. The male also helps to take care of the goslings. Usually the mother birds leads the way while the male stays in the rear, keeping an attentive eye on his precious family.

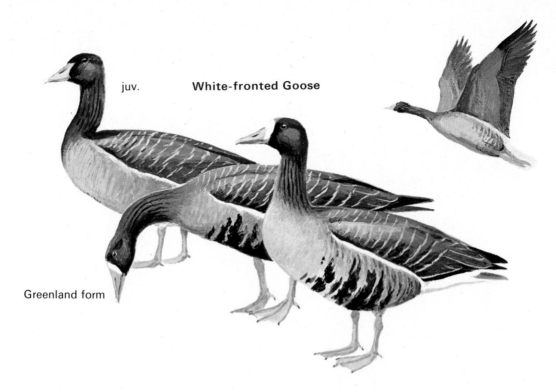

juv.   **White-fronted Goose**

Greenland form

WHITE-FRONTED GOOSE *Anser albifrons* L 28"
Locally common. In winter found on open pasture and on coasts, moors and rivers, and more rarely on cultivated fields. Nests on the Arctic tundra. The adult bird is easily identified by the black belly and white front. Immature birds are best told by orange legs and unspotted bill. The much larger size distinguishes it from the Lesser White-fronted Goose, which also has a distinctly smaller bill. The subspecies nesting in Greenland *(A.a. flavirostris)* is slightly larger with a yellow bill and winters in the British Isles. Like other geese it is gregarious in its behaviour. The call is more highly pitched than that of other large grey geese and consists of a laughing 'kow-yow'. W

When the goslings are half-grown, the parent birds moult their flight feathers and do not regain the power of flight until the goslings are themselves fledged. When flightless, geese are even more wary and unapproachable than usual.

The Greylag Goose is the most widespread of our geese and, with the exception of the introduced Canada Goose, the only species breeding south of Scandinavia. It nests on sheltered islands or on marshes and lakes with extensive reed-beds.

The White-fronted Goose, nesting on the tundras of the far north, has been increasing in numbers at the expense of the Bean Goose. The Pink-footed Goose, which is regarded by some

Lesser White-fronted Goose

juv.

LESSER WHITE-FRONTED GOOSE *Anser ery-thropus* L 24" W 52" Only stragglers reach western Europe. In summer found on Arctic mountain slopes, in winter on pastures and fields. Looks like a small edition of White-fronted Goose, but told from this species by the high front, the extension of the white front on to the crown, the much shorter and smaller bill and, even at a distance, a characteristic yellow rim around the eye. The immature bird also has this yellow ring and, at all stages, the wings extend beyond the tail. In western Europe it is usually seen in flocks of other grey geese. The call is higher pitched than that of the White-fronted Goose. V

Below Greylag Geese

authorities as the westernmost race of the Bean Goose, has, on the other hand, recently increased somewhat in numbers.

The Lesser White-fronted Goose is eastern in its distribution and only rarely seen in western Europe, as its wintering grounds are in south-east Europe and Asia.

There are two subspecies of the Brent Goose: the light-bellied race breeding in Greenland, Spitzbergen and Novaya Zemlya, and the dark-bellied form indigenous to Arctic Russia and Siberia. The distribution of the Barnacle Goose coincides somewhat with that of the light-bellied Brent Goose, although it is rather more southern.

Bean Goose

tundra form

forest form

Pink-footed Goose

Snow Goose

juv.

juv.

BEAN GOOSE *Anser fabalis* L 30" W 60" Local. In winter prefers pastures and fields close to open bodies of water, in summer tundras and the open northern woods. Distinguished from Greylag Goose by lack of pale forewing, and black and orange colour pattern on bill (varies considerably). Also told from immature White-fronted Goose by colour pattern of bill, and from the Pink-footed Goose, which by some is regarded as a subspecies of the Bean Goose, by the yellow legs, longer and lighter coloured neck, and larger bill. It is often met in large flocks, and like other grey geese it flies between the feeding grounds and lakes (where the night is spent) at dawn and dusk. Sometimes other geese are mixed with the flocks. The call is lower and more honking than that of other grey geese.   W

BAR-HEADED GOOSE *Anser indicus* Escapes of this Asiatic goose are sometimes met with, usually in the company of other grey geese. It is easily told from other geese by the white crown with two black bars. Immatures lack the black colours but are very light grey.

PINK-FOOTED GOOSE *Anser brachyrhynchus* L 28" W 58" Locally common. In winter found in pastures and fields near open water. Considered by many a subspecies of the Bean Goose, which it resembles in its habits. Breeds in Greenland, in Iceland and Spitzbergen. The neck and head are very dark, contrasting sharply with the light grey forewing seen in flight. The bill is patterned pink and black and comparatively short. The feet are pink. Most difficult to tell from immature White-fronted Goose, but notice some black on smaller bill and pink feet of the Pink-footed Goose. Because of the smaller bill-size, the shape of the head is more rounded than in the other grey geese. The call is very similar to that of the Bean Goose, but slightly higher pitched.   W

SNOW GOOSE *Anser hyperboreus* L 28" W 59" A North American bird occurring as an accidental visitor and, more often, as an escape in western Europe. Usually in the company of grey geese. Unmistakable with pure white colours and black wing-tips. Immatures are so light they cannot be mistaken for any other European goose. The grey phase, the so-called Blue Goose, has white neck and head and grey body and is even rarer in Europe. Most have been observed in winter and autumn.   V

The most beautiful of our geese, the small Red-breasted Goose, nests on the Siberian tundra, wintering along the shores of the Caspian Sea, and only stragglers reach our shores.

Bar-headed Goose

Dabbling Ducks

The dabbling ducks, or surface-feeding ducks as they are also called, form the largest group of ducks. They all have very short legs, rather long flat bills, and the sexes usually differ greatly in plumage. The males or 'drakes', often have bold and beautiful colour patterns with an iridescent patch on the wing (the speculum) as a constant feature. The colour and pattern of the speculum play an important role in the identification of ducks, particularly in the summer when the males attain their so-called eclipse plumage. This plumage, which is almost identical to that of the female, is attained after the breeding responsibilities of the males are over. The bird loses all its flight-feathers, and until new ones have grown out is very vulnerable to predators. The females also become flightless. The bird in eclipse seeks places where it can hide and often tries to escape danger by diving. Like a rail it slips through the dense reed-beds and like a grebe it submerges at the slightest sign of danger. The eclipse plumage is only present for a very short time (and the flightless period is, of course, much shorter), and by early autumn it is replaced by the breeding plumage with its bold and striking colour patterns. The eclipse moult differs from the moults of other birds in the very short period the actual plumage is kept. Most other birds keep their 'autumn' plumage well into winter and spring. The moult leading to the breeding plumage in autumn is probably an adjustment to the mating season. Unlike most other birds in the northern hemisphere, dabbling ducks pair off in autumn and remain together all winter, breeding in spring.

The dabbling ducks are primarily birds of shallow lakes and marshes; each species has its own preference, but this is not as pronounced as in many other bird groups and families. The least particular in its choice is the Mallard. From woodland ponds to sheltered seashores, from city parks to tundra lakes,

MALLARD *Anas platyrhynchos* L 23" W 36" Most common and widespread surface-feeding duck. Found in lakes, ponds, rivers and along sheltered coasts and in marshes. Drake easily distinguished by dark green head, chestnut breast. Both drake and duck have conspicuous blue speculum. Duck most easily confused with Gadwall and Pintail, but note heavier bill and blue speculum. Often found in flocks or pairs. Duck's voice is loud quack; drake is quieter. RWP

GADWALL *Anas strepera* L 20" W 35" Widespread but uncommon. Found in ponds, lakes, rivers and flooded meadows, rarely in salt water. Seen in pairs or very small flocks, sometimes mixed with other surface-feeding ducks. At a distance, drake looks greyish, but note characteristic red-brown, black and white speculum of both sexes. Also note white belly of duck distinguishing it from Pintail and Mallard. Call is very low and reedy. RW

PINTAIL *Anas acuta* L 28" W 35" Common, found on lakes, ponds and bays, usually in pairs or small flocks. Slim and very agile with slender, pointed wings. Female has longer neck and longer, more pointed tail than other mottled ducks. White on wing not as extensive as on Gadwall, with which it is most easily confused. Call is short whistle. RWP

WIGEON *Anas penelope* L 18" W 32" Common in marshes, meadows and swamps where it breeds. In winter also found in lagoons, lakes and bays. In winter usually seen in large flocks. Note whitish forewing. More compactly built than other surface-feeding ducks. Flies in tight flocks, not in long open V's. Walks well and often grazes on land. Call, a high descending whistle, often reveals presence of flocks. RWP

and from salt marshes to mountain tarns, the Mallard can be found. Its demands are small: vegetation on the surface of the water, or at least no deeper than it can reach by up-ending, a certain minimum requirement of peace, and a tussock of grass or reed where it can place its nest.

More demanding is the Gadwall, which is a little smaller than the Mallard and has its main distribution in Asia, only breeding sporadically in western Europe. This species prefers more peaceful lakes and ponds, where it can easily find cover. Both the Pintail and the Wigeon are found in the nesting season in tundra pools, marshes and moors, as is the Teal, which also occurs both in reedy swamps and quite far from water on dry ground. The Garganey, only slightly larger than the Teal, is

Mallard

Gadwall

Pintail

Wigeon

AMERICAN WIGEON *Anas americana* L 20" W 34"
American counterpart to Wigeon; a rare straggler to
western Europe. Drake unmistakable. Duck closely
resembles Wigeon duck but has greyer appearance with
more contrast between coloration of head and neck and
breast, and scapulars are white, not dusky. Call is two or
three soft whistles.   V

TEAL *Anas crecca* L 14" W 24" Very common. Smallest
of the surface-feeding ducks. In summer it is found on
smaller ponds, lakes, bogs and marshes, while in winter
it also frequents bays, lakes and flooded marshes.
Usually prefers fresh water. The female is distinguished
from other small ducks by her green speculum. A very
fast flier, usually in very tight flocks and only rarely in
lines or V's. Most active at dusk. Call is a short whistle.
                                                      RWP

BLUE-WINGED TEAL *Anas discors* L 15" W 24" Rare
straggler from North America. The drake is unmistakable.
The duck is much like Garganey duck but is darker, with
bright blue forewing and a longer bill.   V

BAIKAL TEAL *Anas formosa* L 11" W 24" Rare straggler
from its Asiatic breeding grounds. Note the drake's
distinctive facial pattern. The duck has a green speculum
and a distinct white patch at base of bill.   V

mainly found in swampy areas with much vegetation and many
ditches. The Shoveler, which is specialized for feeding on
vegetable and animal matter floating on the surface, prefers
muddy and shallow water in pools, marshes and meres.

In winter and on migration the various members of this
group are often found together in marshes and shallow lakes, and
some, like the Mallard, Pintail and Wigeon, also resort freely
to sea coasts.

In migratory habits the dabbling ducks vary, particularly
in regard to the extent of migration. In general, the northern
and eastern populations migrate to the Atlantic coasts of
Europe where many spend the winter, while some move further
south to the African lakes and shores. The Icelandic birds show

American
Wigeon

Teal

Blue-winged Teal

Baikal Teal

Falcated Teal

Garganey

FALCATED TEAL *Anas falcetta* L 20" Very rare straggler to eastern Europe from its Asiatic breeding grounds. The drake is unmistakable. The duck resembles Gadwall duck, but speculum is different.

GARGANEY *Anas querquedula* L 15" W 25" Widespread but not very numerous. Found in ponds and lakes and flooded meadows with rich shoreline vegetation. Notice conspicuous white stripe over eye of drake. The duck has pale forewing but is best told from Teal duck by facial pattern. See also Blue-winged Teal. Usually met with in pairs or very small flocks. The call of male is a strange crackling sound. SP

an interesting pattern, as part of the population migrates to the western part of the Atlantic (Wigeon, Teal and Pintail ringed in Iceland have been recovered in numbers in the United States), while many travel to western Europe and some endure the winter on the island itself. The more southern populations of several species are resident and only move over short distances. Ducks wintering in the northern parts of Europe are often forced to move south if the winter proves hard and ice covers their haunts.

The dabbling ducks travel mainly by night, usually in flocks. They also feed mainly at night, and at dusk move from the coast or waters where they have sought refuge during the day to swamps and lakes, rich in food but also in danger, as they often lie close to human habitation. In Europe duck shooting concentrates on these dusk and dawn flights. In America, on the other hand, ducks are drawn to decoys put out by the hunter. This has, among other things, led to the development of very beautiful decoys much sought after by antique collectors in North America.

Other ways of hunting ducks have also been developed to satisfy man's eternal hunger for delicacies. Large traps are used in many places, and huge guns in permanent emplacements are a more bizarre (and dangerous) way of obtaining the desired game.

But ducks can be enjoyed in other ways than on the plate. Many of our parks offer the best opportunity of watching and enjoying their everyday life, particularly the Mallard, which occurs so often in a semi-domesticated state on ponds and moats.

Dabbling ducks are paired in October and display begins in early autumn, being continued with varying intensity throughout the winter until breeding takes place. This is the time to see spectacular social displays in which several drakes more or less simultaneously make different but characteristic movements. One of these movements consists of the drake throwing a small cascade of water in front of him with a sudden movement of the bill; a rather grotesque-looking manoeuvre. In another, he lifts his tail and lowers his breast, appearing to contract his body while increasing its height.

Besides social display in which several drakes and sometimes several ducks participate, there is the display before mating. This

Shoveler

Marbled Teal

SHOVELER *Spatula clypeata* L 20" W 31" Common, found mainly in ponds and flooded marshes where it feeds in shallow water. The drake is unmistakable. Note the flat head, long spatulate bill and large blue wing patch of both sexes. On the water it rides low in front with bill held downwards. Often met with in small flocks, sometimes consisting only of drakes. Quacks like a Mallard; also has a low clucking.   RWP

MARBLED TEAL *Anas angustirostris* L 16" W 25" Uncommon and local. Prefers sheltered ponds and swamps with much vegetation. Notice very light colours, dark eye-stripe and lack of speculum. Large head and long neck visible in silhouette. Often hides and is difficult to approach. Usually met with singly or very few together.

is in many respects different from the social display and the drakes prefer to be on their own when courting so intimately. As an introduction to mating, both birds move their heads up and down as if getting ready to fly. During mating itself, which takes place on the water (as with all other waterfowl), the duck is completely submerged.

The basic patterns of display are common to many of the dabbling ducks, although all show variations on the general theme.

When Mallard ducks are sitting on their eggs, the drakes congregate, often on park lakes where they attain an artificially high density, and pursue any duck that comes off the nest to feed or preen. Sometimes their combined attentions end by drowning her. Aerial chases of a duck by several drakes are also commonly seen at this time.

Dabbling ducks lay from six to sixteen eggs, which are pale-coloured and unspotted. The nest is usually lined with down, which the female plucks from her breast. The down differs in pattern from species to species so the nest is often more easily recognized by the down than by the eggs.

The different species site their nests differently. The Mallard is probably the least particular of all. Its nest has been found among waterside plants, in fields, in old crow and magpie nests, in natural cavities of trees, and probably most commonly in thick low vegetation. Other species are more confined to grass tussocks and rushes.

The eggs are incubated for twenty to twenty-five days and the down-covered ducklings leave the nest immediately to follow their mother into the world. When the nest is placed in a tree they jump out without hesitation to join the mother, who is standing on the ground below, calling them nervously. No harm comes to the ducklings from their fall, which is often from a great height. The young are usually able to fly after three to seven weeks. Until then their lives are filled with danger and their only protection against numerous marauding enemies is their camouflaging coloration, the warning of the mother bird, and their ability in diving, an ability that they to a certain degree lose or seldom make use of once they become adults.

While the ducks are busy taking care of their offspring, the

drakes get together in parties on the open water and soon start moulting. The drakes of most species do not take the slightest interest in the rearing of the next generation, once their essential function in perpetuating the species has been performed.

The Mallard is by far the most common of the European dabbling ducks but may be exceeded in world numbers by the Pintail with its elegantly elongated tail-feathers and long, thin neck; the latter species is common in Europe and the most numerous of the dabbling ducks in North America.

The more elusive and, in distribution, more eastern Gadwall is scarce in western Europe, although it breeds here. The drake's plumage is not showy and the duck so resembles the Mallard duck that it probably often escapes notice.

The Wigeon, the drake showing a beautiful red head and white front, resembles the geese in some respects, due to its regular habit of grazing on land. It walks more like a goose and the bill is short and high as is the case with most geese. The ducks' melodious whistling chorus, which may be heard both day and night in autumn and spring, is a pleasant variation from the usual quacking of most of the dabbling ducks. Its close relative, the American Wigeon or Baldpate, is only a very rare visitor from its home on the western side of the Atlantic.

The Teal is the smallest and one of the most beautiful of our dabbling ducks. Its flight is very fast, 30-40 mph, and the tight flocks or 'springs' are able to wheel and turn as speedily as flocks of Dunlins and Starlings. In spite of its small size, the Teal is a prized game bird because of its delicate meat. The almost identical North American counterpart, the Green-winged Teal, is a rare visitor only, as are the Baikal Teal and Falcated Teal, which are both Asian in origin.

Only slightly larger than the Teal is the Garganey. It is easy to identify by the bright blue areas on the wings, also found on a rare vagrant from North America, the Blue-winged Teal, and on the bizarre Shoveler. The Shoveler is distinguished by the spoon-shaped bill with which it sifts plant material and insects off the surface of the muddy water of the swamps and lakes where it lives. The colour pattern of the drake, black, white and chestnut with blue wings, is particularly striking when a party of five or six are pursuing a female over the reedy swamps of its springtime home.

The Marbled Teal, a greyish brown, wary, but sluggish duck of the western Mediterranean, is occasionally encountered as a rare vagrant to the other countries of our continent.

Differing considerably from the dabbling ducks are the shelducks. They are much larger, almost goose-like, and the sexes are almost alike in plumage. They feed on the surface of the water like dabbling ducks and can also up-end as most dabblers do to get hold of the seaweed and animals found in low water.

MANDARIN DUCK *Aix galericulata* L 18″ W 28″
Escapes have established themselves in a feral state, particularly in some parts of England. Prefers ponds with wooded edges, nesting in tree-holes. The beautiful drake is unmistakable. The duck is less strikingly coloured, but notice the characteristic facial pattern. The flight is direct and swift. Feeds mainly on land.   R

Mandarin Duck

SHELDUCK *Tadorna tadorna* L 24" Common on coastal flats and estuaries; sometimes found on inland lakes and swamps, nesting in holes and under bushes along shores. Drake and duck are similar and share the striking pattern of dark green, black, chestnut and white. Drake has large red knob on bill. The immature looks much whiter than the adults. The flight is low over the water with rather slow wing-beats. Sometimes seen in very large flocks and in huge numbers when moulting. Ducklings often appear in large flocks attended by one or few adults during moulting season. They are strikingly coloured black and white. The call is a characteristic 'ag-ag-ag', rather like the flight call of divers.　　RS

RUDDY SHELDUCK *Casarca ferruginea* L 24" Uncommon, but escapes may occur well outside usual range. More terrestrial than Shelduck. In winter found along river banks, sandy lakeshores and in fields and steppes. Usually seen in pairs or small flocks. The orange-brown colour is characteristic and white area on wing is striking in flight. Male has narrow black neck-band. Resembles Shelduck in shape and habits. Flight resembles that of Shelduck with rather slow wing-beats. Nests in burrows and holes. The call is nasal, Shelduck-like.　　V

EGYPTIAN GOOSE *Alopochen aegyptiacus* L 28" Very rare straggler to south-easternmost Europe from breeding grounds in Africa, but escaped birds established in parts of England. The sexes are similar. Notice large white area on wing and long legs.

The Shelduck is brightly coloured and spends most of its life along sheltered seashores, but in the east of its range it is an inland breeder. It nests in burrows or under boulders and bushes, but may also site its nest in the open. The same is true of the Ruddy Shelduck of eastern Europe, which only rarely visits western parts. Shelducks congregate in large flocks in favoured areas, for instance the Heligoland Bight and Bridgwater Bay, Somerset, to moult in late summer. Here thousands of these beautiful birds can be seen at a single glance. Often several broods of ducklings are merged and left in the care of a single pair while their parents migrate to their moulting grounds.

The Egyptian Goose of the Nile valley and other parts of Africa is a rare visitor to the eastern Mediterranean and Black Sea coasts. It is the largest of the shelducks. It is kept in captivity in many countries and has in some cases established itself in the wild, for instance in England. The same holds true of the small Mandarin Duck, the most ornamental of all our ducks. Its original home is in the Far East, but it has been able to establish itself in many places where it has been introduced and with its extreme beauty it is a great asset to the ponds and lakes where it is found.

juv.　　**Shelduck**

Ruddy Shelduck

Egyptian Goose

RED-CRESTED POCHARD *Netta rufina* L 22"
Uncommon, local, but escapes occur. Breeds by ponds
and lakes with reeds; in winter also found on open lakes,
sometimes along seashores. Resembles surface-feeding
ducks in many aspects of behaviour. Red bill, broad
white wing-band very distinctive. Facial pattern of duck
resembles Common Scoter duck. Usually seen singly or
in pairs, sometimes with other species.   P

SCAUP *Aythya marila* L 18" W 31" Common in winter
along coasts, often on deeper water than Tufted and
Pochard. Flocks usually smaller than those of Tufted,
but very large aggregations can occur in favoured places.
Notice grey back of male, marked white area around bill
of female. Head looks noticeably rounded.   WP

RING-NECKED DUCK *Aythya collaris* L 17" W 28"
Very rare winter straggler to western Europe from North
America. Drake easily told from male Tufted by head
shape and vertical white stripe on side. Duck harder to
identify, but head shape, facial pattern and grey (not
white) wing-bar of both sexes are characteristic.   V

TUFTED DUCK *Aythya fuligula* L 17" W 28" Most
numerous bay duck, nesting near lakes and swamps. In
winter found in large flocks on lakes, bays, seashores,
often with other species. Black back and long tuft of
drake diagnostic. Ducks and immatures usually have a
hint of a tuft and some white at base of bill. Under-tail
area of female can be pale but not as white as in smaller
Ferruginous. Flight fast; flocks usually fly in irregular
formation with lines or V's interspersed.   RW

Small Diving Ducks

These rather diminutive, plump, diving ducks are most closely
related to the dabbling ducks, with which they share many
characteristic features. Although Goldeneyes are considered by
many to be more closely related to the sea ducks, they are
discussed here because of their preferred habitat outside the
breeding season.

The bills of these ducks are rather long and spatulate like those
of the dabbling ducks, whereas their feet are placed further back
and apart, reflecting their diving habits.

In summer they nest by freshwater ponds and swamps or in
sheltered bays; in winter they are found in flocks in ice-free
lakes, rivers and bays, only rarely going out into the open sea.
As is the case with most of our ducks, the male and female have
distinct plumages.

They live on plant material, insects, molluscs and other
animal matter which they obtain on the bottom of shallow
waters rarely exceeding a few feet in depth. The different
species have differing preferences in food; thus the Pochard
lives almost exclusively on vegetable matter, whereas the

Red-crested Pochard

Scaup

Ring-necked Duck

Tufted Duck

Pochard

Ferruginous Duck

POCHARD *Aythya ferina* L 18″ W 31″ Common, nesting in reeds near open fresh water; in winter on larger lakes and sheltered bays, often with Tufteds. Triangular head shape and heavy, compact bill help identify. Drake easily told from other red-headed ducks by black breast, grey back. Female more drab, but notice facial pattern and steel-grey ring on bill. Both sexes have grey wing-bars. RW

FERRUGINOUS DUCK *Aythya nycora* L 16″ W 26″ Common, nesting by freshwater lakes and in swamps with much vegetation. In winter found on larger lakes, sheltered bays. Rarely occurs in salt water. Smallest bay duck. Notice rich brown colour of male, white eye, distinctive white under tail-coverts. Wing-bar white. Floats higher than relatives; holds tail higher, revealing striking white of under tail-coverts. Duck more drab, lacking white eye. W

Scaup has a great preference for animals, especially molluscs. The dive does not usually last more than about thirty seconds. Although these ducks obtain their food mainly by diving, they can also be seen up-ending on very shallow water.

All are more or less migratory. The degree of ice-cover is of great importance, as many populations only move on when forced to do so by severe frost. All have characteristic wing-bars, the showing of which plays an important role in their display.

The nests of these ducks are usually placed well-hidden in grass or rushes. Here they lay six to eleven light, uniformly coloured eggs which are incubated for about four weeks. The ducklings leave the nest shortly after hatching and follow their mother into the water. The first few times the mother brings food to the surface for the ducklings to devour, but soon they are able to find food by themselves by diving in the shallows. After about six weeks the young have attained their full juvenile plumage and are able to fly.

The Pochard shows an interesting tendency to place its eggs in the nests of other ducks. This tendency is further developed in its American counterpart, the Redhead, and most of all in the South American Black-headed Duck *(Heteronetta atricapilla)* which habitually lays in the nests of other ducks.

The Red-crested Pochard resembles the Pochard in having a red head, but the shade is brilliantly orange rather than the more subtle brownish-red of the Pochard. It is also considerably larger and is the member of this group most closely resembling the dabbling ducks. It is a rare visitor to the British Isles, whereas it is found breeding locally in many parts of continental Europe.

The Tufted Duck is the most numerous of the small diving ducks. In its choice of nest site it shows a great affinity for gull and tern colonies, these aggressive birds offering some protection from maurauding crows. The American counterpart, the Ring-necked Duck, is a rare vagrant to the extreme west of Europe.

The Scaup prefers deeper water for its feeding grounds than the other small diving ducks, and feeds almost exclusively on molluscs and snails, but at night it often joins the other species

Goldeneye

Goldeneye displaying

GOLDENEYE *Bucephala clangula* L 19″ W 31″
Common on lakes and rivers and in forested country of the north, where it nests in cavities and even nest boxes. Winters along the coasts and on larger lakes and rivers. The shape of the head of both sexes is characteristic and the large, white wing patches are striking when seen in flight. The wings make a loud, musical whistle. The drake has a rather small, round white facial spot. The duck has a white collar. Usually seen in pairs or small flocks, sometimes mixing with other species. Flight is very fast. They are the best divers of this group and go further out to sea than any related species. The display is characteristic and often seen in early spring on the wintering ground, the drakes throwing their heads back with bills pointing upward.   WP

which are found closer to the shore. The smallest of these is the Ferruginous Duck which has earned its name through the deep reddish-brown colour of the drake. It is widespread in the southern and central parts of Europe, but only rarely wanders as far from its breeding grounds as the British Isles.

Two species of goldeneye inhabit our continent. One, the Goldeneye, is widespread and numerous, while the other, Barrow's Goldeneye, only nests in Iceland, which it has invaded from its main breeding range in North America. To the rest of Europe it is an accidental visitor.

The black-and-white colours of these charming birds are in perfect harmony with the ice-covered bays, rivers and lakes which they frequent in winter. Small parties of Goldeneye may be seen diving repeatedly, and when they take flight a whistling noise from the fast-moving wings rings through the crystal-clear winter air.

Even in winter Goldeneye often perform their social display, in which several drakes court the duck. The drake characteristically throws its head backwards with the neck completely stretched.

In winter Goldeneye are usually met with in small flocks. In early spring they move north to breeding grounds in the Baltic area. The nest is often sited in old nest holes of the Black Woodpecker or in natural cavities, but nest boxes are used if these are set up for it, as is the case in many areas. The same nest hole is often used year after year by the same duck. Barrow's Goldeneye also nests in tree cavities, but in Iceland, where no such things are found, it makes its nest in cracks and crevices in the old lava rocks.

The tree chosen for a nesting site is often far from the nearest water and the Goldeneye duck sometimes has to fly many miles to her feeding grounds. Similarly the ducklings, once hatched, have to travel overland to reach the relative safety of water. This journey through the woods, which starts as soon as the duck, calling from below, has encouraged the ducklings to dare the long jump, is most dangerous for these soft little creatures. Many are lost to foxes and birds of prey, but once in the water their dexterity in diving saves them from many dangers. The duck-

Barrow's Goldeneye

White-headed Duck

BARROW'S GOLDENEYE *Bucephala islandica* L 21″ W 31″ Very rare outside its only European breeding ground, Iceland. Nests along mountain streams and lakes. In winter also found along coasts and in rivers. The drake is told from Goldeneye by the crescent-shape of the white facial spot, completely different shape of head, purple (not green) gloss of the black head and much more extensive black on back and wings. The duck has less white on wings than Goldeneye and in breeding season the bill is all yellow, lacking the Goldeneye's black base. Like the Goldeneye, an expert diver.

WHITE-HEADED DUCK *Oxyura leucocephala* L 18″ Uncommon in freshwater swamps and lakes with much vegetation and in brackish lagoons. Very characteristic shape with large head, short neck and long tail which is often jerked upwards, revealing white under tail-coverts. Outside breeding season often associates with bay ducks. Notice facial pattern of both sexes.

lings follow their mother in single file and often the foremost one gets a free ride on the back of the adult. Soon this harmony is broken and long before the ducklings are able to fly the family is divided into smaller groups or single individuals. Both goldeneyes are good divers and they usually stay under water for about half a minute, which enables them to reach the bottom where they find molluscs and snails, their favourite food.

Sea Ducks

The sea ducks form a group of rather large diving ducks, in winter usually encountered on salt water, often quite far from shore. As with most ducks, the drake is strikingly coloured, whereas the duck is duller and less conspicuous, which helps it to stay undetected when sitting on the nest. The Long-tailed Duck is the most maritime species and is circumpolar in its distribution. But all the sea ducks have northern breeding grounds, most of them only moving south to the west European shores in winter.

Two scoters breed in northern Europe, while the third, the Surf Scoter, is a scarce but regular visitor to the western coasts from its home in North America. Two eiders, Common and King, nest in Europe, the King Eider only in the extreme north The smaller Steller's Eider is a regular visitor to the Norwegian and northern Baltic coasts from its breeding grounds in Siberia. The Harlequin Duck, so called because of the rich variation of colours displayed by the male, is only found breeding in Iceland along the swift-flowing rivers of this lava-covered island and seldom reaches the rocky coasts of the rest of Europe. This small sea duck is only really at home in fast-moving water—in waterfalls and in roaring surf. With great ease and elegance it overcomes the pressure of the water, never for a minute letting itself be carried away by the swift-flowing torrent. In summer it is found along rivers, sometimes making its nest in the rocks behind a waterfall, through which it has to fly to reach the six or seven glossy eggs, but most often it nests on a small rocky

Eider

♂ imm.

♀

♂

♂ imm.

♂

King Eider

♀

EIDER *Somateria mollissima* L 24" W 41" Common and by far the most numerous European eider. Nests along seashores, rarely far from water. In winter found along seashores, only occasionally resorting to large freshwater lakes or rivers. In winter, may form large flocks numbering 10–1000, usually outside the surf. Often mixes with scoters. Flocks of Eiders are usually more loose in formation than those of scoters. Most often flies in lines or V-formation low over the water. The head is held low, and the wing-beats are rather slow and deliberate. White back and black belly are diagnostic of Eider drake. Immature drake has mainly dark-brown plumage, but usually some white on the back distinguishing it from immature King Eider. Duck is uniformly brown with black mottling. At close range duck and immature drake told from female King Eider by sloping profile and long slender frontal shield, which extends much farther up the forehead than in King Eider (twice as far from the nostril). Best-known note is conversational 'oo-oo' of drakes when courting.   RW

KING EIDER *Somateria spectabilis* L 23" W 37" Common in the Arctic where it breeds along seashores and on shores of freshwater lakes and rivers. Very rare south of Arctic Circle. King Eider behaves very much like Common Eider with which it often occurs. Black back, white neck and breast, and heavily shielded bill are good field marks for the drake. Large white wing patches are distinctive against the black back. Duck told from Common Eider by bill profile and often richer brown plumage. Immature drakes never show white on back and differ from Common Eiders in shape of head.   V

STELLER'S EIDER *Polysticta stelleri* L 18" W 29" This small Asiatic eider is uncommon, usually found along rocky shores. General shape is like a Mallard, but bill is stubbier and tail longer. White upper parts and reddish-brown underside of drake are characteristic. Duck is uniform dark brown except for blue speculum bordered with white. Both sexes have tiny rounded crest. Wings whistle in flight like Goldeneye's. In take-off, Steller's Eider is not as heavy as other eiders, and flight and wing-beats are faster. Usually very tame but most often encountered far out at sea.   V

All sea ducks are excellent divers, living on molluscs and other animal matter which they pick from the bottom of the sea. Their bills are strong and well adapted to crushing the hard shells protecting their prey. The Long-tailed Duck is probably the best diver of them all and has been encountered as deep as fifty feet or more, staying below up to one and a half minutes.

All sea ducks, together with the auks, are faced with the danger of waste oil deposited accidentally or through thoughtlessness by ships. An oil slick covers many square miles and causes the sea to look calm. Passing ducks settle, only to be hopelessly fouled by the sticky oil, which destroys the waterproofing of their plumage. Birds trapped in this horrible way act as decoys for others, and thus thousands of these unfortunate creatures may succumb. There is now an international agreement which prohibits the clearing of oil tanks in certain parts of the sea by ships of the signatory powers, thus protecting shores and areas rich in bird life. But it is not always observed.

Steller's Eider

♀

♂

Red-breasted Merganser

Goosander

Smew

Mergansers

The three species of mergansers, the Smew, Goosander and Red-breasted Merganser, are easy to tell from other waterfowl by their long, narrow bills, long heads and bodies, and general impression of streamlining. They are all excellent divers and the serrated edges of the bill (an adaptation of the *lamellae* found in other waterfowl) make a perfect tool with which they grab and hold small and slippery fish which they pursue and catch under water.

Smew and Goosander both nest in tree cavities and in nest boxes put up for them. Here the Smew often comes into close contact and competition with the Goldeneye with which it also associates outside the breeding season. This association has even been carried so far that wild hybrids between the two species have been recorded. The Red-breasted Merganser, on the other hand, makes its nest on the ground, but usually under bushes or rocks, and this species also often nests in boxes laid out for it. The clutches are rather large, eight to ten, and the incubation time rather long, twenty-five to thirty-two days. The young are able to swim and dive immediately after being hatched and often get a ride on the back of the mother bird.

All three species are partial migrants and although Scandinavian Red-breasted Mergansers can move as far as the Mediterranean, this is exceptional. The three species can be met with on larger lakes and along the shore, but the Goosander has a particular affinity for inland lakes and waters bordered by woods.

RED-BREASTED MERGANSER *Mergus serrator* L 22″ W 33″ Common, in the breeding season found along freshwater and saltwater shorelines, placing nest under bushes or hidden among rocks or dense vegetation. In winter almost exclusively found in salt water. Both sexes have shaggy crest. Drake distinguished by reddish-brown chest patch. Duck, which has more crest than female Goosander, lacks the contrast between head and throat. Smaller and more slender than Goosander. Often encountered in flocks after breeding season. Call consists of low short quacks. RW

GOOSANDER *Mergus merganser* L 25″ W 37″ Common, usually found on lakes and rivers with wooded shores. Nests in tree holes and other cavities (will use nest boxes). At a distance, drake looks much whiter or salmon-coloured than male Red-breasted Merganser and green head has only the hint of a crest. Duck is more crested and distinct white throat and sharp contrast between neck and breast distinguish it from duck Red-breasted Merganser. Usually seen in small flocks. Call consists of low short quacks. RW

SMEW *Mergus albellus* L 16″ W 26″ Locally common, found on lakes and rivers surrounded by trees. In winter also found on sheltered bays in salt water. Nests in tree cavities. Drake unmistakable with very white plumage. Female much greyer, with distinctive dark chestnut cap. Also notice very short bill. Often associates with Goldeneyes, even in breeding season, and hybrids between the two are known. Most often seen in small parties with other ducks. W

Birds of Prey
order *Falconiformes*

With their dashing flight and predatory habits, birds of prey have always commanded an awesome respect in the minds of men. Sometimes figuring in mythology, sometimes regarded as robbers, sometimes feared, they have always been associated with mystery and power. Both the Rok and the Phoenix were birds of prey. The proud eagles were symbols of the victorious Roman legions and the once-mighty Russian empire. But many species have fared no better than the declining empires they symbolized, and today conservationists are struggling to preserve a number of species from extinction.

The connection between man and birds of prey goes back to time immemorial. The ancient art of falconry was a pastime for noblemen and kings and was surrounded with meticulously observed rites and laws. The falcon and the vulture played a major role in Egyptian mythology, and both birds made their way into the written language as symbols. The Horus Falcon was identified with the sun-god Re. The vulture was the symbol of Nekhebt, the goddess of childbirth. But in spite of this rise to divine status, the greed of humans, a greed not allowing any kind of competition, led to a relentless persecution with devastating consequences. This short-sighted persecution of birds of prey reached its climax in the late nineteenth century. Wherever and whenever met, the bird of prey was an outlaw to be slain, perhaps to leave more game for the human hunter or to avenge the loss of a neighbour's chicken. But greater understanding of the true importance of the balance of nature and of the role played by predators has in the present century led to a desperate attempt to protect what is left of a once plentiful stock and to restore as much as possible of what has been lost. But on the British Isles the Golden Eagle, although it may survive in Scotland, is unlikely to return to the ancient eyries of England and Wales, and the stock of the Kite seems likely to remain at a few pairs.

The order is ancient, remains of the first vultures dating back some fifty to sixty million years to the early Eocene. It is divided into five families, the most primitive being the New World vultures, members of which, as fossils show, once roamed the Old World too. The snake-hunting Secretary Bird is placed in a family by itself, as is the Osprey. The largest family is that of hawks and eagles; falcons are grouped in a family by themselves.

The birds of prey are persecuted because of the predatory habits for which they are so well adapted; within the order, numerous ways of selecting and catching prey have developed. All birds of prey have strong, hooked bills, perfect for tearing meat. Most are strong fliers, some with pointed wings for fast, dashing flight like the falcons, but the majority with long, wide wings perfect for support in a soaring flight high in the sky. The feet usually have long, sharp claws to give a firm hold on their prey. They are almost all diurnal in habits, unlike most owls, which become active when dark falls. They are usually long-lived compared with other birds of their size. Most birds of prey lay small clutches of eggs. Found in all continents except the Antarctic, they form an important and interesting element in nature, giving the greatest pleasure to the careful and patient observer.

Opposite Goshawk

Hawks and Eagles

order *Falconiformes,* family *Accipitridae*

This family includes such diverse birds as the large, carrion-eating Griffon Vulture, the robust, pigeon-hunting Goshawk, and the elegant, insect-eating Black-winged Kite. The family is defined by internal anatomical features, but can generally be distinguished from the family of falcons by the lack of the notch in the upper bill characteristic of that family. It may be divided into nine subfamilies.

The vultures with their broad, strong wings are found only in the southernmost parts of Europe. In endless circles they soar high in the sky, watching for any movement on the ground below them. With their keen eyesight they are able to spot dying animals at a great distance and at the same time keep an eye on the other vultures in the area. When a vulture spots a carcass, it descends and approaches the prey with great care in case some life should still be present. Its descent will be noticed by other neighbours in the air, and soon there will be a large congregation around the dying prey. When the last breath of life has left the unfortunate animal, the vultures set to work with much fighting and noise.

Four species of the vulture subfamily nest within the European continent. They have bare heads, an anatomical feature which is probably an adaptation to their feeding habit, as it is characteristic of other carcass-eating birds, for example some of the African storks. The two most typical species, the Griffon Vulture and the Black Vulture, have long necks and very big, strong bills. Their wings are broad and square, and the tail is short. In flight the head is tucked between the shoulders, which makes the soaring bird look like a flat board. The longer, more rounded tail of the larger and darker Black Vulture distinguishes it from the Griffon Vulture, which is the more common of the two. Both are carrion-eaters. They have been reduced in numbers as sanitation in Europe has progressed and fewer carcasses are left in the open for them to eat. The Griffon Vulture is the more sociable of the two; it often occurs in flocks at favourable feeding grounds and usually nests colonially. The nest is placed on a ledge or in a cave on a mountain slope. The Black Vulture nests in large isolated trees and only rarely resorts to cliffs. It is a stronger bird and will at times attack small mammals while they are still alive. In the hierarchy of carrion-eaters it ranks higher than the other European vultures, the Griffon usually giving way to the powerful bill of the Black Vulture.

At the bottom in social rank is the small Egyptian Vulture, which is not only a carrion-eater, but will eat almost any refuse offered and often congregates near refuse dumps. By ridding the streets of refuse, it performs a very important duty in countries with poor sanitation facilities. It does not have such broad wings as the two preceding species, but is nevertheless able to stay aloft for hours on its lookout for food. More often, it is seen perched in trees and on rooftops patiently waiting for somebody to discard some refuse on which it can feast. It breeds on inaccessible cliffs, where it places the crude pile of branches forming the nest on a ledge or in a small cave, but it will sometimes even nest on buildings. While the two larger vultures, the Griffon and Black, lay only one egg, the clutch of the Egyptian Vulture consists of two. The young are ready to leave the nest after about six weeks. Until then they are fed disgorged, half-digested carrion.

EGYPTIAN VULTURE *Neophron percnopterus* L 23–27" W 57–59" Smallest and most numerous European vulture. Encountered in almost all habitats, but most commonly in mountainous areas. Often frequents refuse dumps. Easily told from other European vultures by smaller size and whitish plumage with black wing-tips. Immatures are brownish, but can be distinguished from all other birds of prey by their characteristic silhouette. Plumage becomes gradually whiter, reaching full adult whiteness after 6 years. Wings pointed. Notice small, pointed head and long, rather thin bill. Often seen soaring. Roosts in treetops or on buildings. Usually silent. V

GRIFFON VULTURE *Gyps fulvus* L 40–43" W 92–109" Common in some open, mountainous regions. In flight looks rectangular as tail and head only protrude slightly. Distinguished from eagles by very large size and very short, square tail. Told from rarer Black Vulture by square tail and (in good light) lighter plumage contrasting with almost black wings. Whitish ruff is rarely visible. Immatures darker brown with brown ruff. Often seen soaring, sometimes several together. Roosts in trees, often in flocks. Various unmusical croaks and whistles are sometimes heard. V

BLACK VULTURE *Aegypius monachus* L 40–44" W 92–108" Uncommon. Usually only found in desolate mountains and plains. Told from eagles by large size and very long wings; from similar Griffon Vulture by longer, more rounded tail, larger head and bill, much darker plumage. Ruff dark brown in immatures, becoming paler with age. Dark pattern on neck and head rarely visible. Immatures have head and neck covered with uniform dark brown down. Although often seen with Griffon Vultures around carcasses, it is more solitary in behaviour. Usually silent.

LAMMERGEYER *Gypaëtus barbatus* L 41–46" W 98–109" Rare. Was almost extinct in Europe but is slowly gaining in numbers. Almost exclusively found in wild, mountainous areas. Easily identified by long, narrow wings, held slightly bent, and long, wedge-shaped tail. From below, notice contrast between creamy front part and dark wings, tail and belly. Immatures have dark head and breast. Although often seen soaring, it is more active than other vultures. More solitary in behaviour. Usually silent, but at breeding grounds utters loud, high-pitched whistles.

Egyptian Vulture

Griffon Vulture

Black Vulture

Lammergeyer

The Lammergeyer or Bearded Vulture bears little resemblance to the other vultures. Its wings are very long and pointed, and the tail is long and wedge-shaped. At the base of the bill a short 'beard' extends forward, lending the bird an exceptionally ferocious look. It frequents remote mountains where the nest is placed in caves on inaccessible cliffs. Although capable of catching small mammals alive, its food consists mainly of bones. When the other vultures have cleaned the carcass, the Bearded Vulture will descend upon it, breaking and swallowing the bones, which are digested in its hardy stomach. The name Lammergeyer means the 'lamb vulture', but in Europe lambs do not constitute a major part of its diet.

But let us turn from these not-so-appealing scavengers to the group admired by every nature-lover and the symbol of so many valiant and bloody episodes in human history, the eagles. The various birds of prey honoured with the name 'eagle' belong to several different genera, and even different sub-families. The term merely means a big bird of prey.

The 'true' eagles belong to the genus *Aquila* and form a rather homogeneous group. It is to this group that the eagles with the impressive names Golden and Imperial belong. The Golden Eagle is the most widespread and the best-known species of the genus. With a wing span of seven feet it is truly a magnificent bird. A few wing-beats will carry it high aloft where it soars silently in wide circles. When hunting, it sweeps down upon the prey, rabbits and hares, birds and smaller mammals, with great speed, grasping the despairing creature from behind with its powerful talons, but quickly ending any suffering with its strong bill. Sometimes the prey is eaten immediately, but often it is carried to a chosen site where the eagle can enjoy its meal more peacefully and securely than at the place of the kill. But the art of hunting is a difficult one for the eagle too, and hard to learn. It is believed that many young eagles simply starve to death before they learn to catch the prey abounding around them. Although it is a great hunter, the Golden Eagle does not find it beneath its dignity to eat insects, mice, fish and even carrion. Pride is unknown among birds, even among eagles: the struggle for survival is too serious a task.

The Imperial Eagle of southern Europe is smaller than the Golden Eagle and is not so mighty a hunter. In food it limits itself to smaller mammals and a larger proportion of carrion. The same is true of the Steppe Eagle of the eastern European steppes. Here the severe conditions force the eagles to become primarily carrion-eaters in the cold season of the year. Both the Imperial Eagle and the Steppe Eagle have bills which are weaker than the Golden Eagle's. The very similar Spotted and Lesser Spotted Eagles, both found primarily in eastern Europe, are also smaller than the Golden Eagle. The Spotted Eagle has a preference for swampy woods and lowlands where it hunts small mammals, insects and frogs. The Lesser Spotted Eagle retires to dense forests with clearings where it hunts rodents and insects on the ground. Whereas the Golden Eagle prefers to place its eyrie on an inaccessible ledge on a cliff, the other eagles nest in trees. Usually two eggs are laid, but often only one young is reared, as the first to hatch will eat the most food and even attack its smaller sibling which may finally succumb. The young eagle does not reach full maturity until four years of age.

Two smaller eagles, Bonelli's Eagle and the Booted Eagle, belong to a different genus, *Hieraaetus*. They inhabit the southern part of Europe. Both are found in mountainous regions, Bonelli's Eagle in the wilder and higher parts devoid of

WHITE-TAILED EAGLE *Haliaeetus albicilla* L 31–36"
W 78–92" Uncommon. Also called Sea Eagle, it prefers
coastal areas or large inland waters. Adult unmistakable
with pure white, wedge-shaped tail. Immature is dark
brown with varying numbers of cream-coloured spots,
gradually attaining adult plumage over 5 years. The
flight silhouette is characteristic with long neck and
head, short wedge-shaped tail and very broad wings
held horizontally. Wing-beats are sluggish. On favoured
haunts several may be seen together. Often seen soaring.
V

PALLAS' SEA EAGLE *Haliaeetus leucoryphus* L 27–
35" W 68–78" Uncommon. Only found in easternmost
parts of European Russia. Prefers open steppe country
close to rivers and lakes. Adult is unmistakable. Immatures very similar to White-tailed Eagle immatures but
have darker, longer tails and shorter wings. In behaviour
and silhouette it resembles the White-tailed Eagle.

GOLDEN EAGLE *Aquila chrysaetos* L 31–34" W 74–
90" Most common of the eagles but declining in numbers. Primarily found in mountainous areas, but sometimes, particularly in winter, in woods and fields. Easily
told from Sea Eagle by more harmonious proportions
(long tail, short neck), stronger, more well-controlled
wing-beats and squarish (not wedge-shaped) tail.
White wing spots and inner tail of immatures are diagnostic. These characteristics are lost when adult plumage
is attained at the age of 5 years. Adult birds have tawny-
golden nape. When soaring, this species holds its wings
above horizontal and the wing-tips point slightly upward and forward. Both the spotted eagles hold their
wings low. Imperial Eagle has proportionally shorter tail
and is smaller. Steppe Eagle has smaller head, narrower
wings. Golden Eagles are usually seen singly or in pairs
and hunt by searching mountainsides and fields from
low flight. R

White-tailed Eagle

juv.

Pallas' Sea
Eagle

Golden Eagle

juv.

IMPERIAL EAGLE *Aquila heliaca* L 31–33" W 69–73"
Uncommon. Prefers open fields, plains and swamps. Silhouette very similar to Golden Eagle, but tail proportionally shorter and wings held at more horizontal level. White scapulars, particularly prominent on Spanish form which also has white leading edge to wing, are diagnostic when present. This characteristic (attained when 3 years old) is lacking in immatures, which are light reddish-brown with streaked undersides (more prominent in eastern subspecies). Very similar Tawny Eagle has less distinct stripes on underside and smaller head. Behaviour more sluggish than that of Golden Eagle.

STEPPE EAGLE *Aquila rapax* L 27–30" W 62–68"
An uncommon eagle of dry, bushy plains or steppes. Adult has dark brown plumage. Flight silhouette is very similar to that of the Golden Eagle, but head is proportionally smaller. Difficult to distinguish from Spotted Eagle, but never has white upper rump. In flight, wings are held horizontal with slight bend. Immatures are very light, almost cream-coloured. Very sluggish in behaviour, rarely soaring high. Often perches on the ground. Tawny Eagle, the African subspecies, is an accidental visitor to the Mediterranean countries and cannot be distinguished from Steppe Eagle in the field.

SPOTTED EAGLE *Aquila clanga* L 27–29" W 63–67"
An uncommon eagle of extensive woods and bushy country, most often found near lakes, rivers and marshes. Adult is uniformly dark brown, sometimes with a little white on upper tail-coverts (diagnostic when strongly marked). Immatures have boldly spotted upper parts. Silhouette is rather disproportionate with short, rounded tail. Wing-tips point downward as wings are held with a downward bend from carpal joints. Wing-beats feeble. At close range seven primaries can be counted, as opposed to only six in Lesser Spotted Eagle. Wings and base of tail are wider than in Lesser Spotted, and wings are held straight out from body, not slightly forward. V

LESSER SPOTTED EAGLE *Aquila pomarina* L 25–27" W 55–63" Uncommon, usually met with in extensive woods, often near water. Adult very similar to Spotted Eagle, but never has clear white upper tail-coverts, although it may have a few white spots. Flight silhouette differs from Spotted Eagle by proportionally longer tail and more slender wings. Six primaries can be counted at close range. Immatures told from immature Spotted Eagle by fewer spots on back and lack of clear white upper tail-coverts.

eastern form

juv.

western form

Imperial Eagle

Steppe Eagle

juv.

Spotted Eagle

juv.

Lesser Spotted Eagle

juv.

Opposite Imperial Eagle

BONELLI'S EAGLE *Hieraaetus fasciatus* L 27–29"
W 62–66" This rather small eagle is uncommon. It prefers open, mountainous areas; in winter also found in more open country. More Goshawk-like in silhouette than other eagles. Adult is recognised by light underside of body contrasting with almost black underside of wings and long, barred tail with broad, black terminal band. Upper side is dark brown. Immature in first year has rusty head, red-brown underside and rather heavily barred tail. In second year it is almost uniformly brown but with black terminal band on tail. Characteristic plumage of the adult is attained after 3–4 years. Flight is swift and strong. Often seen in pairs, gliding along mountain sides. Exceptionally swift and aggressive in its hunt. Call resembles that of Goshawk.

BOOTED EAGLE *Hieraaetus pennatus* L 18–20"
W 43–46" Uncommon. This is the smallest European eagle, the size of a Buzzard. Found in mixed and deciduous woods with clearings, usually in low mountains but also in flatter country. Flight is swift and agile. Does not soar as often as Buzzard. Told from Buzzard by much longer and narrower tail. Occurs in two colour phases, a more common pale and a rarer dark phase. Pale phase is told from all other birds of prey by light wing linings and dark primaries. Scapulars are white, forming a characteristic white V when seen from above. Dark phase is uniformly dark brown with paler tail. Immatures resemble adults of the same phase, but in pale phase they have buffish, not white underparts. Call is a high-pitched, trilling cry.

SHORT-TOED EAGLE *Circaetus gallicus* L 26–27"
W 61–63" Uncommon. Prefers mountain slopes, gorges, secluded marshy plains and woodlands, where it hunts snakes and lizards. A very pale eagle with entire underside of wing white except for wing-tips. Two colour phases occur, a more common with rather dark head and breast and a rarer almost pure white. Tail is long and head exceptionally large. Wings are held at horizontal level with tips pointing slightly forward. Often seen soaring but will also hover like a Kestrel with dangling feet; an almost diagnostic feature for so large a bird. Easily told from Osprey by larger size, broader wings and dark upper side. Does not hover over water.

juv.
Bonelli's Eagle

dark phase
Booted Eagle
light phase

juv. light phase

light phase

Short-toed Eagle
dark phase

forests, the Booted Eagle in the forested lower parts. Bonelli's Eagle is the larger of the two and lives on medium-sized and small mammals and birds. An excellent flyer, it is even able to catch its prey in the air, a skill uncommon among broad-winged predators. Although often seen soaring, the Booted Eagle is primarily a forest-dweller, catching its prey of small mammals and birds on the ground, in much the same way as the Common Buzzard. It has a definite preference for ravines, mountain slopes and the edge of forests.

Bonelli's Eagle places its nest on a ledge or crevice on steep cliffs, while the Booted Eagle nests in trees, the nest always being skilfully adorned with fresh leaves and branches. The two white eggs are incubated for about forty days, for the most part by the female, the male only occasionally taking over this duty. The Booted Eagle occurs in two different colour-phases, a light and a dark. This phenomenon is not uncommon among birds of prey and is particularly common among birds of the genus *Buteo,* which are closely related to the *Hieraaeti.*

More widespread, but still mainly found in the southern parts of our continent, is the Short-toed Eagle. This large eagle belongs to a separate subfamily, *Circaetinae,* of which it is the only European representative. Characteristic is the disc of facial feathers giving it an almost owl-like look *en face.* Its staple food items are reptiles and snakes, although occasionally it may take other small animals. Since snakes are disappearing in many parts of Europe, so is this elegant, long-winged eagle. It prefers large, quiet woods interspersed with sunny clearings, or forest edges close to heaths and mountain slopes where reptiles are found in abundance. It sometimes hunts in the fashion of the Buzzard, slowly flying over the ground on the lookout for a snake or lizard warming itself in the sun, but more often it will sit on a low perch, patiently waiting for its prey to come within striking distance. Then it swoops upon it with a single wing-beat. It nests in trees and lays only a single egg.

The largest of the eagles are the sea eagles, of which two breed within our boundaries, the White-tailed Eagle and Pallas' Sea Eagle. Pallas' Sea Eagle is primarily an Asiatic species, and its breeding range only extends into the furthest south-east part of Europe. The White-tailed Eagle was probably once common throughout the continent, but today its scattered distribution bears witness to the relentless persecution it has suffered. Although it is very large with an enormous wing span (more than seven feet), the White-tailed Eagle nevertheless does not impress the observer with the majesty of the Golden Eagle. The silhouette is slightly disharmonic, with a short tail and rather long neck suspended on a pair of wide, almost soft-looking, board-like wings. But it is a powerful hunter and its approach is feared by the waterfowl on which it preys. Flying low over the water it selects its victim, for instance an eider, which it will relentlessly pursue. In panic the eider will dive and not until its oxygen-starved lungs demand it will it come to the surface again, only to see the shadow of its enemy grow as the eagle in a fast swoop descends upon it. Forced to keep diving, the duck will finally tire itself out and the eagle can pick it out of the waves with its strong talons. It is then carried to the shore where it is eaten. The White-tailed Eagle will also eat fish washed ashore, not rejecting even the most foul-smelling specimen. The gulls which usually rid our shores of these fish washed up on the beaches respectfully keep their distance from the feeding eagle, and only occasionally feign an attack to which the self-confident eagle pays no attention.

BUZZARD *Buteo buteo* L 20–22" W 46–54" Common. In summer, in wooded areas with openings and surrounding fields; in winter also on moors, plains and extensive open areas. In Britain, on rocky coasts and hillsides in both seasons. Plumage varies from almost pure white to almost black. Told from Long-legged Buzzard adult by barred tail, from Rough-legged by dark band on upper breast, lack of white rump and of black wing patches. Sometimes difficult to tell from Honey Buzzard but is generally heavier and without pellucid wings. Often seen soaring on migration in flocks. Often seen perched on poles or branches. Usually silent but in breeding season gives high-pitched, drawn-out mewing call. Sometimes hovers.   RP

ROUGH-LEGGED BUZZARD *Buteo lagopus* L 20–25" W 51–60" Common. Nests in mountainous, barren country. Winters in open habitats, marshes, fields and moors. Black carpal patches, black shield on belly and white rump diagnostic. Varies somewhat in colour and immatures have less pronounced characteristics than adults. Feathered tarsi only visible at very short range. In flight very similar to Common Buzzard, but heavier. Soars like the Buzzard but is often seen hovering.   W

LONG-LEGGED BUZZARD *Buteo rufinus* L 24–26" Uncommon, but probably often overlooked. Inhabits dry, open plains and steppes, more rarely mountains. Occurs in two colour phases, a more common light and a rarer dark phase. Light phase can be told from Buzzard by very light head and unbarred tail. Chocolate-coloured dark phase looks almost black at a distance but has light, unbarred tail. Immatures of both phases are difficult to distinguish from Buzzards. Habits closely resemble those of Buzzard.

The White-tailed Eagle uses the same nest year after year. The nest sometimes reaches enormous dimensions and both diameter and height can reach more than seven feet. It is usually placed in a large tree or on a rocky ledge and is visible from far away. Among the branches sparrows and other small birds will often find a nesting site, the eagles leaving them in peace. The two young ones eye their tenants with curiosity but usually do not try to catch them.

In the United States, the Bald Eagle, a close relative of our White-tailed Eagle, is faced with a new danger from the insecti-

medium phase

dark phase

Buzzard

Rough-legged Buzzard

Long-legged Buzzard

dark phase

light phase

HONEY BUZZARD *Pernis apivorus* L 20–22" W 47–50" Common. Nests in open forests with clearings; on migration more varied habitats. Very variable in plumage — ranges from chestnut brown to creamy white, but more sombre brown with greyish head most common. Immatures often very light with large brown spots. Easily confused with Buzzard with which it often mixes during migration. Notice longer, broadly barred tail, outstretched neck and narrower, pellucid wings. Not as sluggish in flight. Migrates in flocks. Does not hover.

SP

GOSHAWK *Accipiter gentilis* L 19–24" W 39–47" Common, but secretive in woodlands with preference for coniferous forests with many clearings. Looks like a large, heavy, short-tailed Sparrowhawk. White fluffy under tail-coverts are characteristic, as is the wide white stripe above the eye. Wing-beats are slower than Sparrowhawk's. Females much larger than males. Adult birds have barred, immatures have spotted undersides. Hunts by quartering wood edges and clearings. Extremely fast. Rarely seen soaring. At nesting site a rapid call similar to Sparrowhawk's and a mewing cry similar to Buzzard's can be heard.

R

cides used in agriculture. The eagle is not necessarily killed by eating prey which has eaten insects killed by the poison, but the fertility of the birds is impaired, bringing an already precariously low reproduction rate to a point where the species might not even be able to hold its own. This has also been found true of the Golden Eagle in Europe in areas where insecticides are widely used and is probably also true for the White-tailed Eagle in the same kind of locality. Already decimated in numbers, this might become the final blow depriving our lands of the already all-too-few eagles, Golden as well as White-tailed. Strict regulations

Honey Buzzard

light
phase

dark
phase

Goshawk

♀

♂

juv.

and restraint in the use of potent poisons in the agricultural countries are an absolute necessity if we are to avoid the alteration and further impoverishment of our wildlife.

The bird of prey most often seen in Europe is probably the Common Buzzard. It is not as big or as bold as the various eagles, but in its silent circling flight it lends equal beauty and charm to the landscape. Although considerably smaller, it has a silhouette similar to that of the Golden Eagle, with broad wings and a rather short, rounded tail. The closely related and slightly larger Long-legged Buzzard of the arid steppes of south-eastern Europe and the Rough-legged Buzzard of the north both have similar flight silhouettes. The Honey Buzzard, more remotely related to the other buzzards, has a similar appearance, but can be distinguished by its longer, more narrow tail.

The three buzzards of the genus *Buteo* feed primarily on

SPARROWHAWK *Accipiter nisus* L 12–15" W 24–31" Common. Mainly found in forested country but also in open country with groves and scattered trees, particularly in winter. Smaller size, longer tail and short rounded wings distinguish this species from buzzards, harriers and kites. Most easily confused with falcons, Kestrel in particular, but has different coloration, stiffer wing-beats and more rounded wings. Male can be quite rufous on underside. Goshawk is bigger and heavier and has white fluffy feathers at base of shorter tail. Very difficult to distinguish from Levant Sparrowhawk in the field. Flies very fast, usually along hedges or wood margins, low over the ground. Sometimes seen soaring with wings and tail more fanned-out than in direct flight. Not sociable. At nesting site a rapid 'leek-keh-leek' can be heard.   RP

Sparrowhawk

Levant Sparrowhawk

rodents, the Rough-legged Buzzard almost solely relying on them in its diet. On its breeding grounds in the far north, the Rough-legged Buzzard eats lemmings almost exclusively, and the number of Rough-legged Buzzards tends to fluctuate slightly with the numbers of this prey. A similar fluctuation, principally dependent on the varying numbers of fieldmice, can also be detected for the Common Buzzard, although it is not as evident.

Buzzards practise two methods of hunting. In one they fly low over the ground on the lookout for any movement in the grass betraying the presence of a small animal. As they spot their prey, they descend upon it in a fast drop, grasping it in

LEVANT SPARROWHAWK *Accipiter brevipes* L 13–15" W 25–31" Less common than Sparrowhawk. Prefers drier, more open country with deciduous woods. Very difficult to tell from Sparrowhawk — can only be identified safely at very short range. In all plumages it has red iris (not yellow) and adults have white underside to wing (not barred). Male has grey, not rufous cheeks. Female is less brown, more grey above with brown-spotted throat, not pure white throat. Immatures have larger drop-shaped spots on very white underside. It has 6–7 rather narrow tail-bands with a wider terminal band whereas the Sparrowhawk has 4 tail-bands with wider terminal band. Besides Sparrowhawk-like calls, it has distinct 'vee-vit'.

RED KITE *Milvus milvus* L 24–26″ W 57–61″ Quite common. Prefers wooded hills and open country with scattered groves and trees. Told from all other birds of prey by long, deeply forked tail and rufous plumage with white patches on underside of wings. Immatures have less deeply forked tail, but can be distinguished from Black Kite by lighter colour of plumage. Soaring flight is characteristic with angled wings. Flight is more buoyant than that of other birds of prey. Long tail is constantly tilted and twisted. On migration often seen with buzzards. Call is buzzard-like. RS

Red Kite

Black Kite

BLACK KITE *Milvus migrans* L 20–22″ W 44–46″ Common. Usually near lakes and rivers bordered with woods or scattered trees. In southernmost Europe also in drier and more open habitats. Not infrequently in or near towns where it scavenges. Quite similar to Red Kite, but has much darker plumage and shorter, less deeply forked tail. Immatures have white patches on underside of wings but have much darker plumage than Red Kite. Adults lack white wing patches. Sociable. Sometimes fishes like Osprey but will also take refuse on the ground or on shores. Often nests in colonies. V

their claws. The Rough-legged Buzzard will often hover above the spot where it suspects the presence of a prey, much in the fashion of the Kestrel. In its other hunting method the bird sits quietly on a perch or on the ground waiting for a prey to come within striking distance. Although the Common Buzzard most often hunts over fields and heaths, it will usually stay close to woods or groves where it spends the night, nests or just rests when full and not in the mood for hunting.

In the breeding season, the Rough-legged Buzzard has a preference for mountain slopes where its eyrie is found on the most inaccessible cliffs. In winter it frequents marshes and open fields where it can be seen hovering low over its prey. The Long-legged Buzzard is a bird of the dry, open steppes, where it places its nest in one of the scattered bushes or trees. The Honey Buzzard prefers forests where it finds the wasps' nests and bees' nests from which it extracts the larvae constituting the principal part of its food. It is well suited for this peculiar feeding habit, as the facial feathers are modified to small, strong and protective structures quite different from the soft feathers found in other birds of prey. It digs out the nests of wasps and bumblebees with its strong feet and picks from the honeycombs the defence-less larvae. It completely ignores the furious attacks from the rightful inhabitants. It also eats other insects, frogs or whatever small animals it is able to catch. It nests in tall trees and adorns its home with fresh branches, even after the two young have emerged from the white eggs.

In early spring one often sees pairs of buzzards wheeling in large circles higher and higher, riding on the rising air currents over the woods and fields. All of a sudden one folds its wings and drops like a stone towards the ground with tremendous speed. It does not spread its wings until just above the treetops. With an elegant swooping manoeuvre, the fall is halted, and the buzzard again starts circling to reach the heights from which its mate has admired the aerial display. It is an exhibition of such beauty that it always leaves the observer with a feeling of reverence for the magnificence of nature and its creatures.

In autumn when the young are well out of the nest, the buzzards of the northern parts of Europe start towards their winter homes further south. The Honey Buzzards, facing the most extensive journey which will bring them to the southern half of Africa, are the first to set off. By the end of August flocks of Honey Buzzards start circling over forest edges, mountain slopes and shorelines offering them strong rising air currents. Spiralling in wide circles, the birds gain height as if on a big screw, each bird on a different turn. When sufficient height has been gained, the topmost bird will stop its soaring flight and start on a straight course in a gradual descent; with hardly a wing-beat it heads toward the south-west, utilizing the momentum gained by the great height. It is followed by the other birds as they reach the top of the screw. When too much height has been lost in the course of the straight flight, a new area with rising air is found and the soaring starts all over again. Only when forced by strong winds will the buzzards travel by using an 'active' flight. Their wing-beats are heavy and laborious, and after three or four strokes they will sail on outstretched wings for a few moments before the wings again have to be used to gain speed and height.

Later in the autumn the Common Buzzards and the Rough-legged Buzzards wintering in Europe start their much shorter travel. They fly in the same way but are even more reluctant to work for their progress. This is also the time when sparrowhawks, harriers, falcons and other northern breeders are on the move to more favourable climates. Because of the reluctance of birds of prey to cross open water, certain narrow points exist where enormous numbers of birds of prey pass by. One such place, passed annually by about 20,000 buzzards and numerous other birds of prey is the south-western tip of Sweden, Falsterbo. On good days in the autumn some fifteen different species of birds of prey can be seen, adding up to a total of several thousand birds. The observer is also rewarded by a large number of migrating passerines crossing Øresund at the same place. Another such locality for migrating birds of prey is the Bosporus. It is passed by birds avoiding the Mediterranean and taking the roundabout route across the Middle East. At the Bosporus it is particularly the eagles which attract attention, but hundreds of other birds of prey and storks pass over this narrow strait. To visit one of these places is an unforgettable ornithological experience.

Among the common birds of prey seen at the points where migrants concentrate is the Sparrowhawk. Together with the almost identical Levant Sparrowhawk and the much larger Goshawk, it represents the subfamily *Accipitrinae*. These hawks are medium-sized with strong, short, rounded wings and rather long tails. Their flight is fast and powerful, and although they can be seen soaring on warm days, they usually fly a straight course only a few feet above the ground. A few strong wing-beats, followed by a period of gliding on stiff wings, bring the birds with great speed towards their destination.

All are forest-dwellers. The Goshawk leads a very secretive life in the dense woods. Both the Sparrowhawk and Levant Sparrowhawk prefer hunting in clearings, along hedges and forest edges. They all eat smaller birds caught in flight. The Goshawk has been used by falconers for centuries and is particularly good at catching pigeons and doves, which also constitute a large proportion of its food.

The Sparrowhawk quietly flies along a hedge and when it sees a small bird, the hunt goes on among the trees and bushes with enormous speed. Turning and twisting, the small bird will try to dodge its enemy, which swings round and as often as not catches the terrified prey in a fast dive.

The nests are placed high in trees. The Goshawk's nest can reach an enormous size as the birds keep adding material to the nest year after year. The Sparrowhawk and Levant Sparrowhawk lay from three to six eggs, while the Goshawk has a smaller clutch of three or four. While the Goshawk is mainly a resident bird, both the Sparrowhawk and Levant Sparrowhawk are migratory, particularly the northern populations. The sexes differ greatly in size, the females being considerably larger than the males. This is true of almost all birds of prey, but is more pronounced in this subfamily. The difference is so great that female Sparrowhawks and male Goshawks overlap in size, making field identification somewhat difficult.

Less homogeneous than the *Accipitrinae* is the subfamily of kites, *Milvinae*. Two species, the Kite or Red Kite and the Black Kite, nest over most of Europe while one, the Black-winged Kite, only breeds on the southernmost tip of the Iberian peninsula. The first two species are rather similar in appearance, both having long wings and long, forked tails. To watch one of these kites in flight is a delightful experience. As it soars rather low, the tail is in constant movement steering the bird into positions and circles where the utmost use is made of the wind.

The Black Kite is often seen over water on the lookout for

BLACK-WINGED KITE *Elanus caeruleus* L 13″ W 29″ Extremely rare and local in dry cultivated areas with scattered trees and bushes in southern part of Iberian peninsula. Colour pattern can be difficult to distinguish at a distance. Often seen hovering like a Kestrel, but also quartering the ground like a harrier. Flight pattern can be almost gull-like.

HEN HARRIER *Circus cyaneus* L 17–20″ W 40–43″ Common. Nests in open country and moorlands. Also seen hunting over marshes and swamps. Although not as large as Marsh Harrier, it is larger, heavier and less buoyant in flight than Montagu's and Pallid Harriers. More white on rump. Male told from male Montagu's by lack of black stripes on wing and unstreaked underside; from Pallid Harrier by more extensive black on wing-tips and grey breast. Females and immatures are similar and very difficult to distinguish from female Montagu's and Pallid Harriers. They are more brownish in general colouring. Usually seen singly flying low over the ground; at favourable hunting grounds sometimes a few together.
RWP

Black-winged Kite

juv.

Hen Harrier

♂

♀

MARSH HARRIER *Circus aeruginosus* L 19–22″ W 44–49″ Common. Nests in large, dense reed-beds. Also seen over open fields and marshes. Colour pattern characteristic. Notice lack of white rump. Heavier and broader winged than the other harriers and wings are held in a more open V. Wing-beats slower. Usually seen flying low over the ground but sometimes soars. On breeding grounds the nasal, high-pitched whistling call can be heard. RS

PALLID HARRIER *Circus macrourus* L 17–18″ W 39–41″ Uncommon. Although frequenting marshes and moorlands, it prefers dry steppes and plains. Male told from Montagu's and Hen Harriers by white breast, unbarred wing and very limited amount of black on wing-tips. Female and immature very similar to female and immature Montagu's. Habits like Montagu's.

MONTAGU'S HARRIER *Circus pygargus* L 16–17″ W 40–44″ Common. Found in marshes, moors, heaths and cultivated land. Smallest and most elegant of the harriers with quite narrow, pointed wings and very buoyant flight. Male easily told from male Hen and Pallid by narrower wing-bars and brown streaks on underside. Immatures have unstreaked rich rufous underside but are indistinguishable from immature Pallid Harriers. Females told from female and immature Hen Harrier by smaller size and more elegant appearance with less well-defined white rump. They are indistinguishable from female Pallid Harrier in the field. Black phase is very rare. Sometimes nests sociably. When hunting, flies low over the ground. S

fish which it catches in a fast plunge like an Osprey. Although it is not as efficient a fisherman as the Osprey, it catches quite large fish which are carried to the shore to be eaten. It is a widespread species in Africa and Asia where it competes with the vultures in devouring refuse of any kind. In Europe, this is not so often the case.

The Red Kite will also take carrion when it finds it, but is a more active hunter. It will attack almost any animal smaller than itself, a habit leading to the great decline in numbers it has suffered. As chickens are not safe from its pursuit, the bird has been persecuted relentlessly by man. All three species nest in trees, the Black Kite close to lakes and rivers, the Black-winged on more arid mountain slopes and plains. The number of eggs is two to five.

Harriers, members of the subfamily *Circinae,* are birds of prey of the open country. Characteristic of the group is the great difference in plumage between the sexes. The adult males of the Hen, Pallid and Montagu's Harriers are greyish-blue birds of the utmost beauty. The male of the slightly larger and heavier Marsh Harrier only has a blue tail and wings, the rest of the plumage being reddish brown. The females of the first three species are all streaked brown with a distinctive white rump. The female Marsh Harrier is dark brown, almost black, with a yellow crown and throat. In flight the harriers hold their wings with the tips pointing slightly upwards forming an open V. Usually flying low over the ground, the harriers are unmistakable as a group, but distinguishing between the females of the

Marsh Harrier

juv. ♀ ♂

Montagu's Harrier

♀ ♂ juv.

Pallid Harrier ♂

three smaller species is exceedingly difficult, sometimes impossible.

The Marsh Harrier is almost exclusively found in marshes and swamps with extensive reed-beds, and only occasionally will it be seen over fields and heaths where the other harriers have their homes. The Hen Harrier prefers open fields, marshes and moors. The Pallid Harrier reaches its greatest abundance on open, dry steppes. Montagu's prefers heaths with low bushes and trees, and here it will sometimes nest sociably. The nests are always on the ground or in reeds, and three to seven eggs are laid. Male and female are often seen flying together, and sometimes the male will throw the prey it has caught to the female which elegantly catches it in the air. The harriers are largely rodent-eaters and as such, highly beneficial to man. All of them will also take birds, particularly young ones, but this does not justify the persecution they have suffered. In this century Montagu's Harrier has extended its range to the north, now breeding commonly in Denmark and more sparsely in the rest of southern Scandinavia.

OSPREY *Pandion haliaetus* L 21–24" W 58–64" Common. Always found near lakes, rivers or sheltered coasts, as it lives almost exclusively on fish. Dark upper parts with white crown, white underparts with poorly marked, narrow breast-band distinguish it from all other birds of prey. Flight silhouette is characteristic. Wings are held at an angle and slightly arched. Usually seen flying slowly 20–30 feet above the water. Often hovers when prey is spotted. Plunges feet-first into the water. Sometimes sociable in nesting. Sometimes soars. Call is a rapid series of descending high-pitched whistles.

SP

Osprey

Osprey

order *Falconiformes,* family *Pandionidae*

The Osprey is the only member of this family. It is almost cosmopolitan in distribution. Although specialized for fishing, it looks very much like the larger members of the family of hawks and eagles with its long, broad wings and rather short tail. It soars well, but will also hover like a Kestrel when it has seen a fish. It plunges into the water feet first and is sometimes completely submerged before its powerful wings make it airborne again. It holds its twisting and fighting prey in a crushing grip with its strong talons. The feet are perfectly adapted for maintaining a secure hold on the slippery fish. The outer toe is opposable, allowing a better grip with two toes in front, two at the back, and the underside of the toes has a rough surface of minute spikes.

At favourable fishing-places the Osprey will sometimes nest sociably. The nests are placed in trees, on cliffs or sometimes even on the ground, and can reach a large size. The Osprey is always found near water, and even on migration does not venture far from lakes, seashores and rivers. Its three eggs are heavily spotted. Incubation takes about five weeks, the female carrying the larger part of this burden. About nine weeks after emerging from the eggs, the young are ready to leave the nest to try their own skill as fishermen. Ospreys sometimes go for larger prey than they can handle, and more than once an Osprey has met its fate below the surface of the water with its claws deeply embedded in the back of a fish strong enough to drag it down.

Falcons

order *Falconiformes*, family *Falconidae*

The fifty-eight members of this widespread family are divided into four subfamilies. Only one subfamily, consisting of the genus *Falco*, is represented on our continent. But among our ten falcons are found the most elegant and powerful fliers of all birds of prey. With their long, pointed wings and tails the falcons can reach incredible speeds in their dives or 'stoops'—a Peregrine Falcon has been measured diving with a speed of 175 mph. Also characteristic of the family is the notch of the upper bill, the 'tooth' of the falcon.

Falcons are formidable hunters. Their great speed and agility makes it very difficult for the selected prey to escape its fate. All its turns and twists are of little avail, and only the closed formation of a flock seems to offer some protection, if the formation can be maintained under attack. When a falcon strikes it depends on its momentum for the blow it gives the prey, which often is heavier than the falcon itself. At tremendous speed the falcon plunges from the sky with closed wings. The impact of

Below Osprey

A. Singer

Gyrfalcon

light phase

dark phase

intermediate phase

GYRFALCON *Falco rusticolus* L 22–24" W 49–52"
Uncommon. Found in mountainous open country.
Outside breeding grounds most often found on sea
coasts and other open areas. Largest of the falcons. Told
from Peregrine by larger size, proportionally longer tail,
slower wing-beats and much broader base of wing.
Lacks the contrast between dark upper side and light
underside so characteristic of Peregrine. Easternmost
birds are very dark, while the Scandinavian are intermediate in colour. The almost white Greenland birds are
very rare. Flies low over the ground but sometimes soars.
Often perches on rocks or poles.   V

PEREGRINE FALCON *Falco peregrinus* L 16–20"
W 32–44" Formerly common, now much reduced in
number, apparently due to the effects of poisonous
chemicals on its prey. Usually found in open or semi-
open country with trees or cliffs, where the nest is built.
Also open woods. Coastal in Britain. Outside breeding
season often found on marshes and moors. Told from
Gyrfalcon by smaller size and greater contrast between
dark upper side and light underside; from Lanner and
Saker Falcon by darker back and head. Female larger
than male. Immatures have brown, not black upper side,
but head is always dark. Moustachial streak is broad and
well-pronounced. Flight swift and strong with fast wing-
beats interrupted occasionally by gliding. Sometimes
soars. Usually solitary. Often perches on stones and
poles in the open.   RP

SAKER FALCON *Falco cherrug* L 18" W 41" Uncommon. A bird of the open plain, semi-desert and desert.
Looks like very pale Peregrine (paler than Lanner). Light
underside, crown and nape finely streaked. Moustachial
streak pale and narrow. Slightly larger than Lanner.
Immatures have darker and bolder streaks on crown and
underside. Behaviour and habits as Peregrine but more
confined to open country.

LANNER FALCON *Falco biarmicus* L 17" W 39"
Uncommon. Found on mountain slopes and plains,
rocky shores and brushland. Very similar to Peregrine,
but has light brown crown and lighter back. Breast in
adult has only few spots; immature more heavily spotted.
Moustachial streak narrow but well-defined. Behaviour
and habits much like Peregrine but less bold.

Peregrine Falcon

juv.

Saker Falcon

juv.

Lanner Falcon

juv.

Opposite Peregrine Falcon

A. Singer

ELEONORA'S FALCON *Falco eleonorae* L 14" W 35"
Local and uncommon. Found on rocky Mediterranean islands and sea cliffs. Occurs in two colour phases: a dark slate grey and a more common light phase with dark upper side and light, heavily streaked underside. Dark phase can be confused with the smaller Red-footed Falcon male, but it lacks the red under tail-coverts. Light phase can be confused with larger immature Peregrine, but has yellow cere, narrower moustachial streak, more heavily streaked underside and longer tail. Immatures of light and dark phases are correspondingly coloured. Larger than Hobby, which it closely resembles in flight. Hunts birds and insects in dashing elegant flight.

HOBBY *Falco subbuteo* L 11–12" W 27–30" Quite common. Found in open woodlands and heaths with many groves. Looks like small Peregrine but is more heavily streaked on underside, and adults have chestnut thighs and under tail-coverts. Immatures are more heavily streaked and lack chestnut areas. Moustachial streak is well defined. Immatures told from immature Red-footed Falcon by dark forehead and more heavily streaked underside. Does not hover like Red-footed Falcon. Manoeuvres with extreme elegance when hunting insects and small birds. Flight silhouette is characterized by long sickle-shaped wings and comparatively short tail distinguishing it from much larger Peregrine Falcon. Does not look as compact as the slightly smaller Merlin. Call is a repeated 'kick'. S

the blow knocks the prey over completely, leaving it to the mercy of the falcon. The falcon can even manoeuvre itself in such a way that it strikes the prey unexpectedly from below.

Falcons also take their prey on the ground. Kestrels habitually hunt in this way and are hardly capable of catching anything on the wing. On the other hand, they are perfect at hovering, hanging unobserved above the small rodents they prey upon. The large Gyrfalcon usually strikes its prey on the ground. It prefers Ptarmigan, but will take any animal from a lemming to a goose. Some of the smaller falcons, particularly the Red-footed Falcon, catch insects in the air, sometimes with their beaks, sometimes with their feet. All falcons have aerial displays varying somewhat from species to species. Elegant dives, loops and turns are part of this magnificent performance high above the treetops. The display is the prelude to breeding.

None of the falcons build nests of their own. Some use old nests of crows or buzzards; some lay their eggs on cliffs and

Eleonora's Falcon

light

juv.

light phase

dark phase

juv.

Hobby

MERLIN *Falco columbarius* L 11–12" W 24–26"
Common. A bird of prey of the open, nesting on moors and tree-less hills; outside breeding season also found on marshes, cultivated fields and along seashores. A very small, very fast falcon. Male has bluish back and tail. Larger female has dark brown back and tail. Told from Hobby by longer tail with broad black band near tip, smaller size and less sickle-shaped wings. From Kestrel by colours, shorter tail and more compact appearance. Moustachial streak ill-defined. Immatures resemble female closely. Easily told from Sparrowhawk by pointed narrow wings. Flies fast low over the ground. Often seen perched low on stones and fence posts. Nests on the ground. Call is a Kestrel-like chattering 'ki-ki-ki'.   RWP

RED-FOOTED FALCON *Falco vespertinus* L 10–12" W 23–28" Common, often seen in flocks. Found on open and semi-open plains, wood edges and open agricultural areas with scattered trees. Male is slate-black with red feet and rusty under tail-coverts, the latter distinguishing it from dark phase Eleonora's Falcon. Female very light rufous, resembling female Kestrel, but with lighter head and unstreaked breast. Immatures resemble immature Hobby but are paler with pale forehead and less bold streaking of underside. Very long wings. Behaviour resembles Kestrel's but it is often seen in flocks hunting insects, particularly at dusk. Often hovers. Nests colonially. Call is Kestrel-like, but higher pitched.   V

ledges or in hollow trees. The Red-footed Falcon is a sociable nester, as is the Lesser Kestrel. The Red-footed Falcons sometimes select a rookery for a nesting site, waiting to lay their eggs until the Rooks have left. The Kestrel sometimes nests on buildings and ruins and, like the Peregrine, can also nest on the ground. The Gyrfalcon prefers ledges on cliffs, but in years when its Arctic home abounds with Ptarmigan it might even place the eggs on big boulders on the open tundra.

The Gyrfalcon was the highest in social rank in the hierarchy of falconry. Particularly valuable was the white race from the rocky shores of Greenland. Very rarely one of these almost pure white birds will make its way across the Atlantic to our shores. The less spectacular grey race nesting in northernmost Europe is also only a rare straggler further south.

The Peregrine is found on the entire continent and is actually almost cosmopolitan in distribution. It will nest in trees as well as inaccessible cliffs, but has declined in numbers dramatically in

Merlin

Red-footed Falcon

juv.

Lesser Kestrel

♂

LESSER KESTREL *Falco naumanni* L 11–12″ W 24–26″ Very common. Often seen in surroundings of villages and towns, hunting in open agricultural country and marshes. Roosts in flocks in trees. Very similar to Kestrel but slightly smaller with smaller bill and white claws (black in Kestrel). Male has unspotted back and wings with clearer blue and red markings. Female indistinguishable in field except for gregarious, noisy habits. Hunts insects in the air and on the ground. Does not hover as frequently as Kestrel. Call is more chattering, not as shrill as Kestrel's. Nests colonially in ruins, cliffs or quarries.
V

KESTREL *Falco tinnunculus* L 12–13″ W 27–29″ Most common and widespread of the falcons. Found in almost all types of open and semi-open habitats. Male has blue head and nape, reddish back and wings with dark spots and blue tail with broad sub-terminal black band. Can only be confused with Lesser Kestrel which has unspotted back and wings. Female and immatures have barred reddish-brown upper side and apart from black, not light claws and more solitary habits, are almost indistinguishable from female and immature Lesser Kestrels. Told from female and immature Red-footed Falcons by spotted breast, dark forehead and broad, dark sub-terminal band on tail. Flight-silhouette is characteristic with long, pointed wings and very long tail. Often hovers at 20–30 feet with tail fanned out on the lookout for prey, insects and small mammals on the ground. Usually solitary in habits. Call is a series of shrill 'keh-leek' notes.
RW

♂ **Kestrel**

♀

recent years. The Lanner and Saker Falcons of southern and eastern Europe have similar nesting habits. Their lives are inadequately studied, but they seem to be very closely related to the Peregrine.

Eleonora's Falcon of the Mediterranean is a very interesting species. Smaller than the Peregrine, it lives on smaller birds such as warblers and pipits. It breeds on rocky cliffs and sea-shores, and the nesting season is delayed until early autumn. This is the time when the small passerines from northern Europe pass through the Mediterranean countries on the way to their African winter homes, and the time when by far the largest concentration of small birds is to be found in this area. Eleonora's Falcons take a heavy toll of these passage-migrants on which they raise their offspring. This is one of the most amazing adaptations of breeding habits and a clever example of the ingenuity of nature.

In open wooded country one is sometimes lucky enough to see a bird looking almost like a giant swallow. It is the Hobby, a small falcon found all over Europe, but never numerous. To a large degree it lives on insects, but it is also able to take small birds like swallows and larks. The eggs are most often laid in an abandoned crow's nest in a wood with many clearings spacious enough for hunting dragonflies and other large insects.

The Merlin is about the same size as the Hobby, but is a bird of the open fields, moors and marshes. Here it hunts larks, sparrows, buntings and other small birds, only rarely taking insects and small rodents.

The Red-footed Falcon is also found in the open, usually nesting in small groves. Like the Lesser Kestrel, it is sociable in behaviour, but unlike it, is not found in cities and villages. The Lesser Kestrel is almost identical in looks to the Kestrel but is much more gregarious in habits. In some southern cities hundreds can be counted, and the roosting place, usually a lonely tree in the outskirts of the town, is lively and noisy when the Lesser Kestrels settle for the night. Several pairs of Kestrels, so familiar in the rural districts of Europe, can sometimes be found nesting in close proximity on buildings or ruins, but usually it is a solitary nester and frequently it takes over an old crow's nest on the edge of a forest or in a small grove. Its hunting grounds are open fields, over which it is often seen hovering. It also likes to perch on telephone poles and cables whence it keeps an eye on what goes on in the grass below. Rodents and insects are its staple food items, and only rarely does a small bird succumb to it, except in cities like London where it takes sparrows.

The sexes of falcons differ considerably in size, particularly in the bigger species. The females are always larger and play a dominant role in the breeding season. The size difference seems to have some survival value in offering a larger choice of prey for the pair, which is particularly valuable when the young are being reared and crave for food.

Falcons lay from two to six eggs, the larger species laying fewer than the smaller. The incubation time for the Kestrel is about one month, and it takes another month before the young are ready to stretch their wings and leave the nest. During incubation and the first week or so after the eggs have hatched, the female stays on duty while the male catches most of the food and brings it to the nest. In most species of birds of prey this is the case, and in many it is always the female which feeds the young, the duty of the male being limited to catching and bringing food to the nest.

Gallinaceous Birds
order *Galliformes*

This order is fairly well defined, its members being ground dwellers with strong feet, short, strong bills and rounded wings. Most have sedentary habits. They all resemble the domestic fowl, the wild form of which, the Jungle Fowl, is still found in south-east Asia. Six families make up this order. Only two of these, the grouse and the pheasants, are represented in Europe. The megapodes of the Australian region are unique in building a pile of leaves which ferments to produce the heat for the incubation of their eggs. The currasows, the turkeys and the Hoatzin are all New World families, while the guineafowl are African.

The order is sometimes called the 'game birds' as many of its members are popular among hunters and gourmets.

Grouse
order *Galliformes*, family *Tetraonidae*

All eighteen species of this family of attractive game birds are found in the northern hemisphere from the temperate zone to the Arctic.

The anatomical characteristics of the family include nostrils covered with feathers, either feathered toes or pectinated toes, and the lack of spurs. They vary in weight from one to fourteen pounds.

All grouse are sedentary although some movements have been observed in the northernmost populations of Ptarmigan. Ptarmigan and Willow Grouse inhabit the high mountains in summer but in winter most of them are forced down the mountain slopes by the snow and only a few hardy Ptarmigan will endure the bitter cold and heavy snow in their lofty summer home. Other grouse are resident, often very strongly attached to a small area where they spend their entire life.

Mysterious fluctuations in numbers are characteristic of almost all grouse, and of Ptarmigan in particular. As with the famous lemmings, the north will see years of overabundance

BLACK GROUSE *Lyrurus tetrix* L male 21", fem. 16" Common on heath and moors, wide open woods, fields, and in winter also in open birch woods. Blackcock (male) can hardly be confused with any other European species except perhaps Capercaillie, which is found in coniferous woods, is much larger, not as black and has rounded, not lyre-shaped, tail. Greyhen (female) has slightly forked tail, is larger and more brownish-grey than hen Red Grouse, and smaller and not as barred as hen Capercaillie. At short range, very narrow white wing-bar can be seen. Flies high for a game bird and takes rather long glides. Sometimes hybridizes with Capercaillie, Red Grouse and Pheasant. Most often seen at dawn and dusk. Displays are picturesque, the cocks performing beautifully with fanned-out tails and puffed-up plumage, on special areas called 'leks'. Feeds on shoots and buds. Cocks are often polygamous and do not help rear the young. R

Black Grouse

WILLOW GROUSE *Lagopus lagopus* L 16″ Common, but abundance varies. Found in moors with low scrub, often near rivers. Usually at lower altitudes than Ptarmigan but not uncommon a little above tree limit. Difficult to tell from Ptarmigan but is larger with proportionally larger bill, more rufous colours in summer, and in winter neither cock nor hen has dark stripe between eye and bill characteristic of cock Ptarmigan. In autumn, Willow Grouse is patchy dark brown and white, and not grey above like Ptarmigan. Winters in small flocks. When flushed, gives rapid laughing call.

RED GROUSE *Lagopus lagopus scoticus* and *Lagopus lagopus hibernicus* L 13–15″ The Red Grouse of Britain and Ireland are now regarded as races of the Willow Grouse. Common on upland moors and heaths. Dependent on heather at different stages for food, nesting and cover. In cold spells may go down to fields. Wings dark in all plumages. Colour predominantly dark rufous, distinguishing them from Greyhen (female Black Grouse), Hazelhen and partridges. Hens paler than cocks and Irish race yellower than British. Voice like Willow Grouse's.   R

followed by seasons when they are hardly to be found. The cycle is six to eight years and influences the numbers of predators. Gyrfalcons and foxes are strong in numbers in the peak years of Ptarmigan, falling back when their prey reaches its low. No full explanation has been offered for this strange fluctuation, although attempts have been made to link it with practically every natural phenomenon, including sunspots.

Grouse live mostly on plant material, seeds, buds and fresh leaves, but the chicks eat insects in summer and the adults also take a share of these. Grouse also swallow a lot of small pebbles which are necessary to help the digestion of hard plant material, seeds in particular. Snow cover is perhaps most dangerous for grouse by depriving them of these small stones, as they will usually be able to find enough food on branches sticking up out of the heavy snow. Gamekeepers in Scandinavia, therefore, are as concerned that pebbles be laid out for the birds as they are for their food.

Ptarmigans—the genus includes the Willow Grouse and its British race, the Red Grouse—have their toes covered with feathers, 'snowshoes', a unique adaptation for walking on soft snow. Their scientific name, *Lagopus,* means the foot of a hare. It refers to the look of the foot in winter when the feathers are much longer than they are in summer.

♂ summer

Willow Grouse

♂ autumn

♂ winter

♂ summer

♀ summer

♂ winter

♂ summer

Red Grouse

♀ summer

♂ summer

An adaptation to the snow-covered areas in which Ptarmigan live is the plumage change. In winter they are almost pure white, in summer brown like the bare mountain slopes on which they live. The similar Red Grouse, the prized game bird of the moors of the British Isles, do not change their plumage in winter, probably an evolution which has taken place since the last Ice Age when the population became isolated from the Continent.

The ptarmigans and the Hazelhen are monogamous while the Capercaillie and the Black Grouse are polygamous. Spectacular as is the display, for instance, of the Red Grouse, in which the male jumps vertically into the air, it cannot compete in magnificence with the performance at the 'lek' of the polygamous species. The Black Grouse in early spring select special display grounds, leks. Here the cocks compete for the attention of the hens. With wings hanging down and the beautiful lyre-shaped tail extended and cocked upwards, they utter their deep chuckling notes. The white under tail-coverts and the red skin flaps over the eyes contrast magnificently with the deep black of the plumage, as the Blackcocks (male Black Grouse) face each other in their bloodless contest early in the morning. Even less vicious is the dawn display of the Capercaillie in the depth of the woods. The males perch on rocks or branches a little above the

CAPERCAILLIE *Tetrao urogallus* L male 34", fem 24" Common in large coniferous woods, sometimes seen at edges and in clearings. Retiring in habits. Enormous size, black plumage and rather long, fan-shaped tail make cock unmistakable. Hen is less characteristic but told from Greyhen (female Black Grouse) by more closely barred plumage, much longer, rounded tail, rufous in colour. In flight, cock easily recognized even at a distance by size, long neck, very short wings with rapid wing-beats and light underside of wings. When flushed, bursts out of cover very noisily. Display of cock is magnificent; he stands on a rock with tail cocked and fanned and bill pointing upwards, calling. Feeds on buds, shoots, berries and some insects. Often polygamous; cock takes no part in domestic duties.   R

PTARMIGAN *Lagopus mutus* L 14" Common in mountain areas, normally above the tree line. Usually found at higher elevations than Willow Grouse. In summer, cock lighter and more yellow than larger Willow Grouse, but hens are virtually identical except for size and bill. In winter both sexes are white with black tail, and cock has black line through eye. Found in pairs in summer, in flocks in winter. When flushed, utters peculiar, dry croaking, very different from laugh of Willow and Red Grouse.   R

courtship display

Capercaillie

♀ summer ♀ winter ♂ autumn

Ptarmigan
♂ summer

♂ winter

♂ summer

♂ winter

ground. With their bills stretched upward, tails fully spread and cocked vertically, they utter their song, a series of whispering and knocking sounds.

Although the Capercaillie is polygamous, it has been observed that the number of males often exceeds that of females. Nevertheless, no pair formation takes place and, unlike the Ptarmigan males which faithfully guard the incubating female, neither the Blackcock nor the Capercaillie cock pays any attention to the rearing of its offspring. Birds of this family produce between five and twelve eggs.

Grouse chicks are delightful little creatures. Covered with soft brown down in different patterns when they emerge from the eggs, they are immediately ready to leave the nest and after ten to fourteen days their wings have grown enough for them to fly short distances.

In winter grouse collect into packs. Those of the Ptarmigan consist of families, while Black Grouse and Capercaillie make up parties all of the same sex. While Ptarmigan and Black Grouse are birds of the open countryside, Hazelhen and Capercaillie are found in dense woods.

Hazelhen

HAZELHEN *Tetrastes bonasia* L 14″ Common but retiring, in woods near rivers and on mountainsides with thick undergrowth. Cock has black throat; hen's throat is whitish. Black band on grey tail of both sexes is very distinctive in flight. General colour of plumage varies from rufous to greyish-brown. Unlike most other grouse, it does not crouch when danger approaches, but immediately takes to wing with characteristic burring sound. Often perches in trees. Usually seen in pairs or families. Call is repeated whistling.

Pheasants, Partridges and Quail

order *Galliformes*, family *Phasianidae*

This, the largest of the families of game birds, contains 178 species, of which five are native to Europe and one, the Pheasant, introduced. Characteristic of the family are the uncovered nostrils, bare and smooth feet and the presence of a spur on the legs of many species.

The Pheasant was introduced into Europe by Roman times and although there is no certainty that the Romans introduced it to England, it was present there as early as the year 1059, when we have the first reference to this colourful bird. Several different subspecies have been introduced all over Europe and most of the Pheasants met with now have blood from a number of these subspecies. Although introduced to parks and estates, it has maintained a wary behaviour which is probably a decisive factor in its enormous success. There are few places in Europe where the Pheasant is not today an integral part of the natural scene. Although originally a reed-bed species, it is not particular in choice of habitat, but flourishes best in cultivated land with hedges, groves and open woods. The food is varied, including leaves, berries, grain and insects of all kinds. With a clutch size up to fifteen or more eggs, the rate of reproduction is enormous, and it is known that fifty Pheasants can swell to fifty thousand in ten years. The dangers faced by the Pheasant are many: the shotgun is the worst, but many a nest and female have been destroyed by harvesting machines. The chicks fall prey to rats, foxes and predatory birds, and many succumb when the weather is particularly cold or wet.

Our native members of this family, the partridges and the Quail, are faced with the same dangers and some, like the Common or Grey Partridge, have trouble holding their own, while the Quail has recently been decimated in numbers in some areas.

The partridges are smaller than the Pheasant. To a much greater degree than the Pheasant they are birds of the open. The Rock and Barbary Partridges are found on dry, rocky slopes covered only with bushes and a few clusters of trees. The Barbary Partridge is limited to Gibraltar and Sardinia in its European distribution, while the Rock Partridge is found in a much larger area covering Italy and the Balkans.

Chukar

CHUKAR *Alectoris chukar* L 13″ Common, preferring open, rocky and barren lands. Closely resembles Rock Partridge but barring on flank more strongly marked and black ring around throat is broken near the eye. Call is chicken-like.

Opposite Black Grouse displaying

95

juv.   ♀   ♂   Partridge

PARTRIDGE *Perdix perdix* L 12" Most widespread and numerous European partridge, found in almost any kind of open land, cultivated or uncultivated. The numbers in Britain have recently declined. Notice small size, rusty tail, orange-brown unbordered throat and face, and chestnut patch on belly. Like other partridges, often encountered in pairs or family groups. When flushed, bursts into flight with noisy wing-beats. Coveys usually do not spread out widely. Rather silent, except during spring courtship, when cocks call 'chirrick, chirrick'. Also calls when flushed.   R

ROCK PARTRIDGE *Alectoris graeca* L 13" Common in rocky evergreen forests and scrub, also found above tree limit. Closely resembles Red-legged Partridge but has larger white throat patch with very distinct, clean-cut black border. Upper parts greyish-brown rather than red-brown. Call is characteristic three-note whistle.

BARBARY PARTRIDGE *Alectoris barbara* L 13" Common in arid scrub. Barbary, Red-legged and Rock Partridges and Chukar are almost indistinguishable at long range. At shorter range, Barbary Partridge told from all others by chestnut-coloured, rather than black, border of the grey, not white, throat-patch. Call consists of fast and slow cackling notes.

PHEASANT *Phasianus colchicus* L male 33", fem 23" Common in open woods and on farmland in scrub, hedgerows and fields. Both sexes have long pointed tails and short, rounded narrow wings. Cock very colourful with distinctive red eye patch on black head and neck. Plumage is variable, depending on the origin of the released stock. Some have distinct white ring on neck. Hen is mottled brown but long, pointed tail is diagnostic. Bursts upward into flight noisily if flushed, and flies strongly but only for short distances. Roosts in trees, often in small flocks. Feeds mostly on waste grains, seeds and berries. Often seen in the open. The cock's loud, two-syllabled call is followed by the muffled sound of rapidly beating wings.   R

Rock Partridge

Barbary Partridge

Pheasant

♀   ♂

Red-legged Partridge

The Red-legged Partridge is found in fields and sandy heaths, usually preferring drier ground than the Common Partridge, which is the most common and widespread of this group and is found in open fields and grass heaths. A characteristic of the partridges is their preference for places with sand and dust where they can 'bathe'.

RED-LEGGED PARTRIDGE *Alectoris rufa* L 13½"
Common on farmland and heaths with preference for more arid regions. At a distance difficult to tell from Partridge, as both have reddish tail and brownish back. At closer range notice red bill and legs, heavily barred sides and lack of chestnut-brown patch on belly. Immatures spotted rather than streaked. Much more reluctant than Partridge to take wing or run long distances. Coveys spread out when flushed. Has characteristic call with repeated first note: 'chuck, chuck-or'. R

QUAIL *Coturnix coturnix* L 7" Formerly abundant but has declined in numbers. Found in grassland and fields. Usually keeps out of sight, hidden in vegetation. Smaller than any other game bird. Sandy coloured, with striped back and sides. Cock is striped on throat, hen unmarked. Best told from Andalusian Hemipode of similar size and build by striped, not spotted, side and sandy, not orange, breast. Very hard to flush. Once on the wing, flight is low and slow with very fast wing-beats and the very short tail looks sandy coloured, not red like that of Partridge, which it resembles somewhat in build and colours. Our only migrating gallinaceous bird. On migration, seen in small bevies (flocks) but otherwise usually solitary. Call can be heard day and night but most often at dusk. Consists of repetition of liquid, three-syllabled notes: 'wet-my-lips'. S

ANDALUSIAN HEMIPODE *Turnix sylvatica* L 6"
Very secretive, usually found in well-covered brush and grassland. Very similar to Quail but has bright orange patch on breast and black spotting on sides. More closely related to the cranes and rails than to the gallinaceous birds. Usually seen singly or in pairs and family groups. Very hard to flush. Call is a characteristic resonant 'hoo-hoo-hoo', heard particularly often on clear nights at dawn and dusk.

Quail

Andalusian Hemipode

In winter partridges are met with in tight coveys consisting of the members of a family. On winter nights the birds cluster together closely on the snow, offering each other protection against the bitter cold. In spring the coveys break up and the males set up their territories in the fields; they can often be heard at night as they warn off competitors and attract females with their squeaky 'song'. If the mate of the preceding year has survived the dangers of the winter, the couple will stay together; if not, another mate will be attracted to the territory. The nest is a hollow which the female scrapes under a bush or in the open. Here the eggs, varying in number from ten to twenty, are laid. The partridge does not start incubating until all the eggs are laid, and the exposure of the eggs at this time leads to the destruction of many clutches if a spell of cold weather sets in. After an incubation period of about twenty-four days the eggs hatch. All the eggs hatch within a few hours and the nest is left almost as soon as the chicks are dry. Both male and female tend the chicks, brooding and protecting them. When little more than a week old, they can flutter along, although they are not able to manage a sustained flight.

Like grouse, partridges fluctuate in numbers. This fluctuation is not as apparent in the field as that of the Ptarmigan, but shows up clearly in game statistics.

The smallest of the game birds is the Quail. The size of a Starling and with a clay-coloured plumage, it easily avoids detection, except in spring when the male courts his mate with his liquid call. Quail are very difficult to flush and only when almost stepped upon will they take to the wing, abandoning the crouching position in which they have been hiding.

As it breeds in fields, harvesting machines take a heavy toll of Quail nests and birds. This is at least part of the reason for the severe decline in numbers noticed all over Europe in recent years. Even more devastating is the hunting of these birds in the Mediterranean countries as they pass through on their migration to north Africa. Migrating at night in small flocks, Quail fly low over the ground and are easily taken in nets put up by hunters. Caught by the thousand in the Middle East, they were exported in such quantities as to be of economic importance. In the peak year 1920, more than three million were exported from Egypt alone, many of them alive in cages. Thanks to conservationists this trade in live birds has been stopped. Quail are mentioned in the Bible when they were picked up by the Hebrews during the Exodus. But the days of abundance have passed never to return, and only through strict enforcement of game laws will we be able to maintain a stock.

Very similar to the Quail is the Andalusian Hemipode, the only European representative of a family belonging to the order *Gruiformes* (Cranes and Rails). It is pictured here because it is most easily confused with a Quail, although differing in both habits and internal anatomical features.

Cranes, Bustards and Rails
order *Gruiformes*

Four of the eleven families within this diversified order are represented in Europe. These are the hemipodes, cranes, bustards, and rails, gallinules and coots, the last three being grouped into one family. The seven other families are distributed over the other continents; each contains not more than three species.

The members of this order are characterized by somewhat similar skeletal and muscular anatomy; in general they are marsh birds, though the bustards and hemipodes show a preference for drier grasslands. They range in length from the five-foot-long Sarus Crane to the five-inch Hemipode.

Hemipodes
order *Gruiformes,* family *Turnicidae*

Of the sixteen hemipodes found throughout the southern part of the Old World, only one, the Andalusian Hemipode, has penetrated as far north as Europe. It nests in the southernmost part of the Iberian peninsula, where it frequents the dry fields and thickets so common in that region. In looks it is very similar to the Quail, but its behaviour is quite different. Hemipodes are extremely difficult to flush and are usually met

Below Common Cranes

with singly or in pairs, never flocking like Quail. As is the case with some shorebirds, the roles of the sexes are reversed: the female performs the courtship and after she has laid the four eggs in a nest on the ground, the male takes over all responsibility for the rearing of the next generation. For ease of comparison the Andalusian Hemipode is pictured together with the Quail on page 97.

Cranes

order *Gruiformes,* family *Gruidae*

The beauty and elegance of cranes have been praised so often and so eloquently that the mere statement that they are large, long-legged, long-necked marsh birds seems almost unnecessary. The Greeks enjoyed the sight of these gorgeous birds flying in long lines high overhead towards their summer homes. Today it is only the fortunate few who get a chance to view these stately birds on their migration and even fewer have had the opportunity to see the graceful bows and jumps which constitute the dance, so often praised in poetry and prose.

Of the fourteen different cranes inhabiting the world, only two nest in Europe and, like most of the species found in other parts of the world, ours have suffered a great decline in numbers. The threat of extinction is not as great as is the case with the Whooping Crane of North America, of which only about forty exist, but our own cranes are also in need of all the protection they can get.

The most numerous of the European cranes is the Common Crane. The Demoiselle Crane is only found nesting in the extreme south-east of our continent. In winter large flocks of cranes usually collect in open areas, both dry and marshy. These habitats are also visited during migration, but in the nesting season, when the flocks break up, cranes are found in wooded regions with open swamps. Here the nest, a mound of branches, hay and grass, is built and the two very glossy, brown eggs are laid. After about thirty days of incubation, a duty shared by both parents, the downy young hatch. For nine to ten weeks they follow their parents on foot through the bogs, but as soon as they are able to fly the families congregate in flocks before the southward migration.

CRANE *Megalornis grus* L 44" W 80" Locally common, nesting in bogs and wooded swamps. Outside breeding season found in marshes and on sandbanks, along rivers, in grasslands and fields. Larger size and outstretched neck in flight distinguish it from herons, grey colour from storks, spoonbills and ibises. Much larger than Demoiselle Crane but in flight can be difficult to tell from this species. Flies in V-formations or long lines, often very high, sometimes soaring. On the ground the tail looks very bushy. In spring both sexes perform the fantastic courtship dance consisting of jumps and bows. Call is trumpet-like. Voice deeper than Demoiselle Crane's. V

SIBERIAN WHITE CRANE *Grus leucogeranus* L 47" Rare, but regular in autumn along coast of Caspian Sea. Extremely rare in rest of Europe. Pure white colour with black primaries diagnostic. Behaviour is like that of Crane.

DEMOISELLE CRANE *Anthropoides virgo* L 38" W 70" Less common than Crane. Breeds on dry ground on open plains and high plateaux. In winter found on grasslands, in marshes and fields. Distinguished from Crane by much smaller size, long white ear tufts, elongated black breast feathers and elongated but not fluffy inner secondaries. In flight very difficult to tell from Crane, but is smaller and has higher pitched call. Often mixes with Cranes. Like Crane, it flies in V-formation or long lines, often at great height. Performs courtship dance more often than Crane.

Crane

juv.

Siberian White Crane

Demoiselle Crane

GREAT BUSTARD *Otis tarda* Male L 40″ W 90″
Fem L 32″ W 70″ Rare and local, found on open plains
and cultivated fields, where it feeds on cereals and other
vegetable matter, also on insects, frogs and other small
animals. Extremely shy and difficult to approach. Easily
told from other bustards by its enormous size. In its
strong flight the large white area on the wing is striking.
wing-beats, resembling flight of game birds. Appears
size difference between males and females is striking.
Females outnumber males. In winter, vagrants can
occasionally be found far away from regular range.
Communal or single displays, usually performed in the
early morning hours, are spectacular, the males bending
their legs and suddenly displaying white under tail-
feathers, underside of wings and moustachial feathers.
Cannot be confused with any other European bird.   V

Bustards
order *Gruiformes*, family *Otididae*

In a recent survey of extinct and almost extinct birds of the
world, one of the two bustards breeding in Europe, the Great
Bustard, was the only European bird considered to be seriously
threatened with extinction. There is no doubt that the reason
for the rapid decline in numbers and limitation of the breeding
range of this species is hunting, as the enormous bird, which
can reach a weight of more than thirty pounds, is much
prized for the table. But, thanks to strict enforcement of game
laws, this stately bird now seems to be holding its own on the
threshold of eradication. Its smaller relative, the Little Bustard,
has fared better and is not threatened seriously.

Another of the twenty-three bustards inhabiting the world,
the Houbara Bustard, is a vagrant to the southern and eastern
parts of Europe from its breeding grounds in north Africa and
western Asia.

Great Bustard display

Great Bustard

Little Bustard

Houbara Bustard

LITTLE BUSTARD *Otis tetrax* L 17" W 35" Fairly common on open plains and farmland. Shy, although not as unapproachable as Great Bustard. Notice black and white neck markings of male in breeding plumage. In winter plumage he resembles the female. Told from larger Houbara Bustard by lack of dark stripes along neck, more extensive white on wing and much smaller size. Flies higher than Great Bustard, with much faster wing-beats, resembling flight of game birds. Appears very light-coloured in flight. Males produce whistling sounds in flight. Seen in small flocks, outside the nesting season often far from the breeding grounds. In the courtship display the male puffs up, raises his tail and occasionally leaps into the air and emits a sharp 'irr' note.
V

HOUBARA BUSTARD *Chlamydotis undulata* L 25" W 60" A very rare straggler from its African and Asiatic breeding grounds. Prefers very dry steppes but can occur in farmland. In western Europe most often seen in autumn, usually singly although it is quite sociable where more numerous. Told from other bustards by having less white on wing, longer wing and tail, and long, black lines on sides and neck. It has a short crest, more pronounced in the male than the female. Flight resembles that of Great Bustard.
V

Bustards are shy birds of vast open country, savannahs and steppes, also cultivated fields. Here the males in spring perform their elaborate courtship displays, assembling around them a harem of females. When mating has taken place, the female lays the three or four brownish eggs in a crude nest built on the ground. After about twenty-two days of incubation, the young emerge, leaving the nest immediately. When the young are able to fly after about six weeks, the flocks start moving over a larger territory, the Little Bustards gathering for their migration southward, the Great Bustards only spreading out into the neighbouring areas.

Rails, Gallinules and Coots
order *Gruiformes,* family *Rallidae*

This family, by far the largest of the *Gruiformes,* comprises 132 species. It is, for convenience rather than for sound taxonomical reasons, subdivided into rails, gallinules and coots.

Five rails are indigenous to our continent and one, the Sora Rail, which is the North American counterpart of the Spotted Crake, is a rare straggler to the British Isles.

Characteristic of all the rails is the laterally compressed body, enabling them to slip easily between reeds and other dense vegetation. Except for the Corncrake, which is found mainly in

Water Rail

juv.

Spotted Crake

juv.

Baillon's Crake

juv.

fields, they are all swamp or marsh dwellers as are the gallinules and coots. In and around a lake with extensive shore vegetation one might find almost all the *Rallidae* occupying their preferred habitats. In the open water and at the edge of the reeds the coots seek their food. In the extensive reed-beds Baillon's and Little Crake are found far out, while the Water Rail prefers to be closer to shore where the reeds are replaced by sedges. Even farther inshore where the vegetation mainly consists of sedges, the Spotted Crake resides, and in the open fields surrounding the lake the Corncrake may be heard claiming ownership. The Moorhen is less specific than most of its relatives in its choice of habitat and can be met with on the edge of reed-beds as well as in the scrub round the edges of marshes, lakes and rivers.

The rails are primarily nocturnal in their habits and are much more often heard than seen. Although many have a large variety of notes, they can with practice be told apart by their calls. They are weak fliers but in spite of this they are all migratory to some extent. Most sedentary in habits is the Water Rail which even in Iceland is resident, surviving the cold of winter by the banks of the rivers leading from the hot geysers. Spotted Crake and Corncrake both perform very extensive migrations, even occuring accidentally on the western side of the Atlantic. They travel only by night.

The nests of rails are always placed in dense vegetation and

WATER RAIL *Rallus aquaticus* L 11" Common in swamps and ponds with dense vegetation. The largest of the rails, with a very long reddish bill, and pure white under tail-coverts. Although secretive in behaviour, less so than the crakes. Most often seen at dusk and dawn. More often heard than seen. Has a large vocabulary of calls which are more penetrating than musical and are most often heard at night, or when birds are disturbed.
RSW

SPOTTED CRAKE *Porzana porzana* L 9" Common in swamps and ponds with dense vegetation. Resembles Water Rail but has short bill and buff under tail-coverts. Can also be confused with Corncrake, but notice dark brown, not reddish, wings. Call is repetition of high-pitched, short 'wheet' notes, rather like the cracking of a whip.
SWP

BAILLON'S CRAKE *Porzana pusilla* L 7" Fairly common in swamps and ponds with dense vegetation. Adult birds are told from male Little Crakes by having boldly barred sides, flesh-coloured legs and no red spot at base of bill. Immatures resemble immature Little Crakes, but are more strongly barred. The call is a trill resembling that of Little Crake but is faster and higher pitched. Both species are most secretive in behaviour.
V

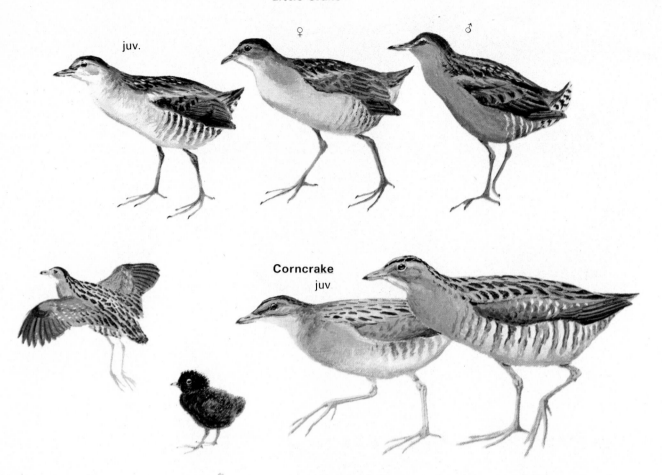

Little Crake

juv.

♀

♂

Corncrake

juv

LITTLE CRAKE *Porzana parva* L 7″ Fairly common in swamps and ponds with rich vegetation. Very secretive in behaviour. Male is distinguished from Baillon's Crake by having less strongly marked barring on sides, green legs and red spot at base of bill. Female is buffish, rather than grey, with green legs and red base of bill. Immatures resemble immature Baillon's Crake but have less distinctive barring on the side. Usual call is a rather weak series of notes ending in a trill.   V

CORNCRAKE *Crex crex* L 10″ Locally common in meadows and fields with dense vegetation. Told from other crakes by buffish plumage and distinctive reddish colour of wings, very obvious in flight. Secretive, but call, which is a repeated 'crex-crex', may be kept up for hours in the breeding season, most persistently at night.
S

well hidden. They are prolific birds, laying from four to twelve eggs, which are incubated for about twenty days. The young have pitch-black down while the coloration of their bills and heads varies from species to species.

Rails take a great variety of food, insects, snails and other animals forming the bulk of their diet, but vegetable matter is also taken.

The biggest and the most striking of the European *Rallidae* is the Purple Gallinule. Because it is found only in the very southernmost parts of our continent, where it is not very numerous, few Europeans have a chance to admire its extravagant beauty as it stalks through the vegetation on its red legs with head held low, ready to pick up anything eatable with its red bill. But all over Europe everyone has a good chance to enjoy the more sombre good looks of its close relative, the Moorhen. This bird is distinctive in its dark plumage with a bright red shield on its forehead and a beautiful pattern of black and white on its short tail, which it constantly jerks up and down as it works its way along the banks of ponds, lakes, canals and slow-flowing rivers. Although the long toes of the Moorhen are especially helpful when it climbs through reeds and other vegetation, they also enable it to swim efficiently.

In spring, when territories are being divided among the rival Moorhen males, one can often see violent fights taking place over the various areas claimed by the birds. Moorhens use both bills and feet when fighting an antagonist. These fights may have a fatal outcome where the population is large, as is often the case in parks. The nest is placed among dense vegetation but sometimes also in trees and bushes. Five to twelve spotted, brownish eggs are laid and both parents incubate for about

Allen's Gallinule

juv.

juv.

Purple Gallinule

twenty days. Often more than one clutch is hatched in a season and in some areas two are the rule rather than the exception, unusual among birds of its size. Sometimes the young of the first brood help their parents bring up the second brood, a habit also recorded for coots.

Two coots nest in Europe: the Common Coot is widespread, but the Crested Coot, which is its African counterpart, is only found in the extreme south. They share with the grebes and phalaropes the anatomical oddity of lobed feet. This adaptation enables them to swim well and they are also good divers. They live mainly on vegetable matter they pick off the bottom in shallow water. To start a dive they have to make a little jump and they are only able to stay under water for a very short time. When they emerge after a dive, they come up tail first. They walk well and can often be seen searching for food on land.

Although primarily found on freshwater lakes when breeding, coots can also nest in sheltered bays and fjords of salt water. The nest consists of a large, rather disorderly pile of vegetation where the coot lays six to nine greyish eggs. During the mating and breeding season one can often see the coot take up its threatening posture: with wings held high and neck horizontally outstretched, the bird swims towards the intruder and if it does not give way immediately, a violent fight develops.

The incubation period is about three weeks, and after another eight weeks the young are able to look after themselves. Often two clutches are hatched in a season. In autumn the coots congregate in large flocks to spend the winter on lakes or along the seashore where the water is shallow enough for them to reach the bottom. They are often seen in flocks with Tufted Ducks and other diving ducks; they sometimes

ALLEN'S GALLINULE *Porphyrio alleni* L 10" A very rare visitor to the Mediterranean countries and occasionally further north from its African breeding grounds. Found in swamps with dense vegetation. Small size, red bill and legs easily distinguish this species from other gallinules.

PURPLE GALLINULE *Porphyrio porphyrio* L 19" Uncommon, preferring swamps with dense vegetation especially extensive reed-beds. Unmistakable, with large, red bill and long, red legs. Immatures best told by large size and shape of bill. Secretive in behaviour. Call is trumpet-like.

MOORHEN *Gallinula chloropus* L 13" Very common in swamps, ponds and lakes with shore vegetation. Often in parks. Swims well. Adult easily distinguished by black colour of body, red base of bill, white line on side and white under tail-coverts with a black line through them. The last two characteristics also distinguish immature Moorhens from immature Coots. Tail is held high and often jerked both when swimming and walking. Flight is weak and fluttering. Calls include a number of harsh, unmusical notes, the most common rendered 'creck' and 'whittuck'.   RW

COOT *Fulica atra* L 15" Very common in lakes and ponds and in winter also in sheltered bays. Adult easily recognized by black plumage with white frontal shield and bill. Immatures are distinguished from immature Moorhens by having black under tail-coverts and the characteristic Coot silhouette. Dives after an upward jump. Swims with nodding movement of head. Takes to the wing only after a long run along the water. In winter it congregates in flocks at suitable feeding areas. Usual calls are a loud 'kowk' and a double 'ke-kowk'.   RWP

CRESTED COOT *Fulica cristata* L 16" Resembles Coot closely and the two red knobs above the frontal shield distinguishing this species are hard to see at a distance. Wing is pure black without the whitish areas found in Coot. Common, and like Coot in habits although more secretive. Call is of two syllables, distinctly different and deeper than call of Coot.

rob these much more capable divers of the snails and molluscs which they bring to the surface. As ice covers more and more of the open water in northern Europe, the coots slowly retreat, but often they are too slow and hundreds succumb to the severity of winter.

Coots are not very good fliers and only take to the wing when forced to do so. They have to patter along the surface for a long time before they become airborne, when their feet dangle clumsily behind them. Only in very cold weather do they draw their legs up among their feathers when they are flying.

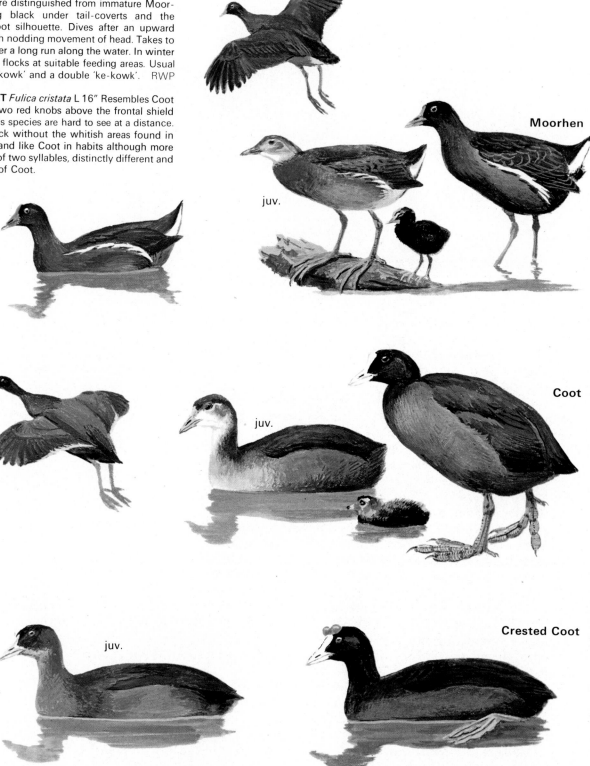

Moorhen

juv.

Coot

juv.

juv.

Crested Coot

Shorebirds, Gulls and Auks
order *Charadriiformes*

Ranging throughout the world, the members of this order are diverse in appearance but show their relationship by internal characteristics such as the arrangement of tendons and structure of voice box. Sixteen families are recognized, of which ten are represented in Europe. These families form three main groups.

The first group, the shorebirds or waders, consists of jaçanas and painted snipes, both tropical in distribution; oystercatchers, plovers, sandpipers, stilts, phalaropes, stone curlews and coursers, all of which are represented in Europe; Crab Plover, which is a tropical family of only one species in Africa and Asia; seed snipes, sparrow-like birds inhabiting South America; and the sheathbills, dove-like scavengers of the Antarctic. These birds range in size from the tiny six-inch stints to the large curlews, nearly two feet in length. They are primarily found on shores, marshes and bogs, although the phalaropes are pelagic in winter, while stone curlews and a few others prefer the drier uplands. Most nest on the ground, and the downy young leave the nest soon after hatching to follow the parents in search of food.

Below Oystercatchers and Grey Plover

The second group consists of the skuas, gulls and terns, which are all placed in the same family, and skimmers, a small family of primarily tropical distribution whose members are the only birds with the lower mandibles longer than the upper. The members of these families all have webbed feet. They are better adapted for flying than the preceding group, although all are capable of both walking and swimming. They nest on the ground in colonies often numbering many thousands of birds, and the young, although covered with down when hatched, stay close to the nest for a considerable time. All the members of this group are more closely attached to water than many members of the preceding group. They range in size from the twenty-seven-inch Great Black-backed Gull to the nine-inch Little Tern.

The third group consists of only one family, the auks, which are found only in the northern hemisphere. All auks are oceanic in behaviour and are excellent divers. Their flight is fast with very rapid wing-beats. Their ecological niche in the southern hemisphere is taken up by the penguins. They come ashore only for a few months to breed. Auks nest in colonies on rocky shores, and the young either stay in the nest hole for the fledging period or take to sea when about two weeks old. They vary in size from the seventeen-inch Common Guillemot to the eight-inch Little Auk.

Oystercatchers
order *Charadriiformes*, family *Haematopodidae*

Of the six similar species making up this family, only one is indigenous to our continent. The Oystercatcher is unmistakable. The black and white plumage, the long, straight, bright red bill and the red legs leave no doubt when it is seen. The very strong, chisel-like bill is the tool with which the Oystercatcher chips molluscs off the rocks, probes deep into the sand to catch worms and skilfully opens even the strongest oyster. In most parts of Europe the Oystercatcher is a bird of the open sandy beaches, but in Scotland, parts of England and some of the North Atlantic islands it is also found in the highlands, on moors and river banks.

In spring one can see the strange display of the Oystercatchers as the pairs are being formed. Parties of four or more run around in curves with a stiff gait and their bills pointed downwards, constantly uttering loud piping trills. Two then leave the piping-parties to find a quiet place where they mate, and a new pair has been formed to bring up a new generation.

The nest is only a scraping on the ground with a few shells or pebbles as lining material. Here the three greyish-green, spotted and streaked eggs are laid. Incubation is by both sexes and lasts for almost four weeks. Sitting in the open, the incubating bird can spot any approaching danger from far away. Quietly it leaves the nest, running several yards in a crouched position and taking to the wing only when far enough from the nest not to raise the suspicion of the approaching enemy. It relies on the camouflage of the eggs, and the nest is very difficult to find.

The young are ready to fly about thirty-five days after being hatched. In winter Oystercatchers congregate in flocks along the tidal beaches of Europe so rich in molluscs, worms and other animal life. Some northern populations migrate southwards. Pairs remain together and will return to their old nesting site year after year. Oystercatchers are very long-lived; one ringed bird reached the age of twenty-seven.

Oystercatcher

OYSTERCATCHER *Haematopus ostralegus* L 17"
Very common along coasts, locally also breeding on inland moors, plains and river valleys. Unmistakable black and white with long coral-red bill. In flight the broad white wing-bar is striking. Immature birds have incomplete white band on the throat. Outside breeding season usually occurs in large flocks frequenting mud-flats and beaches. Flight is strong and direct. Flight formation lines or V's. Probes deep into mud when feeding but also takes shellfish from rocks. Very noisy. Call is a shrill, loud 'bleep'. Song, heard on breeding ground only, is a high-pitched trill ascending in frequency and volume.

Plovers

order *Charadriiformes*, family *Charadriidae*

This family of wading birds, consisting of sixty-three species, is rather distinctive. Plovers are plump with short bills swollen at the tip. Most are sociable in behaviour, and many are boldly coloured. Ten species breed in Europe (Spur-winged Plover, Sociable Plover, and Caspian Plover only in the extreme southeast). The Killdeer is an almost regular visitor to the British Isles from North America, and another, the Lesser Golden Plover, is a visitor from the Siberian Arctic.

The most familiar of the plovers and probably the most familiar of all wading birds is the Lapwing. It is commonly found over almost the whole of Europe. The sad call 'vee-veet' is often heard on open fields and marshes. In spring flight it throws itself about erratically in constant dives and turns, the broad, rounded wings beating slowly to keep it aloft. The arrival of the Lapwing on nothern European fields is for many a farmer the sign that spring is coming and the long, dark nights of winter are to be left behind. With its bold, metallic-black back, solid black breast, rufous undertail and long, curved crest, its beauty and charm are unsurpassed by any of our shorebirds.

The erratic flight is the way the male Lapwing marks his territory and tries to impress the female. When the pair is formed, the male will make several scrapings on suitable nesting sites, and the female selects one. Here she lays her four pear-shaped eggs, which are brown with black spots. Lapwings defend their territory and nest with great courage. Any intruder, regardless of size, will be attacked furiously from above in steep dives, while a constant chorus of alarm calls neighbours to help. Lapwings are often successful in driving away their enemies in this manner. Another method of protecting the eggs and young is by feigning injury. When an enemy approaches, the Lapwing will run away with one wing hanging down and flapping as if it were helplessly trying to take flight. The foe starts chasing the bird in the vain hope of catching an easy prey, but as soon as he has been lured away from the danger spot where the eggs are lying exposed or the young are crouching, the Lapwing takes flight and elegantly swings itself into the air, leaving the surprised and rather baffled enemy below. This manner of luring predators away from nests and eggs is common among ground-nesting birds, waders in particular, and it is always an intriguing experience to watch the bird trying so hard, often very successfully, to look injured.

After about four weeks' incubation the eggs hatch. The young leave the nest as soon as they are dry. They look a little like their parents with their tiny crest, brown spotted crown and back, and dark breast-band. With their soft down and slightly clumsy walk they are very attractive. They can be very hard to find, as they immediately seek cover and crouch when the parents give their warning signal. Even when picked up, they will remain flattened out with the neck stretched and head down. They can fly when about one month old and at this time the immatures congregate in large flocks, moving about at random over long distances before they start on their regular migration towards their winter quarters in southern Europe and Africa. In Great Britain about one-half of the population migrates, the other half performing local movements.

The Sociable Plover, common on the south-eastern Russian steppes, is a rare straggler to western Europe. Its legs are longer than those of the Lapwing, and it does not have a crest. In behaviour it is somewhat similar. The Spur-winged Plover of north Africa and Asia is found regularly only in north-eastern Greece and Turkey. It is boldly coloured black and white, but has only a small crest. Less distinctive, but almost as charming as the Lapwing is the Ringed Plover. Two other closely related species, the Little Ringed Plover and the Kentish Plover, nest on our continent. They share rather similar habitats. The Ringed Plover is the least particular of the three in this respect. It nests on sandy beaches, marshes and sometimes inland near lakes and rivers. The Kentish Plover prefers barren sandy beaches and mud-flats, while the Little Ringed Plover is found in freshwater localities, river shingle-beds and old gravel-pits being particularly favoured. All three are aggressive inter-specifically, not allowing any of the others within the territory. They are very active birds, always on the move. When they run, they appear almost to roll over the ground. They run with great speed then stop suddenly to make a quick survey of the situation.

Besides a display performed on the ground, they also have aerial displays, when with very slow wing-beats, sometimes gliding with the pointed wings held in a narrow V, the male flies above the female. The two ringed plovers lay four eggs in a hollow on the ground with only a little lining, while the Kentish Plover usually lays only three eggs on the bare sand. The eggs of the Kentish Plover are often almost completely buried in the sand, thus giving them both protection and heat. About three weeks after the eggs are laid the young pick their way out. Like little balls of grey down rolling along the beach, they scoot about, their parents frantically trying to keep all within sight and out of danger, an almost impossible task. When hiding among the stones of the beach, the young are perfectly camou-flaged and only rarely is the eye of a marauding gull keen enough to spot them. Three weeks later the young can fly, and they soon move to more southern shores. The Ringed Plover is the hardiest of the three, being able to endure the winter as far north as the British Isles. The other two species prefer to move to the warmer climate of the African shores.

The Caspian Plover inhabiting the south-east Russian steppes is larger than the Ringed Plover and more like the Golden Plover in behaviour. It is only a rare straggler to the shores of western Europe. The Killdeer is a large, long-tailed North American plover with two distinct black breast-bands. It is a visitor of almost annual occurrence in the British Isles.

Beaches and mud-flats are the winter home of the Grey Plover. The strikingly beautiful breeding plumage is unfortunately not often seen on our shores but is reserved for the season spent on the nesting grounds in the Arctic. In winter the more uniformly grey plumage is characteristic. Grey Plovers can be seen in loose parties running about on mud-flats and banks and picking up all kinds of snails, worms, insects and molluscs revealed by the retreating tide. The generally grey

SPUR-WINGED PLOVER *Hoplopterus spinosus* L 11" Uncommon and local, in marshes and irrigated fields. Black and white pattern makes this species unmistakable. It has a slight crest but distribution of black and white and the brownish upper parts easily distinguish it from Lapwing. In behaviour it resembles Lapwing, but lacks the characteristically rounded wings of this species and usually flies lower over the ground. The call is a noisy 'zeet-zeet-zeet'.

LAPWING *Vanellus vanellus* L 12" Abundant, in marshes, meadows, moors and fields. Easily identified by long, thin crest, black and white colour pattern and, in flight, the broad, rounded wings, unique among waders. Immatures have shorter crest and less distinct black and white pattern. Outside breeding season usually recorded in flocks of varying sizes, sometimes mixed with Golden Plovers. Flock pattern is either that of a 'cloud' or an irregular line with a larger group at the head. Wing-beats are rather slow and in breeding season the erratic display flight is conspicuous. The call is a nasal 'vee-veet', hence the alternative name 'Peewit'. RSW

SOCIABLE PLOVER *Vanellus gregarius* L 12" Nests on steppes. A very rare visitor to western Europe, mainly in autumn, when it occurs on shores, meadows and fields. Black crown bordered with white and black and white pattern of wings and tail characterize the species. Very characteristic chestnut colour of belly is almost lost in winter. Standing on the ground at a distance the bird looks greyish brown. The call does not resemble that of Lapwing. It consists of a short whistle and a harsh chatter. V

Spur-winged Plover

Lapwing

juv.

Sociable Plover

imm.

Ringed Plover
juv.

Little Ringed Plover
juv.

Kentish Plover
juv.

juv.

Caspian Plover

Killdeer

RINGED PLOVER *Charadrius hiaticula* L 7" Common along shorelines, on tundra and sometimes marshes. Notice prominent wing-bar and orange legs and bill (tipped with black). Flight is fast and low, with fast wing-beats. Outside breeding season often encountered in small flocks, sometimes mixed with other small shore-birds. Call is a mellow 'choo-ee'. Best told from Little Ringed Plover by wing-bar and voice. Immatures do not always have complete breast-band but are told from Kentish Plover by tail pattern and yellow legs.   RSWP

LITTLE RINGED PLOVER *Charadrius dubius* L 6" In summer locally common on inland localities: shores of lakes, river shingle beds, gravel pits and sandy ground. Often difficult to distinguish from Ringed Plover, but in all plumages notice lack of white wing-bar and pale pink legs. Also notice facial pattern and bill colour of adult, and prominent yellow eye-rim. Call is a character-istic high-pitched, two-note whistle. In winter found along coasts.   S

KENTISH PLOVER *Charadrius alexandrinus* L 6" Fairly common on sandy and stony beaches. Upper parts paler than in the ringed plovers, neck-band interrupted and in flight shows white wing-bars. Legs are always black, distinguishing it with certainty from immature Ringed Plover. Also notice tail pattern. Usually encoun-tered singly or in pairs. Call is a low-pitched 'chu-uu-ee'.   P

CASPIAN PLOVER *Charadrius asiaticus* L 7½" Breeds on steppes. Very rare in western Europe, mainly during summer when found on open land. Reddish-brown breast-band of summer male indistinct in winter and in female. Notice whitish head and Golden Plover's upright stance.   V

KILLDEER *Charadrius vociferus* L 10" A rare visitor to western Europe from North America. Usually met with on marshes and farmland. Notice large size, long rufous tail and two black breast-bands. Call is a loud and characteristic 'kill-deer'.   V

GREY PLOVER *Pluvialis squatarola* L 11" Common. Breeds on tundra. In winter found on shorelines with mud-flats and sandy beaches. Resembles Golden Plover, but can be distinguished by white rump and striking black axillaries under the wing. It is greyer above than Golden Plover and bill is larger. Does not migrate in large flocks like Golden Plover, but is usually encountered singly or in small groups. Call is plaintive, slurred whistle. WP

GOLDEN PLOVER *Pluvialis apricaria* L 11" Common except in southernmost part of its range where it is becoming increasingly scarce. Nests on moors; in winter found in fields, on mud-flats and meadows. Distinguished from Grey Plover by golden-brown upper parts, lack of wing-bar and white rump. Outside breeding season often encountered in very large flocks, sometimes mixed with Lapwings. Call is a sad-sounding, melodious, single-note whistle. Also note white axillaries distinguishing it from Grey Plover (black axillaries) and Lesser Golden Plover (grey axillaries); habit of raising wings when standing helps in using this as a field mark. RWP

LESSER GOLDEN PLOVER *Pluvialis dominica* L 10" Very rare visitor from Arctic Asia and North America. Mainly seen in autumn. Resembles Golden Plover closely but not as heavy and has grey, not white axillaries. Wings and legs are proportionally longer than those of Golden Plover. Habitat similar. Call is a clear, short, whistled 'oodle-oo'. V

DOTTEREL *Eudromias morinellus* L 9" Rare, nesting usually on tundra and mountains. Outside breeding season found on fields and marshes. Adult with its cinnamon underparts is unmistakable. Female is slightly larger than male, who incubates and rears brood. In autumn could be mistaken for Golden Plover, but broad white stripes over eyes meet on nape, and at close range pale breast-line is visible and diagnostic. Usually seen singly or in small groups. Call is a soft trill. SP

appearance, with a pronounced wing-band and black axillaries, distinguishes them from the rather similar Golden Plover.

The summer plumage of the Golden Plover is basically the same as that of the Grey Plover: jet-black belly, breast and throat bordered with white. But whereas the Grey Plover has a greyish back, the Golden Plover is a rich spangled yellow-brown on the upper parts. In Europe two distinctive subspecies are found: the Southern and the Northern Golden Plover. In summer plumage they are quite easily told apart, the southern subspecies (breeding in the British Isles and the adjacent Continent) having the black underside much less well defined

winter   summer

Grey Plover

Golden Plover

southern form summer

northern form summer

winter

Lesser Golden Plover

winter

Dotterel

winter

summer

than the northern subspecies. In winter the two are indistinguishable. The Southern Golden Plover is a bird of the upland moors and heaths. Here it whistles its plaintive call during the breeding season and here the three or four boldly blotched eggs are laid in a hollow among moorland grass or short heather. The Northern Golden Plover is more a bird of the Arctic tundra, but frequents similar habitats. In autumn Golden Plovers congregate in large flocks for their migration. During migration and on the wintering grounds, they are most often met with on pastures and stubble fields as they are much less fond of shores than the Grey Plover.

Closely related is the Lesser Golden Plover inhabiting the Siberian tundras. It is slightly smaller than the Golden Plover and has grey axillaries (white in Golden). It is only a rare vagrant to western Europe. The last of the plovers is the dainty little Dotterel. It is slightly smaller than the Golden Plover and much rarer. It nests in mountainous areas and tundras though it has recently colonized low ground in Scotland. The male does most of the incubation and cares for the young. In winter small flocks or 'trips' of four or five birds visit moors, marshes and shores in lowlands.

Sandpipers
order *Charadriiformes*, family *Scolopacidae*

A heterogeneous group of some eighty-two species, this family is characterized by a long bill and generally rather uniform plumage. It is divided into four subfamilies: turnstones, snipes, *Tringinae* (the long-legged sandpipers), and *Eroliinae* or 'peeps' as the Americans call these small, short-legged waders. Further subdivisions are often used, particularly among the *Tringinae*,

TURNSTONE *Arenaria interpres* L 9" Common along rocky and stony shores, rare inland. Also frequents sandy beaches. Prefers rocky types of shores, feeding among seaweed. Note head and breast pattern and short orange, red or yellow legs, and in flight the striking black, brown and white pattern of wings, rump and tail. Usually seen singly or in small groups. Sometimes found with other small waders. Call, one to eight fast, low, slurred, whickering notes.   WP

SNIPE *Gallinago gallinago* L 10" Very common in marshes, meadows and swamps. The most numerous of the snipes. Told from Great Snipe by white belly, only little white on tail and when flushed, by characteristic zig-zag flight; from Jack Snipe by pattern on crown, larger size, longer bill and tail pattern. Outside breeding season it can be encountered in rather large, loose flocks. Call is a low, rasping note. In display flight, produces strong vibrating sound with under tail-feathers, called 'drumming', as it dives almost vertically from great height.   RWP

Turnstone
summer
winter

Snipe

as they naturally fall into easily distinguishable groups.

The Turnstone is one of the most northern breeding birds, extending far into the Arctic. With its harlequin plumage, short, conical bill and short legs it is unmistakable as it searches the rocky shores for insects and worms. Its name comes from its habit of turning small stones over to reveal hidden items of food. It nests on rocky and stony islands, often close to gull and tern colonies. The proximity of these aggressive birds offers it so much protection that it dares place its nest in the open rather than hidden under rocks and vegetation as it does when nesting alone. The four eggs are incubated for twenty-four days, during the daytime by the female, at night primarily by the male. Ringing has shown that most of the Turnstones breeding in Europe migrate to Africa in winter, while those met with on our rocky and stony shores in winter are visitors from Greenland and eastern Canada. Even in winter they are often seen singly or in small flocks.

The subfamily of snipes, *Scolopacinae*, includes the Woodcock as well as the three kinds of snipe breeding within the boundaries of our continent. These birds are plump with rather short legs and very long bills. They obtain their food by probing deep into the soft ground or mud and, as the tip of the bill is furnished with many nerve-endings, they are able to feel when they touch their prey inches below the ground. All snipes are able to open the outermost quarter of the bill while keeping the rest closed, and are therefore able to obtain a grip on prey found in rather hard soil. The colours of the snipes and Woodcock are dark brown, mottled with darker areas and lighter stripes. These colours offer a perfect camouflage on which the birds rely heavily. They are almost impossible to spot when hiding and very hard to flush, especially when they are brooding. The Common Snipe

GREAT SNIPE *Gallinago media* L 11″ Uncommon, declining in numbers. Breeds in marshes and swamps or on drier land with small streams. Outside nesting season found on fields and marshes. Told from very similar Snipe by slightly larger size, barred belly, white outer tail-feathers and straight, heavy flight (immature Snipes sometimes have similar flight pattern). Usually silent when flushed. Communal display is seen at dusk. During display a twittering sound is produced, but also a characteristic drumming.   P

JACK SNIPE *Lymnocryptes minimus* L 8″ Uncommon, in marshes and swamps. Distinguished from the larger Snipe by shorter bill, crown pattern and brown unmarked tail. Very difficult to flush. Silent when flushed, and the flight is then usually short without the characteristic zig-zag of the Snipe. During spectacular display flight, a call resembling the sound of a galloping horse is produced.   WP

Great Snipe

Jack Snipe

Woodcock

Curlew

Whimbrel

Slender-billed Curlew

WOODCOCK *Scolopax rusticola* L 14" Common in woods with bogs and wet ground. Easily told from Snipe by larger size and more rounded wings. Flight is fast and agile among the trees. When flushed, a clattering of wings is heard. Solitary in behaviour although it can occur in very scattered groups on migration. In the breeding season the soft, croaking call, 'roding', of the displaying male is heard at dusk and early in the morning.   RSW

CURLEW *Numenius arquata* L 22" Common, nesting on moors, marshes and fields. Outside breeding season also on mud-flats. Very large, with very long down-curved bill. Lacks distinctive crown pattern of Whimbrel and underparts are striped rather than spotted (compare with Slender-billed Curlew). Usual call is a mellow whistle: 'curlee'.   RWP

WHIMBREL *Numenius phaeopus* L 16" Common, nesting on moors and upland meadows. In winter found in fields, marshes and on mud-flats. Told from Curlew by smaller size and much shorter bill and characteristically striped crown. Often mixes with Curlew. Call is a short, mellow whistle, repeated rapidly 6–7 times.   SP

SLENDER-BILLED CURLEW *Numenius tenuirostris* L 16" Uncommon, breeding on wet steppes. In winter found in marshes and mud-flats. Told from Whimbrel by lack of crown pattern, from Curlew by smaller size and shorter bill. From both by rounded spots on underside. Call resembles Curlew's but is higher pitched and shorter.

almost explodes into one's face when flushed and disappears in a zig-zag flight which it is tempting to believe was designed to avoid the blast of a shotgun. The Jack Snipe and the Great Snipe fly a straight course, while the Woodcock flutters away among the trees in a more erratic fashion.

All three snipes nest in bogs, wet marshes and meadows. The nest is lined with grass and is usually well hidden in a tussock of grass. The Woodcock usually makes a simple nest of leaves under cover of dead bracken and other woodland vegetation, but occasionally nests in the open. All normally have a clutch of four eggs, the snipes' pear-shaped, the Woodcock's more rounded.

One of the most spectacular habits of these birds is the display flight. Each species has its unique way of courting. The Common Snipe is best seen and heard at dusk or early dawn. After introducing himself with a repeated 'kip-kip-kip' call uttered on the ground, the male takes to the wing and climbs very high, sometimes disappearing from view. Suddenly he starts on a very fast and steep descent. He spreads his outermost tail-feathers widely and the air pressure causes them to vibrate producing the characteristic and well known 'drumming' or 'bleating'. As he passes over the female, she invites him with a hoarse call and like a stone he drops to her side. The aerial display can be performed by both sexes, but most commonly by the male. Often the dive will be repeated again and again.

The Jack Snipe also dives during display. While diving it utters a knocking call which has been compared with the distant galloping of horses. Great Snipe on the contrary have a collective display ground where the males give their song, a series of bubbling notes, in a chorus. Where it is plentiful, the Woodcock may be polyandrous. The males will fly at dusk low above the treetops keeping a keen eye on what goes on in the wood and carefully listening for the inviting call of the female on the ground. When she calls he drops to her side and starts courting her with drooping wings and tail cocked upwards. After mating he will continue on his route. The male's flight is called 'roding' and is characterized by a deep gobbling call and a high-pitched 'chissick' which sound quite unrelated.

While the Common Snipe and Woodcock breeding in the British Isles are mostly sedentary, the more northern populations are migratory, as are both the Great Snipe and the Jack Snipe, both of which are rather uncommon birds. The Great Snipe has suffered a great decline in this century and has disappeared from almost all its former breeding areas in western Europe, its stronghold being now in the eastern part of its range. The reason is probably excessive hunting, combined with the drying out of many bogs and marshes where it formerly nested.

The *Tringinae,* the third group of shorebirds, are divided into several smaller groups. The long decurved bill of the curlews is so characteristic that the three European species are unmistakable as a group. It is much more difficult to tell the three apart. All are large long-billed shorebirds with rather nondescript brown plumage. The upper rump is white, and the head of the Whimbrel clearly marked with dark and light stripes. The Slender-billed Curlew, which nests on the marshy steppes of south-east Russia and migrates via the Balkans to the eastern end of the Mediterranean, is the size of the Whimbrel but paler and has distinctive heart-shaped spots on the flanks. It is only rarely met with in western Europe. Here the large Curlew and the somewhat smaller Whimbrel dominate the scene.

Black-tailed Godwit

summer

winter

winter

summer

Bar-tailed Godwit

On migration these two species often mix and the differences between them are easier to observe. First of all the Curlew is considerably bigger. It also has a proportionally much longer bill than the Whimbrel with its strongly marked head. Outside the breeding season both occur on marshes and estuaries; stubble fields and meadows are also used as feeding grounds. During migration, melodious whistles are often heard as these dignified birds in long lines cross the glow of the evening sky.

In spring when the male Curlew has set up his territory on an open heath or meadow, one will often see him perform his magnificent display flight. With very fast wing-beats he climbs abruptly, stops his ascent and on quivering wings utters his far-reaching bubbling trill. Sometimes he will also glide to the ground on stiff wings, giving his liquid song. As he lands he will stand with his magnificent long wings stretched upward, displaying the white under wing-coverts to his admiring mate. The Whimbrel, which usually inhabits the upland moors and heaths, has a similar display.

The nest of both species is a hollow on the ground lined with grass or small twigs and sheltered by a tussock of grass or heather. The four eggs are incubated for about twenty-four days before the downy brown young emerge from their pear-shaped shells. They are adorned with narrow dark bands on the crown and have not yet acquired the long curved bill of the adults, but have a rather short, straight bill better suited for picking up small insects on the ground. The adults feed by probing deep into soft ground or mud.

The godwits are almost as big as the curlews, but they have straight bills. Their breeding dress is also different from the winter plumage, the rich red colour of head and breast being

BLACK-TAILED GODWIT *Limosa limosa* L 16"
Fairly common, nesting in meadows and marshes, wintering on mud-flats and marshes. In all plumages easily distinguished by long bill, distinctive white wing-bars and solid black band on tail. In summer, chestnut breast, neck and head. Call is a loud 'wicka' repeated three times.   RWP

BAR-TAILED GODWIT *Limosa lapponica* L 15"
Common, nesting in Arctic marshes. In winter found along shores and on mud-flats. In all plumages told from Black-tailed Godwit by barring of tail, lack of wing-bar and comparatively shorter legs and bill. In summer, chestnut colours cover entire underside. Flocks are usually very closely packed. Call is a harsh two-note 'irrick'.   WP

Common Sandpiper

Green Sandpiper

COMMON SANDPIPER *Tringa hypoleucos* L 8″ A very common sandpiper breeding along freshwater shores, wintering along freshwater as well as saltwater shores. Characteristic stance is with body tilted forward, head lowered. It bobs the tail up and down almost continuously. In flight the wings are held stiffly downward, with very shallow wing-beats. Usually seen singly or in small flocks, nearly always along water edges or flying low above the water. Sometimes associates with Dunlins or Ringed Plovers. Call is a shrill piping, often rendered 'kitty-wiper'.
SP

GREEN SANDPIPER *Tringa ochropus* L 9″ Common, breeding in woodland swamps and marshes using old nests of songbirds. Outside breeding season usually found in freshwater marshes and shores. Notice dark upper parts, strikingly white rump and dark underside of wings. The dark breast ends abruptly in front of the white belly. Usually seen singly or in small parties. When flushed it often throws itself from side to side a few times. Call is a musical, penetrating three-note whistle: 'tit-looet'.
WP

lost in autumn and replaced by a more sombre greyish brown. Two species, the Black-tailed and the Bar-tailed, nest in Europe. The Black-tailed is the more southerly in distribution; the Bar-tailed is only found nesting on the Arctic tundras. The Black-tailed Godwit is a splendid-looking bird in its breeding plumage. The rich chestnut-brown colours match beautifully the bold patterns of black and white on the tail and wings. This beauty is displayed most magnificently in the courtship flight which the male performs over his territory on the wet meadows. Continuously calling, he rises on fast, clipping wing-strokes. Reaching a height of about two hundred feet, he starts circling in a rolling flight, tipping from side to side with the tail spread wide. After a few turns he suddenly drops to the ground.

Black-tailed Godwit often nest in loose colonies on suitable marshes and meadows. The nest is made of grass, and the four pear-shaped eggs are incubated for about twenty-four days by both male and female. In autumn the birds congregate in small parties and move south to the wintering grounds. On migration Bar-tailed Godwit are usually seen in much larger flocks and frequent seashores more often than Black-tailed Godwit. They wade out into the water as deep as they can without submerging and probe their long, slightly upturned bills deep into the bottom whence they extract molluscs and worms.

The genus *Tringa* is indigenous to the northern hemisphere. In Europe seven species nest and four are stragglers to western European shores, especially those of the British Isles, from the North American continent. The genus is characterized by the long, straight bill, long legs and rather delicate build of its members. In size they range from the Greenshank with a total length of twelve inches to the Common Sandpiper only eight inches long. They are birds of marshes, meadows, grasslands, moors and tundra, close to water, but each has its particular preference for a nesting site. The Common Sandpiper is practically always found nesting on river-banks or by freshwater lakes. The Green Sandpiper breeds in forest regions with open swamps where it uses old Blackbird or thrush nests. The Wood Sandpiper will also often take advantage of the nests of other birds left from the preceding year, but prefers more open ground on heaths and tundras. The Redshank is less particular in its choice and can be found in a great variety of open marshes, moors and meadows. The Spotted Redshank and the Greenshank both prefer similar areas, dry, open stretches in forest regions not far from water, though the Greenshank nests on rocky moorlands in Scotland. The Marsh Sandpiper of the European south-east is more a bird of open swamps and marshes in inland steppes and lakes. All lay four spotted eggs and in all species both parents partake in the incubation.

The Common Sandpiper is perhaps the easiest to identify of the group. It is practically always encountered at the water's edge by rivers, lakes or seashores. The bird is in continuous movement. Bent slightly forward, it nervously bobs its tail up and down, and when taking flight it will swing out low above the water, wings held with tips pointing downward in a characteristic jerky flight which is almost diagnostic. Also characteristic is the shrill, piping call, 'kittywiper', which it gives several times when flushed. The Common Sandpiper and the Redshank are the only members of the genus which have distinct wing-bars. But the Redshank can hardly be confused with the much smaller Common Sandpiper. The striking red legs and red base of bill together with the white wing-bar and white upper rump make it easy to identify. The Redshank is very common in most of Europe, and there are few marshes which do not harbour one or several pairs of Redshanks during the spring. Aggressive and noisy, Redshanks cannot be missed; only when leaving or approaching their nests are they silent and unobtrusive.

In winter Redshanks are found mainly on estuaries and open mud-flats along the shores where they congregate in loose flocks. Here in the time of autumn migration, all the other *Tringae* can be found too, although Marsh Sandpiper and to a certain degree Green and Wood Sandpipers, are more often seen in freshwater marshes and swamps. The autumn migration starts, as with most shorebirds, in July. Often the females leave the males to take care of the young. When the young can care for

WOOD SANDPIPER *Tringa glareola* L 8″ Fairly common, nesting in marshes and on the tundra. Outside breeding season found in marshes and swamps and along shores. Notice yellowish legs, spotted upper parts, white rump and light underwing. The striped breast and sides merge into the white belly. More elegantly built than Green Sandpiper. Usually seen singly but can occur in small flocks. Call is a high-pitched, three-note whistle.
SP

Wood Sandpiper

themselves, the males start moving south and last come the juveniles. Both male and female Greenshanks do, however, tend the young. When about one week old the family will split up, each parent taking care of one or two of their offspring.

The Greenshank is also unique in having three different territories. One is the mating place, usually close to the water's edge. Here the male tries to attract the attention of the female and, once he has succeeded, this is the place where the mating takes place. The second is the actual nesting territory which can, and usually does, lie far from the water. The third territory is less well defined in its boundaries. It is the feeding territory, the stretch of shore and mud-flat where the birds find the insects and worms on which they live, and the place where they take their young when hatched.

The Spotted Redshank is unique among the *Tringae* in having communal display grounds where the males meet and perform the 'helicopter' flight.

The four American species which British and Irish bird-watchers have a good chance of seeing are the Spotted Sandpiper, Solitary Sandpiper and the Lesser and Greater Yellowlegs. The Spotted Sandpiper is the New World counterpart of our Common Sandpiper. It is almost identical to it but in summer has the underside covered with large, round spots. The Solitary Sandpiper is very similar to our Green Sandpiper but has a dark upper rump. Like the Green Sandpiper, it uses the nests of thrushes and is in summer a woodland species. The two yellowlegs, of which the Lesser most often crosses the Atlantic, look like our Greenshank but both have bright yellow legs. Besides being slightly larger, the Greater Yellowlegs can be told from the Lesser by its long, slightly upturned bill and its three-syllable whistle. The Lesser has only one or two syllables in its plaintive call.

The Terek Sandpiper of eastern Europe is closely related to the *Tringae*. It has proportionally short legs and a very long, upturned bill. The size of the Wood Sandpiper, its behaviour is close to that of the Common Sandpiper, and it is found along inland lakes and swamps. While most of the *Tringae* in northern Europe migrate towards the south-west and are therefore common all over western Europe, the Terek Sandpiper takes a straight southward course in autumn. Therefore it is only a very rare vagrant to western Europe, though a few pairs do nest in Finland.

Two waders closely related to the snipe are the dowitchers. They are only stragglers to our western shores from the New

TEREK SANDPIPER *Xenus cinereus* L 9″ Uncommon, nesting on inland marshes. Outside breeding season also encountered along seashores and on marshes. Notice relatively short yellow legs and long upturned bill. On the wing, note white rump and edge of wing. In habits it resembles the smaller Common Sandpiper. Call is a fast repetition of flute-like notes.　　　P

Terek Sandpiper

winter

summer

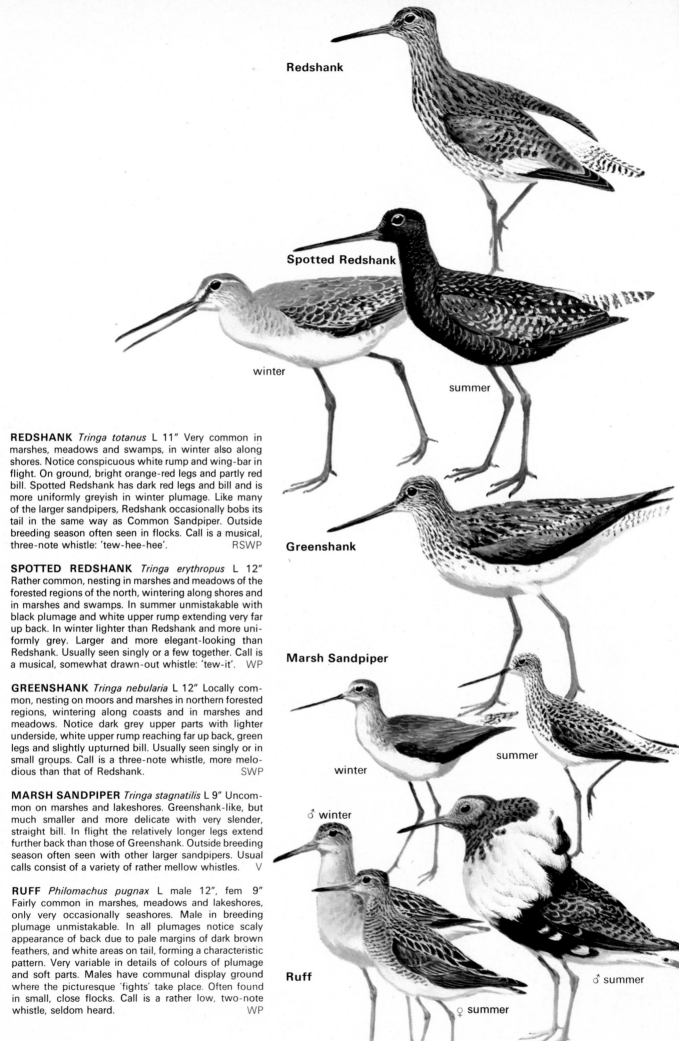

Redshank

Spotted Redshank

winter

summer

Greenshank

Marsh Sandpiper

winter

summer

♂ winter

Ruff

♀ summer

♂ summer

REDSHANK *Tringa totanus* L 11" Very common in marshes, meadows and swamps, in winter also along shores. Notice conspicuous white rump and wing-bar in flight. On ground, bright orange-red legs and partly red bill. Spotted Redshank has dark red legs and bill and is more uniformly greyish in winter plumage. Like many of the larger sandpipers, Redshank occasionally bobs its tail in the same way as Common Sandpiper. Outside breeding season often seen in flocks. Call is a musical, three-note whistle: 'tew-hee-hee'.   RSWP

SPOTTED REDSHANK *Tringa erythropus* L 12" Rather common, nesting in marshes and meadows of the forested regions of the north, wintering along shores and in marshes and swamps. In summer unmistakable with black plumage and white upper rump extending very far up back. In winter lighter than Redshank and more uniformly grey. Larger and more elegant-looking than Redshank. Usually seen singly or a few together. Call is a musical, somewhat drawn-out whistle: 'tew-it'.   WP

GREENSHANK *Tringa nebularia* L 12" Locally common, nesting on moors and marshes in northern forested regions, wintering along coasts and in marshes and meadows. Notice dark grey upper parts with lighter underside, white upper rump reaching far up back, green legs and slightly upturned bill. Usually seen singly or in small groups. Call is a three-note whistle, more melodious than that of Redshank.   SWP

MARSH SANDPIPER *Tringa stagnatilis* L 9" Uncommon on marshes and lakeshores. Greenshank-like, but much smaller and more delicate with very slender, straight bill. In flight the relatively longer legs extend further back than those of Greenshank. Outside breeding season often seen with other larger sandpipers. Usual calls consist of a variety of rather mellow whistles.   V

RUFF *Philomachus pugnax* L male 12", fem 9" Fairly common in marshes, meadows and lakeshores, only very occasionally seashores. Male in breeding plumage unmistakable. In all plumages notice scaly appearance of back due to pale margins of dark brown feathers, and white areas on tail, forming a characteristic pattern. Very variable in details of colours of plumage and soft parts. Males have communal display ground where the picturesque 'fights' take place. Often found in small, close flocks. Call is a rather low, two-note whistle, seldom heard.   WP

Solitary Sandpiper

Spotted Sandpiper

winter

Stilt Sandpiper

summer

SPOTTED SANDPIPER *Tringa macularia* L 8″ Very rare. In winter plumage indistinguishable from Common Sandpiper, of which some authorities consider it to be the American race. In summer distinguished by spotted underparts and yellow base of bill. V

SOLITARY SANDPIPER *Tringa solitaria* L 8″ Very rare autumn visitor. Told from rather similar Green Sandpiper by lack of white upper rump. Call is a shrill, high-pitched 2–3 note piping. V

STILT SANDPIPER *Micropalama himantopus* L 8″ Very rare late summer, early autumn visitor. Unmistakable in breeding plumage with barring and rusty facial pattern. In winter plumage notice white upper rump, greenish legs and 'drooping' bill. Call is a low, rather hoarse, single-note whistle. V

Ruffs displaying

World. The Long-billed and the Short-billed Dowitchers, inhabiting the Arctic parts of North America, look like snipe. They have short legs and very long bills. In summer their undersides are reddish-brown in colour; they are grey in winter when they become tropical shorebirds occurring in closed flocks almost like Dunlins. In Europe they are usually seen singly. Formerly regarded as subspecies, the two almost identical forms are now considered distinct and separate species. The Long-billed inhabits the western part of the range, the Short-billed the eastern.

Perhaps the strangest among European birds and certainly unique in several respects is the Ruff. Unfortunately this astonishing species can no longer be enjoyed as a breeding bird in the British Isles. In the last century it was found nesting in several parts of England, but after a sharp decline in numbers it ceased to breed, though there is some hope it may re-establish itself in Norfolk. It can still be admired as it passes through the country on its way to its breeding grounds in the northern part of the continent. While the female (Reeve) is plain in looks, the Ruff in spring and summer is adorned with extraordinary features in the form of a magnificent ruff and two ear tufts. These outstanding ornaments differ in colour from bird to bird and no two are completely alike. The ruff can be white, the ear tufts black, or both can be the same colour; sometimes they are uniform, sometimes barred or spotted. The coloration is inherited as has been shown by comparing the percentage of various basic colour combinations of different populations. Besides these striking ornaments the males also have wart-like protuberances on the face which disappear in late summer together with the ruff and ear tufts. One of the most fascinating experiences any nature lover can have is to watch the display on one of the ancient display grounds of the Ruff. Promiscuous in sexual relations, the males congregate in a certain area—usually a meadow or marsh—on traditional hillocks where each male has his own stand. Here great fights take place as the ownership of a

GREATER YELLOWLEGS *Tringa melanoleuca* L 14"
Very rare autumn visitor (occasionally spring). Notice
white upper rump and rather long, slightly upturned bill,
yellow legs and characteristic sharp, 3–4 note whistle.
                                                        V

LESSER YELLOWLEGS *Tringa flavipes* L 10" Rare
autumn visitor (occasionally spring), but more numerous
than Greater Yellowlegs. Notice yellow legs and white
upper rump. Bill is shorter and more slender than that of
Greater Yellowlegs. Call is a soft, 1–3 note whistle.   V

LONG-BILLED DOWITCHER *Limnodromus scolo-
paceus* L 12" Very rare autumn visitor. Notice very long
bill, plump build, rather short legs and white upper rump
reaching far up on the back. Told from Short-billed
Dowitcher by barred flanks (summer) and more finely
barred tail (winter). Call is a single, thin, piping note, or a
series of notes.   V

SHORT-BILLED DOWITCHER *Limnodromus griseus*
L 12" Very rare autumn visitor (occasionally spring).
Only told from Long-billed Dowitcher with difficulty.
Best distinguishing feature is the call, a low, mellow
three-note whistle.   V

stand is challenged by other males skimming the outskirts of the
arena. Charging and fending with erected ruffs and tufts, the
males attack each other, but although the conflict gives the
impression of great violence, seldom is even a drop of blood
shed. The females circle the arena with a completely disinter-
ested look and carefully select their mates. After fulfilling their
obligation to posterity, they leave the display ground, perhaps
to return or visit a neighbouring arena the next day. Males with
white ornaments seem to take up a privileged position among
females as well as males. The males take no part whatsoever in
the rearing of their offspring, and as their display activity slowly
tapers off, they assemble in small flocks concentrating their
energies on feeding, putting on enough fat to last for the long
journey ahead of them. Males are considerably bigger than
females, a trait which is obvious later in the season when flocks
of both sexes are met with in swamps and marshes.

The Ruff has a shorter bill than the members of the genus
Tringa, with which it is most often confused, and it is more
likely to pick its food—insects, worms and other small animals—

Greater Yellowlegs

Lesser Yellowlegs

Lesser
Yellowlegs
in flight

Long-billed
Dowitcher

summer

Long-billed
Dowitcher

Long-billed
winter

Short-billed Dowitcher

winter

off the ground, rather than probing as the *Tringae* and many other shorebirds do.

The Upland Sandpiper, a brown, plain coloured visitor from America, is of rare occurrence in the British Isles. It is a bird of dry habitats and has characteristic habits. When alighting, it habitually holds its wings stretched upward, displaying the heavily barred axillaries, and when seeking its food it runs about with sudden stops in a plover-like fashion. It perches freely on posts and poles.

The *Eroliinae* are a large group of small sandpipers. The American term 'peeps' is a good name for these dainty shorebirds, characterized by short necks and legs, rather plump bodies and medium-long bills. They usually occur in flocks ranging in size from just a dozen birds to several thousand. Characteristic of the flocks is their fantastic unity in movement, the whole host twisting and turning as if it were one single organism and not thousands of individuals. The flocks often consist of several different species. Most are typically found on mud-flats and estuaries outside the breeding season, but several

UPLAND SANDPIPER *Bartramia longicauda* L 11″ Very rare autumn visitor. Notice brown colour, long tail, small head and short bill. Call is a mellow whistle.   V

KNOT *Calidris canutus* L 10″ Common. Breeds in the high Arctic, wintering along seashores with mud-flats. In red summer plumage unmistakable. In winter greyish, but notice rather large size, light rump and tail, and faint wing-bars. Usually seen in flocks sometimes with other small sandpipers, when larger size of this species becomes obvious. Bill is comparatively short. Usual calls are a single, rather quiet 'wut' or a whistling 'thu-thu'.   WP

PURPLE SANDPIPER *Calidris maritima* L 8″ Fairly common on rocky coasts and in harbours. Nests on Arctic tundra. The darkest of the small sandpipers. Orange-yellow base of bill and yellow legs are noticeable at a long distance. Usually seen in small flocks, often with Turnstones or Sanderlings. Call is a short 'wit', sometimes repeated.   WP

Upland Sandpiper

winter

summer
Knot

winter

winter

Purple Sandpiper
summer

winter

have certain preferences and are most often seen in these characteristic places together with shorebirds of other groups with the same preference of habitat. Thus Purple Sandpipers are most often met with on rocky beaches or piers and often in the company of Turnstones. The Sanderling is typical of the open sandy beach where the Grey Plover is also often encountered.

Seven species breed within the boundaries of Europe, the Knot and the Sanderling only on Spitzbergen (but otherwise they are circumpolar in distribution). The Broad-billed Sandpiper, Temminck's Stint and Little Stint are Palearctic species found only in Scandinavia and northernmost Russia. The Purple Sandpiper is circumpolar, but its breeding grounds reach south to southern Norway, Iceland and the Faeroes; and the Dunlin, the most numerous of the group, is found nesting as far south as the British Isles and Germany. One species, the Curlew Sandpiper, so called from its slightly down-curved bill, is a migrant through Europe. A further seven species are irregular visitors from Asia and North America.

All the *Eroliinae* are migratory, some of these fragile little creatures travelling for thousands of miles between their winter homes and breeding grounds. The Sanderling is found in winter as far south as South Africa, faithfully following the shores on its way both south and north. Just as spectacular is the migration of the Curlew Sandpiper. From the breeding grounds in northernmost Siberia it travels west in late summer and early autumn. Upon reaching western Europe it starts heading south towards the African continent. Apparently some of these migrants overshoot their goal when travelling west, as the species is regular on the eastern shores of North America. It also occurs in North America in spring; but the birds encountered on the 'wrong' side of the Atlantic at this time have probably crossed the ocean near the Equator, passing from Africa to the South American coast whence they continue their northerly course. The Ruff occurs similarly in North America, and in its migratory habits it has much in common with the Curlew Sandpiper, particularly the almost westward direction of the first part of its autumn voyage.

With their pointed wings and stiff flight, the various birds within this group are able to cover incredibly long distances in a very short time. A Little Stint, ringed on Öland in the Baltic, was recovered only two days later in northern Italy more than 800 miles away. Generally, however, the autumn migration is taken rather at leisure, the birds slowly working their way towards their final wintering areas. Most of the actual travelling takes place at night, and at dusk one can sometimes see the flocks getting restless on the mud-flats. All of a sudden they take flight and in their tight formation set off for another shore further south. In spring the migration is much swifter, and only a short time is set aside for resting and feeding. This is why, for instance, the Curlew Sandpiper is so seldom recorded in spring as compared with numerous observations in autumn.

All the peeps change their plumage in spring. Most drastic is the difference between the sombre grey winter plumage of the Knot and the Curlew Sandpiper and the magnificent red underparts assumed by both species in spring. When passing through northern Europe, only a few individuals have attained their bright breeding plumage and by early autumn, when returning to our shores, most have lost it again; so we see few of these extravagantly coloured individuals. On the other hand, we have a good chance to observe the beauty of the Dunlin in its nuptial plumage. The pitch-black patch on the lower breast

DUNLIN *Calidris alpina* L 7" Most numerous of the small sandpipers. Nests on moors and marshes; outside breeding season found in flocks along seashores and on mud-flats of fresh as well as salt water. In summer plumage notice bright rusty back and black belly. Winter plumage is grey-brown above, white below. Distinguished from Curlew Sandpipers and larger Knots by dark upper rump. Call is a rapid, low, grating reel. SWP

CURLEW SANDPIPER *Calidris ferruginea* L 7" Common, more numerous in autumn than spring. Nests in the Arctic. Outside breeding season found on mud-flats and marshes, fresh as well as saltwater. In red summer plumage unmistakable. In winter plumage resembles Dunlin, but has white upper rump and more pronounced down-curved bill. Stance is more upright than that of Dunlin. Call is a soft whistle 'chirrup'. P

LITTLE STINT *Calidris minuta* L 5" Fairly common, breeding in the Arctic tundra. In winter found in marshes and mud-flats. On migration and in winter often seen with other small waders. Little Stint and Temminck's Stint are easily picked out in these mixed flocks by their smaller size, shorter and straighter bills and more active behaviour. This greater activity is most characteristic of Little Stint. Told from Temminck's Stint, which is the same size, by more distinct light V-pattern on back and dark outer tail-feathers. It is lighter on breast and face and has noticeably longer legs. Call is a sharp, short, high-pitched note, quite distinct from the trill of Temminck's Stint. P

TEMMINCK'S STINT *Calidris temminckii* L 5" Fairly common, nesting on mountain moors, tundra and along lake and seashores. Outside breeding season found on mud-flats and marshes, primarily of fresh water. Differs from the similar Little Stint in having more uniform dark back, white outer tail-feathers and pale legs (black in Little Stint). Breast and face darker. Often mixes with Dunlins although it has a greater tendency to occur in small unmixed flocks than the more active Little Stint. Call is a short, high-pitched trill, very different from the sharp, high-pitched note of the Little Stint. P

winter

winter

summer

Dunlin

winter

Curlew Sandpiper

winter

summer

winter

winter

summer

Little Stint

winter

winter

summer

winter

Temminck's Stint

summer

BROAD-BILLED SANDPIPER *Limicola falcinellus*
L 6" Uncommon, nesting on mountain moors and tundra.
In winter found on mud-flats and marshes. Notice very
dark colours with Snipe-like pattern, extremly short legs.
White belly distinguishes it from Dunlin in summer.
Rather sluggish in behaviour. Only at very short range is
the drooping, flattened tip of the bill noticeable. In winter plumage, prominent white eye-stripe and dark spot
on the front of wing are the best field marks. Only rarely
mixes with other small sandpipers, usually occurring
singly or in small flocks. Call is a rather deep trill,
'crrrooit'.   V

SANDERLING *Calidris alba* L 8" Common, breeding in
the Arctic. Outside breeding season found along sandy
beaches at the water's edge. In winter plumage notice
very white appearance with prominent black spot on
front of wing, in summer replaced on the upper parts by
rich brown. In flight the white wing-bar is striking. Very
active, keeping close to the retreating waves. Often
allows a close approach before flying off. Usually occurs
in unmixed flocks. Flight call is a sharp, distinctive 'plick'.
                                                            WP

and belly and the rich brown upper parts are reminiscent of the
Golden Plover, but the colours are much warmer. When a
flock of Dunlin manoeuvres with fast turns and twists low over
the mud-flats, it seems to flash as all the birds turn and their
white and black underparts glitter in the sun. In the other
species the changes are less striking and most turn from a
brownish colour in summer to become more grey and white in
winter.

When the sandpipers arrive at their breeding grounds, the
flocks dissolve and the nesting sites are occupied. This is the time
when the displaying birds hover and sing over the northern
tundra. Almost like a lark, Temminck's Stint hovers in the air,
its trills ringing loudly over the open moor. Sometimes several
Dunlin can be seen chasing each other in very fast flight low
over the ground. Twisting and turning, the birds keep up a
constant reeling trill.

All the sandpipers have aerial displays which are somewhat
similar, but they also display on the ground. Here the tail is
spread showing its contrasting brown and white colour patterns.
The nests are usually built in a tussock but vary a little in situation from species to species. The Knot and the Sanderling place
their nests on stony ground almost free of vegetation, while the
two stints (Temminck's and Little) sometimes prefer the shelter
of willow scrub.

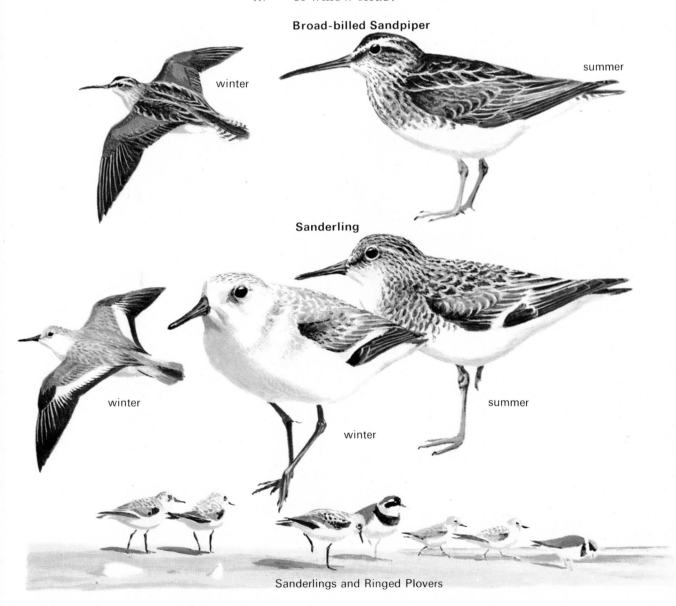

Broad-billed Sandpiper

winter

summer

Sanderling

winter

winter

summer

Sanderlings and Ringed Plovers

The number of eggs is usually four. They are greenish-brown with darker spots. Like the eggs of most shorebirds, they are pyriform. Incubation takes about twenty days; and after another twenty-five days the young are able to fly. Although both parents share the incubation, there is a tendency for the male to carry the heavier burden, and he also is the one who most carefully tends the young when hatched. The male Purple Sandpiper alone takes care of the young while the female starts her southward journey. Nesting as far north as many of these small birds do, they have only a very short season in which they can breed. It is characteristic that usually only one brood is reared and the time spent in preparatory work (display and nest-building) is very short. Also, the immediate departure from the breeding grounds after the young are able to fly is an adaption to the concentrated time in which so many duties have to be performed.

For the beginner, sandpipers are often difficult to tell apart, but practice soon perfects this ability. The Knot is easy to recognize by its large size. The two stints are set apart from the others by their smaller size, but they can be hard to tell from each other. Temminck's is more uniform in colour though, and the outer tail-feathers are white, not grey as in the Little Stint. In behaviour the Little Stint resembles the Dunlin with which it flocks, while Temminck's Stint keeps more to itself and resembles the Common Sandpiper. Of the medium-sized sandpipers the Dunlin is by far the most numerous. The Purple Sandpiper is much darker and is usually encountered on rocks, while the Curlew Sandpiper has a very distinct white upper rump clearly exposed in flight. The Sanderling is found almost exclusively on sandy beaches and its very distinctive white wing-bar is easily seen in flight. In winter plumage its clean white and grey colours with a black shoulder patch tell it apart from any of the other sandpipers. The Broad-billed Sandpiper, which is quite rare in western Europe, is slightly smaller than the Dunlin and has much shorter legs. Its plumage is striped almost like a snipe, distinguishing it from all the other sandpipers.

The question of identification becomes much more difficult when one has to consider the stragglers from Asia and North America. These occur almost annually and are particularly numerous in Britain and Ireland. The Pectoral Sandpiper from the New World and the Sharp-tailed Sandpiper from the Siberian Arctic are very similar and very closely related. Slightly larger than the Dunlin, the colours and patterns of the back are much more like those of the Little Stint with rather strongly marked stripes. The Pectoral Sandpiper's brown breast ends sharply, the contrast with the pure-white belly being very pronounced. But the breast colour of the Sharp-tailed Sandpiper fades away more gradually. The Buff-breasted Sandpiper from the New World has a preference for dry fields. The entire underside is buff, distinguishing it from all other sandpipers. Baird's Sandpiper is about the size of a Dunlin but has a much shorter bill and longer wings. Its breast is buffish and the back looks barred rather than striped. The White-rumped Sandpiper has a distinct white rump like the Curlew Sandpiper but the bill is much shorter and is straight. The Least Sandpiper and Semi-palmated Sandpiper are both the size of our Little Stint and Temminck's Stint. In general the Least Sandpiper looks quite like the Little Stint but has pale yellowish legs, while the Little Stint has black legs. The Semi-palmated Sandpiper resembles Temminck's Stint but has black legs. It is almost

LEAST SANDPIPER *Calidris minutilla* L 6" Very rare visitor from North America. Resembles Temminck's Stint, but has brownish outer tail-feathers and is slightly darker above. Bill is thin and short. Legs are yellow. Call is a distinctive high 'breep'.   V

SEMI-PALMATED SANDPIPER *Calidris pusilla* L 7" Very rare visitor from North America. Resembles Little Stint, but back pattern less well-defined and bill thicker and heavier. Call, a short 'kripe', is lower pitched than Least Sandpiper's.   V

WHITE-RUMPED SANDPIPER *Calidris fuscicollis* L 7" Rare visitor from North America. Has distinctive white upper rump but differs from Curlew Sandpiper in having short, straight bill and more horizontal stance. Call is a thin 'jeet'.   V

PECTORAL SANDPIPER *Calidris melanotos* L 6" Rare visitor from North America, often found in drier locations than other small sandpipers. Note the abrupt border between streaked breast and white underparts. When flushed, zig-zags like Snipe. Call is a low 'prrrp'.
V

SHARP-TAILED SANDPIPER *Calidris acuminata* L 7" Very rare visitor from Asia. Resembles Pectoral Sandpiper, but in autumn its breast is buffish, narrowly streaked at sides, and there is no abrupt border between breast and underparts. Legs are darker than those of Pectoral Sandpiper. Call is a high-pitched 2-note whistle.

BAIRD'S SANDPIPER *Calidris bairdii* L 7" Very rare visitor from North America, often found on drier ground than other sandpipers. Notice scaly back, horizontal stance and relatively long wings. Call is a rather liquid 'keep'.   V

BUFF-BREASTED SANDPIPER *Tryngites subruficollis* L 8" Rare visitor from North America. Prefers short grass habitats. Notice buffish colour with distinctive white underwing and upright stance. When flushed, zig-zags rather like Snipe. Call is a low trill.   V

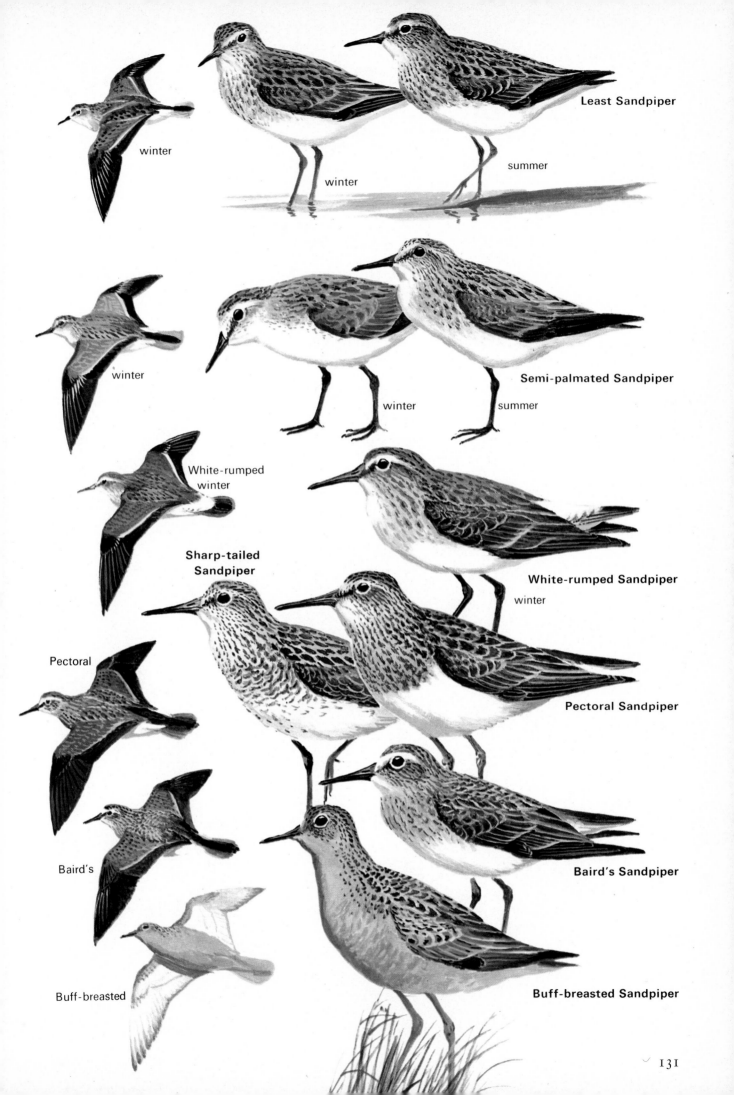

winter

Least Sandpiper

winter

summer

winter

Semi-palmated Sandpiper

winter   summer

White-rumped
winter

White-rumped Sandpiper

winter

Sharp-tailed
Sandpiper

Pectoral

Pectoral Sandpiper

Baird's

Baird's Sandpiper

Buff-breasted

Buff-breasted Sandpiper

indistinguishable with certainty from the Little Stint, but the broader tip of the bill should be of some help. In general, the identification of these stragglers is so difficult and refined that it should be reserved for the specialists, and even they venture into this field with some hesitation.

Interestingly the North American shorebirds met with in western Europe are the species which breed in the western part of North America and only occur in small numbers on the eastern coast. This is at least partially explained by the almost direct eastern direction of the first part of their autumn migration. They then have a tendency to fly too far towards the east bringing them out over the Atlantic, where they continue until they reach land in western Europe.

Stilts and Avocets

order *Charadriiformes*, family *Recurvirostridae*

These long-legged birds are undoubtedly the most elegant of all shorebirds. There are seven species, of which two breed in Europe. The Avocet is about the size of the Oystercatcher and similarly it is black and white. But the similarities go no further. Where the Oystercatcher is strong and solid, the

Below Purple Sandpipers

AVOCET *Recurvirostra avosetta* L17" Locally common. Prefers sheltered bays and lagoons. Elegant white and black with extremely long, lead-coloured legs and thin, black, upturned bill. Flight graceful with rather slow wing-beats. Often in large flocks. Sometimes flies in V-formation but more often in loose cloud formation. Nests in colonies of varying size. Call is soft, melodious 'klui-it', hence Dutch name Kluut. SWP

BLACK-WINGED STILT *Himantopus himantopus* L 15" Locally common. Prefers marshes and lagoons with open water. Extremely long pink legs and thin, straight bill are unmistakable. Easily told from Avocet by these, and by solid black back and upper side of wing. Nests in small, loose colonies. Can be seen in small groups but not as sociable as Avocet. Call is a sharp, repeated 'kik'. V

Avocet is thin and graceful. The very fine bill is curved upward, lending the bird a look of refined aristocracy. The long, lead-coloured legs carry the bird with the grace of a ballet-dancer. And the call, a somewhat worried 'bluuit', seems to plead for protection and shelter. But the Avocet is quite capable of protecting itself. Anyone approaching a colony is attacked relentlessly, and even cattle are driven away from the exposed nests and eggs.

Avocets nests in colonies on flat marshes at the edge of lagoons. The four eggs are laid in a simple scraping on the ground. After an incubation time of about twenty-three days the young pick their way out of their narrow confinement. With silky grey down and thin bills which soon take on an upward bend, the little creatures are as appealing as their parents. After about thirty days of flightless life, their wings are strong enough to carry them aloft and they have happily passed the most hazardous stage of their lives. In late summer the European Avocets congregate in large flocks at favoured lagoons before their migration which only carries them to the shores of southern Europe.

The Black-winged Stilt has pitch-black back and wings, the rest of the plumage being snowy white except for the brownish

Avocet

Black-winged Stilt

♂ winter

♀

♂ summer

juv.

head of the male. The red legs are even longer than those of the Avocet and the gait even more deliberate and graceful. The bill is very thin and straight, and it feeds by picking insects from the water rather than by skimming the surface sideways which is the way of the Avocet. Colonial when breeding, it prefers tussocks in low water or on dry ground as a base for its nest. It is very erratic in its occurence, and although definitely a southern species, it has once bred in England, a single colony of three nesting near Nottingham. Both the Avocet and the Black-winged Stilt are strong flyers and with their long bills, necks and legs they are unmistakable.

Phalaropes
order *Charadriiformes*, family *Phalaropodidae*

Resembling the Dunlin superficially, these small shorebirds are nevertheless very different from their relatives. There are three species, of which the two breeding in Europe are Holarctic in distribution. The third is indigenous to the New World.

The Phalaropes have lobed feet, small flaps of skin attached to the sides of the toes enabling them to swim very well. They are pelagic in their habits and usually only come near land for the purpose of breeding. They nest by small ponds and lakes in the north, and upon arrival in spring the females set up their territories here and vigorously defend them against intruders of their own sex. When a male approaches the territory, the aggressiveness of the female is suppressed although at first she apparently has trouble restraining herself from attacking. Soon a pair is formed. When a nesting site on the shore has been selected, the female lays the four eggs and takes off, leaving all family duties to the male, who alone tends to the eggs and the young. The roles of male and female are comple-tely reversed from what is normally the case among birds. The

WILSON'S PHALAROPE *Phalaropus tricolor* L 9" Rare visitor from N. America in late spring, summer and autumn. More likely seen inland than other two phala-ropes. Bill very thin and rather long. With white rump and dark wing, it resembles some of the larger sandpipers, but notice chestnut pattern in summer plumage. Very active. Call is low and grunting.   V

GREY PHALAROPE *Phalaropus fulicarius* L 7" Un-common pelagic species most often seen during storms along the coast. Breeds on Icelandic coastal lagoons. Yellow bill is short and much stouter than Red-necked Phalarope's. Notice also less bold pattern on back in winter. Usually seen singly or in small flocks flying low, far out to sea. Call suggests Turnstone's.   P

RED-NECKED PHALAROPE *Phalaropus lobatus* L 6½" Uncommon, though more numerous than Grey Phalarope. Nests by tundra lakes. Bill longer and thinner than Grey Phalarope's. Flying birds in winter plumage resemble Sanderling, but have darker back, more slender bill and black line through eye. Usually seen singly or in small flocks. Call consists of low, short, scratchy notes.   SP

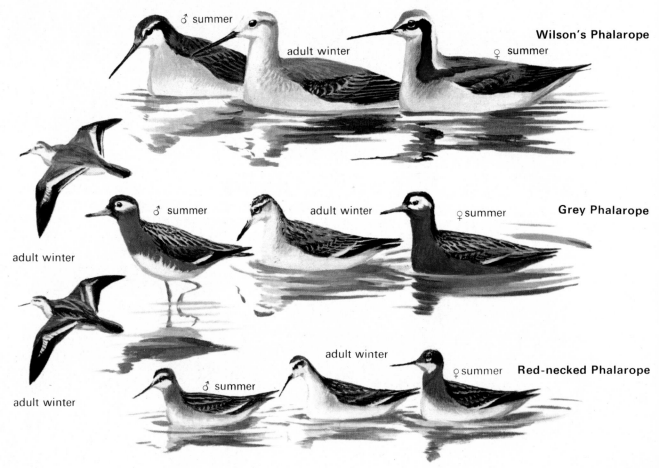

♂ summer   adult winter   ♀ summer   **Wilson's Phalarope**

adult winter   ♂ summer   adult winter   ♀ summer   **Grey Phalarope**

adult winter   ♂ summer   adult winter   ♀ summer   **Red-necked Phalarope** females are the more brightly coloured.

As soon as the young can fly, they take to the sea where they spend the rest of the year. In flocks they move about on the open ocean, where they pick crustaceans and other organisms from the surface while they swim. They lie rather high on the water. On the breeding grounds they feed on various animal life from the surface, but they can also be seen swimming around in narrow circles. Apparently the whirlpool they create brings insects and larvae closer to the surface where they can be picked up.

Stone Curlews
order *Charadriiformes,* family *Burhinidae*

Of the nine species of this widespread family only one breeds in Europe. The Stone Curlew leads a very inconspicuous life and is much more often heard than seen. In spring the plaintive whistle 'cur-lee', reminiscent of the Curlew's call, is repeated over and over again at dusk. But, once spotted, the bird is easy to recognize. Generally the shape of a large plover, it has a very large head with bright yellow eyes. The light brown plumage gives it perfect camouflage against the dry, stony ground it frequents, and it relies heavily on this protective coloration as it crouches when an enemy is approaching. Once flushed, the strong wings carry it with ease low above the ground, and the slow wing-strokes interrupted by glides make the distinct black and white markings of the wing clearly visible.

The Stone Curlew is nocturnal in habit and spends the daylight hours dozing on the ground. The nest is just a plain scraping where the two blotched, ground-coloured eggs are laid. The light brown young with their black stripes are hatched after an incubation period of about twenty-six days. They are fully fledged about six weeks later, after which the families join

STONE CURLEW *Burhinus oedicnemus* L 16″ Scarce or locally common on dry, open localities. Notice large head and eyes and streaked plumage. Often escapes danger by running in a crouched position. Sometimes stands very erect, when characteristic head shape and large eye are prominent features. Flight is usually low over the ground with deliberate wing-beats and the wing pattern is distinctive. Outside breeding season often seen in small flocks. Largely nocturnal in habits. Call is Curlew-like but higher pitched.   S

PRATINCOLE *Glareola pratincola* L 10″ Locally common on mud-flats, marshes and open plains. Notice tern- or swallow-like silhouette in flight and dark brown underwing. Stance horizontal but runs very well on rather short legs. Can only be told from the more eastern Black-winged Pratincole by the reddish-brown, not pitch-black, underwing. Nests colonially and is usually encountered in flocks, which are often very noisy. Call is tern-like.   V

Stone Curlew

Pratincole

imm.

to form flocks varying in numbers from 10 to 200. In autumn most of the British and central European breeders leave to spend the winter in southern Europe and north Africa.

Coursers and Pratincoles
order *Charadriiformes*, family *Glareolidae*

Sixteen species belonging to two subfamilies, the coursers and the pratincoles, make up this aberrant family of shorebirds. Only one species of the coursers, the Cream-coloured Courser, is regularly met with in Europe. It does not breed within the boundaries of our continent, but is a bird of the African and Asian steppes and deserts. Its almost uniform buffish plumage is only interrupted by two distinct eye-stripes meeting at the nape and blends so perfectly with its normal surroundings that it almost fades into the background. But when it takes off the black underwing strikes the eye as the bird flies for a short distance before settling on the ground again. Its actions are similar to those of the plovers as it runs swiftly with short abrupt stops. In Europe it is usually seen singly or in pairs and it is most frequently met with in southern Italy.

Two species of pratincoles nest in Europe. The only difference

Below Stone Curlews

between the two is the colour of the underwing, which in the species nesting in the western part of Europe, the Pratincole, is chestnut, while in the eastern species, the Black-winged Pratincole, it is black. Some authorities regard the two as different colour phases of the same species. But as the ranges of the two overlap at several places without interbreeding, it is more likely that we are dealing with two closely related species.

In flight pratincoles look like huge swallows, and like swallows they hunt insects in the air. But on the ground the long-bodied bird is surprisingly good at running, moving about like a plover. Pratincoles nest in colonies, usually not very large, on dried out mud-flats and shores. They lay three spotted eggs on the bare ground. The colonies of the Black-winged Pratincole tend to be larger than those of the Pratincole.

Skuas
order *Charadriiformes*, family *Stercorariidae*

The four species of skuas all breed within our territory although they are confined to the extreme north. They are robbers and thieves, obtaining most of their food by chasing other sea birds and forcing them to give up the prey they have caught.

BLACK-WINGED PRATINCOLE *Glareola nordmanni* L 10" Locally common on open steppes and dried-out mud-flats. Has pitch-black underwing with no white or brown. Otherwise almost identical with Pratincole, of which some authorities consider it a race.   V

CREAM-COLOURED COURSER *Cursorius cursor* L 9" Rare straggler to most of Europe from its African breeding grounds. Usually encountered in localities resembling its desert home, such as sandy beaches and dried-out fields. Notice very light brown colour with black eye-stripes and black tips to wings. Runs very fast, interrupted by sudden stops. Often tries to escape danger by crouching. Call is unmusical and harsh.   V

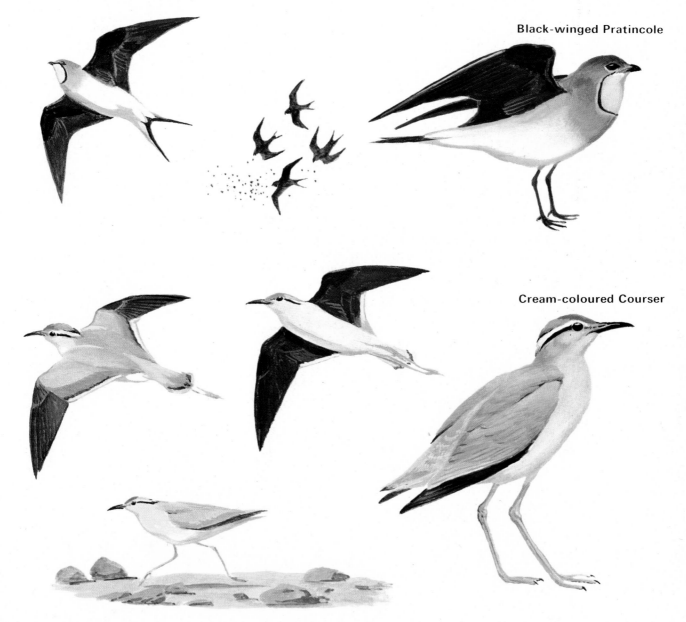

Black-winged Pratincole

Cream-coloured Courser

Harassing its victim by constantly swooping down upon it, the skua forces the unfortunate bird to drop or regurgitate whatever food it has obtained. As it reluctantly lets go of its food, the skua in an elegant dive picks it out of the air and swallows it, only to return to pester the victim until nothing is left to rob.

Superficially gull-like in appearance, skuas nevertheless possess traits resembling those of birds of prey. Their wings are pointed, their flight is as fast as that of a falcon and the hooked bill is a formidable weapon. The skuas are more maritime in their habits than most gulls, with the exception of the Kittiwake, a favourite target for robbery. Immature skuas are speckled brown, almost black, as is the adult Great Skua. The smaller skuas have two colour phases, a light phase in which the underside is cream-coloured, and a dark phase in which the entire plumage is sooty-brown. The dark phase is common in the Arctic Skua, rarer in the Pomarine Skua, and so rare that it is practically non-existent in the Long-tailed Skua.

Although piracy is the main way in which all the skuas obtain their food, they will also eat refuse of all kinds found at sea and on the shores. In summer both the Pomarine Skua and the Long-tailed Skua prey heavily on the lemmings so abundant on their nesting grounds in the Arctic. They are so dependent on this item of food that in years when the lemming populations are low the skuas will not breed, but only stay at the nesting sites for a few weeks, trying to support themselves on insects, carcasses and berries before they return to the open sea.

Skuas spend most of the year far out to sea. On migration they are regularly observed along the coasts of Europe, but only in small numbers, the majority passing south further out to sea. In winter skuas are found throughout the length and breadth of the Atlantic.

The Great Skua is the giant of the four. Subspecies are found in Antarctic waters and this species is the only bird breeding in both the Antarctic and the Arctic. As big as a Herring Gull, it does not limit its parasitism to gulls, terns and auks, but will also successfully harass the giant Gannet, with whose breeding range in Europe it approximately coincides. Its nests are in colonies but rather far apart, as the Great Skua demands a large territory and vigorously attacks all intruders.

The Arctic Skua, by far the most common of the other three species, also nests in colonies on the open moor but its nests are much closer together. Often the colonies are found close to those of terns, gulls and auks and the Arctic Skuas not only steal the prey caught by these birds but also eat their eggs and young if they are left unprotected.

Both the Pomarine and the Long-tailed Skua are solitary nesters on the open tundra, the Pomarine preferring wetter situations, the Long-tailed the high fells. Here they hunt lemmings, other rodents and insects and, if given the chance, they will not reject eggs and young of other birds. The Long-tailed Skua, which on the breeding ground is very tame, hovers like a Kestrel when hunting, and at a distance it can be confused with this falcon in the Scandinavian highlands where they both nest.

Gulls and Terns
order *Charadriiformes*, family *Laridae*

Nearly every shore and harbour has its gulls and terns. To most Europeans the wail of a gull or the penetrating call of a tern is symbolic of the seashore and the rolling waves. In any harbour

GREAT SKUA *Stercorarius skua* L 23" Very local. At a distance it looks like a dark short-tailed Herring Gull, but it can be distinguished by the large white patches at the base of the primaries. More of a scavenger than other skuas and often seen soaring with gulls. Like the other skuas, it nests colonially on moors and tundra. SP

POMARINE SKUA *Stercorarius pomarinus* L 20" Uncommon. Larger than Arctic Skua. Bill is proportionally larger than those of Arctic and Long-tailed. Flight is heavier and more steady. The long central feathers are broad and twisted. In the light phase, sides are barred and breast-band is more distinct than in other skuas. Immatures only told from Arctic Skua by larger size and broader wings. Dark phase is rare. P

ARCTIC SKUA *Stercorarius parasiticus* L 18" Most common skua, frequently seen pursuing terns. Adults are told from larger, heavier Pomarine Skua by short, flat, pointed central tail-feathers; from Long-tailed by tail length alone. Proportion of dark to light phase birds is greatest in the south of the breeding range. Immatures are browner than Long-tailed and have more white on wing. Immatures very hard to tell from Pomarine Skua immatures, but notice smaller size and narrower wings. SP

LONG-TAILED SKUA *Stercorarius longicaudus* L 21" Uncommon except on breeding grounds. The smallest-bodied and slimmest of the skuas and the one least inclined to rob other sea birds. Central tail-feathers of adult extend 5–8" behind the others. On nesting grounds it often hovers over its prey, the Lemming. Dark phase is almost unknown. Immature is also grey rather than brown and has less white on wing. Flight is more graceful and tern-like than that of other skuas. P

Great Skua

dark phase

light phase

Pomarine Skua

imm.

dark phase

light phase

Arctic Skua

light phase Arctic

juv.

Long-tailed Skua

the cries of gulls mingle with the sounds of human activity. Although they belong to the same family, the gulls and the terns are so distinctly different that they are best treated separately.

Gulls are cosmopolitan in their distribution and although found primarily along the coasts, only the driest deserts are not visited by them at some time or another.

Forty-three different species of gulls inhabit the world, some species, like the Herring Gull, covering almost a complete hemisphere. Europe has fourteen breeding species, while three are visitors from other parts of the world. Ross's Gull, one of the least known, occasionally occurs on the coast as a visitor from its north-east Siberian breeding grounds. The small bill and wedge-shaped tail make it look pigeon-like in flight, the narrow neck-band and rosy-white plumage adding to the beauty of this rare bird.

The Iceland Gull, which is observed more often along the shores of northern Europe, does not breed in Iceland at all, but is indigenous only to Greenland. Bonaparte's Gull, hard to tell from the familiar Black-headed Gull, is another stray visitor from the New World. It breeds in the interior of North America and is a scarce winter visitor to the Atlantic coast of our continent.

Gulls are large to medium-sized birds. They have short tails and long wings held at a characteristic angle. The bill is rather large, downward curved at the tip and a perfect tool for handling the many different types of food which gulls enjoy. The legs are short, the feet webbed; gulls are good swimmers and walkers, but they do not possess the tern's skill and dexterity in diving.

In their migratory habits gulls vary from being resident, like the rare Audouin's Gull of the Mediterranean and many southern

Above Arctic Skuas

IVORY GULL *Pagophila eburnea* L 18" Rarely encountered outside the Arctic. During breeding season found along the coast, otherwise over open water and along pack ice in the Arctic Ocean. Ivory is much smaller than other all-white gulls; it is easily distinguished by the short black legs and black bill (yellow-tipped in adult). Immatures are speckled with black on the upper side. Flight is elegant and light. Call is tern-like. V

GLAUCOUS GULL *Larus hyperboreus* L 27" Uncommon, usually seen along the coast in the company of other large gulls. Distinguished from Iceland Gull by size (larger than Herring Gull), heavier bill and by relatively shorter wings, which do not extend beyond the tail when at rest. Immatures of both Glaucous and Iceland Gull easily told from other immature gulls by their very light colouring, particularly of the wings. Immatures told from immature Iceland Gulls by heavier bill and more extensive flesh colour at its base. In all plumages of Glaucous and Iceland, note in flight the transluscent 'windows' at base of primaries. Yellow eye-ring of adult very hard to see. Fiercely predatory in its behaviour. Call resembles that of Herring Gull. W

ICELAND GULL *Larus glaucoides* L 22" Rare, usually seen along the coasts, often in company with other large gulls. Slightly smaller than Herring Gull but has no black on wings. When sitting, folded wings protrude beyond the tail in most individuals. Head looks small for the body and bill seems still smaller. Like Glaucous Gull, immatures are very light in plumage. Immatures are best told from immature Glaucous Gulls by smaller size, longer wings and much smaller and darker bill. Reddish eye-ring of adult is very hard to see. The feet are always flesh-coloured in both species. Call resembles that of Herring Gull. W

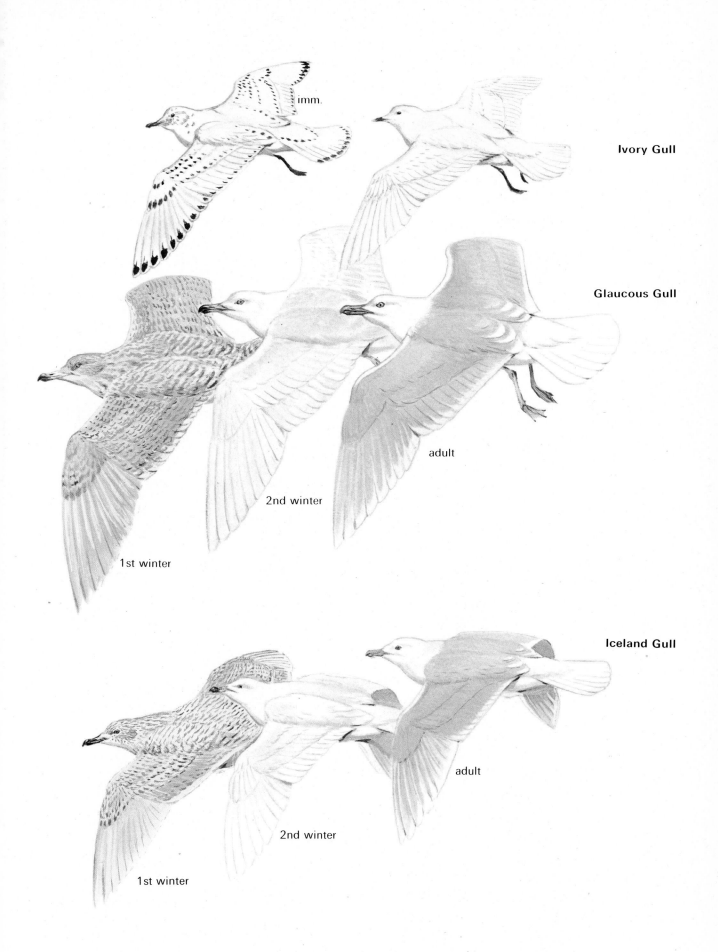

imm.

Ivory Gull

Glaucous Gull

1st winter

2nd winter

adult

Iceland Gull

1st winter

2nd winter

adult

Great Black-backed Gull

1st winter

adult

L.f.graellsii

Lesser Black-backed Gull

2nd winter

L.f.fuscus

Herring Gull

adult

1st winter

2nd winter

adult

GREAT BLACK-BACKED GULL *Larus marinus* L 27"
Common along coasts, rarely found inland. Nests singly
or colonially, often with other gulls. Distinguished from
similar Lesser Black-backed by larger size, noticeably
larger and heavier bill, more solid black of wing and
back, pinkish legs and, from below, by lesser extension
of black on wing-tips. Wing-beats measurably slower
than Lesser Black-backed's. Immatures difficult to tell
from immature Lesser Black-backed and Herring Gulls,
but note shape and extent of black band on tail, contrast
between light head and dark back, and heavy bill. Sometimes follows ships but not as much as Herring Gull.
Predatory, especially on nesting colonies of other sea
birds. Call is low pitched 'kow-kow-kow'. RSW

LESSER BLACK-BACKED GULL *Larus fuscus* L 21"
Very common, usually along coasts and in harbours but
also inland. Scandinavian subspecies migrates along
European rivers towards the south, and is also becoming
more common in southern areas. Nests colonially on
islands, beaches and moorland. Adults of both British
and Scandinavian subspecies told from Great Black-
backed by smaller size, lighter bill, yellow legs and more
extensive black on underside of wing. British subspecies
L.f. graellsii has much lighter (slatey-grey) mantle and
wings than Great Black-backed, whereas Scandinavian
subspecies *L.f. fuscus* is much darker. Immatures very
hard to tell from immature Herring Gulls. In the second
winter, legs become yellow and contrast between dark
and light areas becomes more pronounced. Call is loud,
clear and bugle-like, only slightly deeper than that of
Herring Gull Often follows boats. RSWP

HERRING GULL *Larus argentatus* L 22" Abundant
along coasts, particularly in harbours and on rubbish
dumps, but also common inland by lakes and rivers.
Breeds colonially on cliffs, islands and beaches. Adult is
best told from Common Gull by larger size and yellow
bill. Leg colour is usually flesh, but legs of subspecies in
Mediterranean and eastern Europe are yellow. Immatures very hard to tell from immature Lesser Black-
backed. Told from immature Great Black-backed by less
contrast in colours and distribution of dark and light on
tail. Primarily a scavenger, Herring Gull will also break
molluscs by dropping them on a hard surface. Sometimes
seen diving clumsily in tern-like fashion in low water.
Commonly seen high overhead, soaring like a hawk.
Usual call is loud, clear and bugle-like. RW

COMMON GULL *Larus canus* L 16" Common inland
and along shores, in harbours, parks and sometimes on
refuse dumps. Nesting colonies are found on islands,
beaches, marshes and moors. Adult resembles Herring
Gull but is much smaller, and greenish colour of bill
should be noticed. Distinguished from rare Audouin's
Gull by green bill and more defined black and white
wing-tips; from Kittiwake by white on otherwise black
wing-tips. Immatures have distinctive black band on tail.
Call is higher pitched than that of Herring Gulls. Often
follows boats. RSWP

AUDOUIN'S GULL *Larus audouinii* L 19" Very rare
and local. Breeds in small colonies on rocky islands. Less
coastal in behaviour, staying further out to sea, than
most other gulls. Distinguished from all other gulls by
characteristic bill pattern and very indistinct border
between black tips and grey upper side of wing. Notice
also wing and head pattern of immature birds, which
have greyish crown and neck and brownish upper parts.

SLENDER-BILLED GULL *Larus genei* L 17" Fairly
common except in westernmost part of its range. Nests
colonially in marshes and swamps. Outside breeding
season usually found along coasts. Resembles Black-
headed Gull but notice white wing-tips of adults, lack of
hood, and long thin bill, which in flight is usually held
pointing downwards. Immatures told from immature
Black-headed Gulls by much fainter markings and shape
of bill. Even at a distance, bill and head shape differ
markedly from those of other gulls. Call is very nasal. V

Common Gull

imm.

Audouin's Gull

Slender-billed Gull

143

populations of the Herring and other gulls, to being highly migratory, as are the Little Gull and the nothern populations of the Lesser Black-backed Gull. Most gulls, however, are what is known as partial migrants. This term simply means that some birds migrate, some do not. In general it is usually the northern and eastern populations of a species which migrate, because they would not be able to survive the conditions on their breeding grounds in winter. But it is also found that immature gulls are much more likely to migrate than adults. This is true of all the partially migratory species. There are also populations where some of the adults migrate while others stay in the area all winter. These populations are found in areas between clearly migratory and clearly resident populations. A good example of this rather confused migratory pattern, which has been revealed by ringing results, is the Common Gull. All the Finnish birds are migratory, many wintering in the British Isles. Danish Common Gulls are partial migrants, about ten per cent staying behind to endure the severity of winter together with visitors of the same species from the Baltic countries. The rest migrate to the North Sea and Channel regions. Scottish Common Gulls are relatively sedentary and, although many immatures venture south to England and south-west to Ireland, very few are known to cross over to the Continent.

Ringing has also yielded interesting results concerning the movements of the Lesser Black-backed Gull. Three races occur in Europe, the Baltic race, the Norwegian race and the British subspecies migrate along the western coast of Europe, continental Europe along the rivers to winter in the eastern part of the Mediterranean and north-east Africa, some reaching as far south as the Great Lakes region. The Norwegian and the British subspecies migrate along the western coast of Europe, wintering here but also reaching the western part of the Mediterranean and the north-western coast of Africa. This distinct difference in migratory habits has undoubtedly influenced the development of subspecies. Recently British Lesser Black-backeds have begun to spend the winter near towns and cities where there is edible refuse.

Some gulls travel far: Black-headed Gulls ringed in Germany have been recovered in America, one in Mexico and one on Barbados. Black-headed Gulls are regularly observed along the entire east coast of North America, but most of them come from the increasing Icelandic population. Another European species, the Little Gull, is among the rare but regular stragglers which American ornithologists enjoy. This dainty bird regularly crosses the northern, stormy part of the Atlantic in late autumn and has even, on one occasion, been found nesting in Ontario, Canada. Apparently late migrants from the Baltic countries move due west and are caught in the storms so prevalent at this time of year.

The Kittiwake, a true maritime species unlike the other gulls which rarely move out of sight of land, regularly migrates to the Newfoundland Banks. Here millions of sea birds assemble in winter to feed on the abundance of fish. Kittiwakes ringed in Iceland, Norway, Russia and even Great Britain are recovered in great numbers in this area. Russian Kittiwakes reach their destination by way of the Greenland coast and British birds are also known to reach this northern island. Outside the breeding season the Kittiwake spends its time far out at sea. Here it catches fish and crustacea and is often encountered in large groups with which skuas associate for the purpose of robbing the less powerful gulls.

MEDITERRANEAN GULL *Larus melanocephalus* L 15" Fairly common, nesting colonially in shallow water in lakes, swamps, and marshes. Outside breeding season found on coasts, in harbours and occasionally inland. Slightly larger and heavier than Black-headed Gull. Adult is told from similar Black-headed Gull by having more extensive, solid black (not brown) hood in summer, no black at all on wing, and heavier, dark, banded bill. Immatures have much darker wing-tips than Black-headed (only a few white spots) without white fore-edges of wing. They usually lack the very wide and distinctive black tail-band of immature Common. Has more distinct black line through eye. Call is lower pitched than that of Black-headed Gull.   V

BLACK-HEADED GULL *Larus ridibundus* L 14" Abundant, nesting colonially in swamps, marshes and lagoons. Occasionally found nesting on cliffs in the far north where the species is spreading. Outside breeding season found along coasts, in harbours, along rivers and lakes and on farmland, often far from large bodies of water. Adult told from other hooded gulls by brown hood which does not extend down the neck. Also note white leading edge of wing, black rear edge of tip. Underside of wing is dark, distinguishing it from rare Bonaparte's Gull. Immatures are told from immature Common Gulls by much narrower black band on tail and characteristic pattern on upper side of wing and on head. From immature Mediterranean Gulls by lighter wing-tips with a white fore-edge of the wing. Smaller than Mediterranean Gull, larger than Bonaparte's and Little Gull. Often encountered in large flocks, following ploughs or boats close to shore. Call is a very harsh cackling 'kwuririp'.   RSWP

BONAPARTE'S GULL *Larus philadelphia* L 13" Rare visitor from its North American breeding grounds to western European countries, where it often associates with very similar Black-headed Gull. Mostly seen in winter months. In summer, adult easily told from Black-headed Gull by solid black (not brown) hood and black bill. In all plumages, undersides of primaries are white, not dark. Smaller and more elegant, particularly in flight, than Black-headed Gull. Immatures resemble immature Black-headed Gulls, but dark wing pattern is more pronounced. Flight buoyant and tern-like, with bill held down. Call is a low quacking.   V

KITTIWAKE *Rissa tridactyla* L 16" Very common, but usually stays far from shores as it is one of the few truly pelagic gulls. Breeds in large colonies on ledges of cliffs on coasts, sometimes on buildings and beaches. Notice square-cut tail and solid black wing-tips of adult bird. When standing, very short black legs are characteristic. Immature resembles several of the dark-headed gulls, but is distinguished by combination of dark neck-band, short black legs, black wing-tips and very slightly forked tail. Flight is elegant, almost tern-like, often in lines low over water. Call is a characteristic 'kittiwake'.   RS

Kittiwake

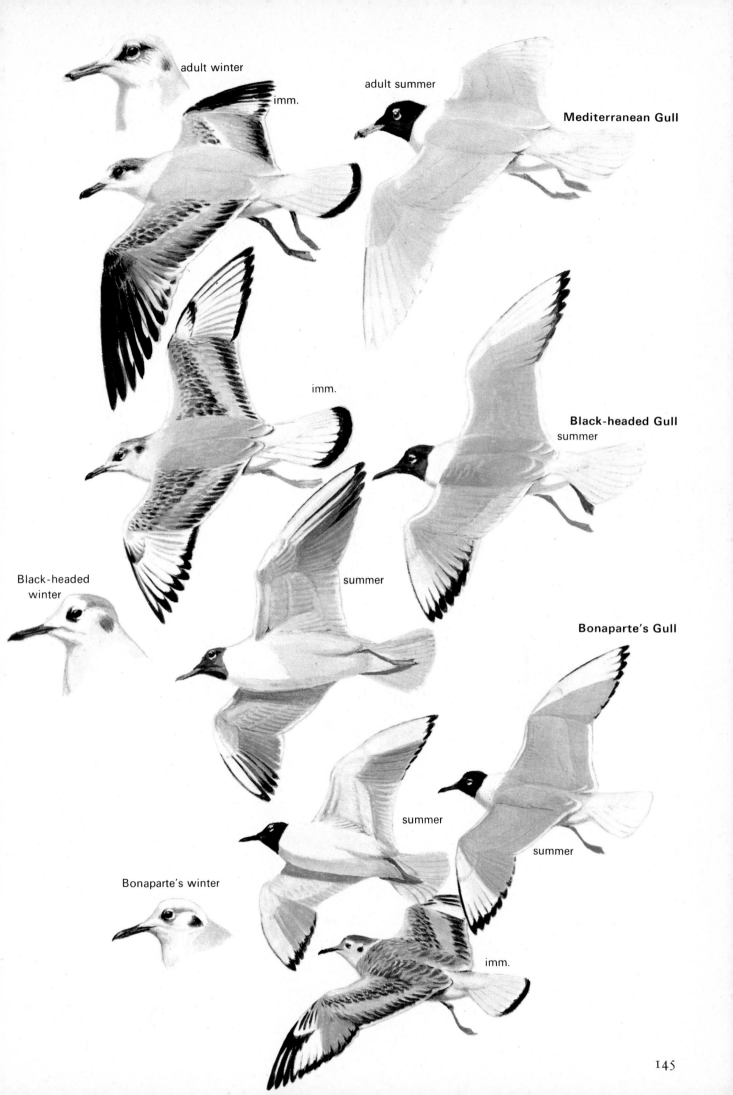

adult winter

imm.

adult summer

Mediterranean Gull

imm.

Black-headed Gull
summer

Black-headed
winter

summer

summer

Bonaparte's Gull

summer

summer

Bonaparte's winter

imm.

145

GREAT BLACK-HEADED GULL *Larus ichthyaetus*
L 25" Fairly common, nesting along lagoons, in marshes
and lakes. Rare visitor to western Europe, with occurrences at all times of the year, usually along sea coasts.
In summer, adult unmistakable by enormous size and
black hood. In winter, yellow bill with black band and
dark feathers on head are characteristic. Immatures told
from other large immature gulls by striking wide black
band on white tail. In habits it resembles the other large
species, but is even more ferocious, often parasitising
other gulls. Call is harsh and crow-like.   V

Unlike the Kittiwake, most gulls are not specialized at all in
their food preference and the increased amount of offal and
refuse discarded by man has offered a tremendous chance for the
omnivorous species. The Herring Gull in particular has
increased greatly in numbers and every harbour and dump has
its Herring Gulls cleaning up everything which is eatable.
The Black-headed Gull has also increased in numbers. Both
species showed a considerable increase in breeding range
in the earlier part of the twentieth century. This rapid expansion
has been particularly conspicuous in Scandinavia, and Iceland
has also been successfully invaded. The great increase in records
of the Black-headed Gull from North America coincides with
this expansion.

adult winter

Great Black-headed
Gull

summer

imm.

The larger gulls can be quite voracious in their feeding
behaviour. In spring and summer they often take eggs and
young of other birds, and when food is really short they even
resort to cannibalism. Adult birds of other species are sometimes taken and I have seen a Herring Gull snatching a Skylark out of the air on a foggy day on the North Sea. I have
also watched a flock of Herring Gulls viciously attacking a
migrating Merlin, forcing it into the sea where it was torn to
pieces. Herring Gulls can quarrel amongst themselves when
competing for refuse in harbours and dumps, or offal thrown
overboard from the ships they so persistently follow. Along the
coasts they eat molluscs and dead fish washed ashore. The shellfish are either broken with their powerful bills or, if that is not
possible, by dropping them from a height onto rocks. Herring
Gulls are even able to make dives in tern-like fashion and
although clumsy-looking they often succeed in catching fish in
this way.

Gulls, particularly the Black-headed Gull, will also eat a large
number of worms and insects which they find on the open
fields, and many follow farmers' ploughs to pick up the larvae
and worms unearthed for them. Herring Gulls and Common
Gulls do the same, as does the Mediterranean Gull.

Black-headed Gulls can also be seen catching insects in the air, particularly at dusk after a warm summer day when many beetles are on the move. The food eaten by the different gulls varies according to the surroundings in which they live. The Kittiwake eats crustacea caught far out at sea, as does the much rarer Sabine's Gull. Of the larger gulls the Herring Gull has made the best adjustment to the environment created by modern man, whereas others still resort to the more natural food found on the seashore. The Great Black-backed and the Glaucous Gulls are giants which often prey directly on other birds. In Britain, Lesser Black-backed Gulls have adjusted to the new possibilities of civilization. Elsewhere, species such as Audouin's Gull of the Mediterranean rocky shores, have stable populations which are not increasing in the same way as most other gulls.

LITTLE GULL *Larus minutus* L 11" Fairly common, nesting in marshes and swamps, often in association with other *Laridae*. Outside breeding season found on inland lakes and rivers as well as along coasts and quite far out to sea. Smallest of the European gulls, in summer plumage easily distinguished by black hood extending far down on neck, uniformly grey upper side of wing and black underwing. Immatures have light underwings, but characteristic Kittiwake-like wing pattern. In spite of the very rounded wings, flight is buoyant and elegant, almost tern-like. Also swims buoyantly, like a paper boat. Usually encountered singly or in small flocks. Often associates with Black-headed Gull. The call: 'kek-kek-kek'. WP

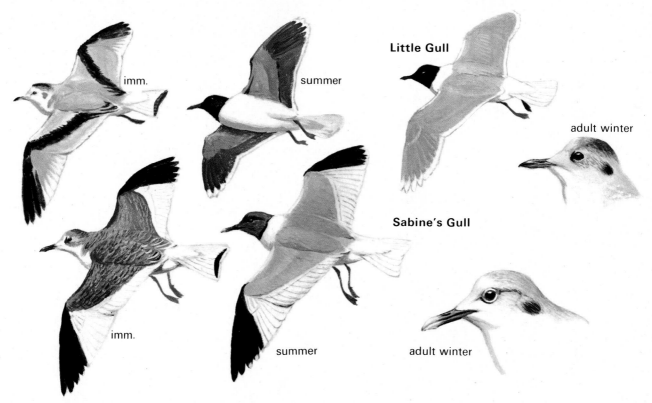

imm.   summer

Little Gull

adult winter

Sabine's Gull

imm.   summer   adult winter

The same stability is true for the Great Black-headed Gull, which is found in south-eastern Europe. This species is known particularly for its ruthlessness in attacking live prey.

The Common Gull represents in its feeding behaviour a combination of the habits of the Herring Gull and the Black-headed Gull. The Slender-billed Gull of south-eastern Europe, which in many ways resembles the Black-headed Gull, seems much more dependent on open water and shorelines and only rarely will it assemble in harbours and other places where offal is available. The Little Gull feeds in summer mainly on worms and on insects caught in the air, in the water or on land; in winter it is more maritime in behaviour, although it sometimes takes refuse like most of its relatives.

All our gulls are social in their nesting habits. Colonies may number thousands of pairs. The territory each pair will defend against intruders varies in size from species to species. In general the rule is: the larger the bird, the larger the territory. For this reason colonies of the larger gulls have a tendency to be spread over a large area, while the smaller gulls often nest very close together. The large gulls site their colonies in the open on sea cliffs or grassy islands and sometimes on moors. The same is true of the Common Gull, which has also been found nesting in bushes. The Black-headed Gull and the Little Gull are more

SABINE'S GULL *Xema sabini* L 13" Common on breeding grounds, elsewhere seen singly or in small flocks, wintering far out to sea. Only rarely encountered inland or along canals. Adult in summer plumage unmistakable with slate-coloured hood and black bill tipped with yellow. In all plumages notice characteristic upper side of wing with triangles of black, white and brown or grey. Tail is forked. Immatures have more dark on head than other hooded gulls. In behaviour it resembles Little Gull but may parasitise Arctic Terns. Flight is very buoyant and tern-like. Call is harsh and tern-like. W

often found in marshes. When colonies of Black-headed Gulls are located on sea coasts, as sometimes occurs, more young are lost than by Common Gulls nesting in the same situation, or by Black-headed Gull colonies in marshes. The reason for this is the chicks' habit of swimming away from the nesting site when danger approaches. While this is of great survival value in marshes where they can find protection among rushes or reeds, the habit often causes disaster at sea as the young venture too far from land to be able to find their way back. The young of Common Gulls do not start swimming when approached but crouch on the spot or seek cover underneath vegetation or stones.

The Kittiwake builds its nest on a ledge on steep sea cliffs, often in association with auks, and unlike all other gulls, the young stay on the nest until they are able to fly. This even happens in the rare instances where Kittiwakes are found nesting on flat ground, unless some immediate danger forces the young to leave the nest.

While gulls nesting on open ground may not make much of a nest, the species nesting in marshes and lagoons, Black-headed Gull, Little Gull, Mediterranean Gull and Slender-billed Gull, build a rough platform of sedge and reeds, raising the nest-cap well above the surface of the water.

The colonial nesting of gulls seems to offer some protection for the members of the colony, as well as stimulating breeding behaviour. Most gulls attack intruders violently by constantly diving upon them. Accompanied by a menacing call, this habit is unpleasant enough to drive most enemies away. Other species often take advantage of the aggressive behaviour of gulls and nest in proximity. This is true of several kinds of grebes, ducks and waders.

The eggs of gulls are greenish-brown with dark spots. They are usually three in number. If the first clutch is removed, which happens where eggs are collected for commercial reasons, the second clutch often contains only two eggs.

When the downy young hatch, they leave the nest after a short time but usually stay close to the colony until they can fly.

During incubation, which takes from twenty to twenty-six days, and fledging, from five to eight weeks, life in a gull colony is hectic. Something is always going on and even in the middle of the night wails and yells can be heard. One often wonders if the gulls sleep at all during this period.

The behaviour of gulls during breeding season has been studied intensively and many separate behavioural movements and ceremonies have been recognized. Although varying slightly from species to species, the basic pattern seems to be the same. The threatening intention is expressed by pointing the bill slightly downward ready for a thrust against the enemy. Fear is expressed by pointing the head and bill upwards as if ready to take to the wing. The reverse of aggression is shown by turning the head and bill away from the other bird, a gesture most often seen exchanged between mates. It has also been found that the young Herring Gull, when begging for food, pecks the bright red spot on the bill of the parent bird. This pecking stimulates the parent bird to feed the young, and it will regurgitate whatever it has brought home to the hungry offspring, which takes the softened food straight from the bill.

As summer passes, the young lose their down and assume their first juvenile plumage, which in most gulls is of a more or less dirty brown colour. In the smaller gulls the plumage of the juvenile has a definite pattern of darker and lighter areas, while the larger species are more uniform in colour. The smaller

ROSS'S GULL *Rhodostethia rosea* L 12" Very rare visitor to the northernmost coasts from its Arctic Asiatic breeding grounds. A very light-coloured gull with wedge-shaped tail (the only European gull to have this). Adult birds are tinged rosy and in summer have narrow black neck-band. Immatures have wing pattern similar to that of Kittiwake immatures, but notice wedge-shaped tail. Flight is pigeon-like.   V

Opposite Great Black-backed Gulls

BLACK TERN *Chlidonias niger* L 9½" Common, nesting in colonies by inland waters, swamps, marshes and lakes. Outside breeding season also found along seashores. Summer plumage unmistakable, with all dark upper parts but white underside of wing and tail. In winter told from White-winged Black Tern by darker upper side and a dark mark on side of lower neck. Black Terns dive little, but take insects from the surface and in the air. Flight is erratic. Call is nasal.   P

species only take one to two years to attain the white adult plumage, but the larger ones may take four years.

Gulls moult twice a year, and in the autumn the hooded gulls lose their hoods, which are usually replaced by dark spots or markings. In the spring moult the dark hood is again acquired and plays an important part in the mating ceremonies.

The second subfamily of the *Laridae*, the terns, forms a very distinctive group of excellent fliers. Thirty-nine species are found along the shores of the world, and few coasts are not regularly visited by these expert fishermen.

imm.

Black Tern

moulting

winter

summer

White-winged Black Tern

summer

imm.

moulting

winter

WHITE-WINGED BLACK TERN *Chlidonias leucopterus* L 9½" Common, nesting in inland marshes, swamps and lakes; in winter also frequents seashores. In summer plumage, told from Black Tern by white upper side of wings, white tail, black underside of wings and red legs. In winter very similar to Black Tern, but is lighter above, particularly rump, and lacks dark mark on side of neck. Wing lining is white at this season. Behaviour like that of Black Tern with which it often associates.   P

In Europe ten species nest, and one species, the Sooty Tern, is a rare visitor from the tropical seas which are its home.

From the large Caspian Tern with a wing span of fifty-three inches to the dainty Little Tern whose wing span hardly exceeds twenty inches, terns are all built much the same way: long, pointed wings for their agile flight above the waves, a forked tail to give them superb manoeuvrability, and a straight, pointed bill to catch their prey. Their legs are very short and they are almost as clumsy on land as they are swimming, in spite of their webbed toes.

Most terns are snowy-white with a pitch-black cap and silver-grey back and wings, but there are exceptions to this rule. Black Tern, White-winged Black and Whiskered Terns (the 'marsh terns') are more dark than white in their summer

WHISKERED TERN *Chlidonias hybrida* L 9½" Fairly common, breeding in marshes, lakes and swamps; in winter also found along seashores. In summer plumage, easily told from other dark terns by white cheeks. Underside more dusky than that of other dark terns. In winter plumage, lighter than other dark terns and has considerably more white on crown. Notice distribution of dark on crown of the three species in winter plumage. Bill slightly heavier on Whiskered Tern than on the other two dark species. Associates freely with Black and White-winged Black. Call is harsher and consists of two syllables. V

plumage, and only in winter do their colours resemble those of the other terns. The Sooty Tern has dark brown or blackish upper parts instead of grey, and this species and the Little Tern have a white forehead in summer. The legs and bill of terns are usually brightly coloured, and the bill colours are particularly helpful in the identification of these elegant birds.

Most of the terns feed on fish and other aquatic animal life. They obtain their food by throwing themselves like a projectile into the water. One never tires of watching the skill and elegance of a fishing tern. Leisurely it flies along the shoreline

Whiskered Tern

summer

imm.

winter

Sooty Tern

SOOTY TERN *Sterna fuscata* L 16" Very rare visitor to Atlantic and Mediterranean coasts from subtropical and tropical oceanic islands. Pelagic in behaviour. Adult is black above with white front and white below (the only European tern to have this distribution of colours). Immature is dark brown with white under tail-coverts. Does not dive; catches surface fish in flight. Call is a nasal 'wide-a-wake'. V

some twenty feet above the surface. The bill is pointed downward as the bird carefully examines the water for a likely prey. When it spots a fish or insect near the surface, it drops with half-closed wings at great speed, hitting the water head first and often completely submerging. Because of the extreme streamlining of the whole bird, the splash is minimal. A second later the bird emerges from the water with a fish dangling from its bill. As it becomes airborne it shakes the water off with a characteristic shrugging movement. Sometimes one can also see the tern stand still in the air on hovering wings as it spots something below. The forked tail is then spread out wide to keep balance. After a few seconds the bird either resumes its searching flight or plunges headlong into the water.

This manner of fishing is the most common but is not the

Gull-billed Tern   imm.   winter   summer

winter   summer

Sandwich Tern   imm.

Caspian Tern   winter   summer

GULL-BILLED TERN *Gelochelidon nilotica* L 15"
Uncommon, nesting colonially on coastal marshes and
sandy beaches. Also seen over land and along shores.
Recognized in all plumages by short, thick, black, gull-
like bill and broad, very white wings. Tail is less forked
than in most terns and legs are black and long. Flight is
more gull-like than that of other terns. Looks considerably heavier and more stocky than Sandwich Tern. When
standing, the long legs are characteristic. Rarely dives
but hawks for insects and small vertebrates over marshes.
In winter plumage has only very little black on head,
easily distinguishing it from somewhat similar Sandwich
Tern. Nasal 2–3 syllable call is characteristic.   P

SANDWICH TERN *Sterna sandvicensis* L 16" Common, nesting in dense colonies on shores and small
islands. Takes its food almost exclusively at sea. No
other European tern has a black bill tipped with yellow.
Note also the long, slender bill, black legs and slight
crest. Forehead of juvenile is mostly black; adult has
white on forehead and crown in winter, although it still
has much more black than somewhat similar Gull-billed
Tern. Immature has less forked tail than adult and sometimes lacks the yellow tip to bill, making it difficult to tell
from Gull-billed Tern, but notice colours on head and
much more 'tern-like' silhouette and behaviour. Fishes
far off shore, often out of sight of land. Call is a loud,
grating 'karrik'. Very noisy.   SP

CASPIAN TERN *Hydroprogne tschegrava* L 21"
Uncommon, nesting singly or in small colonies on
islands and sandy beaches. Outside breeding season
usually along seashores but occasionally on larger inland
waters. Enormous size (almost as big as Herring Gull)
makes it easy to identify. Large, bright red bill is a very
prominent characteristic. Wider wings give it a more gull-
like appearance than most terns, and its behaviour is
also more gull-like. Alights on the water, occasionally
soars, robs other sea birds, and eats eggs, but fish is its
chief diet. The huge coral-red bill is noticeable even at
a distance. Call is a very deep and characteristic 'caw-
caw-cah'.   V

COMMON TERN *Sterna hirundo* L 14" Very common,
nesting colonially on islands, sandy and marshy sea
coasts and on inland lakes. Most common along seashores. Flocks with Arctic and Roseate Terns. Wing-tips
are noticeably darker than in Roseate, tail is shorter and
bill in summer brighter coral-red (black tip varies in
extent). Best told from Arctic Tern by black tip of bill,
lighter underside, shorter tail, longer legs and more
extensive black underside of wing. Retains red legs in
winter whereas they become black in Arctic Tern. Often
seen in large groups. Call is a harsh 'kee-urr'.   S

winter   summer

Common Tern

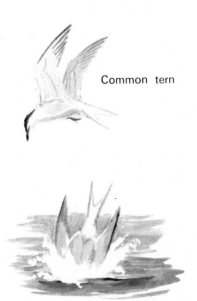

Common tern

only method used. The three marsh terns in summer hunt
mainly by snatching insects off the surface of the water rather
than by plunging into it, and they often catch flying insects in the
air. The rare Sooty Tern, which is highly pelagic in its habits,
also prefers to keep its plumage dry by picking food items off
the surface. The Gull-billed Tern in summer catches frogs,
lizards, rodents and insects on land and will even resort to the
eggs and young of other birds if given the opportunity, as will
the giant Caspian Tern.

Often terns can be seen fishing in flocks along coasts where
shoals of fish are found. This is particularly true of Arctic,
Common and Sandwich Terns.

All our terns are migratory and only the Caspian and the
Sandwich Terns sometimes winter in the Mediterranean. The
world record as a traveller is held by the Arctic Tern. Journeys
by ringed birds of up to 10,000 miles have been recorded,
including one from Angelsey, Wales, to New South Wales,
Australia, and one from Denmark to Antarctic waters. The
latter is the first recovery from this area, long known to be a
wintering place for these far-travelling birds.

The migration of the Arctic Tern in the Atlantic has been
thoroughly studied. When the European birds start their
southward flight in autumn, they are joined in European
waters by their relatives which have nested on the western side
of the Atlantic, in Canada and Greenland. Together the terns
move south along the African coast and once across the Equator
they spread out to reach their wintering grounds, stretching
from the southern tip of South America in the west to Australia
in the east. In spring they retrace their route to reach their
nesting grounds in late April and May. The Arctic Tern therefore experiences more sunlight than any other animal, spending
the summer in the land of the midnight sun and the winter in the
Antarctic, which at this time of the year is also enjoying
continuous sunlight.

Although the Arctic Tern is unsurpassed in its travels, other
terns also move over great distances. For instance, Sandwich
Terns ringed in Europe have been recovered from the Carib-

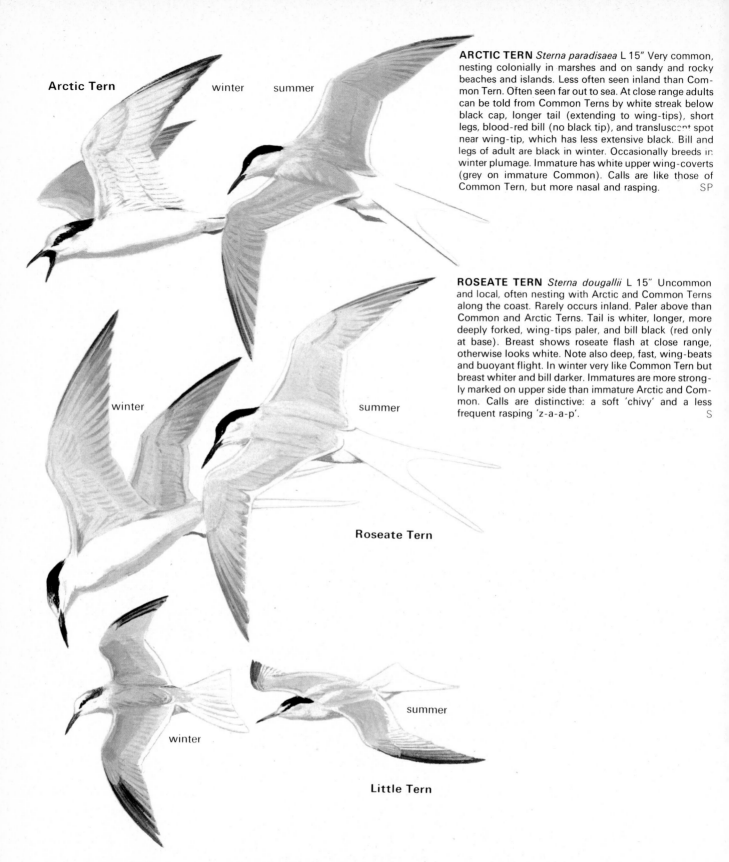

Arctic Tern winter summer

ARCTIC TERN *Sterna paradisaea* L 15" Very common, nesting colonially in marshes and on sandy and rocky beaches and islands. Less often seen inland than Common Tern. Often seen far out to sea. At close range adults can be told from Common Terns by white streak below black cap, longer tail (extending to wing-tips), short legs, blood-red bill (no black tip), and transluscent spot near wing-tip, which has less extensive black. Bill and legs of adult are black in winter. Occasionally breeds in winter plumage. Immature has white upper wing-coverts (grey on immature Common). Calls are like those of Common Tern, but more nasal and rasping. SP

ROSEATE TERN *Sterna dougallii* L 15" Uncommon and local, often nesting with Arctic and Common Terns along the coast. Rarely occurs inland. Paler above than Common and Arctic Terns. Tail is whiter, longer, more deeply forked, wing-tips paler, and bill black (red only at base). Breast shows roseate flash at close range, otherwise looks white. Note also deep, fast, wing-beats and buoyant flight. In winter very like Common Tern but breast whiter and bill darker. Immatures are more strongly marked on upper side than immature Arctic and Common. Calls are distinctive: a soft 'chivy' and a less frequent rasping 'z-a-a-p'. S

winter summer

Roseate Tern

summer winter

Little Tern

bean. But most of our terns spend the cold season off the African coast, and the marsh terns by the inland lakes of that continent.

The return of the terns marks the true arrival of spring and their rasping call is a sign of the warm summer to come. Most terns migrate along shores and rivers, even the 'inland' marsh terns, and mixed flocks are often encountered in spring. All terns are colonial in their breeding habits and their breeding behaviour has been studied intensively by several ornithologists.

Almost all the terns have a characteristic 'fish flight'. This can be observed even before the birds are paired. With a fish in the

LITTLE TERN *Sterna albifrons* L 9" Common, nesting colonially on sandy beaches, usually along the coasts, occasionally inland. Smallest of the European terns, with a comparatively short tail. Notice the rapid wing-beats, white forehead, yellow bill (spring), and legs, yellow or yellowish at all seasons. Immature has contrasting wing pattern, similar to that of other white terns, but small size distinguishes it at a glance. Very active and noisy. Call is a rapid series of paired notes. S

Opposite Black Terns

154

Razorbill

winter

summer

imm.

Bridled Guillemot
summer

Guillemot

winter

summer

winter

Brünnich's Guillemot

summer

RAZORBILL *Alca torda* L 16" Common, nesting in colonies on sea cliffs, sometimes associated with Guillemots but usually not on as steep cliffs. Outside breeding season usually stays far off shore. Notice thick bill which, when the bird is swimming, is uptilted, as is the short tail. In flight, back is more arched than in Guillemot. Razorbill also looks more thick-necked and has different head shape which makes it possible to distinguish it from Guillemot even at some distance. It is also more black, rather than brownish. At sea usually seen in small flocks which fly in lines low above the water. Sometimes seen singly off rocky coasts.   RS

GUILLEMOT *Uria aalge* L 16" Common. Nests in colonies on ledges of steep cliffs along seashores. Winters at sea; rare within sight of land. Best told from Razorbill by long, narrow bill. In winter plumage, has a narrow black streak back from the eye which, when seen, is diagnostic. In a proportion of birds, Bridled Guillemots, there is a furrow along this streak which shows white in summer. In flight, back is held less arched than Razorbill. Other useful field characteristics distinguishing this species from Razorbill are long, narrow bill, thinner neck, more pointed head shape, and colour: dark brownish rather than black. Told from Brünnich's Guillemot by longer and more slender bill, and in winter plumage by characteristic facial pattern. Like other auks it is often seen in small flocks, flying in lines low above the water.   RS

BRÜNNICH'S GUILLEMOT *Uria lomvia* L 16" Common, but more northern in distribution than Guillemot and Razorbill. Like Guillemot, it nests colonially on sea cliffs. In all plumages note shorter, thicker bill and narrow white streak at base of mouth. In winter plumage there is no white above the black eye-line. In habits it resembles the Guillemot, but often roams further out to sea.   V

bill, one will fly around in the area where there are other terns, constantly calling its excited and rather harsh 'keer-keer'. Soon it is joined by another tern which flies in front of the fish-carrier. Twisting and turning at great speed, the two terns will stay together for some time but all of a sudden they break up and return to whatever occupied them before the pursuit. The fish-carrier does not give up its prey, but swallows it when the ceremony has ended. It has been shown that any combination of sexes in this display is possible in the beginning of the breeding season, but later, when the male has occupied his territory, he alone becomes the fish-carrier.

Another aerial display consists of two birds following each other as, in great circles and with constant calling, they rise to a height of several hundred feet. Suddenly the two shiny white birds start a steep descent during which they constantly change places, one being in front one moment, the other the next. When they are just above the water, they part or repeat the display.

When the male has occupied his territory on the nesting ground and the time has come for pairing, he attracts a female by his fish flight, but instead of parting as they do earlier in the season, both birds land within the territory and the male feeds the female, who assumes the posture of a begging young one with the head low and the bill pointed upward. As soon as pairing has taken place both mates feed each other, a ceremony which probably serves to strengthen the ties between them.

The size of the territory required by each pair in the colony varies somewhat from species to species. Sandwich Terns nest very close together while the Arctic Tern prefers an area of at least several feet around the nest. This arrangement reflects itself in the behaviour of the terns towards intruders. When a Crow approaches a colony of Arctic Terns, the nesting birds will immediately rise and attack the intruder long before it has reached the colony, while Sandwich Terns simply stay put, the nesting birds forming an impenetrable phalanx with their sharp bills pointed towards the marauder.

While the 'white' terns mainly nest on small islands or on beaches along seashores, the 'dark' marsh terns prefer the shores of lakes and swamps. Here they often site their nests among reeds and sedges in low water, building large platforms to support the three eggs. When the Common Tern and the Little Tern nest inland, as they do particularly in eastern Europe, they place their nests on dry land, and their colonies are often smaller than when they nest along the seashores of western Europe.

The 'white' terns usually lay only two eggs, although clutches of three are quite common among the smaller species. The eggs are incubated by both male and female for about twenty days and the charming downy young take three to four weeks before they are able to fly. Until then Common Terns stay within the territory, while young Sandwich Terns move in packs to the beach. As soon as the young one is able to fly, it starts following the parent birds on their fishing trips but it is not yet able to catch fish itself and is fed for a considerable period before it learns to feed itself.

Auks
order *Charadriiformes*, family *Alcidae*

Approaching one of the bird cliffs of the North Atlantic by boat, one is astonished to observe the teeming life on the water around its base and it can often be recognized far away

LITTLE AUK *Plautus alle* L 8" Abundant in the Arctic, nesting in enormous colonies in holes in sloping cliffs. Outside breeding season truly pelagic, only rarely coming within sight of shore. After severe westerly storms, 'falls' or 'wrecks' occur far inland. Much smaller than any of the other auks. Note very short body, neck and bill, whirring wing-beats and distribution of black and white. White areas much more extensive in winter plumage. At Sea usually seen in small flocks, flying in lines very low

W

BLACK GUILLEMOT *Cepphus grylle* L 13" Common, nesting singly or in small groups among rocks along sea-shores, sometimes in holes dug out in cliffs. Less maritime in behaviour than other auks, staying closer inshore winter and summer. In summer notice black plumage with large white area on wing. In winter much whiter but white wing area is still delineated in black. Red legs seldom visible, but red gape of mouth may show up. In immatures, wing patch is usually mottled. Wing-beats are extremely fast. Always fly very low over the water. Usually seen singly or in very small flocks, often in openings in the ice. In spring quite often heard giving its characteristic, high-pitched twittering 'vee-bee' calls.

R

by the whiteness caused by the droppings of the thousands of birds resting on the ledges. Kittiwakes and Fulmars are everywhere but the majority of birds seen in and on the water and swiftly flying to and fro low over the surface belong to various species of auk. Their flight is straight and direct, the weight of the birds and their short, pointed wings leaving no scope for more intricate manoeuvres.

The family of auks is probably North Pacific in origin as the largest number of species is found there, but of a total of twenty-one living species, six breed in the North Atlantic (Common, Brünnich's and Black Guillemots, Puffin, Little Auk and Razorbill). One other species, the flightless Great Auk, lived in

Little Auk

winter

summer

Black Guillemot

winter

summer

PUFFIN *Fratercula arctica* L 12" Common, nesting in colonies in burrows on mountain slopes along seashores. In winter far off shore, reaching further out to sea than most auks except for the Little Auk. Notice chunky body and large head and bill. On breeding grounds the small fish held in the bill give it a characteristic 'bearded' appearance. The outer layers of the bill are shed in late summer, so winter adults and especially immatures have smaller bills (rectangular at base). Although face is largely dark in winter, characteristic facial pattern is still present. When swimming, holds its fore-parts higher above water than other auks, giving it a characteristic silhouette. Usually seen in small or large flocks. Flies low above the water in short lines. In flight the very large head is characteristic. Call, heard on the breeding grounds only, consists of unmusical guttural notes. R

the North Atlantic until it became extinct in 1844.

Although superficially the auks resemble the penguins of the southern oceans, the two families are not related to each other but illustrate converging adaptations to the similar environments they inhabit. While penguins are flightless, auks, except for the extinct Great Auk, have retained the power of flight, a trait of tremendous survival value in a part of the world where predation by man is intensive. The streamlined body and high specific gravity, the webbed feet set far to the rear and the short wings enable them to dive and swim under water with supreme speed and agility.

They live on small fish which they pursue under water, but

Puffin
imm.
summer
winter

the items preferred by the different species vary so there is little interspecific competition. On the nesting cliffs there are also specific preferences. The Common and Brünnich's Guillemots lay their single, rather pointed eggs on the narrow ledges; the Razorbill prefers a rather open cavity or crevice; the Little Auk lays among boulders and rocks on the slopes; and the Black Guillemot incubates its two eggs in deep crevices and under rocks. The Puffin digs its own burrow on the gentle slope on top of the cliff. The burrows are several feet deep and a single white egg is laid in a chamber at the end. The pointed shape of the eggs of the species nesting on ledges prevents the eggs from falling into the sea, as they will roll in a very narrow circle. The young of the Common Guillemot and Razorbill have a short fledging period, only about two weeks, while that of the Puffin is seven weeks. This discrepancy reflects the different exposure to predators. In the shelter of the burrow a slow and complete development can be afforded, while on the ledges the young of Razorbill and Guillemot are constantly exposed to the predation of gulls. They therefore leave the dangerous position on the ledge before their development is complete and face the dangers of life from a safer position in the water. In many places the colonies are preyed upon heavily by both man and beast. While gulls constitute an ever-present danger to eggs and young, the harvest taken by man for food is usually controlled, after generations of experience, so that a constant population of birds is maintained. At many sites, eggs are collected early in the season, young birds (especially Puffins) later, and the adults are caught in nets and snares. Sea-bird cropping is now important only in the Faeroes and Iceland.

In autumn auks spread over the seas and do not return to land until the next spring when a new generation is to be raised. Black Guillemots however remain in coastal waters.

Auks are generally black and white. The summer plumage has more black than the winter plumage and the horny ornaments on the bills of Razorbills and Puffins are shed to give way to more sombre colours.

Below Puffins

Pigeons and Their Allies
order *Columbiformes*

Three families make up this order of ground- and tree-dwelling birds. The families of sandgrouse and pigeons are both represented on our continent by several species, whereas the third family, the dodos and solitaires, has no living representatives. The Dodo, known from pictures (in many of which the artist let himself be carried away by his imagination), was found only on one island, Mauritius in the Indian Ocean. By the late seventeenth century European sailors, looking for fresh meat as a change from their salty diet, had killed the last members of this species. Two species of solitaires closely related to the Dodo lived on neighbouring islands and also became extinct in the seventeenth and eighteenth centuries.

The species of this order are characterized by having thick and dense plumages and a large, strong gizzard in which seeds and fruit are 'minced' before their high content of starch is utilized. Also characteristic of the sandgrouse and pigeons is their unique method of drinking. They are the only birds to dip the bill into the water and suck it up without the backward jerk of the head by which other birds let the water run from the bill into the gullet.

Sandgrouse
order *Columbiformes*, family *Pteroclidae*

Sandgrouse are medium-sized, terrestial birds found in large numbers in the arid steppes of Africa and Asia. Sixteen species inhabit the world, two of which breed in southern Europe, a third, Pallas' Sandgrouse, sometimes invading Europe from its breeding grounds in western Asia.

Sandgrouse look rather like pigeons. The head is small, the wings rather long and pointed, and many species have long pointed tails. The flight is fast, around 40 mph, with fast wing-beats. The feet are very short and in some species the three front toes are almost fused. On the ground sandgrouse move about with an ungraceful, waddling gait and are incapable of hopping or jumping. Their plumage is sand-coloured with varying amounts of black, brown and red in patterns resembling the dry ground on which they live. When approached, they usually crouch in an attempt to avoid detection and only when almost stepped upon do they take flight with rattling and whistling wing-beats. Although the plumage of male as well as female blends perfectly with the background, the patterns on the

BLACK-BELLIED SANDGROUSE *Pterocles orientalis* L 14" Fairly common, found on steppes and outlying fields. Very rare outside breeding grounds. Tail is shorter than that of other sandgrouse. Much darker below and on underside of wing than any other European sandgrouse, easily distinguishing it in flight. On the ground, neck and breast pattern distinguish it from other sandgrouse. Female is more spotted than male. Call is a deep 'djur-djur-djur'.

Black-bellied Sandgrouse

161

Pin-tailed Sandgrouse

Pallas' Sandgrouse

female are somewhat less well defined. They are social in behaviour, are usually encountered in flocks and nest in colonies.

The Black-bellied and Pin-tailed Sandgrouse, both inhabiting the Iberian peninsula, are residents, spreading over a somewhat larger area outside the breeding season in their search for food. Unlike them, Pallas' Sandgrouse at infrequent intervals makes eruptions of fantastic proportions into Europe. From their breeding grounds on the steppes of western Asia the birds travel in large numbers across the European continent and have reached as far as the Faeroe Islands and the British Isles. On occasion they have even tried to breed in the British Isles, and in Denmark they have successfully reared young. The largest of these far-reaching mass movements took place in 1888 and 1908. The reason for the exodus is probably prolonged drought in the breeding areas. Sandgrouse are also famous for their drinking flights, most often observed in South Africa and India. As they live in very arid country, they often have to travel far to reach water-holes where they may congregate in tremendous numbers at dawn and dusk.

The nest is a mere scrape in the sand in which the two or three eggs are laid and incubated for about twenty-three days. The young are covered with sand-coloured down and leave the nest immediately after hatching. Both male and female share the incubation as well as protecting and feeding the young. The young are fed regurgitated food and the adult birds even carry water to the young in the nest. The food consists almost exclusively of seeds and other plant material and large amounts of

PIN-TAILED SANDGROUSE *Pterocles alchata* L 13"
Fairly common on dry steppes and other dry, flat areas. Very rare outside its normal range. Lighter in colour than the other sandgrouse, with a brown breast-band bordered with black. Central tail-feathers elongated. It is the smallest of our sandgrouse. In flight, easily told from Black-bellied Sandgrouse and Pallas' Sandgrouse by its distinct white wing-band. Female lacks the black throat of male. Usually seen in flocks, larger than those of Black-bellied Sandgrouse. In flight, which is fast, the characteristic far-reaching call 'catar, catar' is often given.

PALLAS' SANDGROUSE *Syrrhaptes paradoxus* L 15"
Common. In some years makes far-reaching eruptions into western Europe in varying numbers. During such invasions it has reached as far west as England and has occasionally settled down to nest. Smaller invasions and sporadic occurrences sometimes take place and it is the sandgrouse most likely to be found outside its normal range. Found on dry steppes; during invasion in sandy and other dry areas. Elongated central tail-feathers and black spot on belly are diagnostic. Notice also the very light underside of wing. Usually encountered in flocks, which are noisy. Call consists of two or three notes. V

Domestic Pigeons

Rock Dove

Stock Dove

ROCK DOVE *Columba livia* L 13″ Locally common; but huge populations of feral domestic pigeons which are descendants of this species are found in cities and resemble it closely. Found in mountains of moderate elevation, mainly along the coasts, also on sea cliffs where it nests in caves or on sheltered shelves. Light above, with pronounced white upper rump, and two black stripes on wings. Underside of wing is white. Resembles Stock Dove most but white rump and wider wing stripes are usually present even on domestic pigeons. Smaller, more compact and has more rapid wing-beats than Wood Pigeon. Flight is very fast. Usually encountered in small flocks. Call is similar to that of the domestic pigeon.   R

STOCK DOVE *Columba oenas* L 13″ Fairly common, nesting in tree-holes in open woodland. Can also place the nest in rabbit holes and in holes in rocks. In winter also found on fields and open farmland. Rather uniformly grey, lacking white upper rump of Rock Dove, and white wing-bars and neck-band of Wood Pigeon. Black wing-bands less prominent than on Rock Dove. Often encountered in small flocks, but also mixes freely with Wood Pigeons, in which case the much smaller size, darker colours and faster wing-beats are evident. Flight usually a little faster and more straight than Wood Pigeon's. Cooing is a monotonous, coughing 'oo-hoo-hoo', more similar to that of Rock Dove than Wood Pigeon.   RP

grit are eaten to help mince up the rough food in the gizzard.

Sandgrouse are hunted extensively where they are common and thousands are shot near the watering holes, a manner of killing which can hardly be called sport.

Pigeons and Doves
order *Columbiformes*, family *Columbidae*

Pigeons and doves, symbols of peace and love, are found almost all over the world. Only in the Arctic and the Antarctic are these graceful birds absent.

A total of 289 species are recognized, of which seven are found in Europe. Six of these species breed within the boundaries of our continent, while one, the Rufous Turtle Dove, is an accidental visitor from its home in Asia.

Our pigeons and doves ('dove' is usually, but not always, used to signify one of the smaller species of the family) are medium-sized birds with small heads, pointed wings, and tails which are either pointed or square. They all more or less resemble the familiar feral Pigeon found in so many cities. In many cities this bird has become so numerous that it is a sanitary problem and a pest, particularly since it has been established that pigeons can carry diseases also affecting man. The feral Pigeon is a descendant of the Rock Dove indigenous to Europe but now declining in numbers. It was domesticated in the Near East by 3000 BC and has since then spread over most of the world.

The European pigeons and doves show great diversity in their migratory habits. The Rock Dove, Collared Turtle Dove and Palm Dove are all resident, many never moving more than a few miles from the site where they were hatched. The Stock Dove and the Wood Pigeon, on the other hand, are partial migrants, the northernmost population spending the winter under more favourable climatic conditions in the more southern part of Europe. The Turtle Dove travels further than the others, wintering in tropical Africa.

The highly developed homing instinct of many pigeons has been known and deliberately used by man for centuries. Pigeon-racing has become a most popular sport and today there may be up to five million homing pigeons in Great Britain alone. The records set by these trained pigeons are truly amazing. A good average speed for homing lies around 40 mph, whereas several have been able to reach speeds exceeding 60 mph, particularly in races over short distances. Homing pigeons are trained to fly on a certain compass direction, which they are then able to determine by the help of the sun and a so-called physiological clock. This manner of navigation is much the same as that used by the European explorers when they so successfully navigated to distant parts of the world, the physiological clock being replaced by the chronometer set at Greenwich time.

imm.

Wood Pigeon

WOOD PIGEON *Columba palumbus* L 16″ Called by many the Ring Dove, it is the most common and widespread European pigeon. Found in farmland, parks, gardens, all types of woods. Has invaded many large cities in recent years. Easily distinguished by large size, white 'ring' on side of neck, and broad white bar on wing. Outside breeding season usually found in flocks, sometimes of enormous size. In flight, dark underwing helps in identification. Wings clatter when it takes flight. Stock Doves sometimes mix in the flocks. In towns and villages often very tame, mixing with domestic pigeons. Cooing consists of five syllables, emphasis on the first.   R

The food of pigeons varies from season to season but is almost exclusively vegetable matter. The food of the Wood Pigeon in particular has been studied intensively because of the harm sometimes done by large flocks of these birds. In late summer and autumn, cereals constitute over three-quarters of its food and a single Wood Pigeon requires about fifty grams of fresh food per day. In winter, when cereals are not available in as large quantities as at harvest time, clover leaves are a favourite diet, often constituting up to half the food eaten. The Stock Dove also eats large quantities of cereals and smaller seeds but takes little fresh vegetable matter. The Turtle Dove eats almost exclusively small seeds. Although it is well-established that large flocks of pigeons can cause considerable economic loss locally, they do not constitute a serious pest in most areas.

Since earliest times, pigeons have been associated with the

image of love and fertility. The reason for this is probably to be found in a particular part of the display of pigeons in which the mates, once 'engagement' has been established, caress each other in a most attractive fashion. But sweet and loving as the pigeon may be to its mate, it can be cruel and brutal to intruders on its territory. The territory in the breeding season is announced by an aerial display in which the pigeon often claps its wings, and on the ground by the strutting and cooing which can be watched in almost any park. If an intruder on the territory does not give way to the rightful owner, a flight usually develops, sometimes leading to the death of one of the participants. In the territory defended in this way, the rather poor nest is built and two, sometimes one or three, white eggs are laid. The nest is only a flimsy platform sometimes insufficient to support the weight of the eggs. Both male and female help to incubate for fourteen to eighteen days, at which time the eggs hatch and the blind and helpless young are exposed to the world. For the first few days the young are fed 'pigeon milk', a unique cheese-like fluid which is produced in the crop of both male and female pigeons when the young are hatching. Later the young are fed cereals and other vegetable matter which the adults regurgitate like the 'pigeon milk'.

Turtle Dove

After eighteen to twenty-two days the young leave the nest and have to fend for themselves, as the parents now start their second brood. Whereas the Rock Dove, which is a shy, wary bird making its home on sheltered cliffs, has declined in numbers, the Wood Pigeon has increased considerably as the agriculture of man has made much more food available. In England alone the population at its peak has been estimated to be about ten million birds of which as many as two million are shot every year. The Wood Pigeon has become more and more common in parks and gardens and, as is the case with the Black-bird, has successfully moved into much closer proximity to man. Whereas the Wood Pigeon places its nest in trees on an open branch, the Stock Dove nests in holes. It has suffered consider-ably from the decline of natural cavities in western Europe, and in many places nest boxes are set up to attract this bird.

TURTLE DOVE *Streptopelia turtur* L 11″ Common in parks and farmland with hedges and groves and in open woodland with plenty of undergrowth. Much smaller than Wood Pigeon. White patches with black stripes on neck are diagnostic. This characteristic is lacking in the immature bird. Tail is conspicuously dark, showing nar-row white edging from above and below. Looks much darker than Collared Turtle Dove of similar size and shape. Smaller and lighter in colour than the very rare Rufous Turtle Dove. Lacks the bright blue areas found on the wing of the slightly smaller Palm Dove. Usually seen in small flocks or pairs. Builds an open nest in trees or bushes. Song is a soft purring coo. SP

The most beautiful of our pigeons is undoubtedly the Turtle Dove, which is primarily found in semi-open park-like landscape and the edges of woods. It is sometimes social in its nesting behaviour, although the colonies never even approximate in numbers to those of the now-extinct Passenger Pigeon of America. The counterpart of the Turtle Dove in Asia, the slightly larger Rufous Turtle Dove, is only a very rare visitor to the British Isles, whereas it has occurred more often in the countries of eastern Europe.

The Collared Turtle Dove has a most astonishing history of distribution which, as it has taken place in this century, is very well-studied and documented. At the turn of the century it only nested in European Turkey but was spreading to the Balkans. In 1930, when its hold in this south-eastern part of Europe was well established, it again started spreading through central

PALM DOVE *Streptopelia senegalensis* L 10" Common but local in cities and villages. Very recent invader. Smallest of the European doves. Speckled band on front part of neck is hard to distinguish. Seems quite dark with white-tipped tail-feathers and brilliant blue areas on wings particularly noticeable in flight. Usually seen in pairs or few together. In behaviour and habitat very similar to Collared Turtle Dove. Cooing is rapid and distinctive, almost resembling call of Cuckoo.

RUFOUS TURTLE DOVE *Streptopelia orientalis* L 13" Accidental visitor west to England from Asiatic breeding grounds, mainly occurring in late autumn and winter. Resembles Turtle Dove but is considerably larger and darker. The white on neck and tail of Turtle Dove is replaced with light blue and grey in Rufous Turtle Dove. Back more finely speckled. Behaviour and habitat similar to Turtle Dove. V

Palm Dove

Rufous Turtle Dove

Collared Turtle Dove

Europe, reaching the Netherlands and Denmark in 1947-8. The spreading continued and Norway and England were invaded in 1954. Since then it has spread from a few breeding pairs in Norfolk to thousands of birds distributed over Britain to the Hebrides and Ireland. It prefers parks and gardens, where it is easily observed, particularly as it is often seen feeding with poultry. This amazing spread, which seems to be continuing, is probably connected with the appearance of a suitable ecological niche for a bird commensal with man but larger than a Starling or Sparrow. The Palm Dove has recently spread from its home in Africa and Asia to European Turkey where it lives in close proximity to villages and towns.

COLLARED TURTLE DOVE *Streptopelia decaocto* L 11" Common in parks and gardens of villages and cities. Sandy coloured with wide terminal white band on tail. Black neck-band bordered with white is diagnostic. Much lighter in colours than similar-sized and shaped Turtle Dove. Usually seen in pairs or small flocks. Often very tame, feeding with domestic fowl. In flight very dark primaries contrast with the otherwise light plumage. Immatures lack black neck-band. The cooing is characteristic: three syllables with emphasis on the second syllable. From the original breeding area in the Balkans this species is still extending its range towards the north-west. This spectacular spread started in the 1930s. R

CUCKOO *Cuculus canorus* L 13" Common in open woods, groves and areas with bushes and hedges, also on moorland. Occurs in two colour phases: the more numerous grey, and a brown form (only juveniles and females). In flight can be confused with smaller birds of prey, but notice very pointed wings, rounded tail, small head, often held slightly upward, and thin bill. Flight is fast, usually low above ground. Often chased by small passerines. Repeated 'cuckoo' song of male is diagnostic; female has babbling call. S

YELLOW-BILLED CUCKOO *Coccyzus americanus* L 12" Rare autumn visitor to western Europe from North American breeding grounds. Secretive in behaviour. Can only be confused with rarer Black-billed Cuckoo, from which it is told by large white spots contrasting with black on undersurface of tail, by bright rufous flash in the open wing, and by yellow lower mandible. Call is guttural and toneless. V

Cuckoos and Their Allies
order *Cuculiformes*

This is a diversified order consisting of two families, the cuckoos of world-wide distribution, and the turacos, eighteen species all found in Africa. The relationship of these two families has long been disputed among systematists, but recent studies of egg-white protein have demonstrated that the two families are closely related. Whereas formerly ornithologists have been limited to gross anatomical characters in establishing the relationship of species, families, and so on, the egg-white analysis, which is biochemical, has given them a new tool in their attempts at classification.

♀ red phase

Cuckoo ♂

Black-billed Cuckoo

Yellow-billed Cuckoo

♂

Oriental Cuckoo

♀

BLACK-BILLED CUCKOO *Coccyzus erythropthalmus* L 12" Very rare autumn visitor to western Europe from North American breeding grounds. Habits and habitat similar to Yellow-billed Cuckoo. Separated from this species by indistinct tail spots, by all-black bill and by showing hardly any rufous in spread wing. Call consists of three or four coos. V

ORIENTAL CUCKOO *Cuculus saturatus* L 12" Fairly common in woods. Two colour phases, grey and brown, also occur in this species, but brown phase is more numerous than is the case with the Cuckoo. Very similar to Cuckoo, but is darker above and bars on underside are usually broader. Underside of wing is not whitish but yellowish. Call is distinctly different from that of Cuckoo, consisting of four syllables rather than two.

Cuckoos
order *Cuculiformes*, family *Cuculidae*

The 127 species making up this family are found in most parts of the world. In Europe cuckoos are rather poorly represented with only three breeding species, Cuckoo, Oriental Cuckoo and Great Spotted Cuckoo, and two accidental visitors from North America, the Yellow-billed and the Black-billed Cuckoos. All are medium-sized, long-tailed birds with short legs. The Cuckoo, which has lent its name to the entire family, has attracted the attention of man to a degree surpassed by few other birds. This is seen clearly in the multitude of superstitions connected with it and the innumerable times it is mentioned in our literature. Two things in particular attract attention to this bird: its far-reaching, characteristic 'cuckoo' which loudly proclaims the advent of spring in woods and over moors, and its parasitic nesting behaviour, which has intrigued and mystified man for centuries.

Not all species of cuckoos are parasitic. The Yellow- and Black-billed Cuckoos indigenous to North America breed normally. Nor is parasitic behaviour limited to cuckoos, but it is found among such families as the cow-birds of the New World and weaver finches of Africa; a South American duck also has parasitic nesting habits. The Cuckoo has, however, developed its parasitism further than any other bird.

In western Europe the unfortunate hosts are warblers, pipits, wagtails, Dunnocks, Robins and other birds of the same size. All in all, more than fifty host species have been recorded. The egg is laid in the host's nest soon after the nest is finished, sometimes even before the host has started laying its own eggs.

To attain a high degree of acceptance by the host, the Cuckoo egg shows many specific features. First of all it is very small for the size of the Cuckoo but almost identical in size to the eggs of the host species. Clans of Cuckoos have developed which lay eggs mimicking in colour the egg of the preferred host species.

Great Spotted Cuckoo

imm.

GREAT SPOTTED CUCKOO *Clamator glandarius* L 16" Common near groves and woods and on open land with scattered trees and bushes. Somewhat resembles Magpie which it parasitizes, but the black and white pattern is quite differently arranged. Often seen in small flocks. Call is rasping, almost tern-like.   V

One Cuckoo may lay light-brown, speckled eggs resembling those of the Meadow Pipit, a very frequent host; while a neighbouring bird will lay light-blue eggs, harmonizing with those of the Redstart and Dunnock. Yet British Cuckoos do not lay blue eggs, though the Dunnock is as common a host as the Meadow Pipit.

If the egg-laying Cuckoo finds eggs of the host in the nest, it will usually remove one in the bill. A female cuckoo lays between fifteen and twenty-five eggs through a season.

The young hatches early, after about twelve days incubation, so early that it is usually out before those of the foster parents. Once out of the egg, the young Cuckoo instinctively works itself underneath the eggs or other young in the nest and ejects them over the edge so that the parents have only the Cuckoo to feed. It is ready to leave the nest twenty to twenty-three days after hatching, when it so large that the foster parents often have to sit on its back to feed it.

The Great Spotted Cuckoo, found mainly in Spain, parasitizes various species of crows, in Spain primarily the Magpie. Unlike the Common Cuckoo, several eggs are laid by the same bird in a single nest, or several Great Spotted Cuckoos may lay in the same nest. But the young do not throw their foster siblings out of the nest and both are reared in harmony together. But if there is a food shortage, the Great Spotted Cuckoo young have a better chance of survival due to their faster development.

All our breeding cuckoos are migratory, wintering in Africa.

Owls

order *Strigiformes*

The members of this order in many respects resemble the birds of prey, but they are far removed on the family tree of birds. The hooked, sharp bill and strong claws are traits shared with falcons and hawks, but we are here again faced with the phenomenon so common in animals where resemblance in food and feeding behaviour has led to the superficial resemblance of otherwise unrelated species. But in the household of nature, owls do play the same role as birds of prey and when hawks and buzzards stop hunting their unfortunate mammalian prey because of approaching darkness, the owls take over and pursue the rodents at night.

On closer examination the differences from birds of prey are easily noticed. The very large head and the facial disc surrounding the eyes are immediately noticeable. The eyes are very large, enabling owls to distinguish better in poor light (they are of

grey form

brown form

Scops Owl

SCOPS OWL *Otus scops* L 8″ Common in gardens, groves and in ruins, usually nesting in cavities. Very small, rather uniformly brown, with ear tufts. Slimmer and not as squat in appearance as Little Owl. Wings rather long. Call is a monotonously repeated 'piuww', usually heard at night, occasionally during the day. ∨

course incapable of seeing in total darkness), and are set facing forward, giving a rather small field of vision but, on the other hand, aiding in the judgment of distance. The ears are also very large and it has been proved that owls are able to locate and catch their prey by using their hearing only. The ear tubes and lobes are often asymmetrical, aiding the exact location of noise.

The outer toe can be moved, so that the owl can grasp with three toes in front and one behind like most birds, or with two in front and two behind, giving a more secure hold on a moving object like a struggling toad or rodent.

There are about 130 species in this order of soft-plumaged birds, but only thirteen breed in Europe. The order is usually divided into two families: the Barn Owl *(Tytonidae)* and owls *(Strigidae)*. Only minor differences in bone structure separate the two families; they have so many traits in common that they are treated together here. Superficially the Barn Owl, the only representative of the *Tytonidae,* is quite easily distinguished from other owls by its heart-shaped facial disc and very long legs.

Our thirteen species of owl vary tremendously in size from the six-inch-long Pygmy Owl to the almost thirty-inch-long Eagle Owl. In spite of this, they show uniformity in their choice of food; almost all find their main source among the rodents. The only exception to this rule is the Scops Owl found in southern Europe, where it lives primarily on insects and only occasionally catches a mouse. The Eagle Owl, usually only found in vast, wild and mountainous regions, also takes a larger number of birds than other owls. Even a bird as large as the Capercaillie has been known to fall prey to this enormous predator. The Barn Owl may take large numbers of shrews, mammals which are usually rejected by most other predators.

Many of the rodents preyed upon show cyclic population variations, the most spectacular and best-known being that of the lemming on the Scandinavian peninsula, where the cycle is from three to four years. The same phenomenon is found among many other small rodents. The animals preying on these rodents show many adaptations to the cycle. This is particularly obvious among the more northern owls like the Hawk Owl and Snowy Owl. When the lemming population is small on the Scandinavian peninsula, hardly any Snowy Owls nest, whereas in peak years, they take advantage of the tremendous food supply and lay as many as six to eight eggs (clutches of up to

TENGMALM'S OWL *Aegolius funereus* L 10" Fairly common in mature coniferous forests. Nests in tree cavities. Populations fluctuate and in some years invasions of areas outside the normal range take place. Distinguished from rather similar Little Owl by more rounded appearance of head (not flat on top), spotted rather than striped head, and more erect posture. Only during the Arctic summer does it feed by daylight. Call is a series of whistles like the sound of water dripping, 12–15 groups per minute.   V

Tengmalm's Owl

juv.

Little Owl

fourteen eggs have been found), an unusually large number for a bird of its size. Seldom do all the eggs hatch, but the large number gives the Snowy Owl a potential change to rear large broods under unusually good food conditions, thus compensating for the meagre years when no breeding takes place.

The variation in numbers of these northern owls is also noticed in countries lying south of their breeding range, as they are forced to emigrate when feeding conditions are less favourable. Thus northern Europe usually sees invasions of Snowy Owls and Hawk Owls in years following good lemming years in Scandinavia. Though often regarded as residents, they can therefore be better described as occasional invasion species.

LITTLE OWL *Athene noctua* L 9" Common in open land with hedges and trees, often near human habitation; introduced to Britain. Notice squat appearance and large head. The white spots on neck form a characteristic V. Partially diurnal. Flight is characteristically undulating, and can hover. Bobs when nervous. Calls are shrill and sharp.   R

Above Eagle Owl

Tengmalm's Owl shows the same tendency, although not as pronounced as in the two preceding species.

The Barn Owl, Eagle Owl, Little Owl, Pygmy Owl, Ural Owl and the most common of all, the Tawny Owl, are all resident, although their numbers change according to the abundance of small rodents in different areas. The Long-eared Owl and Short-eared Owl are both partial migrants, leaving their more northern breeding grounds in favour of areas lying slightly further to the south with less dense snow cover to protect their prey. Scops Owl is a typical migrant (as it lives on insects), most spending the winter in northern Africa, although a few may linger in the Mediterranean area.

171

Eagle Owl

Snowy Owl

♂

♀

Great Grey Owl

Great Grey Owl

Ural Owl

EAGLE OWL *Bubo bubo* L 27" Uncommon, found in large tracts of undisturbed land, woods, mountains and even open country. Usually nests on the ground or on rock leges, but also in hollow trees. Huge, with large ear tufts. It is the largest European Owl. Female is larger than male. Colour pattern is similar to the smaller and slimmer Long-eared Owl, but Eagle Owl's ear tufts are larger and farther apart. Hunts medium-sized mammals and birds at night, spending the day perched upright in trees. Like all owls, it is often harassed by smaller birds. Call is a far-ranging, deep 'boo-hu'.   V

SNOWY OWL *Nyctea scandiaca* L 24" A rather uncommon diurnal Arctic owl. Nests on the ground. Populations fluctuate and in some winters it occurs south of its normal range in considerable numbers reaching the southern part of middle Europe. Most adult birds are almost pure white. Immatures, which are darker, go farther south than adults in winter. Large size, pale plumage, and lack of ear tufts are diagnostic. Perches near the ground in open country and often allows itself to be approached. Feeds on lemmings and other rodents and rabbits. Usually hunts during the day. On breeding grounds a 2-note crow is occasionally heard; otherwise silent.   V

GREAT GREY OWL *Strix nebulosa* L 27" Rather uncommon, in mature coniferous forests. Uses old nests of other large birds. In some years winter range extends south of normal range. Very large. Looks greyish. Easily told from other large owls by enormous rounded head, bold, concentrically-barred facial disc, striking facial pattern and lack of ear tufts. The eyes are rather small. In flight notice long tail and pale wing-bar. Call is a deep, booming series of 'whoos', each lower in pitch.

URAL OWL *Strix uralensis* L 24" Uncommon, in coniferous as well as mixed woods, primarily in mountain regions. Nests in hollow trees. Large, without ear tufts, but with very long tail. Underside strongly streaked. Facial disc unmarked. Resembles Tawny Owl, but is larger with longer tail and rather small dark eyes. Also diurnal in habits. In flight told from Eagle Owl by shorter tail and more streaked underside, from Great Grey Owl by shorter, narrower wings and more brownish colour. Call is a deep 'how-how-how'.

Although most owls are nocturnal in their habits, some are quite frequently encountered hunting in the daytime, particularly at dusk. This is true of the brilliant white Snowy Owl, the long-tailed Hawk Owl, the Short-eared Owl and, to a certain degree, the Barn Owl, but these species are also active at night. The Little Owl is crepuscular: most active at dusk and dawn.

Owls are much more often heard than seen and although they hoot all year round, they are most noticeably noisy in the early days of spring. It is usually easy to tell the various owls apart by their voices, and although each species has several different calls, one or two are characteristic and most often heard. Hooting occupies the same role for the owl as does song for the diurnal song-birds—it is an announcement of territory and an attempt to attract the attention of members of the opposite sex in the area.

Owls do not build nests but either use those of other birds such as Buzzards, Rooks, Crows, Magpies, or cavities in trees or in buildings; some species even lay their eggs on the ground.

The eggs of owls are unspotted white and rounder than the eggs of most other birds. As already indicated, it is difficult to establish an average clutch size since it can vary from none to as many as fifteen, according to species and year. The eggs are incubated for periods varying from twenty-four days by the Scops Owl to thirty-five days by the Eagle Owl. They are usually incubated by the female alone while the male brings food to her. The young often show great difference in size as the female starts incubating when the first egg is laid, and the eggs therefore do not hatch at the same time. Often the smallest young of the brood will succumb to its more mature siblings, and cannibalism is a far from unknown phenomenon among owls. The young are hatched blind, covered with whitish or greyish down, which is soon replaced by a fluffy, downy plumage. After they have left the nest, this downy plumage gives way to the normal adult plumage.

The Barn Owl is probably the most beautiful of our owls. It occurs in two colour phases, a western form with white underparts, and a darker race in eastern Europe. As the name indicates, Barn Owls are often found around farms, where they are of great benefit to the farmer, ridding him of many mice.

The Eagle Owl is the largest of the European owls with a wing span of about five feet and weight of around five or six pounds. It is a truly magnificent bird and the ear tufts (which have nothing to do with the ears) and the large yellow-orange eyes give it a particularly sinister and ferocious look. Unfortunately it is now very rare as it has been persecuted by man for centuries.

The Snowy Owl is almost as big as the Eagle Owl but does not have ear tufts. The male can be almost completely white, whereas the female is white with dark bars. The Great Grey Owl and Ural Owl are both found in the far north and in the east, and their habits are not very well known. The Great Grey Owl looks almost as big as the Eagle Owl, but its extremely fluffy plumage and long wings and tail contribute to its impressive-looking size.

The Long-eared Owl is one of the most common owls. It is often found in small fir plantations and at the time of migration it can even be encountered in small flocks (most other owls are solitary). When approached, it stretches out and raises its ear tufts so that it looks almost exactly like a broken-off branch, thus often avoiding detection. Its close relative, the Short-eared Owl, prefers open moors and swamps where it is often seen at dusk, coasting low over the vegetation on the lookout for the small mammals on which it preys. The tiny Scops Owl also has ear tufts, but is so much smaller it can hardly be confused with any of the preceding species. It nests near villages and houses, in gardens and parks, and has a characteristic repeated call which is often heard when one is outdoors at night-time in the Mediterranean countries. The Hawk Owl of the northernmost parts of Europe has got its name from its resemblance to a Sparrowhawk. For an owl it has a very long tail, which it often wags in a

Below Snowy Owls

A. Singer

distinctive manner. It is one of the most beautiful and most rarely encountered of our owls. The Pygmy Owl is even smaller than the Scops Owl. As a small bird requires proportionally more food than a larger bird, this species has developed a habit of storing mice and voles in tree cavities for consumption when food is short or unobtainable.

The Little Owl is one of the owls most often seen, as it is not unusual for it to be active in daytime. It has a preference for old willow trees, in the cavities of which it nests. The Little Owl

PYGMY OWL *Glaucidium passerinum* L 7" Fairly common in dense coniferous forests, where it nests in tree cavities. Very small with rather small rounded head and short, wide tail. The flight is undulating, woodpecker-like. Partially diurnal in habits. The short tail is often jerked upwards. Call is a monotonous repetition of soft whistles, sometimes on a rising scale.

LONG-EARED OWL *Asio otus* L 14" Common in coniferous forests, occasionally in deciduous. Notice very long ear tufts held erect when nervous. Told from Eagle Owl by smaller size; from Short-eared by longer ears, habitat and erect posture. Wing-beats deep but slow. Outside breeding season occasionally found in small parties. Generally silent except near nest, where it makes various low hoots, whistles and shrieks.   RWP

SHORT-EARED OWL *Asio flammeus* L 15" Fairly common in open country, over plains, moors and marshes. Ears very short and hard to see. Note black patch near bend of underwing and large, buffish area on upper wing surface. Active before dark, quartering low over fields in irregular flight. Wings are tilted upward like harriers'. In winter occasionally found in small groups. Usually silent.   RW

Pygmy Owl

Long-eared Owl

Short-eared Owl

Tawny Owl

grey phase

brown phase

Hawk Owl

Barn Owl

light-breasted form

dark-breasted form

is the only bird other than game birds and waterfowl which has been successfully introduced to Britain. Tengmalm's Owl is found in the woods of northern and eastern Europe where it is very common. After good breeding seasons in these regions, it will sometimes invade western Europe in some numbers. It is closely related to the most common of our owls, the Tawny Owl. The Tawny Owl is the owl we hear around houses, in small woods and in parks. Tawny Owls live largely on mice and voles and are of great service round a farm. As is the case with almost all owls, the Tawny Owl swallows its prey without tearing it apart and regurgitates the indigestible parts. These pellets are found on the ground and are the most obvious proof of the beneficial role played by the owl, as they contain the hair and bones of rodents. The Long-eared Owl has the habit of delivering these pellets from its favourite perch, under which large piles can be found. Most other owls drop them wherever they are, so the pellets are found spread over larger areas.

Owls are protected by law in almost all European countries and rightfully so, as they are some of our most efficient allies in the attempt to control rodent populations.

TAWNY OWL *Strix aluco* L 15" Most common and widespread European owl. Found in woods, parks, gardens, often near human habitation. Black eyes and lack of ear tufts distinguish this species. Occurs in two colour phases, grey and more rufous. Song consists of a deep hooting. Another common call is a rather shrill 'kuvvitt'. R

BARN OWL *Tyto alba* L 14" Common, but local, usually near buildings or ruins. Only owl with a heart-shaped facial pattern. The west and southern European subspecies is dark-breasted but still lighter than most other owls except for Snowy. Usually nocturnal, hunts rats and mice in farmyards, marshes and fields. Has a peculiar habit of lowering its head and moving it back and forth. Does not hoot, but has a soft, ascending, wheezy cry and a shriek. At the nest it gives a toneless hiss, compared to human snoring. RP

HAWK OWL *Surnia ulula* L 15" Fairly common in northern birch and coniferous forests. Sometimes invades areas south of its range. No other owl has the long, slender tail that gives this bird a falcon-like appearance. Perches in the open on treetops, where it raises and slowly lowers its tail. Sometimes sits with tail cocked up at an angle. Flight is straight and swift, usually very low, with alternate flapping and gliding. Also hovers somewhat as the Kestrel does. Calls are a series of whistles, 10–15 groups per minute. V

Nightjars and Their Allies
order *Caprimulgiformes*

This is a rather homogeneous order of nocturnal birds which are medium-sized with mottled brown plumage and a very large gape. The order is divided into five families. There is only one

Nightjar

NIGHTJAR *Caprimulgus europaeus* L 11" Fairly common, found in open woods and clearings, or open land with scattered trees and bushes and even in sand dunes. Usually seen at dusk when hawking insects. Flight is silent, but during display wings are clapped together; twists and turns with great ease and elegance and sometimes hovers like a Kestrel. Notice white spots on wings and tail of male only. Told from slightly larger Red-necked Nightjar by dark throat and lack of reddish neck-band, from smaller Egyptian Nightjar by darker colours. Solitary in behaviour, except on migration when flocks occur. Migrates at night. Song, which is given at dusk and at night in spring and summer, is an unmistakable churring trill which often leads to the detection of this bird. It is very different from the 'cutek' note of the Red-necked Nightjar.   S

species of the *Steatornithidae*, the Oilbird, which is quite unique in its habits and is found in the Caribbean and South America. It feeds exclusively on fruits which it picks at night, bringing them back to eat in the caves where it spends the daytime. It has earned its name by the extreme obesity of the young bird which used to provide cooking oil for the Indians of Venezuela. Potoos *(Nyctibiidae)* are five species confined to Central and South America (the name refers to the call of the bird). The frogmouths *(Podargidae)* are a family of twelve species found in Australia and the Far East. They catch insects in the same manner as flycatchers: from a perch on an exposed branch they throw themselves into the air or to the ground when a prey is spotted. They eat not only insects but will also take mice and frogs. The family of owlet frogmouths *(Aegothelidae)* contains seven species which are found exclusively in the Australian region. Characteristically they sit upright like owls, giving them a superficial resemblance to members of this other nocturnal order. The nightjars *(Caprimulgidae)*, or goatsuckers as they are also called, are the largest family within the order and the only one represented in Europe..

Nightjars

order *Caprimulgiformes*, family *Caprimulgidae*

World-wide in distribution, this family of about seventy species is fairly homogeneous. Three species are found within our boundaries. The Nightjar, which has given its name to the family, has a wide range in Europe and is well known in most European countries, where it has given rise to many legends due to its nocturnal and elusive habits. The Red-necked Nightjar, which closely resembles it, is restricted in breeding range to the Iberian peninsula. The Egyptian Nightjar is only a rare visitor to the Mediterranean countries and occasionally further: it has even visited the British Isles.

Red-necked Nightjar

display

Egyptian Nightjar

Nightjars have long, pointed wings and long tails. The eyes are large, as is to be expected in nocturnal birds. They are best seen at dusk when they dash through the waning light in their erratic flight, hunting insects which they catch in their wide gapes. All through the breeding season their churring calls are heard at dusk and early in the night and are a characteristic part of the summer atmosphere in areas where the bird is found. Nightjars spend the days on the ground or perched vertically on a branch, almost impossible to detect because of their cryptic colours. Only reluctantly do they take flight.

The nest, which is a bare scrape on the ground, usually contains one or two white eggs which are incubated for eighteen days by both male and female. The young stay on or near the nest for the same length of time, after which they are able to fly. In most parts of Europe two broods are reared every year; when the female lays her second clutch, the male takes care of the young from the first clutch. All our nightjars are migratory, but an American relative, the Poorwill, has been found to hibernate in crevices in the mountains. This most interesting phenomenon has not been proved for any European species of bird.

RED-NECKED NIGHTJAR *Caprimulgus ruficollis* L 12" Fairly common, found in evergreen woods and on dry, bushy wasteland. Nocturnal in habits like the Nightjar. Resembles Nightjar closely, but is larger with longer tail, has lighter colours, reddish neck-band and pure white throat. Spots on wing and tail are more distinctive than on Nightjar and are present in both sexes (only the male Nightjar having white spots). Much larger and darker in plumage than rare Egyptian Nightjar. Song, distinctly different from that of Nightjar, is fast repetition of 'cutek' notes.   V

EGYPTIAN NIGHTJAR *Caprimulgus aegyptius* L 10" Very rare visitor in summer from African and Asiatic breeding grounds. Found in deserts but usually near water. Smaller and much paler and more uniformly coloured than Nightjar and Red-necked Nightjar, which it resembles in habits and silhouette. White spots are ill-defined. Churring song resembles that of Nightjar. V

Swifts and Their Allies
order *Apodiformes*

Two very different families, swifts *(Apodidae)* and humming-birds *(Trochilidae)*, make up this order. Hummingbirds, among which are the smallest of all birds, are found in the New World only, whereas swifts are world-wide in distribution. Internal anatomical features and great aerial dexterity are the only traits common to the two families.

Swift

White-rumped Swift

Swifts
order *Apodiformes*, family *Apodidae*

Swifts, which have a superficial resemblance to swallows, have carried life in the air further than any other group. Not only do they find their food in the air, but they even mate and sleep on the wing. There are about sixty-five species of these small to medium-sized birds. All have extremely long scythe-shaped wings, lending them perfect support in the air and enabling them to attain great speed. Their streamlining reduces the air pressure to a minimum and for their size swifts are probably the fastest flying birds in existence. In cruising flight their speed is around 30 mph, but the top speed they can reach is over 60 mph. There is one record of a Swift flying about 175 miles at an average speed of about 40 mph. For comparison it is worth mentioning that Starlings (which are considerably bigger than Swifts) reach speeds of about 40 mph whereas Chaffinches only cruise at 25 mph. Geese and ducks fly at speeds ranging from 40 to 60 mph.

Swifts hardly ever sit on the ground. Their feet are degenerate and adapted for clinging to walls and rocks. Nevertheless a

SWIFT *Apus apus* L 6½" Very common. Can be seen in the air almost anywhere, but most often near towns and villages which offer nesting sites. Nest is placed in hollow trees, chimneys and other protected cavities. Colonial in breeding. Larger than any of the swallows, with narrower and stiffer wings. Very dark, with black underside (Pallid Swift has brownish underside). Often flies very high, usually in small flocks. Flight is extremely fast. Call is a shrill screaming. S

WHITE-RUMPED SWIFT *Apus caffer* L 5" Very rare summer visitor to southern Iberian peninsula where it has recently begun to breed. Small and generally black with white upper rump and marked forked tail. Its behaviour is typically swift-like.

swift stranded on flat ground is able to get on the wing again although only with difficulty. Most swifts are sooty in colour.

The Swift, which is common over most of Europe, builds its nest in chimneys or other crevices and holes in buildings, sometimes resorting to its natural site in rock crevices. The Pallid Swift nests in the same places as the Swift but has a greater affinity for coastal regions. The large Alpine Swift, however, has retained its natural habitat and is indigenous only to Alpine and Mediterranean mountain areas.

Two or three white eggs are laid and incubated by both sexes in eighteen to twenty days. The young leave the nest after six to seven weeks. In the fledging period the young are able to starve for several days and can even reach a torpid state in which their metabolism is considerably diminished. This is a typical adaptation to the great variations in food supply (flying insects) which swifts encounter, even at the height of their breeding season.

All swifts are migratory, wintering in tropical Africa.

PALLID SWIFT *Apus pallidus* L 6½" Rather common, with a preference for rocky shores and mountains. Often mixes with Swift and Alpine Swift. Resembles Swift closely but is paler with brown on underside (not black like Swift). Silhouette differs slightly from that of Swift, as head is broader. When seen with Swift, the slower wing-beats of this species can be noticed. Call is like that of Swift.

ALPINE SWIFT *Apus melba* L 8" Common, found in mountains and towns. Much larger than the two other swifts, with white underside and brown breast-band. Flight even faster than that of Swift, wing-beats slower. Like Swift, often encountered in flocks. Nests colonially. Call is distinctly different from Swift's, consisting of a loud, descending and ascending trill.   V

Pallid Swift

Alpine Swift

KINGFISHER *Alcedo atthis* L 7" Fairly common along slow-running rivers and streams and by ponds rich in fish. Blue and green upper parts and orange-red underside distinguish this species. Notice the relatively enormous head, short wings, legs and tail. Perches on poles and branches by the water, often sitting motionless for long periods of time, but also has characteristic jerking of head and tail. Flight fast and direct, low over the water. Occasionally seen hovering for brief moments. Plunges headlong into the water from perch to catch fish. Call is a high, ringing repetition of 'cheet' notes. R

PIED KINGFISHER *Ceryle rudis* L 10" Very rare, usually spring visitor from African and Asiatic breeding grounds to eastern and south-eastern Europe. Black and white plumage, large size and kingfisher silhouette easily distinguish this species from any other European bird. Male has two, female one, more or less complete breast-band. Soars and hovers above the surface of the water before plunging head-first to catch fish. Fishes in salt and fresh water. Call is short and penetrating.

Kingfishers and Their Allies
order *Coraciiformes*

This is a cosmopolitan order of extremely diversified birds. Common features are limited to brilliantly coloured plumages and the fusing of some of the front toes. There are nine families, of which four—kingfishers *(Alcedinidae)*, bee-eaters *(Meropidae)*, rollers *(Coraciidae)* and the Hoopoe *(Upupidae)*—are represented in Europe. Other families are the quaint todies *(Todidae)* of the West Indies, the long-tailed motmots *(Momotidae)* of Central and South America, the cuckoo-rollers *(Leptosomatidae)* of Madagascar, and the African wood-hoopoes *(Phoeniculidae)*. The most bizarre family of the order are the hornbills *(Bucerotidae)*, found in the tropical parts of the Old World.

Kingfishers
order *Coraciiformes*, family *Alcedinidae*

By a quietly flowing stream one suddenly sees a flying diamond-shape swoop low over the water and hears a penetrating rattling

Kingfisher

Pied Kingfisher

call. This is the Kingfisher, the only European member of the family to which it has given its name. A closer look at this brilliantly coloured bird, as it perches on a branch overhanging the water, reveals its peculiar shape: a very long, straight bill and huge head, very small body and short tail, small weak feet. This strange build reflects its feeding habits and is a perfect adaptation to its way of obtaining fish. Like a projectile, it dives from its perch in a headlong plunge into the water when it spots a fish. The bill is the tool with which the Kingfisher grasps the fish before knocking it against the perch to kill it, and then either swallowing it or taking it to its brood.

Other kingfishers, for instance the Pied Kingfisher, which is a very rare visitor to the Mediterranean countries from its African haunts, fly over the water when on the lookout for prey. When a fish is spotted, the bird stops its flight, perhaps hovering for a second or two before dropping head first into the water like a tern.

Kingfishers dig their nests in banks along the water's edge. Well protected in a chamber at the end of a tunnel about two and a half feet long, the six or seven eggs are incubated for about twenty days. The young are fed fish carried to the nest by both parents. Three to four weeks after hatching, the young are able to care for themselves and the parents start their second brood. Only the northernmost elements of the European population of Kingfishers are migratory; the rest are resident along ice-free streams and they may suffer badly in a very severe winter.

Bee-eater

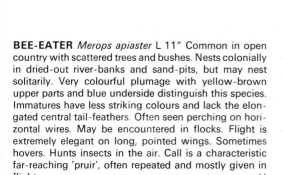

BEE-EATER *Merops apiaster* L 11″ Common in open country with scattered trees and bushes. Nests colonially in dried-out river-banks and sand-pits, but may nest solitarily. Very colourful plumage with yellow-brown upper parts and blue underside distinguish this species. Immatures have less striking colours and lack the elongated central tail-feathers. Often seen perching on horizontal wires. May be encountered in flocks. Flight is extremely elegant on long, pointed wings. Sometimes hovers. Hunts insects in the air. Call is a characteristic far-reaching 'pruir', often repeated and mostly given in flight. V

Bee-eaters
order *Coraciiformes,* family *Meropidae*

This family of brilliantly coloured birds is limited to the Old World, where twenty-four species are recognized. Only one species breeds in western Europe, the Bee-eater; the Blue-cheeked Bee-eater is a very rare vagrant from North Africa to western Europe, and there are isolated colonies in the northern Caucasus.

The bright and striking colours of the Bee-eater make it a pleasure to see whenever it is encountered. Adding to the pleasure is the unwariness which often permits a close approach. It may be seen perched horizontally on telephone wires, where its weak feet can get sufficient grasp, or darting elegantly through the air on its long, pointed wings, hunting insects, mainly wasps and bees.

Bee-eaters breed in colonies, the nest being placed at the end of a tunnel which can be up to nine feet deep. The tunnels are dug out in banks along roadsides and rivers. The nest contains five or six shiny white eggs which are incubated by both sexes.

European Bee-eaters are migratory, wintering in tropical Africa. Sometimes they occur far outside their regular breeding range and can even settle down to nest for a season or two, as has happened in England and Denmark.

Rollers

order *Coraciiformes*, family *Coraciidae*

The European avifauna has only one species of these brightly coloured birds of which seventeen different species are spread over most of the world. Superficially resembling the crow family, the Roller nevertheless is far removed from these much clumsier birds.

It has earned its name from the habit of rolling and wheeling through the air during its display flight. It prefers well-wooded land with old trees and clearings, and plenty of tree cavities in which it can nest. In a clearing or at the edge of a wood the Roller often shows itself on an exposed perch, looking out for

BLUE-CHEEKED BEE-EATER *Merops superciliosus* L 12″ Fairly common in open steppes. Local in very restricted European range. Very rare summer visitor to western Europe. Nests colonially in holes in river-banks or sand-pits. Green colour without any brown on upper parts and reddish underside of wing distinguish it from the Bee-eater. Habits are similar to Bee-eater. Often encountered in flocks on breeding grounds but in western Europe singly. Call resembles that of Bee-eater but is shriller and not as far-reaching.

ROLLER *Coracias garrulus* L 12″ Fairly common in open country with scattered trees and bushes, and in open woodland. Nests in hollow trees or other cavities. Blue colour with chestnut back make this species unmistakable. Sexes similar. Often sits in the open on a perch from which it catches insects on the ground or even in flight. Flight resembles that of Jackdaw, but is faster and more erratic. On the ground it is rather clumsy. Has characteristic 'rolling' display flight. Call is a loud, crowlike 'kraack'. V

Blue-cheeked Bee-eater

Roller

imm.

insects, which are taken on the ground.

Incubation of the four or five white eggs takes about eighteen days and the young are able to leave the nest after twenty-seven days.

The Roller is migratory and winters in Africa.

Hoopoe

order *Coraciiformes*, family *Upupidae*

With its gorgeously displayed crest this sole member of its family has attracted the attention of man for centuries. This long-billed, unwary bird is the subject of folklore in many countries throughout its range. For instance its appearance in some countries has been taken as a sign of approaching war. So sinister a thought would hardly occur to the modern bird-watcher who is lucky enough to see it searching the ground with its long, curved bill for whatever insects might come its way. Like the other members of its order, it occupies cavities, trees, rocks or buildings, where five to eight, or even more, usually whitish eggs are laid and incubated for eighteen days.

Most Hoopoes migrate and only in southern Spain can one encounter these beautiful birds all the year round.

HOOPOE *Upupa epops* L 11″ Fairly common in open land with many trees and groves, parks and open woods, nesting in tree cavities. Erectile crest, long decurved bill, light pinky brown plumage and striking black and white wing pattern identify this species at a glance. Crest is often raised and lowered. Sexes are similar. Immatures have shorter crest. Wings are very rounded and flight is undulating. Runs well on the ground. Often seen perching on bushes, trees, rocks and buildings. Call is a characteristic deep 'hoo-poo-poo'. P

Hoopoe

Arthur Singer

Woodpeckers and Their Allies
order *Piciformes*

As diverse as it is cosmopolitan, this order consists of six families of which only one, the woodpeckers *(Picidae)*, is represented on the European continent. The other five families are the brightly coloured jacamars *(Galbulidae)* and puffbirds *(Bucconidae)* of South America, the barbets *(Capitonidae)*, found in the tropical parts of the Old as well as the New World, the honeyguides *(Indicatoridae)*, which lead animals and men to bees' nests, and the curious toucans *(Ramphastidae)* of South America with their enormous bills.

Different looking as they are, the families in the order are bound together by various structural similarities, among which is zygodactyly: two toes point forwards and two point backwards. They all live in woods, the young are hatched naked and helpless, and neither they nor their parents have down as most other birds do.

Woodpeckers
order *Piciformes*, family *Picidae*

Except for Australia, all continents enjoy the presence of these busy carpenters, of which more than 225 species are recognized. We on our continent have but a poor selection, only ten species being indigenous to Europe.

Woodpeckers are small to medium-sized birds, highly specialized to their way of obtaining food. The bill is chisel-shaped and the feet are adapted for clinging to the bark of trees, the stiff tail-feathers lending the bird perfect support for the hard work of drilling through the bark and wood to get at insects hidden underneath. The woodpecker's tongue is also specially developed. It is very long and lies in a sheath which may even reach around the skull to make it extra long, so that it can project far into the holes of wood-boring insects and worms. At the tip of the tongue many species have hooks and barbs to which the insects stick. Salivary glands are well developed to keep the long tongue sticky, making it almost impossible for the prey to escape its fate.

Most woodpeckers obtain their food by drilling holes in the bark over the holes bored by insects and their larvae. They insert their tongues into the holes and extract the insect. But the Great Spotted Woodpecker, the most widespread in Europe, is an exception as, in some areas at least, it lives largely on pine seeds, whereas other species do so only occasionally. It is this source of food which is probably the secret of the Great Spotted Woodpecker's success as it is the most widespread and common European woodpecker. It takes the pine cones and presses them into a slit in a tree where it hacks them apart to reach the seeds, the only parts which are eaten. Underneath such a favourite slit, which the Great Spotted Woodpecker can actually make for the purpose, piles upon piles of empty pine cones may be found. Although they are difficult to distinguish from cones emptied by crossbills, woodpeckers are much more violent in their attacks on the cones. The Green and the Grey-headed Woodpeckers live to a large degree on ants' nests, picking the ants out of them with their tongues.

Almost all woodpeckers are resident, although the northernmost populations may move southward in winter. In some

GREEN WOODPECKER *Picus viridis* L 12" Common in deciduous woodlands with a preference for areas with large clearings and rides. Also found in more open land with scattered trees and groves. Where range overlaps that of Grey-headed Woodpecker, Green is usually found at lower elevations. Notice green upper parts with conspicuously yellow upper rump. Only other greenish Woodpecker in Europe is the Grey-headed, but Green is told from this species by larger size and more red on crown (both male and female) and more black on face. Juveniles are spotted and are greener than juvenile Grey-headed Woodpeckers and have more red on crown. Often seen on the ground in the open, feeding on ants. Carriage on the ground is upright. Hops clumsily. Perches across branches more often than other woodpeckers. Call is a far-reaching laughing cry. Seldom drums. R

GREY-HEADED WOODPECKER *Picus canus* L 10" Fairly common in open deciduous and mixed woods, open areas with scattered trees and open mountain forests (less numerous than Green Woodpecker). Where range overlaps that of Green Woodpecker, usually found at higher elevations. Resembles Green Woodpecker, but is smaller and has less red on head (male a little, female none, juvenile very little or none) and less black on face (limited to narrow lines). Juveniles are browner in colour, not spotted, and have no red on crown. Like Green Woodpecker, often seen on ground, where it finds ants. Call resembles that of Green Woodpecker, but is not as harsh and dies away slowly. Unlike Green Woodpecker, it drums frequently.

years the Great Spotted Woodpecker occurs in very large numbers and may emigrate to other places if there is a food shortage, particularly when the crop of pine cones fails. The Wryneck, which in many respects differs from the other woodpeckers, is migratory, wintering in tropical Africa.

Many woodpeckers announce a territory by drumming on trees, particularly old and dry ones; telegraph poles are sometimes preferred, perhaps because sound from them carries further. Not only does this indicate to other males the territory already occupied, but it also attracts females (which are themselves able to drum). The calls of woodpeckers are rather unmusical but often wide-ranging and distinctive. Drumming is heard particularly in spring and this is the time when the nest holes are excavated. The male is the most active carpenter and sometimes the female does not even make a pretence of participating in the hard work of boring into a partly live tree. In spite of this, it only takes about a week to finish a hole completely, which means about five hours work daily for the woodpeckers. They bore horizontally into the trunk, then sink

Green Woodpecker

Grey-headed Woodpecker

imm.

imm.

GREAT SPOTTED WOODPECKER *Dendrocopos major* L 9" The most common and widespread of the woodpeckers, found in both deciduous and coniferous woods, in gardens and parks with many trees. The black and white plumage distinguishes the spotted woodpeckers as a group at a glance. To tell the species apart it is important to note the head, neck and back pattern. Great Spotted Woodpecker has two large white areas on back, as does the Syrian Woodpecker from which it is told by bold black line across side of neck, and Middle Spotted Woodpecker from which it is told by black line reaching bill, by only a little red on neck of adult male (female has none), and by unstriped flanks. Juveniles have red crown, but black on side of head and neck extends further than on any other spotted woodpecker. Call is a loud, short 'kik'. Often drums; drumming is very fast. RW

SYRIAN WOODPECKER *Dendrocopos syriacus* L 9" Common in open woodland and parks, preferring less dense woods than the Great Spotted Woodpecker. Very similar to Great Spotted Woodpecker, but told from this species by lack of black stripe across side of neck. Immatures are told from Great Spotted Woodpecker immatures in the same way, from Middle Spotted Woodpecker by moustachial stripe extending forward to the bill. In call and behaviour like Great Spotted Woodpecker.

MIDDLE SPOTTED WOODPECKER *Dendrocopos medius* L 8" Fairly common in mature deciduous forests, staying rather high in the canopy. Has white patches on shoulders, like Great Spotted Woodpecker, but has red crown in all plumages and less black on sides of head and neck. Sides of flanks striped with black. Told from immature Syrian Woodpecker by shorter moustachial stripe which does not reach bill. In mating season it has a distinct slow cry, 'gait-gait'. Does not drum as often as Great Spotted Woodpecker.

LESSER SPOTTED WOODPECKER *Dendrocopos minor* L 6" Common in rather open deciduous and mixed woods, orchards and parks. Smallest of the European woodpeckers. Lacks white shoulder spots of Great Spotted, Syrian and Middle, but has boldly barred back. Usually stays well up among small branches of old trees. Sometimes mixes in flocks of tits. Call is a repetition of high-pitched 'kee' notes. Drums frequently, but a little less powerfully than Great Spotted. R

Great Spotted Woodpecker

Syrian Woodpecker

Middle Spotted Woodpecker

Lesser Spotted Woodpecker

WHITE-BACKED WOODPECKER *Dendrocopos leucotos* L 10" Rather uncommon in old deciduous forests and mixed woods with old, rotting trees. The largest of the *Dendrocopos* group, with a distinct white upper rump and lower back, and black upper back (diagnostic). The white back of the smaller Three-toed Woodpecker extends all the way to the neck. Bill is longer than that of any of the spotted woodpeckers. In flight the white lower back and upper rump are very distinctive. Female has a black instead of red crown; immatures have only a little red on the crown. Call is similar to that of Great Spotted Woodpecker.

THREE-TOED WOODPECKER *Picoïdes tridactylus* L 9" Rather uncommon, in coniferous and birch forests up to tree limit on mountains. Head is large and very dark, the male having yellow on crown. White back and upper rump are diagnostic. Flanks are barred. The white on the back of the much larger White-backed Woodpecker does not extend as far as on the Three-toed Woodpecker. Flight is stronger and faster than that of other woodpeckers. Less vocal and active than other woodpeckers, drumming infrequently. Call is rather similar to that of the Great Spotted Woodpecker.

BLACK WOODPECKER *Dryocopus martius* L 18" Fairly common in old coniferous and deciduous forests, particularly in mountain tracts. Largest of the European woodpeckers. Enormous size and uniform black plumage make this bird unmistakable. Male has a red crown, female only a red spot on the neck. Flight is more straight than that of other woodpeckers, and heavier. Call is a far-reaching ringing 'kleoh'. Drums commonly and extremely loudly.

imm.

White-backed Woodpecker

Black Woodpecker

Three-toed Woodpecker

a shaft in the dead and often rotting centre.

No nest material is used and the four to eight whitish eggs are placed on the bare bottom of the hole. The eggs are incubated for twelve to nineteen days which, for some of the larger species, is a comparatively short time. The young, which are very noisy in their holes, are fed for about three weeks before they leave the nest and fend for themselves. The Syrian Woodpecker, resembling the Great Spotted Woodpecker, differs from most other species by feeding the young on fruit and berries, whereas the others feed their young on insects.

Usually woodpeckers excavate new nest holes each year. They can even make holes outside the breeding season, where

WRYNECK *Jynx torquilla* L 7" Fairly common but retiring in parks and open land with plenty of bushes, trees and hedgerows. Does not resemble woodpeckers at all. Plumage is lilac and brown with a dark area down the neck, tail is long, and bill is short. Flight is undulating. Banded tail is distinctive when the bird is in flight. It is often seen on the ground where it feeds on ants. Often turns its head at queer angles (hence name). Can hardly be mistaken for any other European bird. Call is a repetition of nasal crying 'gyeeh' notes. Does not drum. SP

Wryneck

Species	Nest-hole diameter	Shape
Lesser Spotted Woodpecker	32 mm	round
Middle Spotted Woodpecker	50 mm	round
Great Spotted Woodpecker	50 mm	oval
Syrian Woodpecker	45 mm	round
White-backed Woodpecker	60 mm	oval
Green Woodpecker	60 mm	round
Grey-headed Woodpecker	55 mm	round
Black Woodpecker	100 mm	oval

they spend the night well protected from the severity of the winter cold. The size and shape of the nest-hole entrance is characteristic and the nest can with some certainty be identified by this.

The Green Woodpecker, which is an extremely noisy bird, is also very aggressive, much more so than the similar Grey-headed Woodpecker, which in many areas has had to leave the better feeding grounds to its relative. They both prefer open or fairly open deciduous woods, but usually the Grey-headed Woodpecker is found at somewhat higher elevations.

The Great Spotted Woodpecker is by far the most numerous of our woodpeckers and this is usually the species concerned when one sees a black-and-white bird with a pinch of red fly through the wood in undulating flight. The very similar Syrian Woodpecker has invaded central Europe from Asia Minor in this century and has recently reached Austria. The extension of its breeding range is probably not over yet. This species is also very aggressive, both towards other species as well as towards members of its own. The slightly smaller Middle Spotted Woodpecker is often difficult to tell from the two larger species but its nasal cry heard in spring is diagnostic. Like the Great Spotted Woodpecker it will sometimes resort to nuts for food.

The Lesser Spotted Woodpecker is the smallest, being only the size of a sparrow. It often feeds on insects on leaves and branches, and in winter sometimes joins company with tits moving about in search of food. The White-backed Woodpecker is of eastern distribution and has a preference for rotten trees and tree-stumps. The rarer Three-toed Woodpecker has, as the name indicates, only three toes. Its home is to be found in the pine woods at high elevations.

The largest of our woodpeckers, the Black Woodpecker, also prefers fir and pine trees. Like the Green and Grey-headed Woodpeckers, it lives partly on ants but it does a lot of carpentry work as well: wear and tear on the bill is so great that in the course of a year it is actually replaced by a new bill which grows as the tip is worn off.

The most aberrant of our woodpeckers is the Wryneck with its elusive behaviour and camouflaged plumage. It is not able itself to drill out nest holes but uses those made by other woodpeckers. Its food consists mainly of ants.

Perching Birds
order *Passeriformes*

Sand Martin colony

This cosmopolitan order to which most of our familiar garden birds such as tits, thrushes and finches belong is by far the largest order of birds. More than 4000 species belong to it, comprising more than half of all the different kinds of birds. In Europe we have 187 breeding species; another 16 have been recorded from our continent more than five times in this century, and 42 have been recorded even more rarely.

The order is subdivided into four suborders: *Eurylaimi,* the broadbills of the old world tropics; *Tyranni,* including such birds as the New World flycatchers, but not represented in the European avifauna; *Menurae,* the lyrebirds and the scrub-birds of Australia; and *Oscines,* the suborder to which all our perching songbirds belong.

The most characteristic anatomical feature of all the perching birds is the construction of the foot, three toes pointing forward, one toe pointing backward and joined at the same level, enabling the bird to get a firm grip on its perch. Another characteristic is the sophisticated quality of the song of many perching birds. The arrangement of the muscles of the voice box is the anatomical basis for division into suborders.

Crag Martin nest

The perching birds are small to medium-sized land birds, the European species ranging in size from the Raven with a length of twenty-five inches to the Goldcrest only three and a half inches long. On land the perching birds exploit almost every type of habitat, and one, the Dipper, even finds food underwater on the bottom of streams.

The young of perching birds are all altricial, or nidicolous, which means they have closed eyes and little or no down when hatched and are unable to care for themselves. In most other respects the perching birds vary so much it is hard to find common characteristics. They are divided into many families each of which with its characteristics will be described in the following sections.

Swallow nest

Swallows
order *Passeriformes,* family *Hirundinidae*

The swallows are elegant flyers, well-adapted to a life on the wing although not as specialized in this respect as the superficially similar swifts. Their flight is not as fast as that of a swift but is more agile.

Swallows are small birds with long, pointed wings, forked tail, short, weak feet and bill, but with a large gape. There are seventy-nine species in the world and five breed on our continent. Swallow, House Martin and Sand Martin nest in all European countries except Iceland, where the first two are annual visitors but do not breed. The Crag Martin and Red-rumped Swallow are Mediterranean in their distribution. All are migratory, the Crag Martin only moving to lower altitudes in the Mediterranean countries, whereas the other members of the family move further, wintering in Africa.

Red-rumped Swallow nest

In late summer swallows congregate in large flocks which are often mixed. Outside the breeding season these flocks often spend the nights in reed-beds, where thousands may congregate. As swallows live solely on flying insects caught in the air they have to seek warmer climates during the northern winter.

House Martin nest

SAND MARTIN *Riparia riparia* L 5" Common near steep river-banks, sea cliffs and gravel pits, where they burrow their nest holes into the banks. Often seen near water. Brown breast-band diagnostic. Also told from Crag Martin by more deeply forked tail, narrower wings and lack of white spots on tail. Nests colonially. Call is a low, unmusical buzz. S

CRAG MARTIN *Hirundo rupestris* L 5" Common but local in mountains and along rocky sea cliffs. Larger than Sand Martin, and lacks breast-band. Wings broader and tail less deeply forked. White spots on upper side of tail visible at short distance only. Nests colonially on cliffs. Call is high-pitched, weak 'tchnin', only rarely heard.

SWALLOW *Hirundo rustica* L 7½" Very common in cultivated open country, where it builds an open mud nest on buildings. Tail very deeply forked. Red throat and front diagnostic. No white on upper rump. Flight extremly elegant. Nests singly and in small, loose colonies. Song is long and twittering. S

RED-RUMPED SWALLOW *Hirundo daurica* L 7" Fairly common in open rocky country where it builds closed mud nest with tubular entrance under cliffs, bridges and buildings. Looks like Swallow, but notice light upper rump, light throat and less forked tail (rump looks long). Flight resembles that of Swallow but is not as elegant. Nests singly or in small, loose colonies. Song resembles that of Swallow. V

HOUSE MARTIN *Delichon urbica* L 5" Common in cultivated country and in towns. White upper rump diagnostic. Tail shorter and less forked than in Swallow and Red-rumped Swallow. Wing action and flight stiffer than in Swallow. Often encountered in large flocks. Builds closed nest. Breeds in colonies. Flight call sharp and high pitched. Song twittering. S

Sand Martin

Crag Martin

Swallow

House Martin

Red-rumped Swallow

Sometimes the cold surprises these delicate birds in spring or autumn and thousands succumb to the adverse conditions.

Safely arrived in spring on their breeding grounds, they soon set about nesting. All three martins are colonial in their breeding behaviour. The House Martin builds its completely closed mud nest under eaves, often so close to its neighbour that the nests touch each other. Sometimes the much stronger and aggressive House Sparrow takes over the nest to the dismay of the rightful owners. The Sand Martin digs long horizontal tunnels in cliffs and banks, usually with entrance holes a few feet under the upper edge of the cliff. Even they are not safe from intruders and Starlings sometimes enlarge the tunnel so they can accommodate themselves, and after the Starlings even Black Guillemots can do the same in certain places. Crag Martins build open mud nests on sheltered cliffs or in small caves in rocky cliffs and gorges. The Swallow also builds an open nest of mud but this is usually placed inside a barn, on a veranda or even in a room with a permanently open window. It is not colonial in its nesting behaviour. The Red-rumped Swallow, least numerous of the European swallows, builds a completely closed mud nest with a long retort-shaped opening. It is often placed under bridges and overhanging rocks.

DUPONT'S LARK *Chersophilus duponti* L 7" Very rare visitor from North Africa to western Mediterranean countries. Frequents dry steppes with scattered bushes. Rather long decurved bill and round head without trace of crest are diagnostic. Whitish eye-stripe is characteristic. No white on wings. Secretive in behaviour, hiding in vegetation. Runs quickly. When perched on the ground, stands more erect than other larks. Song, given in flight, contains rasping notes.

Short-toed Lark

Dupont's Lark

juv.

The song of swallows is a subdued, pleasant twitter, but they all have shrill and far-reaching calls which are more often noticed. The Swallow and House Martin have associated themselves very closely with man, taking advantage of his dwellings as nesting places and his technological advances in the form of telephone wires and electric wires as resting places. But with their gracefulness and charm, they are always welcome visitors and enjoy widespread protection, in spite of the notorious piles of excrement accumulating under their nests each summer.

Swallows lay three to six white or spotted eggs. The female does most of the incubation, which lasts about two weeks, but both sexes share equally in the feeding of the offspring. Many pairs are double brooded.

SHORT-TOED LARK *Calandrella cinerea* L 5½" Common in open, dry country and on dried-out mud-flats. Rather small and pale. Underside unstreaked except for a few spots on juvenile. Dark patches on neck difficult to see. Centre of tail looks very dark in flight. Resembles Lesser Short-toed Lark closely but told from this by lack of striping of underparts, more rufous colours and, at short range, dark patches on neck. Usually flies low. Song is rather high-pitched, less varied than that of Skylark, given in flight as well as on the ground.   V

Larks

order *Passeriformes,* family *Alaudidae*

There are seventy-five different species of larks. All are found in the Old World and one, the Shore Lark, is also found in the New World. In Europe we have ten breeding larks, of which one, the Skylark, is among the most widespread and numerous of European birds. One, Dupont's Lark, is a rare visitor to the Mediterranean countries from its African breeding ground.

Larks are small to medium-sized, mainly brown and grey birds. Their rather indistinct plumage tends to be coloured so as to camouflage them against the earth in whatever region they are found. In most species the sexes are very similar in plumage. A striking exception is the Black Lark, the male of which is beautifully rich black in the breeding season whereas the female has the duller plumage of the other members of the family. Most larks have a long hind claw. If it were not for their beautiful song, larks would be among our most inconspicuous birds.

Larks are typically birds of the open land, steppes and deserts. With the clearance over the past 2000 years of much of the vast forest which once covered most of Europe, a completely new

LESSER SHORT-TOED LARK *Calandrella rufescens* L 5½" Fairly common in dry, open country and on dried out mud-flats. Resembles Short-toed Lark closely, but has streaked upper breast and is darker, greyer and more uniform in colour. It also lacks the dark neck patches of the adult Short-toed Lark. Song, given in high circling flight, is rich and varied with characteristic short notes.   V

Calandra Lark

Lesser Short-toed Lark

CALANDRA LARK *Melanocorypha calandra* L 8" Common in dry, open country. Very large with comparatively short tail and broad wings with white trailing edge. Bill thick. Large black neck patch sometimes difficult to see and less prominent in females. Flight usually low and undulating. Call is short and nasal. Song musical, resembling that of Skylark, usually uttered on the wing from a height.   V

habitat has been opened up for many species of larks—the agricultural fields. Larks were probably very restricted in their European distribution before man modified the landscape. Thus the spread of the Skylark has been associated with the introduction of the different cultivated plants into western Europe in Roman times. Although most of our larks are found in open country, the Woodlark is an exception to this rule, preferring areas with scattered bushes and trees, but it is not found in true woodlands.

The migratory habits of our larks vary: the Crested Lark is a resident, while the Short-toed Lark leaves Europe altogether in the cold season. Most larks wander about in flocks in winter, and even the Crested Lark and Thekla Lark can be encountered far from their breeding grounds. The wings of the larks show an unexpected adaptation in that the wing areas of the migratory species are usually smaller than those of their relatives which do not travel as far. But for a migrant the shape and development of the flight feathers is more important than the surface area.

Most larks live on insects and seeds picked off the ground. During the summer about half the food of, for instance, the Skylark consists of animal matter, the other half vegetable. In winter they eat very little animal matter, but rely almost solely on seeds. Here again an exception is found; the Shore Lark in winter seeks its food mainly along seashores, where it finds snails, insects and other small animals surviving among the seaweed washed ashore.

The most striking feature of the group is their beautiful songs. Song is usually delivered in a circling flight and helps to announce the ownership of the territory; a more pleasant sound than the liquid notes which in spring and summer fill the air over the open fields is hard to find. The song and the flight high above the ground, almost beyond the reach of the eye, have inspired many poets; both Shakespeare and Goethe refer to this familiar bird. In January and February the first Skylarks begin to announce their ownership of a certain strip of land by their circling flights or by hovering high overhead.

All larks build a rather simple nest on the ground, sometimes

WHITE-WINGED LARK *Melanocorypha leucoptera* L 7½" Common in dry grasslands. Annual in eastern Europe, very rare in western Europe, mainly in winter, where it reaches as far as the British Isles. Similar to Calandra Lark, but large white wing patches, very prominent in flight, are diagnostic. Wings narrower than Calandra Lark's. Crown rich brown in male, more greyish in female. Song is loud, resembling Calandra Lark's. Usually does not rise as high as Calandra Lark during song-flight. V

BLACK LARK *Melanocorypha yeltoniensis* L 8" Fairly common on steppes, often near water. Rare winter visitor to central Europe, where it has reached as far west as Belgium. Male easily told from other larks by black plumage with brown feather margins. Female best told from Calandra Lark and White-winged Lark both of which also have heavy bill, by lack of black neck patch and lack of white wing patch. From other larks by heavy bill and plump build. Underwing is dark brown. Song resembles that of Calandra Lark.

White-winged Lark

Black Lark

juv.

CRESTED LARK *Galerida cristata* L 6½" Common in dry open country with sparse vegetation, by roadsides, and in open spaces in towns. Crest is larger than that of any other lark except Thekla. Sandy edge of short tail characteristic in flight as are sandy underwings. Where range overlaps that of Thekla Lark (Iberian peninsula), identification is extremely difficult and probably only possible when direct comparison can be made. Tail is rather short, wings rounded compared with other larks. Immatures have less prominent crest and are more spotted above. Runs rapidly. Often very tame. Usually encountered in small groups. Call is a characteristic 'dee-dee-doo'. Song resembles that of Skylark but is shorter and less melodious. Usually delivered from the ground or from low perch on rock.   V

THEKLA LARK *Galerida theklae* L 6" Common in dry open country with sparse vegetation, usually preferring rockier landscape and higher elevation than the Crested Lark, from which it can be distinguished only by direct comparison. Slightly smaller, with shorter and heavier bill. Greyer and paler with grey underside to wing. Breast spots clearer. Often perches on trees (which the Crested Lark rarely does), from which song resembling that of Crested Lark is given.

hidden in a tussock. The Calandra Lark sometimes adds a little hill of pebbles on the side of the nest, but the function of this is unknown. The eggs, three to seven in number, are white to green and usually spotted with brown. They are incubated by both sexes or by the female alone for about two weeks. After hatching, the young only stay in the nest a little more than a week and can soon be found in the vicinity still unable to fly any distance and far from fully grown. The early departure from the nest is of high survival value as the brood becomes scattered and much more difficult for predators to find.

The growth and development of Skylarks have been studied in some detail and can be given as an example of the general development of many small songbirds. The freshly laid egg weighs 4.1 gram. At the time of hatching the weight has dropped to 3.1 gram of which the egg shell accounts for about 0.2 gram. The newly hatched young seems to be little more than gape and belly and only weighs 2.9 gram. But in the course of four days the weight is more than quadrupled. The rate of increase then slows down and it takes eight more days before this weight is doubled and reaches the 26 gram of the flying young. The young then slowly gain another 10 gram before they are ready to breed.

Larks have been regarded as great delicacies, especially on the Continent, and many ingenious contraptions have been

Crested Lark

Thekla Lark

Skylark

Woodlark

Shore Lark

juv.

SKYLARK *Alauda arvensis* L 7" Abundant in open cultivated and uncultivated country. Boldly striped with small crest and long white-edged tail. Told from Corn Bunting by characteristic lark-like undulating flight, horizontal posture when perched, brownish rather than greyish colours, white-edged tail and more slender bill. Told from rather similar Woodlark by longer tail with white edges and less conspicuous and striking stripe over eye. From Calandra Lark by longer tail, more slender bill, less triangular wing and lack of black spot on side of breast. Crest is much smaller and more rounded than that of Crested and Thekla Lark. Outside breeding season usually seen in loose flocks. Call is melodious 'treek-e'. Song, usually given from flight high-up, is liquid, varied and sustained. Often remains at the same spot in the air for long periods of time, sometimes beyond sight of the naked eye. RSWP

WOODLARK *Lullula arborea* L 6" Common in wood margins and clearings, heaths and mountains with scattered bushes. Resembles Skylark but has much shorter tail without white edges, and characteristic stripes over the eyes meeting on the nape. Small crest is much more rounded and less prominent than that of Crested and Thekla Lark. Has small dark spot on back of wing, but this is not nearly as obvious as the black spot on neck of Calandra Lark. Flight is more undulating than that of Skylark. Short tail is particularly noticeable in flight. Often perches on trees, bushes and even telephone wires. Outside breeding season sometimes mixes with Skylarks in the loose flocks so characteristic of larks, but more often seen in small unmixed groups. Call is a musical, liquid 'diedelie'. Skylark-like song, which is sometimes given from perch but more often in flight, is characterised by interspersed trilling 'lu-lu-lu-lu-lu'. Sometimes sings at night. RP

SHORE LARK *Eremophila alpestris* L 6½" Fairly common, breeding on dry tundras above or north of the tree limit, wintering along shores and on fields with short vegetation. Facial pattern of black and sandy-yellow diagnostic, but can be somewhat obscured in winter, particularly on females and immatures, but it is always present to some degree. Outer tail-feathers are white. In winter usually encountered in small flocks, sometimes associated with Snow and Lapland Buntings. Flight is usually low and undulating. Call consists of faint pipit-like notes. Song, which is given from perch or in flight, is weak, high-pitched and repetitive. W

TREE PIPIT *Anthus trivialis* L 6" Common in open woods, clearings, heath and more open landscapes with bushes and trees. Resembles Meadow Pipit from which it is told by unstriped upper rump, pink legs, short hind claw and stouter build, but best by voice. Call note is a characteristic coarse 'teezee'. Song, which is given from perch or more often in short song-flight with slow descent, is canary-like, ending with a repeated 'zeea'. SP

INDIAN TREE PIPIT *Anthus hodgsoni* L 6" Common in its limited European range where it is found in the taiga. An extremely rare autumn visitor to north-western Europe. Resembles Tree Pipit closely but is slightly smaller, more olive-green above with less bold streaks, whereas underside is more striped. Eye-stripe more prominent. Upper rump unstriped. Song, given from perch, is not as varied as that of the Tree Pipit and is higher pitched. V

devised to catch the birds, of which it takes many to make a meal. Luckily this practice is declining, although larks are still eaten in numbers in southern Europe. One of the devices originally contrived to catch larks for culinary purposes, a plate covered with tiny mirrors which attract the larks as an Eagle Owl attracts crows, has in recent times been used to attract and catch Skylarks for ringing.

Pipits and Wagtails
order *Passeriformes*, family *Motacillidae*

The *Motacillidae* are divided into two groups, pipits and wagtails. The family as a whole consists of medium-sized to small birds, slender and delicately built, with long tails.

Pipits are streaked and brown, in their colours resembling larks, whose habitats, the open spaces, they share to a large degree. Although dull coloured, pipits at a closer look display a build which is of an elegance and beauty surpassed by few other birds. The slender bill, relatively long tail and legs, with rather long pointed wings, give the birds a charm which is perhaps even accentuated by their unobtrusive plumage patterns.

Wagtails are more brightly coloured, black, white, yellow and green. They have extremely long tails which are constantly wagged up and down, thus the name.

There are about forty-eight species of pipits and wagtails in the world. The exact number is not certain as different authorities disagree whether some forms should be regarded as species or subspecies. Six species of pipits and four of wagtails breed in Europe and two, Indian Tree Pipit and Richard's Pipit, are rare stragglers from their Asiatic breeding grounds.

The question of subspecies within this family illustrates the problem that taxonomists face in their attempts to establish the relationships between animals. Taxonomists fully agree that the

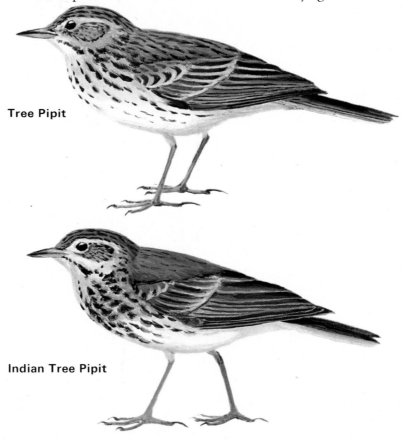

Tree Pipit

Indian Tree Pipit

Arthur Singer

PETCHORA PIPIT *Anthus gustavi* L 6" Common in scrubby and wooded tundras. A very rare autumn visitor to north-western Europe. Resembles Tree Pipit but has long hind claw, two pale stripes down the back, buffish (not white) outer tail-feathers and more striped underside. Upper rump is striped. Call is a characteristic, hard 'pipit', usually repeated three times. Song, given from perch or song-flight, consists of Wood-Warbler-like phrase followed by low warble.   V

RICHARD'S PIPIT *Anthus novaeseelandiae* L 7" A rare but probably annual, autumn (sometimes spring) visitor to Europe from Asiatic breeding grounds. Usually seen in open wet country near coasts. Large, long-legged with very long hind claw and boldly streaked plumage. Stands erect. Call is rather harsh 'r-reep'.   V

MEADOW PIPIT *Anthus pratensis* L 6" Very common on moors, meadows, dunes and grasslands. Resembles Tree Pipit but is more white on breast and has brown legs and long hind claws. Upper rump is less striped than back, distinguishing it from Red-throated Pipit. Outside breeding season often encountered in loose flocks. Call is a thin 'zeep', very different from that of Tree Pipit and Red-throated Pipit. Song, usually given in song-flight, is weak, ending in a trill.   RSWP

Petchora Pipit

Richard's Pipit

Meadow Pipit

Opposite Pied Wagtail

Water and Rock Pipits are of the same species, although superficially they show greater dissimilarity in plumage than do, for instance, the Tree Pipit and Meadow Pipit. Yet these two are distinct species with different songs and different habitat preferences. In the large areas where both species occur commonly they do not interbreed. The Water and Rock Pipits on the other hand have similar songs but occupy two completely different habitats and their distributions do not overlap at all. The Rock Pipit is found along rocky shores, whereas the Water Pipit is a bird of the high mountains. Other subspecies are found in many other parts of the world.

juv.

Tawny Pipit

Red-throated Pipit

winter   summer

Water Pipit

winter   summer

Rock Pipit

TAWNY PIPIT *Anthus campestris* L 6½" Fairly common in open, dry and sandy country with sparse vegetation. Sandy colour, rather faint streaking and large size distinguish it from other pipits. Immatures in autumn are streaked like Richard's Pipit but distinguished by longer, more slender bill. Usually seen singly or in small groups. As in other pipits voice is of great importance in identification. Call is drawn out or of two notes. Song is a repeated 'tsili', given in flight or on the ground.   V

RED-THROATED PIPIT *Anthus cervinus* L 6" Fairly common on tundra with low bushes. Uncommon visitor in west and central Europe. In summer easily distinguished from other pipits by rosy throat. In winter resembles Meadow Pipit but has more prominently streaked upper rump and more heavily streaked underside. Call is a hoarse 'tseeh' quite different from that of Meadow and Tree Pipit. Song resembles that of Meadow Pipit and is given in flight.   P

GREY WAGTAIL *Motacilla cinerea* L 7" Common along mountain streams, in winter also frequenting sewage farms by water in lowlands, even in towns, and lakesides. Yellow underside, grey back and extremely long tail distinguish it in all plumages. Male in summer has black throat. Yellow underside distinguishes it from similar Pied and White Wagtails. Immatures have less yellow on underside and are more greyish-brown above but always have yellow under tail-coverts, distinguishing them from immature White and Pied Wagtail, which have pure white under tail-coverts and usually some black on breast. Usually seen singly but a few can associate at favourable feeding grounds. Call resembles that of Pied and White Wagtail, but is higher pitched and shorter. Song, seldom heard, is twittering.   R

The White Wagtail and the Pied Wagtail also belong to the same species. The Pied Wagtail with its beautiful contrasting black and white colours is found in the British Isles and in isolated areas on the adjoining coast of the Continent. The White Wagtail, which is found in the rest of Europe and is only a passage migrant in the British Isles, has a less contrasting plumage, particularly the upper back which is grey rather than black.

Most complex of all is the problem of subspecies among the Yellow Wagtails of which more than eight are found within the boundaries of Europe and even more in Asia. The different subspecies can be told apart mainly by the differently coloured males in breeding plumage. These vary from the bright yellow of the British race to the startlingly beautiful deep black of the Balkan subspecies. Further complicating the issue is the fact that variants resembling other subspecies occur within the breeding range of almost all the different races. This is

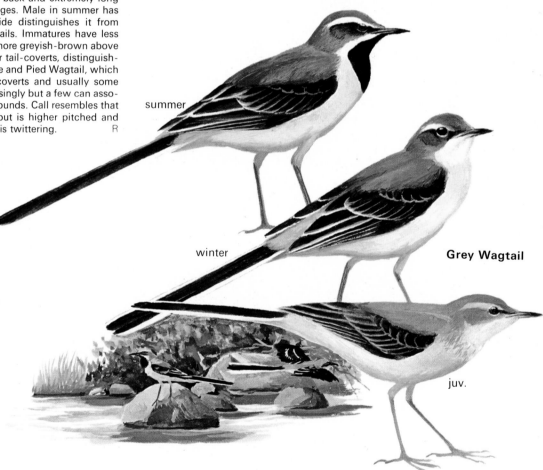

summer

winter

Grey Wagtail

juv.

WATER PIPIT *Anthus spinoletta spinoletta* L 6¼" Common on mountains above the tree limit, in winter in open country of lower elevation. In summer greyish-brown upper side and unstreaked underside separate it from other pipits. In winter resembles Meadow Pipit but distinguished by black leg colour and darker plumage. Distinguished from very similar Rock Pipit by white, not grey, outer tail-feathers. Call and song more metallic than those of Meadow Pipit.   WP

ROCK PIPIT *Anthus spinoletta (petrosus* group) L 6½" Subspecies of Water Pipit. Common on coasts, particularly where rocky. Resembles winter plumage Water Pipit but is more olive on back and has greyish outer tail-feathers. Distinguished from other pipits by dark legs. Often found in association with Meadow Pipits outside the breeding season. Call and song similar to those of Water Pipit.   R

possibly because of the occurrence of recognizable mutations more frequently in this than in any other species. For the field observer it is perplexing, and he is constantly faced with the problem of the different-looking Yellow Wagtails and cannot be certain if what he observes represents a true straggler to his region or is a variant of local origin. He resigns himself and just enjoys the pleasure of watching the bird, an experience far too often overlooked in the excitement of seeing a rarity. The following are the different subspecies found in Europe; the features distinguishing the male and the breeding areas for the various European subspecies are given.

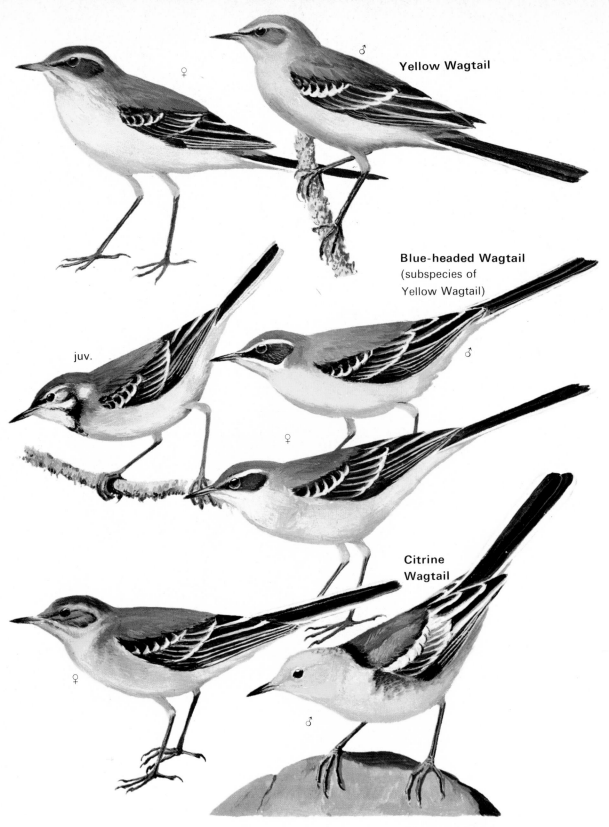

Yellow Wagtail

♀

♂

Blue-headed Wagtail
(subspecies of
Yellow Wagtail)

juv.

♂

♀

Citrine
Wagtail

♀

♂

YELLOW WAGTAIL *Motacilla flava* L 6½" Very common in moist open areas. Long tail, yellow underside and green back distinguish it from all other species. Colour of head and neck variable according to race (see table). Flight undulating. Outside breeding season usually seen in loose flocks. Often associates with grazing cattle. Call is loud mellow 'tseep'.

SP

CITRINE WAGTAIL *Motacilla citreola* L 6½" Fairly common in limited European range, usually in wet open country. A very rare autumn visitor to north-west Europe. Told in all plumages from Yellow Wagtail by grey back and two distinct white wing-bars particularly noticeable in flight. Immature is very pale, whitish on underside, grey on upper side. Often associates with Yellow Wagtail. Call shorter than that of Yellow Wagtail.

V

M.f.flava

M.f.flavissima

M.f.iberiae

M.f.cinereocapilla

M.f.beema

M.f.thunbergi

M.f.feldegg

Race	Summer plumage (male)	Summer distribution
Blue-headed Wagtail. *M.f. flava*	Blue-grey head, yellow throat with stripe over eye from bib to neck	Southern Scandinavia, western Europe except Great Britain and Iberian peninsula and western part of east Europe
Yellow Wagtail. *M.f. flavissima*	Olive-yellow head, yellow throat, yellow stripe over eye	Great Britain and locally adjacent coasts of continent
Spanish Wagtail. *M.f. iberiae*	Grey head, white throat, white stripe over eye to neck	Iberian peninsula. south and south-west France, Balearic Islands
Ashy-headed Wagtail. *M.f. cinereocapilla*	Grey head, white throat, no stripe over eye	Italy, central Mediterranean islands, Albania
Sykes' Wagtail. *M.f. beema*	Pale grey head, white throat, white stripe over eye from bib to neck	South-east Russia
Kirghiz Steppes Wagtail. *M.f. lutea*	Yellow head, throat and stripe over eye	South-easternmost Russia (Lower Volga)
Grey-headed Wagtail. *M.f. thunbergi*	Grey head, yellow throat, no stripe over eye	Northern Scandinavia and Russia
Black-headed Wagtail. *M.f. feldegg*	Black head, yellow throat, no stripe over eye	Balkan and Black Sea coasts

Pipits and wagtails are insect-eaters. Most of them are found in open country, the Tree Pipit usually in more wooded areas. The White and Pied Wagtails are often found close to farms, and in towns and suburbs where they add so much by their beautiful looks and their fascinating tail-wagging. This species often builds its nest in cavities among rocks or in houses. The Grey Wagtail also chooses a site well-hidden in a cavity, but almost always close to a fast-running stream. The other wagtails and pipits nest on the ground or in banks. Four to eight eggs are laid, usually streaked or mottled grey or brown, but the Tree Pipit's show a remarkable variety of colours and markings. Incubation takes about two weeks and the female does most of it, although the male will help her for short periods. Two broods are often reared.

The songs of pipits and wagtails are rather simple although pleasant. Pipits often deliver their songs in a short song-flight. For the birdwatcher the flight calls of pipits are very important in identification and in most cases he will be able to distinguish the species much better by its call than by the much more

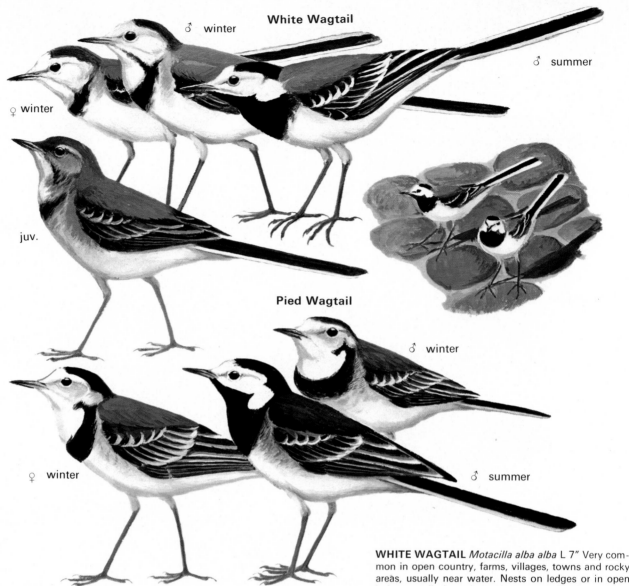

White Wagtail

♂ winter

♀ winter

♂ summer

juv.

Pied Wagtail

♂ winter

♀ winter

♂ summer

subtle and difficult plumage differences.

In the autumn pipits and wagtails assemble in loose flocks; Tree, Tawny and Red-throated Pipits and Yellow Wagtails leave Europe altogether, whereas the Meadow and Rock Pipits endure the winter of our temperate climate together with Grey and Pied Wagtails.

Shrikes

order *Passeriformes*, family *Laniidae*

These miniature birds of prey have earned their name from their rather harsh voices—shrieks. More dramatic is the term 'butcher bird'. This name was given because of their habit of impaling prey on thorns or other suitable pointed objects. Whether this habit, which is shared by all the European species, serves the purpose of creating a 'larder', or is merely of help when the prey is dismembered and eaten, is not known, but it is certainly characteristic of the family.

In Europe five species nest. The remainder of the family is distributed over the Old World, but only poorly represented in the New World.

The plumages of shrikes, with their bold patterns, are

WHITE WAGTAIL *Motacilla alba alba* L 7" Very common in open country, farms, villages, towns and rocky areas, usually near water. Nests on ledges or in open holes, usually low above the ground. Black, grey and white plumage and long, constantly-wagged tail distinguish it from all other birds except Pied Wagtail. Immature resembles immature Grey Wagtail, but has white (not yellow) under tail-coverts and a dark area on breast. Sometimes has greenish and yellowish areas on head. Male in spring has more extensive black than female, particularly on side of neck. On female grey back also extends further up. In winter both have white throat, but distinctive crescent-shaped black area on upper breast. Outside breeding season usually seen in small flocks but sometimes congregates in large roosts in reedbeds in winter. Tail-wagging and bobbing of head when walking are characteristic. Runs very fast. Lives on insects taken on the ground but will occasionally catch them in the air like the flycatchers. Flight very undulating. Call is two-syllable 'tsweep'. Song, which is seldom heard, is twittering. RSWP

PIED WAGTAIL *Motacilla alba yarrellii* L 7" Subspecies of White Wagtail limited to British Isles and sporadically on adjacent continental coasts. (Locally in Norway, Germany, Holland, Belgium and north-western France). Habitat similar to that of White Wagtail. Adult bird easily told from White Wagtail by solid black back. Male told from female by more extensive black bib and side of neck. One year-olds resemble White Wagtails but upper rump is blackish, not grey. Immature resembles female White Wagtail in winter plumage closely but has whiter front and darker crown. Voice and behaviour similar to White Wagtail.

Red-backed Shrike

Masked Shrike

Woodchat Shrike

conspicuous. Except for the Red-backed, the sexes are similar. Most striking is the strong, hooked bill with which the prey is seized. The tail is rather long and the hawk-like impression is accentuated by the vicious expression given by the dark line through and over the eye, like a criminal's mask.

All our shrikes are migratory to some extent, but the Great Grey Shrike does not go very far. It preys mostly on rodents and birds and therefore is not deprived of its food by the northern winter.

Most of their hunting is done from an open perch on a wire or treetop in the bushy semi-open landscape that shrikes frequent. When a prey is spotted the shrike swoops down on it, seizing it with its powerful bill. The Great and Lesser Grey Shrikes may hover over the ground in the manner of the Kestrel. Great Grey Shrikes can also pursue small birds over some distance. Often the victim is not completely eaten at once, but speared to a thorn, barbed wire or broken-off branch. Such a store can contain remnants of many victims, mice, reptiles, birds and insects. Shrikes are solitary in their hunting and only few are seen together, even on migration.

Although the harsh call is the voice most often heard, shrikes are gifted songsters and their songs have a sweetness and

RED-BACKED SHRIKE *Lanius collurio* L 7" Common in open country with bushes. Notice chestnut-red back and wings of male. Female and juvenile are brown with closely barred breast. Told from juvenile Woodchat by uniform colour of upper side. Call is grating 'chaek'. Song, seldom heard, is an attractive warbled medley.
SP

MASKED SHRIKE *Lanius nubicus* L 8" Common in open, dry country with trees and bushes. Notice largely black upper side and long tail. Call is harsh. Song is subdued and monotonous.

WOODCHAT SHRIKE *Lanius senator* L 7" Common in open, dry country with trees and bushes, sometimes in more wooded areas. Notice black upper side with white shoulder patches and upper rump and striking red neck patch. Juvenile resembles juvenile Red-backed but has lighter upper side with traces of white shoulder patches and upper rump. The head is more square in shape. Hides among foliage more often than other shrikes. Call is harsh.
P

207

musical quality which it is surprising to find in such a pugnacious animal.

Both Red-backed and Woodchat Shrikes mimic other birds in their songs. The song of the Masked Shrike has been compared with that of the Olive-tree Warbler, an excellent songster even within its own family.

The nest is built in a bush or tree. Four to seven whitish to bluish eggs, with spots and streaks tending to form a zone, are laid. Incubation is by both sexes, except for the Red-backed where the female, which is much less boldly coloured than the male, alone incubates, often being fed on the nest by her mate.

Orioles

order *Passeriformes*, family *Oriolidae*

Only one of the twenty-eight species of this tropical Old World family is found in Europe. The Golden Oriole is thrush-like. The male is strikingly yellow and black, the female green. Every year the bird returns to the tropics whence it originally came.

The Golden Oriole lives secretively in the treetops where it finds fruit and insects to eat. Even though boldly coloured, the male is difficult to spot in the foliage and the far-reaching flute-like whistle is often the only evidence of its presence. The nest is a beautiful woven cup suspended from a horizontal branch high above the ground. The construction of this very sturdy nest is a complicated task performed by the female in the course of about a week. Three to five whitish eggs spotted with black are incubated for about two weeks.

Opposite Golden Orioles

LESSER GREY SHRIKE *Lanius minor* L 8" Common in open country with scattered trees and bushes. Resembles Great Grey Shrike but is stouter with shorter tail, more prominent white markings and more extensive mask. Call is harsh 'chek'.   V

GREAT GREY SHRIKE *Lanius excubitor* L 9½" Common in open country but prefers more well-wooded areas than most shrikes. Large size and pattern of black and white distinguish it. Compare with similar Lesser Grey Shrike. Often hovers. Call notes include shrill cries and rattles. Song is subdued with harsh notes interspersed.   WP

Lesser Grey Shrike

juv.

♂

juv.

♂

Great Grey Shrike

Arthur Singer

Golden Oriole

Rose-coloured Starling

Starling

Spotless Starling

Waxwing

♀

♂

juv.

juv.

summer

winter

summer

winter

GOLDEN ORIOLE *Oriolus oriolus* L 9½″ Fairly common in parks and old woods. Male unmistakable. Female and juvenile difficult to see as they stay high in the canopy but once spotted cannot be confused with any other European bird. Solitary in behaviour. Flight undulating. The simple song is a flute-like calling of its name: 'or-i-ole'; and it utters harsh, cat-like cries.　　P

ROSE-COLOURED STARLING *Sturnus roseus* L 8¼″ Common in open country. Irregular in west of breeding range. Rare vagrant to western Europe (particularly in late summer). Adult unmistakable. Juvenile resembles juvenile Starling but is paler. Gregarious. Mixes with Starling, which it resembles closely in habits and call.　　V

STARLING *Sturnus vulgaris* L 8½″ Abundant, especially near human habitation. Nests in boxes and holes in trees, walls, cliffs, etc. Notice short tail, speckled plumage and long bill. Flight silhouette characteristic with short tail and pointed wings. Gregarious. Flies in tight flocks, often numbering thousands of birds. Congregates in large roosts outside breeding season. Song is long, varied, with much mimicry. Call and flight call are squeaky.　　RW

SPOTLESS STARLING *Sturnus unicolor* L 8½″ Replaces Starling in south-westernmost Europe. Resembles Starling, but blacker in all plumages, in summer without white spots. Nests colonially. Song resembles that of Starling but is more powerful.

WAXWING *Bombycilla garrulus* L 7″ Common, breeding in coniferous woods. In winter also in parks and gardens. Erratic in occurence, with mass movements in certain years. Unmistakable with large crest. Flocks compact. Resembles Starling in flight. Call is trilling 'shree'.　　W

Starlings
order *Passeriformes,* family *Sturnidae*

The Starling is, next to the House Sparrow, the most widely known European bird. Its close relationship with man has made if familiar to everyone.

The starling family comprises 107 species, all of the Old World, though the Starling itself has been introduced into both North America and Australia where it has flourished. Besides the omnipresent Starling, two other species are found in Europe, the Spotless Starling, which is very similar to the Starling, and the Rose-coloured Starling, or Pastor, of south-east Europe.

The Starling is a partial migrant. The northern populations migrate whereas the southern are resident. Thus both native and foreign birds winter in the British Isles, but the two populations remain fairly distinct, and some British birds maintain their territories through the winter.

The Rose-coloured Starling has occurred very sporadically in most European countries. In some years invasions take place. These invasions are not spurred by lack of food in the normal range but rather by the opposite. Rose-coloured Starlings live mainly on locusts. When vast numbers of locusts occur in an area, migratory or wandering forms appear and soon leave the area in enormous swarms. Rose-coloured Starlings follow these swarms and may thus wander as far as the westernmost parts of Europe. They sometimes start nesting outside their regular breeding ground but these populations soon dwindle and disappear.

Starlings live on animal as well as vegetable matter. Over the year about half their food is animal matter (mainly insect pests), the other half vegetable, of which fruits are an important part.

Starlings are hole-nesters, taking advantage of almost any available cavity. In these they build their sometimes massive nests. Five to six bluish eggs are laid. Sometimes they raise two broods in a season. The Starling is an ardent vocalist although not necessarily a very beautiful one. The song consists of a large variety of whistles and notes often mimicking the calls and noise not only of other birds but also of trains and other mechanical sounds.

In late summer Starlings congregate in large flocks, often numbering thousands of birds. These flocks do not break up until the next spring, and pose problems by fouling and killing woods when they roost in them or by endangering aircraft on airfields where they sometimes settle. The large communal night roosts on large buildings present a similar problem. Thousands of pounds have been spent in finding and testing methods by which Starlings can be discouraged and chased away from these special areas. Methods tried so far include playing recordings of Starling warning calls, suspending hawks from balloons, and laying electric wires along the ledges of buildings.

Starlings were the first birds to be ringed in the modern way. This was done in Denmark in 1899 and the first group of 150 Starlings ringed yielded returns from the British Isles as well as from several continental countries. The success of the method led to the rapid spread of ringing for studies of migration; today hundreds of thousands of birds are ringed each year, and ringing recoveries give important information on the vital statistics of birds as well as on their movements both local and migratory.

Waxwings

order *Passeriformes*, family *Bombycillidae*

The Waxwing is the only representative of its family in Europe. It is related to the silky flycatchers of the New World, the Hypocolius of the Near East and the Palm Chat of the Caribbean. In fact this family is quite heterogeneous and ill-defined.

The Waxwing is a medium-sized passerine with a short erectile crest and a stubby tail. Its extremely beautiful colours enliven the monotony of the northern European winter. It breeds in north-eastern Europe in pine and fir woods and it is social in behaviour outside the breeding season. Normally Waxwings migrate south to return the next spring like most other migratory birds, but in some years immense flocks of Waxwings go on the move, reaching as far west as Ireland and south to Africa. These invasions are the more impressive as the birds appear in great numbers in places where they usually do not occur at all. The reason for an invasion is a great increase in population in years with large crops of berries on which the Waxwings depend in their northern breeding ground. This phenomenon of dense populations erupting into mass emigration is characteristic of many other animals, notably the lemmings, but we have very little understanding of the fundamental function of these wanderings. The years after an eruption usually see very small numbers breeding within the regular range of the species, and even though migrants may try to nest in other places, these attempts are generally unsuccessful.

Four or five spotted eggs are laid in a nest built in a tree. Incubation takes about two weeks. The nestlings are fed on insects but start eating berries as soon as they have left the nest.

Crows and Their Allies

order *Passeriformes*, family *Corvidae*

The crow family is considered by many to be the highest developed of all bird families, in a way corresponding to the primates among mammals. Their intelligence far exceeds that of most other birds but is of course not comparable with that of the more advanced mammals. In Scandinavian mythology, Odin, the chief god, had two Ravens, Hugin and Munin, who kept him informed about all that went on in the world, an example which shows that not only modern animal psychologists have ranked the Raven among the most intelligent of birds.

The family is almost world-wide in distribution, being absent only from New Zealand and most of the Pacific Islands. Twelve out of a total of 102 species breed in Europe.

Crows are the largest of all *Passeriformes*, the Raven having a total length of about twenty-five inches. The rest of our European species are medium-sized to large.

The family can be divided into several groups: the jays, which are colourful woodland birds; magpies with their striking plumage patterns and long tails; nutcrackers, whose bills are long and pointed so that they were once considered to be related to the woodpeckers; the choughs, inhabiting rocky and barren mountain country; and finally the true crows, the highest developed of all.

These birds all show the same heavy build and strong legs. Their flight is powerful and several of the larger species often soar very high in the fashion of birds of prey and storks. The choughs are probably the best fliers of all. They are usually seen

SIBERIAN JAY *Perisoreus infaustus* L 11" Fairly common. Almost exclusively confined to coniferous woods of the far north. Although resembling Jay in build, the longer tail, weaker bill and greyish-brown and reddish coloration distinguish it. The reddish colour of rump, tail and primaries is characteristic in flight. Flight silhouette resembles that of Jay but notice much longer, tapered tail. When searching for food in trees, movements resemble those of Great Tit. Call is loud, nasal 'pee-ach'.

JAY *Garrulus glandarius* L 14" Common. Prefers deciduous woods and parks. Notice white upper rump, and characteristic flight silhouette with weak, flapping flight on broad wings. Has habit of raising slight crest, giving head a square shape. Very restless, always on the move. Frequently jerks its tail. Usually encountered singly but in some winters in flocks. Often chased by smaller birds. Quite noisy, the call is an unmelodious 'skaaak'. RW

AZURE-WINGED MAGPIE *Cyanopica cyanus* L 14" Common but very local in its limited range (which represents a relic population as the main distribution is in China). Found in park-like and wooded landscapes. Builds open nests in small colonies. Unmistakable with black hood, blue wings and long blue tail. Juveniles have short tail. Usually seen in small groups. Flight is like Magpie's but not as heavy. Call is unmelodious 'kree-eek'.

MAGPIE *Pica pica* L 18", Tail 9" Very common. Prefers open and park-like landscapes, with scattered trees in which it builds its large domed nest. Often seen near human habitation but usually quite wary. The striking white and black colour pattern and extremely long tail are diagnostic. (Juveniles have short tails.) Flight is characteristic, with fast flapping followed by short glides. Usually seen in pairs; large flocks are rare and only seen at times of migration in northern part of range, but may roost in numbers. Call is fast, harsh chatter. R

Siberian Jay

Jay

Azure-winged Magpie

Magpie

juv.

213

Nutcracker

juv.

Chough

Alpine Chough

Jackdaw

NUTCRACKER *Nucifraga caryocatactes* L 13" Fairly common in coniferous forests in the mountainous areas of central Europe. Erratic in occurrence, as Siberian sub-species *N.c. macrorhynchos* (with thinner, longer bill) occasionally invades eastern, central and even western Europe in winters. Speckled plumage and characteristic flight silhouette with short tail and rounded wings make identification easy. Juveniles have fewer spots and are lighter brown. Notice broad black band on white under-side of tail. Flight is heavy. Outside breeding season usually seen in small flocks. Has preference for hazel nuts. Often perches in the open. Call is raucous 'grair'.
V

CHOUGH *Pyrrhocorax pyrrhocorax* L 15" Common in high mountains. Local along steep rocky coasts. Black with very rounded wings and square tail. Long decurved red bill distinguishes it from similar Alpine Chough, which has shorter, yellow bill. Juveniles have orange-red bill; otherwise similar to adult. Often seen in small parties and flocks. Flight strong and elegant and often soars. Nests colonially in crevices and caves. Call is high-pitched 'kiah' resembling Jackdaw, and other shrill, unmusical notes.
R

ALPINE CHOUGH *Pyrrhocorax graculus* L 15" Common in high mountains to the snow limit, going into valleys in winter. Nests colonially in crevices and caves. In winter often seen in mountain villages. Closely resembles Chough but has shorter, yellow bill and shorter tail, and is less glossy. Juveniles have darker legs. Bill yellow (orange in Chough). Habits similar to those of Chough but soars more often. Calls include loud, weird trills.

JACKDAW *Corvus monedula* L 13" Very common in old open woods, in villages, towns and around farms. Black plumage, with grey nape and sides of face, distinguishes it. Walks erect with bobbing movement of head. Head shape characteristic with high front. Flocks can in winter be mistaken for Pigeon flocks but notice slower wing-beats and more rounded wings of individual bird and more loose flock formation. Often soars and performs acrobatics in the air. Flight strong and agile. Social in behaviour. Flocks often mix with Rooks, Crows and Starlings in fields. Nests colonially in holes of trees or buildings. Call is rather high-pitched nasal 'jack', often repeated.
RSW

in flocks, soaring in the mountains, where they take advantage of the winds sweeping through the valleys and across the ridges. Suddenly they can be seen dropping into a ravine, looping, turning on their backs and performing a marvellous variety of impressive aerial acrobatics. Jackdaws, so common in many villages and towns, can likewise be seen performing beautifully in the air, appearing to play with the wind. Jays, on the other hand, have a much weaker flight and normally dislike flying any distance though some from the Continent move into Britain.

Most are sedentary, but the northerly populations of Magpie, Crow (or Carrion Crow), Rook and Jackdaw migrate to more favourable haunts in western Europe. The Alpine Chough, which inhabits high mountains, moves a little down the slopes in winter, thus displaying what is known as vertical migration, a characteristic of many other mountain birds.

The Jays of the north-east in some years move south in large flocks. The reason for this is probably shortage of food, particularly acorns. The invasions made by Nutcrackers are certainly caused by shortage of food. Two subspecies of Nut-cracker occur in Europe: the western Thick-billed and the more eastern Slender-billed. The Thick-billed is highly specialized in diet, preferring hazelnuts above all foods. During the autumn it hides deposits of nuts in the moss on the ground in the woods. The Slender-billed does the same with seeds of the cembra pine. During the winter, when the ground is covered with snow, they are able to find these stores by digging through the snow, often feet deep. It has also been shown that they are able to remember which stores they have already emptied, certainly an impressive feat of memory.

Jays are known to do the same with acorns, and the Siberian Jay hides berries and other food in trees, enabling it to survive in the most inhospitable of winter climates.

The other crows are much less specialized in their choice of food and will eat almost anything. Ravens and Crows often eat carcasses and Ravens are even known to attack sick small animals such as lambs and rabbits. Almost all, including the Jay, are egg-robbers in the breeding season and certainly do not reject the young of other birds when they get the chance. The Rook is more of a grain eater and can do some harm when occurring in large flocks on newly sown fields. The members of the crow family have been persecuted all over Europe for the harm they supposedly do (which is probably far less than most people think), but all except the Raven have been able to hold their own, proof of their great ability to adjust to circumstances.

Crows are noisy birds. Their call is hoarse and raucous. They do have real songs but these are very low and only heard over short distances. The primary function of the song is probably to coordinate the breeding behaviour.

Crows are social in their behaviour. Outside the breeding season they are usually seen in flocks of various sizes. Even the Magpie and the Siberian Jay, the least social of our crows, often assemble in groups in late winter, and may be seen chasing each other and posturing. These assemblies are supposed to bring the unpaired birds into contact with each other, a contact which is difficult for these highly sedentary species to accomplish otherwise. Some nest colonially. Best known are the colonies of Rooks in parks and woods, often close to human habitation, but Jackdaws are also colonial where nesting holes are available in sufficient numbers, for instance in ruins and churches. The Alpine Chough also nests colonially in caves and on sheltered ledges.

Arthur Singer

CARRION CROW *Corvus corone corone* L 18" Very common in all types of fairly open country, but also in cities. Black with only a little gloss. Best told from Rook by black base of bill (young Rooks also have this), heavier, more curved bill and much harsher crowing call. Generally more stout-looking than Rook and lacks characteristic 'thigh feathers' of this species. In flight broader wings and slower wing-beats distinguish it, even at a distance. Distinguished from Raven by smaller size, smaller bill and square tail. Forms flocks especially for roosting, but does not have same social organization as Rook, and pairs nest separately in trees or sea cliffs. RW

HOODED CROW *Corvus corone cornix* L 18" Sub-species of Carrion Crow but unmistakable with grey and black plumage. In abundance, habitat and habits similar to Carrion Crow, with which it often mixes and inter-breeds where ranges overlap. Birds intermediate between Hooded Crow and Carrion Crow are not uncommon in this zone. The light grey areas are then replaced with much darker colours. RW

RAVEN *Corvus corax* L 25" Common only in remote mountains and other undisturbed areas. Nests singly on ledges or in trees. Often frequents garbage dumps of mountain villages. Largest passerine. All-black with large bill and long, wedge-shaped tail distinguishing it from Crows as well as birds of prey. It flaps less and soars more than Crow. Often performs acrobatics in flight. Wary. Usually seen singly, in pairs or, at favoured feeding grounds and around carcasses, in small groups. Call is very deep and hoarse croak. RW

The Jackdaw's complex social behaviour has been studied in detail by Konrad Lorenz. Jackdaws have a highly developed 'pecking order' in which one is the leader who has right of way over all the others in the group. After him is another bird which has right of way over all except number one, and so on. Females do not marry below their social rank and are raised in social rank when marrying a male of higher status. The members of a colony accept each other to a very great degree even near their own nests whereas outsiders are attacked by the group unless 'introduced' by a member. If young ones get lost away from the colony, older birds will set out to find them and lead them back. Attacking enemies is a communal affair in which all take part very vocally.

Many crows pair for life. The nest is built in early spring. The

Carrion Crow

Hooded Crow

Raven

Rook

ROOK *Corvus frugilegus* L 18" Very common in cultivated fields with groups of trees or small woods. Glossy black plumage, with rather long straight bill and pale area around base of bill, distinguishes it from Carrion Crow. On ground, notice more loosely feathered thighs. Juveniles lack pale area around base of bill and have less prominent iridescence of plumage. Told from Carrion Crow by straighter, weaker bill and slimmer build. Usually seen in flocks. Wings narrower and wingbeats faster than those of Carrion Crow. Nests colonially in groves or wood edges. Social throughout the year and in winter Jackdaws, Starlings and Crows often associate in foraging flocks. In colonies, Jackdaws and sometimes Long-eared Owls are found nesting in unoccupied Rook nests. Call is more nasal but less harsh than Crow's.
RW

northern species, like the Siberian Jay and the Nutcracker, often start nesting long before the snow is off the ground, and their nests are extremely well insulated. Except for the Nutcracker, which often lays eggs in sub-zero weather, only the female broods the two to six green or blue eggs, spotted or streaked with brown. The males of most species feed the females while they are on the nest. The nests of choughs and Jackdaws vary in size with the cavity in which they are built. The Magpie builds large domed nests, a familiar sight around farms. Jackdaws and Magpies often adorn their nests with shiny objects, a habit which has given them a reputation as thieves.

The gorgeous Azure-winged Magpies build open nests, usually in scattered groups. In Europe they occur only in the Iberian peninsula, but another population is found in China. The reason for this strange distribution is unknown.

Dippers
order *Passeriformes*, family *Cinclidae*

Only one of the four species of this unique family is found in Europe. The four species resemble each other closely. They are starling-sized and plump-looking, with rather long legs and a short tail. The European species is brownish black with a large white 'bib'.

DIPPER *Cinclus cinclus* L 7" Fairly common along swift-flowing mountain streams, in winter sometimes along shores. Notice short tail cocked slightly upward and large white breast patch. Constantly bobs up and down when perched (usually on rocks). Lies low in water when swimming. Flight low and direct. Call is short 'zirb'. Song, which can be heard even in winter, resembles that of Wren with grating notes. Continental populations lack chestnut on the underparts.
R

Dipper

juv.

The Dipper specializes in an aquatic life and is the only passerine so adapted. Although superficially it appears to be built like any other passerine, closer examination reveals small specialized traits such as the lack of air sacs in the bones, the ability to close the ears and nostrils, and feathers especially water tight: all adaptations to its diving habits. The Dipper is always found near running water, often very turbulent streams where the lively bird can be seen dashing in and out of even the most violent cascades of water. It finds its food on the bottom, and though it is able to cling to stones and pebbles with its claws, it propels itself mainly by means of its short wings. Even though it lacks the webbing of the toes common to most other swimming birds, it swims well. The flight is fast and direct, usually very low over the surface of the water. It can dive directly from flight and commonly becomes airborne immediately after the dive. Most often the Dipper is seen by mountain streams, and in winter it only moves when forced to do so by freezing of the northern rivers and streams.

The Dipper has a very pleasant song, which it utters from a bank or a rock. The song is quite similar to the Wren's, which the Dipper resembles considerably in general body shape.

The nest is domed, usually placed very close to the water's edge in steep river banks. It can even build a nest under a waterfall so that it has to fly through the falling water to reach the site. The four or five white eggs are incubated for about two weeks. When the young leave the nest, they are not yet able to fly but swim very well.

Wrens

order *Passeriformes*, family *Troglodytidae*

The single European representative of this otherwise American family is among our smallest birds. Although it is skulking in behaviour, most people have seen this tiny bird as it flies low over the ground to disappear into a thicket or among rocks and boulders. It is small and plump with a pointed bill with which it extracts pupae, snails and other minute animals from cracks and crevices. The tail is very short, often cocked straight into the air giving the bright brown little bird a rather comical look.

Most of the European Wrens are residents and in severe winters many succumb, but the populations are soon re-established because of the great fertility of the species.

The beautiful song of the Wren can be heard in all months of the year. It is very loud for a bird its size. By the song the males announce their territories which they maintain all year round, and in spring they attract the females to the many unfinished domed nests they have built. The female selects one of these and finishes it by lining the inside with feathers and other soft materials before laying her five or six eggs, which are white, spotted with brown. She alone incubates and while she does so, the male may be successful in attracting another female to take advantage of one of the other nests he has built. This polygamous behaviour of the Wren only occurs in some areas, usually where living conditions are particularly favourable and the female is able to rear the young without help. When the young leave the nest, they stay together for some time and the parents may even lead them to special roosts, cavities or old nests, to spend the night huddled up together. Much larger roosts have been recorded in winter.

WREN *Troglodytes troglodytes* L 4″ Common among thick undergrowth in woods and gardens, but also found on remote islands and among rocks high in the hills. Small size, tail cocked upward and brown plumage identify it. Keeps low, well in cover. Call is harsh and grating. Song is rapid succession of very high, clear notes and trills.   R

Wren

Accentors

order *Passeriformes*, family *Prunellidae*

Accentor is the name of the family to which the familiar Dunnock or Hedge Sparrow belongs. Accentors are sparrow-sized grey and brown birds with thin pointed bills. They are truly Palearctic. Most of the twelve species are montane, the Alpine Accentor breeding as high as the snow limit. The Siberian Accentor is found in northern Asia, reaching the Ural Mountains in the west. It winters in east Asia and individuals are reported in Europe only rarely.

The Dunnock inhabits scrub and hedges and is often found in gardens. It visits feeding stations, where it is easily told from the sparrows by its more delicate build. Rather skulking in behaviour, it seems afraid of everything and prefers to remain

Alpine Accentor

Siberian Accentor

Dunnock

ALPINE ACCENTOR *Prunella collaris* L 7″ Common in high mountains above tree limit. Resembles Dunnock but notice spotted white throat and brown spots on flanks. Call is a short vibrating trill. Warbling song is given from ground or in song-flight.　　　　V

SIBERIAN ACCENTOR *Prunella montanella* L 7″ A very rare visitor from Asia to eastern Europe. Notice prominent ochreous stripe over eye.

DUNNOCK *Prunella modularis* L 6″ Common in gardens and woods with thick undergrowth but also on scrub-clad hills. Notice slate-coloured head and breast and striped, brown back. Song is short, high-pitched tinkling usually from exposed perch.　　　　RP

hidden under bushes, creeping about in a mouse-like way.

The Dunnock's nest is an open cup placed a few feet above the ground in a tree or bush. It contains three to six pure blue eggs, which are incubated for eleven to twelve days. In Britain the Dunnock is one of the Cuckoo's favourite hosts.

The song of the Dunnock, which is delivered from the top of a low bush or tree or from cover, is high-pitched but very pleasant-sounding. The Alpine Accentor, indigenous to the high mountains of southern and central Europe, is not often encountered outside its normal haunts. But in the high mountains it is commonly seen among boulders and low bushes, sometimes even in small loose flocks. Like the Dunnock it is unobtrusive. The nest is usually built in a crevice. It contains four or five pale blue eggs, which are incubated by both male and female for about two weeks.

Tits

order *Passeriformes*, family *Paridae*

Almost everyone with a garden or a bird-feeder knows the tits, the small active birds with chunky appearance and short stout bills. Some of the tits associate themselves closely with man, others not, but most can be approached and observed easily and their breeding habits can be followed in the greatest detail as they readily use nest boxes.

MARSH TIT *Parus palustris* L 4½″ Common in deciduous wood with undergrowth, thickets and parks. Resembles Willow Tit but has shorter black bib, glossy cap and uniformly coloured wing. Juveniles cannot with certainty be distinguished from juvenile Willow Tits. In the hand note that all tail-feathers are same length, whereas tail of Willow Tit is rounded (outside feathers a little shorter than central feathers). Best distinguished from Willow Tit by voice. Typical calls are loud 'pitchu' and repeated, scolding 'tzee'. Usual song, a repeated 'tschuppi'.　　　　R

Willow Tit
Scandinavian
subspecies

Marsh Tit

Willow Tit

The family *Paridae* has other members than the familiar tits: the nuthatches (subfamily *Sittinae*) and the Wallcreeper (subfamily *Tichodromadinae*), which will be discussed later in this section.

The tits belonging to the subfamily *Parinae* are the ones we know best. Alert, active and usually distinctly coloured, particularly on the head, they are welcome and frequent guests in almost every garden.

Nine of the forty-three recognized species breed in Europe. The Sombre Tit is confined to the extreme south-eastern part of Europe, the Siberian Tit to the north, and the astonishingly

WILLOW TIT *Parus montanus* L 4½″ Common in deciduous, mixed and coniferous woods with stronger affinity for wet situations than Marsh Tit. Most striking characteristic of the northern subspecies *Parus montanus borealis*, found in Scandinavia and northern Russia, is the pure white cheek. In rest of Europe resembles Marsh Tit more but has larger bib, no gloss on cap, and light area on wing. Juveniles cannot safely be distinguished from juvenile Marsh Tit. Call is a repeated nasal 'tchay'. Usual song is drawn-out 'tew tew tew', but there is also an unexpected warbling song, seldom heard in some areas.　　　　R

Sombre Tit

Siberian Tit

SOMBRE TIT *Parus lugubris* L 5½″ Fairly common in deciduous and mixed woods and thickets in rocky country. Large, with long bill and bib. Has much less brown in plumage than Marsh, Willow or Siberian Tit. Not social in behaviour and more wary than most tits. Call resembles that of Great Tit.

SIBERIAN TIT *Parus cinctus* L 5¼″ Common in coniferous and mixed woods. Large tit, with brown cap and large black bib which is not sharply delineated from the buffish underside. Plumage more loose than that of other tits giving it a rather untidy look. Call resembles that of Willow Tit but is even more drawn out.

beautiful Azure Tit to the extreme east. As all three of these species are sedentary, there is little chance of seeing them outside their regular ranges, although the Azure Tit has been recorded as far west as eastern France. Generally the tits are resident, although some of the northern populations will move south particularly in years of high population density. This is true of the Great, Blue and Coal Tits in particular. They do not reach very far south and scarcely need to, as they are hardy little birds, well able to survive severe weather conditions.

Tits live mainly on insects and seeds. The smallest of our tits, the Coal Tit, has a very thin bill with which it extracts insects from narrow cracks, most commonly in evergreens. The Crested Tit, frequenting the same type of woods, prefers larger insects as does the Willow Tit. All three also eat large amounts of fir and pine seed, particularly in winter.

Blue Tits and Marsh Tits, found together with Great Tits in deciduous woods and parks, take larger prey and seeds. The Blue Tit finds its food higher in the trees and bushes than the Great Tit. These three species are often attracted to feed at bird tables. Here they are particularly fond of fat and meat although seeds are also eaten with pleasure. Some tits, especially the Great and Blue Tits, have found a rather unusual way of obtaining the fats they like: they pierce the tops of milk bottles left outside a door by the early milkman and drink the top layer, often to the distress of the late arising rightful owner. The spread of this habit, which has taken place in the last ten to fifteen years in Britain, shows the ease with which tits are able to learn from chance experience, an ability which has also been demonstrated in the laboratory.

Crested Tit

Blue Tit

CRESTED TIT *Parus cristatus* L 4½″ Common in coniferous and mixed woods. Prominent crest diagnostic. Greyish. Black facial markings characteristic, also of the juvenile which has smaller crest. Sometimes associated with Coal Tit, which it resembles in habits, but is less sociable than most tits. Rarely uses nest boxes. Call is characteristic purring trill.   R

BLUE TIT *Parus caeruleus* L 4½″ Very common in all kinds of woods, parks and gardens. Outside breeding season frequently found in reed-beds. Blue cap diagnostic. Characteristically explores branches and trunks of trees and bushes, less often coming to the ground than Great Tit. Quite aggressive in behaviour. Call varied, but most commonly a high-pitched 'zee', often repeated several times and sometimes introducing trilling song.
                                                                                        RP

Another curious habit of the tits is the hoarding of food. This is particularly common among the northern populations, and in the season of more plentiful food (late summer and early autumn) they will be very active, finding food and hiding it under bark, in the earth or among the needles of the trees in their home areas. This store is then eaten in winter when food is scarce. This habit is characteristic of the Crested Tit, Coal Tit, Siberian Tit, Willow and Marsh Tits. Blue Tit and Great Tit rarely hoard food.

In the winter most tits move about in flocks, usually consisting of several different species, and even Lesser Spotted Woodpeckers, Nuthatches, Treecreepers and Goldcrests will join them. The distances covered by these flocks are usually quite small and within a limited area of the wood; only occasionally dothey venture more than a few miles. Great, Blue and Marsh Tits often move from the woods into nearby gardens where they have a greater chance to obtain food deliberately or inadvertently left out for them. During the winter many tits spend the night in old nest holes and boxes, well protected from the cold and snow outside.

In spring individual territories are set up and song activity increases. The very familiarity of the song of the tits makes them pleasant to hear. The 'saw-sharpening' of the Great Tit is a well-known sound in woods, gardens and parks; it has a great vocabulary to choose from, though most of its songs are rather metallic. The other tits also have rather repetitive calls and songs, but they are not renowned for the quality of their vocal performance.

All tits are hole nesters, preferring old woodpecker nests or

Azure Tit

Coal Tit

Great Tit

other tree cavities. The Coal and Sombre Tits often use holes among stones on the ground. Blue, Great and Marsh Tit will often, if there are no tree cavities available, use other locations for their nests: old tins, letter-boxes, etc. Blue, Great, Marsh and Coal Tits will readily use nest boxes. Willow Tit and Crested Tit prefer to excavate their own holes in rotting tree stumps. Although many tits will be happy to use nest boxes with any size of hole or cavity, experience has shown that the diameter of the entrance hole is particularly important if one wants to attract certain species and to exclude others, like House Sparrows and Starlings. The best diameters for the entrance hole are given below:

Great Tit: $1\frac{1}{8}$ in.   Coal Tit: $1\frac{1}{8}$ in.
Blue Tit: $1-1\frac{1}{8}$ in.   Marsh Tit: $1-1\frac{1}{8}$ in.

The nest cavity has a basis of moss and the cup of the nest is neatly lined with hair or feathers, or both. Four to fourteen, sometimes up to eighteen, eggs are laid and incubated by the female alone for about two weeks after the last egg is laid. The female is often fed on the nest by the male.

After the young hatch comes the busiest time for the parents. To satisfy the hunger of the numerous offspring they have to be constantly on the move. They may make more than nine hundred visits bringing food to the nest in a day. In years with comparatively few insects, many young die from starvation

AZURE TIT *Parus cyanus* L $5\frac{1}{4}$" Common in deciduous and mixed woods around lakes and streams. Very rare visitor to central and western Europe. White head and blue back diagnostic. Rather long-billed. Much more blue than Blue Tit. Two white wing-bars are prominent, particularly in flight. Call 'tseerr'. Song is loud and trilling.

COAL TIT *Parus ater* L $4\frac{1}{2}$" Common in coniferous and mixed woods. Outside breeding season sometimes associated with Crested Tit, more often in unmixed flocks or mixed with other tits. Black head, with white on cheek and nape of neck, and buffish white underside are diagnostic. Short-tailed. Often feeds near trunk of trees but also in the outermost branches of evergreens. Call is a thin 'tset', more plaintive than that of other tits. Song is a repeated 'weetse'.   R

GREAT TIT *Parus major* L $5\frac{1}{2}$" Very common in all kinds of woods, parks and gardens. Large size and black central stripe through yellow underside diagnostic. Stripe broader in male than female. Often seen in flocks mixed with other tits, when its larger size distinguishes it at a glance, but less gregarious than most species. Often searches for food in low bushes and even on the ground. Calls numerous, and usually stronger than those of other tits. Song is a very characteristic penetrating, metallic series of 'zee-de' notes.   RP

Opposite Great Tit and Blue Tits

224

Arthur Singer

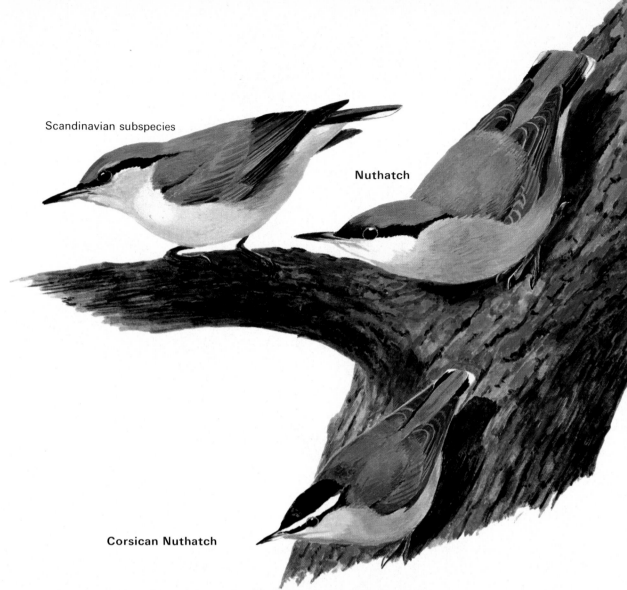

Scandinavian subspecies

Nuthatch

Corsican Nuthatch

NUTHATCH *Sitta europaea* L 5½″ Common in mature deciduous and mixed woods, parks and gardens. Besides woodpecker-like silhouette, distinguished by bluish-grey upper side and chestnut-coloured flanks. Colour of underside in adults varies from white in *Sitta europaea europaea,* found in Scandinavia and northern Russia, to clear buff in *Sitta europaea caesia* of western Europe. Intermediates occur. Best told from very similar Rock Nuthatch by habitat, stronger colours and white spots on tail. Calls are tit-like. Typical song is a characteristic, repeated, musical 'tueeh'. Does not drum like wood-peckers, but hammering on nuts of various sorts to open them can often be heard. Nests in tree holes, often reducing size of entrance hole with mud. R

CORSICAN NUTHATCH *Sitta whiteheadi* L 4½″ Fair-ly common in mountain woods and groves. Resembles small Nuthatch but notice distinct head pattern, with black crown and distinct white line over the eye. Female and juveniles are duller in colours, but pattern is dis-tinctive. Underside is clean white. Habits resemble those of Nuthatch, but more retiring. Excavates its own nest in trees. Call is much more nasal and quieter than that of Nuthatch. Song consists of two phrases of different pitch.

in the nest, but in good years most survive. The large clutch size seems to be of survival value for the species, as it insures maximum use of the available food supply.

The young are ready to leave the nest when about two and a half weeks old, after which Blue and Great Tits often rear a second brood, though this is unusual in Britain. Tits are extremely easy to attract both by feeding and by supplying them with nesting cavities. They are therefore ideal for the birdwatcher who wants to study a species at close range.

Nuthatches
family *Paridae*, subfamily *Sittinae*

These are small, woodpecker-like birds. They climb trees and rocks with great dexterity and can even run downward head first, a unique accomplishment among birds. There are three species nesting in Europe, the Nuthatch, Neumayer's Rock Nuthatch and the smaller Corsican Nuthatch, all of which are sedentary in behaviour. Nuthatches are found almost exclusively in deciduous and mixed woods where they use old woodpecker holes or natural cavities as nesting sites. They have a peculiar habit of reducing the size of the nesting hole with mud. This habit has been developed even further by the Rock Nuthatch which finds a half-open crevice or hole in rock which it encloses completely and furnishes with an entrance tube of mud. Six to eight eggs are laid and incubated for about two weeks. The young spend about three and a half weeks in the hole before venturing outside.

Nuthatches have very penetrating, monotonous calls, usually a long series of repetitions of the same note.

Wallcreepers
family *Paridae*, subfamily *Tichodromadinae*

This subfamily is represented in Europe by one species which is confined to the higher mountains of continental Europe. It looks very different from the other members of the family, with very broad wings and a long decurved bill. It is exquisitely beautiful but unfortunately quite rare and not often seen. It

Neumayer's Rock Nuthatch

finds its food among steep rocks, which it negotiates with great elegance. The nest is placed in a crevice. In winter the Wallcreeper moves to a lower altitude in the same area.

Long-tailed Tits
family *Paridae*, subfamily *Aegithalinae*

The eight species of this subfamily differ from other tits in many ways. The Long-tailed Tit is the only European representative. It looks like a cotton ball on a stick, the tail being extremely long in proportion to the size of the bird. Its bill is small and the Long-tailed Tit lives mostly on insects. Most Long-tailed Tits are resident although the northern and particularly eastern populations in some years may undertake rather extensive movements to milder climates. In winter they form small flocks which roam the woods. The flocks rarely exceed ten to fifteen birds and sometimes mix with other tits. The flock is tightly knit and individuals stay close together. At the roost, usually a branch or root in a well-protected place, the birds sleep close together. When two birds have settled, the other members will squeeze in between them. This is repeated until the whole flock has settled so close that it would be almost impossible to distinguish each individual bird if it were not for the long tails hanging below the branch.

The Long-tailed Tit does not nest in holes, but builds a beautiful and elaborate domed nest, completely covered on the

NEUMAYER'S ROCK NUTHATCH *Sitta neumayer* L 5½" Common on rocky slopes and mountains with scattered bushes. Resembles Nuthatch closely but colours are paler and it lacks white spots on tail. Very active, darting among the rocks. In movements and stance it is very similar to Nuthatch except that it climbs rocks instead of trees. Nests in crevices and holes in rocks, adding funnel-shaped entrance of mud. Very noisy, with loud and high-pitched calls, less musical than those of Nuthatch. It has a large variety of calls. Song is a loud, descending trill.

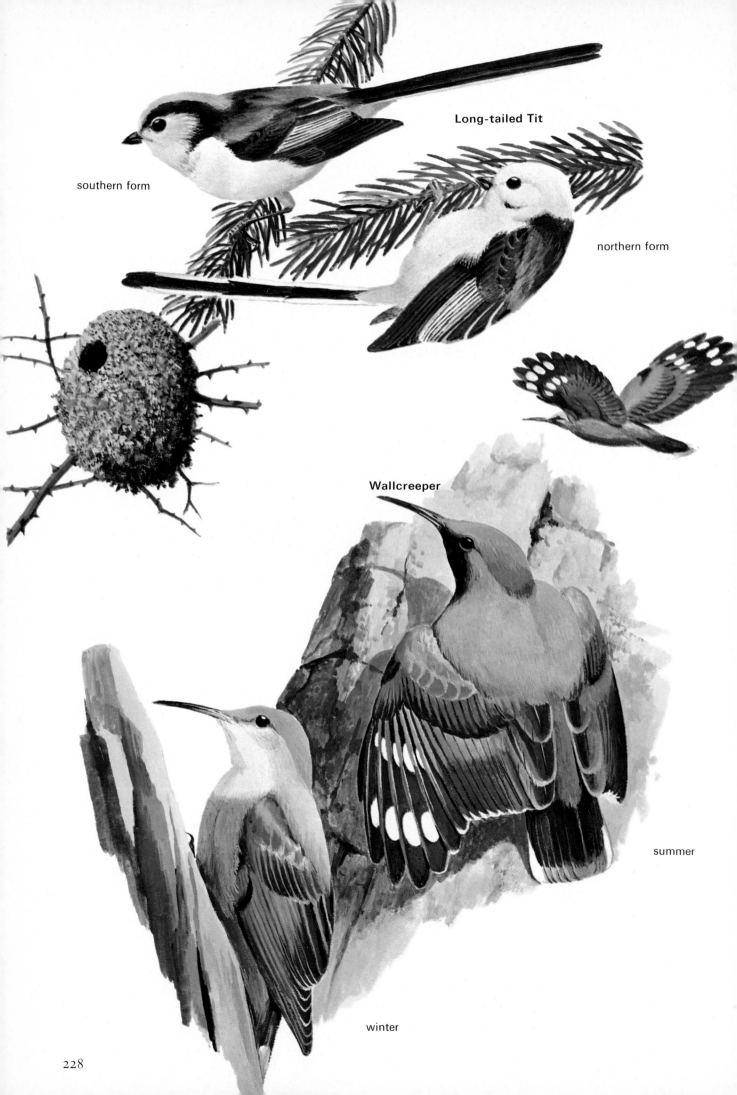

Long-tailed Tit

southern form

northern form

Wallcreeper

summer

winter

LONG-TAILED TIT *Aegithalos caudatus* L 5½" Common in undergrowth in woods, thickets, parks and gardens. In winter often seen with other tits. Small size, black and white plumage with very long tail distinguish it from other tits. Northern subspecies *Aegithalos caudatus caudatus* has completely white head and is found in Scandinavia, Baltic states and northern Russia. Southern subspecies *A.c. rosaceus* has wide black stripe above the eye. Intermediates found in central Europe. Resembles other tits in habits but rarely feeds at bird tables. Nest is domed, lichen-covered and built in bushes or forks of trees. Call is a repeated trilling 'tsimp' and thin 'see-see-see'. Song, rarely heard, is a mixture of these notes.   R

WALLCREEPER *Tichodroma muraria* L 6½" Uncommon and local in high mountains to snow limit, moving further down in winter. A very rare visitor outside its normal range in autumn, winter and spring, when it also occurs on buildings and ruins. Characterized by long, decurved bill, greyish upper parts and in summer black, in winter whitish, underside. Most striking are the wide, rounded wings with large red areas and white spots. Flight characteristically fluttering. Climbs on rocks looking for insects, but can also be seen perched in trees. Call is thin and piping. Song is a repeated, accelerated and rising, high-pitched 'zee-zee-zee-tui'.   V

PENDULINE TIT *Remiz pendulinus* L 4¼" Locally common in riparian bushes and thickets. Sporadic in occurrence, extending its range towards the north-west. Black mask on generally brown bird distinguishes adult. Juvenile lacks the black mask and is more greyish brown but is easily told from juvenile Bearded Tit by much shorter tail. Habits somewhat resemble those of tits. Call is a drawn-out, sweet 'zee-eh'. Song is twittering, but it is quiet and only heard for a short time.   V

outside with moss and lichen, and lined with as many as two thousand feathers. The construction, by both male and female, takes about three weeks. The six to twelve round, white, faintly speckled eggs are incubated for a little more than two weeks by both parents and the young stay in the nest for another fifteen to sixteen days.

Penduline Tits
order *Passeriformes*, family *Remizidae*

Although the penduline tits resemble the other tits in looks and movements, they differ in many other aspects, both in choice of habitat and in particular breeding habits. The family is small and only one species, the Penduline Tit, is found in Europe, where it occurs locally and widely scattered. At first sight the conical, pointed bill is strikingly different from the bill of the true tits, which the bird otherwise resembles in proportion and build. It lives on insects but also takes some seeds. Its preferred habitat is always close to water, usually in lush vegetation with many trees. It often searches for food in reeds, where it climbs about with great dexterity.

It has earned its name from the beautifully constructed globular nest which is suspended from one of the outer branches of a tree. The male starts the nest by making a ring suspended from the branch. From this ring the rest of the nest is constructed, and finally a tubular side entrance is attached. While constructing the nest, he only takes a short time off for feeding and singing. The similar nest of one of the African species is so solidly constructed that it is used locally as a purse.

A female attracted by the male's song will join him, but her activity at the nest is limited to providing the inner lining. Once

Penduline Tit

juv.

finished—the whole construction takes from two to three weeks—she will lay the five to eight white eggs and start incubating them. The male will then start constructing another nest and may be successful in attracting a second female to take possession of it. Energetic males may even repeat this behaviour several times.

The male does not take any part in the rearing of the young, and ignores all such activities in his territory. The female incubates for about two weeks and the young, which are fed by her alone, stay in the nest for another two weeks before they start venturing outside. For some time they will return to the nest for the night. The exhausted female may retain enough energy (and hormones) to start a second brood, but this is uncommon.

In autumn and winter Penduline Tits leave the nesting area and spend most of the cold season in the south, but not much is known about their life outside the breeding season.

Treecreepers
order *Passeriformes*, family *Certhiidae*

Treecreepers are among the most unobtrusive of all birds. Speckled brown, with a usually low call and timid, unaggressive behaviour, they tend to escape notice. They share with nuthatches and woodpeckers the habit of climbing tree trunks and branches. The treecreepers' tail is short and stiff and is used as a support. The bill is rather long, slightly decurved and very thin. It is a far cry from the 'chisels' of woodpeckers and nuthatches and treecreepers have to pick what is on the surface or in crevices of the bark. Sometimes a treecreeper will follow a woodpecker up a tree, picking what the larger bird has left behind. The food is mainly insects and spiders and their eggs, but sometimes small seeds are taken as well, mainly in winter when animal food is scarce.

It is interesting to watch a treecreeper feeding: it goes more systematically about the chore than most birds, starting at the bottom of a tree trunk or branch, working its way upward in a spiral. When it reaches the top, it drops to the bottom of another tree to start its search there.

Treecreepers are not very sociable but sometimes they join flocks of tits in the winter. Most are resident, although some of the northernmost birds move a little southward in winter. During this migration treecreepers can sometimes be seen miles

TREECREEPER *Certhia familiaris* L 5" Common in mature woods, parks and gardens, both coniferous and deciduous. In southern Europe where occurring with Short-toed Treecreeper, shows greater preference for coniferous woods at higher elevations. Inconspicuous but easily told from other birds except Short-toed Treecreeper from which it is distinguished by more distinct stripe over eye, lack of buffish brown on flank and more contrasting reddish rump. Call is a single very high note. Song is high, faint and accelerated.   R

SHORT-TOED TREECREEPER *Certhia brachydactyla* L 5" Common in mature deciduous woods, parks and gardens, usually at lower elevations than Treecreeper, particularly in southern part of its range. Resembles Treecreeper closely but has less distinct stripe over eye and has buffish brown flanks. The rump is not as rusty as that of the Treecreeper. In the hand it can be distinguished by its shorter toes. Bill is a little longer than that of Treecreeper. Habits like Treecreeper's. Call is a firm 'zeet'. Song is more plaintive than that of Treecreeper, and may be delivered from exposed perch.

Treecreeper

Short-toed Treecreeper

away from the nearest tree, a most unusual thing for a bird so tied to woods. Treecreepers have characteristic high-pitched calls and each species has a simple but rather elusive song.

The nest is usually sited behind dead bark or in other crevices. One has even been found built in the foundation of a Goshawk's nest. Four to eight speckled eggs are incubated for two weeks, and another two weeks elapse before the young are ready to leave the nest.

Treecreepers have special cracks where they spend the night. Usually they sleep alone but occasionally several birds will join and thus diminish the loss of heat. The two European species, the Treecreeper and the Short-toed Treecreeper, are very similar and are best told apart by their different songs and calls. Only shades of colour distinguish their plumages.

Warblers and Their Allies

order *Passeriformes*, family *Muscicapidae*

When the term 'songbird' is used, most people associate it offhand with members of this large heterogeneous family, although it refers to all the *Oscines*. Many of the *Muscicapidae* are certainly among our best singers.

These birds are mainly insectivorous, but many also take berries. Their bills are slender and pointed and they are in general delicately built. In Europe four subfamilies occur: the warblers (subfamily *Sylviinae*), or Old World warblers to distinguish them from the superficially similar New World warblers which are members of a completely different family (*Parulidae*); the Old World flycatchers (subfamily *Muscicapinae*); the thrushes and their allies (termed 'chats' by some) (subfamily *Turdinae*); and the Bearded Tit, the only European representative of the babblers (*Timaliinae*). Other, non-European subfamilies are the parrotbills (*Paradoxornithinae*), rail babblers (*Cinclosomatinae*), gnatcatchers (*Polioptilinae*), Australian wrens (*Malurinae*) and thickheads (*Pachycephalinae*). All are primarily found in the Old World. In the following pages the four subfamilies will be treated separately.

CETTI'S WARBLER *Cettia cetti* L 5½″ Common in dense low vegetation of ditches, streams and swamps where it stays well hidden and is difficult to see. Notice unstriped, dark, rich chestnut-brown upper side, greyish white underside and white stripe over eye which distinguishes it from all related species. There is a small whitish area below the eyes. Tail wide and rounded, rather untidy-looking. Wings are short and rounded. Flicks tail downward. Bill is thin and pointed. Sexes similar. More often heard than seen. Call is a short 'teck'. Song, which starts and ends abruptly, is very loud and consists of repeated variations of 'cettee', given from well-hidden perch.   V

Cetti's Warbler

Warblers

family *Muscicapidae*, subfamily *Sylviinae*

Even before the sun has risen above the horizon, as the darkness of the spring night is slowly retreating, the early wanderer will hear the songs of many birds. While walking through the woods, he will notice how the voices are at first few, and the songs given at long intervals. As daybreak approaches and the dark masses of trees and bushes take definite forms, the air seems to explode in song. From every bush and tree the voices greet the coming day. Perhaps he notices a particularly liquid song which keeps ringing pleasantly in his ear. In his attempt to find the bird which sings so persistently, he may have to spend some time, and his search may disappoint him because the songster is a small inconspicuous bird, greenish in colour and remarkable only for its song. It is the Willow Warbler, one of the most numerous European birds and a typical leaf-warbler.

In general warblers are inconspicuously coloured. They are small, thin-billed birds, usually very active and found in woods,

SAVI'S WARBLER *Locustella luscinioides* L 5½" Common but local in dense reed-beds and swamps with scattered bushes. Unstriped reddish olive-brown above, whitish below with poorly pronounced stripe over eye. Darker than the other swamp warblers. Tail long, wide and rounded. Call is a subdued 'tsek'. Song resembles that of Grasshopper Warbler but is shorter, deeper and with a much higher frequency. Song is more monotonous than that of River Warbler, which is broken up into short sections. Song often starts slowly. Sings from exposed perch in reeds or bushes.   S

RIVER WARBLER *Locustella fluviatilis* L 5" Common among dense bushes and other vegetation in moist areas of woods and clearings. Unstriped olive-brown above with warmer brown tail, whitish below with faint spotting on throat, breast and flanks. Has whitish stripe above the eye. Tail wide and rounded. Under tail-coverts are brownish with white tips. Stays well hidden in dense vegetation. Call is harsh. Song, which is given from exposed low perch, is trilling, resembling Grasshopper Warbler, but with individual notes clearly separated. Less monotonous, more broken, than that of Grasshopper and Savi's Warblers. Sings mostly at dusk, even at night.   V

Savi's Warbler

River Warbler

PALLAS' GRASSHOPPER WARBLER *Locustella certhiola* L 5" A very rate autumn visitor to north-western Europe from Asia. Found in swamps, marshes and meadows with dense vegetation. Resembles Sedge Warbler but has more pronounced stripe over eye, darker upper side and dark tail contrasting with lighter rump and lighter underside, usually with a few breast spots. Leg colour is pink but this is difficult to see. Told from Grasshopper Warbler by having reddish, dark, streaked rump and greyish tail becoming gradually darker towards the tip, which has narrow whitish vein (difficult to see and not always present). Immatures have less pronounced stripe over eye but more often spots on breast. Habits resemble those of Grasshopper Warbler; keeps well hidden in dense vegetation. Sharp two-note call.   V

PADDY-FIELD WARBLER *Acrocephalus agricola* L 5" Common in dense vegetation of swamps and lake-sides. A very rare autumn visitor to western Europe. Resembles Reed Warbler closely but is paler greenish brown, with more pronounced stripe over eye. Rump more rust-coloured than in other *Acrocephalus* species. Wings more rounded. (2nd primary shorter than in Marsh and Reed Warbler). Call is described as 'schick'. Song resembles that of Marsh Warbler.   V

bushes or reeds, rarely venturing into open country. During the summer warblers can be found almost anywhere where there are bushes or other dense vegetation and their beautiful songs have become an integral feature of all but the most open landscape. Nearly fifty different species of this subfamily are found in Europe, and as many of these vary only in details of plumage, this group is a nightmare to the beginner in bird-watching. With a certain amount of practice identification becomes less confusing and certain helpful patterns emerge, as well as the characteristic songs of the different species. First, there is the habitat in which the bird is seen.

In swamps and reed-beds occur a large number of species of brown warblers. Some show particular preferences, like that of the Marsh Warbler for thickets of nettles. They are rather long-tailed with long, thin bills. Some have distinctly striped backs, like the Sedge Warbler; others are uniformly coloured above, like the Reed Warbler. But specific identification is based on more subtle characteristics, such as shades of colour, pattern of eye-stripes, and colour of legs and bill. Some are so much alike that they are only safely separated in the field by their

Pallas' Grasshopper Warbler

imm.

Paddy-field Warbler

yellowish underparts

whitish underparts

Grasshopper Warbler

GRASSHOPPER WARBLER *Locustella naevia* L 5″
Fairly common in dry as well as moist open land with
thick vegetation and scattered bushes. Main coloration
somewhat varied. Striped olive-brown upper side, faint
stripe over eye, whitish underside with a few indistinct
breast-spots, and characteristically graduated tail distinguish it. The less distinct stripe over eye in combination
with the strongly striped back is best field mark when
seen, but best identification feature is song. Very secretive in habits, staying well hidden in dense vegetation
and only reluctantly takes to the wing when flushed. Call
is short 'tirk'. Song, given mostly at dusk and dawn, from
low perch which it leaves at the least disturbance, is a
characteristic high-pitched, fast trilling sustained for
very long periods, often appearing to vary in volume as
the bird turns its head. Savi's Warbler has somewhat
similar song, but it is shorter, deeper in tone and of
higher frequency. Song of River Warbler is not as
monotonous as it is broken up into short sections.   S

songs, which usually are characteristic for each species, although
a reeling trill is shared by Savi's and Grasshopper Warblers and
their songs can be hard to tell apart.

In thickets of bushes and scrub, on the edges of woods, and in
parks, members of the genus *Sylvia* predominate. They are
long-tailed, rather heavy-looking warblers with short but heavy
bills. Many have rather characteristic colours on their heads,
most notably the Blackcap. Several have prominent moustachial
stripes which help in identification. Generally these warblers
are the easiest to recognize by their plumage. They are also more
often seen in the open, although most of their time is spent in
cover. Several have characteristic song-flights, for instance
those of the Whitethroat and the Barred Warbler. The most
strikingly coloured is the male Rüppell's Warbler. The black
colour of the head and throat contrast sharply with the white
underside, and the deep red eye and the thin moustachial stripe
give the bird great character. It is found in south-easternmost
Europe along the rocky shore of the Aegean.

Found in both scrub and tall woodland are the members of the
genus *Hippolais*. They are greenish or brownish above, yellow
or whitish below, with characteristic long bills. They are
excellent songsters.

In woods, often hidden in the canopy, we find the leaf
warblers, members of the genus *Phylloscopus*. Like the Willow
Warbler, which belongs to this group, they are greenish above,
paler below with short, thin bills. It is often difficult to get a good
look at them and even when seen well, they are difficult to tell
apart in the field. In this group as well as in other warblers the
wing formula is of importance in identifying the species.
It is only possible to use this when the bird is in the hand, caught
in a trap to be ringed, or found dead. The term refers to the
relative length and form of the primaries. In some species this is
the only means, apart from the song, by which positive
identification can be made.

Lastly there are the Goldcrest and Firecrest, tiny green birds
with characteristic crown patterns. They look more plump

Lanceolated Warbler

LANCEOLATED WARBLER *Locustella lanceolata*
L 4½" Fairly common in dense vegetation of marshes,
swamps and the edges of lakes. A rare autumn visitor, to
north-western European islands in particular. Resembles
Grasshopper Warbler, but is smaller, more densely
striped on upper side and has characteristic streaking of
breast. Some streaks on flanks and sometimes on throat.
Stripe over eye poorly pronounced. As in Grasshopper
Warbler, colours are somewhat variable. Habits and
voice resemble those of Grasshopper Warbler and the
bird stays well hidden among vegetation. Can sometimes be approached very closely.   V

than the other warblers and are less proficient songsters. They
were previously placed in their own family, the kinglets.

Warblers are found nesting in all European countries except
Iceland. In Finland, with its extensive woods, the Willow Warbler is the most numerous bird, an estimated five and a half
million pairs breeding every year. The second most numerous
species in that country is another woodland bird, the Chaffinch,
with five million pairs.

Because their food is insects, the warblers are almost all
highly migratory. Only a few southern warblers stay within the
European continent. Some Chiffchaffs and Blackcaps winter in
Britain. The Blackcap has a fondness for berries, on which it
subsists while enduring the severe weather. Warblers migrate
at night. This is necessary as they need all the hours of daylight
to find food. While searching for food among trees and bushes,
they may slowly move in the direction of their migration, but
the long stretches are flown during the dark hours as indicated
by the many warblers killed on migration at lighthouses.

Warblers do not travel in flocks like so many other birds but
on occasion they can be seen in large concentrations, often in the
company of other night migrants such as Pied Flycatchers. Such
'falls', where thousands of birds appear one morning in an area
where few were the evening before, are quite common,
especially along sea coasts. In Britain spectacular falls of millions
of birds, of which a large number are warblers, usually follow
a period of good weather in Scandinavia, which encourages the
departure of large numbers of birds. If while crossing the North
Sea they encounter foul weather, they will seek landfall as soon
as possible and will therefore by concentrated on the coast
rather than spreading over a larger area inland.

This brings up the question of the way in which birds
orient themselves. What makes it possible for the warbler to
travel thousands of miles and yet return to the very same garden
in which it reared its young the preceding year? This fascinating
ability has been studied in many birds; some of the most
interesting experiments have been performed on the Lesser

MOUSTACHED WARBLER *Lusciniola melanopogon*
L 5″ Common in reed-beds and swamps with dense vegetation, often together with Sedge Warblers. Resembles Sedge Warbler but is darker brown above with white and more pronounced stripe over eye and white throat. Cocks tail frequently, a habit not seen in any similar species. Sings from perch in high reeds with tail depressed. Song is rapid and varied, resembling that of Sedge Warbler, but includes Nightingale-like 'too-too-too-too' notes, which are not present in song of Sedge Warbler. V

Whitethroat. As warblers and many other birds migrate at night, they cannot, as the Starling does, orient themselves by the sun. Since they show as great an ability in orientation as daytime migrants do, they must have some other means of knowing in which direction to fly. It is a reasonable hypothesis that they would use what man has used since time immemorial, the stars. To prove this, Lesser Whitethroats were exposed to different skies in a planetarium. From ringing, it is known that Lesser Whitethroats first migrate towards the south-east, and then, when they have reached Africa, they turn south. By studying the direction in which the caged birds set off when getting restless, it was shown to be south-east as long as the

Moustached Warbler

Aquatic Warbler

AQUATIC WARBLER *Acrocephalus paludicola* L 5″
Fairly common in dense vegetation of low height and limited extent near open water. Resembles Sedge Warbler but is paler, and has striped head. Stripe over eye is buffish, not white. Stripes on back extend down to rump. Indistinct stripes on breast and flanks. Tail is more pointed than that of Sedge Warbler. More secretive than Sedge Warbler, staying well hidden in dense vegetation. Song, which resembles that of Sedge Warbler, is also given in short song-flight. V

artificial sky was a northern one, but changed to the south when the birds were exposed to the more southern skies of Africa. When exposed to skies of more eastern latitudes, the birds counteracted this by 'flying' towards the west to 'reach' their normal route. To be able to orient itself in this way the bird must, like the species using the sun, have a keen sense of time, an internal clock. How this operates is unknown.

Although the direction during migration can be maintained, some birds are occasionally seen far from their normal haunts. This has been particularly evident since the many coastal bird observatories have been opened, and a particularly favourable spot for such rarities is Fair Isle, between Orkney and Shetland. Here birds from eastern Europe often alight. These stragglers have become disoriented during their migration and have been unable to correct for the displacement early enough. As they then seek land as soon as possible, they are often first found on offshore islands.

In spring, when the warblers have rushed through northern Africa and southern Europe, they immediately settle down to occupy a territory where they intend to rear the next generation. It is then that they start singing.

The ability to sing is almost as closely associated with birds as are feathers and the ability to fly. Song is not the only vocalization by birds, although it is the highest developed. Call-notes of various types and functions are used all through the year.

Sedge Warbler

Fan-tailed Warbler

Bird-song has fascinated man from time immemorial and it is probably the natural phenomenon which has received the greatest attention from poets throughout the centuries. One of the reasons for bird-song being so pleasing to us is the fact that the bird's ear functions and perceives in much the same way as our ear does. This is different from many other sound-producing animals, for instance insects, which have a range and perception completely different from those of human beings, and fish, which use a different (and better) sound-carrying medium, namely water. Recent studies have shown that although the range of frequency perceived by the avian ear corresponds well with ours, the bird has a greater ability to distinguish separate notes. What to us sounds like a single drawn-out note may be

Blyth's Reed Warbler

Marsh Warbler

BLYTH'S REED WARBLER *Acrocephalus dume-torum* L 5" Fairly common in swampy scrub, edges of woods and clearings with dense shrubbery. A very rare autumn visitor to north-western Europe. Resembles Marsh Warbler but slightly greyer above; more rounded wings (2nd primary shorter than that of Marsh Warbler) identify it with certainty. Bill is longer than Marsh Warbler's. Song resembles Marsh Warbler's but is even more musical and often given from high perch. It is delivered at a more leisurely pace than that of Marsh Warbler. Like the Marsh Warbler it is an expert mimic.
V

MARSH WARBLER *Acrocephalus palustris* L 5" Common in dense, low shrubbery in swamps and other wet locations. Closely resembles Reed Warbler but has pale pink legs and is more greenish-brown above. Also distinguished by habitat (not in reeds), less secretive behaviour and more musical song, which lacks the harsh notes interspersed in the song of Reed Warbler. An expert mimic. Practically indistinguishable from Blyth's Reed Warbler in field except for faster delivery of song, warmer brown colours and shorter bill. In the hand, told by more pointed wing (2nd primary longer than that of Blyth's Reed Warbler). Sings from low perch.
S

perceived as a series of notes by birds.

The sound-producing organ in birds differs from ours. We produce sound by means of our vocal cords and this sound is modulated by resonance in throat, mouth and nose, which we are able to vary in shape and size. The bird, on the other hand, does not have vocal cords. Instead, at least one set of vibratory apparatus is found in its syrinx, a chamber made of cartilage situated at the lower end of the trachea, where the main passages of the bronchi meet.

Some species also have very elaborate chambering of the trachea which may play a part in the production of sound, although this has not yet been thoroughly investigated. Of greatest importance are the fine muscles attached to the syrinx, best developed in the songbirds. That more than one vibratory system is functioning in some species is shown by the fact that they are able to sing two, three or even four different songs simultaneously.

Some birds have special ways of producing sound, for instance the drumming on trees by woodpeckers and the buzzing sound produced by the outer tail-feathers of the Snipe in its display

Reed Warbler

Great Reed Warbler

REED WARBLER *Acrocephalus scirpaceus* L 5″ Very common in reed-beds and other water edges with dense vegetation. Unstreaked brownish upper side and lack of stripe over eye distinguish it from Sedge Warbler found in similar habitat. More brown on upper side than Marsh Warbler and usually has dark brown legs. In flight the tail is spread out. In the hand, 2nd primary is the same length as that of Marsh Warbler but is more pointed. Song is varied and musical, with repetition of same notes several times, but contains harsh chattering notes. It is not as rapid and varied as that of the Sedge Warbler. Like others of the *Acrocephalus* group it imitates other bird-songs. Sings normally from perch.   S

GREAT REED WARBLER *Acrocephalus arundinaceus* L 7½″ Common but local in reed-beds and in reeds along the edge of lakes. Very large warbler with long bill and thin stripe over eye. Resembles Reed Warbler most but is much larger and the thin eye-stripe is more pronounced and well defined. Less secretive in behaviour than other *Acrocephali*. Perches in the open. Fans tail in flight. Song loud and strident with characteristic 'car' and 'cier' notes. Sings from exposed perch on reed.   V

flight. The clapping of wings by pigeons and the clattering of the bill by storks are other examples of this 'instrumental' sound production. This phenomenon is not restricted to birds and man but is found throughout the animal kingdom.

In modern times it has become possible to study bird-songs much more closely because of our technical advances. First of all, we are now able to record sounds with great accuracy, a branch of ornithology which has attracted many amateur ornithologists. Secondly, the invention of the sound spectrograph has made it possible to show sound graphically and to analyze it in much greater detail than was previously possible. This field of work is still young and much has yet to be learned. Only a few species have been studied in detail, notably the Chaffinch, but from our present knowledge it appears that many of the conclusions apply to almost all birds.

The function of both song and call-notes is communication. An exception to this may be the subsong, given outside the regular singing season, which does not seem to have any direct communicative function but is probably a form of schooling in the real song. It is freer in composition than the normal song

and often contains portions of songs of other birds. There is evidence that it is functionless and it may be a phenomenon which can truly be called artistic in the sense that most human song is. Another exception is the clicking sound given by Oilbirds and some cave-dwelling swifts. This is used for echo location in the same manner as the high-frequency calls of bats.

If we examine the various call-notes of birds, we find a number of situations to which they are related. Members of the species in which the same calls are inborn react instinctively to them; and other species may learn to profit by them. Alarm calls may even be differentiated further according to whether the predator approaches flying or on the ground. In the first case the reaction is that of dropping headlong into the nearest bush; in the second case it may be one of more careful exploration, and may even lead to mobbing the enemy. Most alarm calls are of such physical properties that their source is very different to locate; and this is how they are of survival value to the individual uttering them. An example of this is the clicking alarm note of the Garden Warbler.

Icterine Warbler

ICTERINE WARBLER *Hippolais icterina* L 5″ Common in deciduous woods with undergrowth, parks and gardens. Greenish-grey upper side and usually bright yellow underside, including belly, distinguish it from all other warblers except the very similar Melodious Warbler, which replaces it in south-western Europe. Very long-winged. Legs bluish. Sits more upright than the *Phylloscopi* and is less active. When excited, often raises crown feathers. Call is short metallic 'teck'. Song is varied and sustained but includes many discordant notes. Song perch usually in open. Bill is wide open and points upward when singing.   P

Flock and flight calls keep the group synchronized in its movements, and food-begging calls by young stimulate the feeding behaviour patterns of parent birds.

True song is generally said to be confined to the *Passeriformes*; but many waders deliver series of notes that in form and function are virtually indistinguishable from true song. The fully developed song as it occurs among the Passeriformes and particularly the warblers consists of a pattern of different notes. The song varies from species to species and it is difficult to find two species which cannot with practice be separated by their songs alone. Sometimes untypical songs of Blackcap and Garden Warbler, or of Reed Warbler and Marsh Warbler, are almost impossible to tell apart. Gilbert White of Selborne drew attention to the differences among the songs of the three *Phylloscopus* warblers, Chiffchaff, Willow Warbler and Wood Warbler. In his own time and for many years afterwards most professional ornithologists scorned the idea of being able to identify small similar-looking songbirds without obtaining a specimen and especially without even seeing the bird. In our time, with a much more sophisticated knowledge of identification, most acknowledge that some species are more safely identified in the field by their voices than by their looks.

Songs vary tremendously in complexity and quality; within a given species there may be individual variations and even dialects confined to certain geographical regions, but the song can usually be recognized as that of the same species.

The functions of the song are twofold. It announces the occupation of a territory and it attracts a female to the singing male. The singing male loudly lets his neighbours know he is in charge and they in turn avoid his territory. If they enter the territory, fights begin. The song is obviously beneficial to the species as it keeps intraspecific fights to a minimum. This aspect of music is not unknown to our own species. The American Indians, for instance, feared the Scottish regiments less for their bravery than for the ferocious music with which they went into battle, and fled from bagpipes rather than bullets.

The second function of song, that of attracting females to the territory, is of importance particularly in those species where the males arrive on the breeding ground first and in areas which are thinly populated.

Song activity is at its highest when territories are being

MELODIOUS WARBLER *Hippolais polyglotta* L 5″
Common in open deciduous woods with rich undergrowth, parks and gardens, riparian scrub. Resembles Icterine Warbler closely but has shorter wings, more rounded crown, brownish legs and less prominent wing patch. Head shape differs in having slightly more rounded crown and more angled front. Habits like those of Icterine Warbler. Song is faster, with fewer discordant notes than that of Icterine.   P

OLIVE-TREE WARBLER *Hippolais olivetorum* L 6″
Fairly common in olive groves, open oak woods and taller scrub. Large size, brownish-grey upper side, whitish underside, striped wings and long pointed bill distinguish it from all other warblers. The wings are longer than in any other *Hippolais* species. Resembles Icterine Warbler in habits but keeps itself better hidden. Song is loud and slow, resembling that of Great Reed Warbler, and is thrush-like in quality.

OLIVACEOUS WARBLER *Hippolais pallida* L 5″
Common in open, damp woods, parks and gardens. Notice brownish-grey upper side with darker wings and tail and whitish underside. Best told from similarly coloured Garden Warbler by typical *Hippolais* build with long, wide bill, angled forehead and short under tail-coverts. Habits resemble those of Icterine Warbler. Song resembles that of Sedge Warbler, rapid with grating notes.   V

Melodious Warbler

Olive-tree Warbler

Olivaceous Warbler

BOOTED WARBLER *Hippolais caligata* L 4½" Common in bushes and scrub. A rare autumn visitor to western Europe. Resembles Olivaceous but is smaller, has brown upper side, rather pronounced creamy stripe over eye, much shorter bill and buffish wash on sides and flanks. Sometimes has pale tips on tail-feathers. Song resembles that of Sedge Warbler.   V

BARRED WARBLER *Sylvia nisoria* L 6" Fairly common in open country with shrubs and hedges, wood edges and clearings. Often nests close to Red-backed Shrike. Barring and pale eye easily distinguish adult. The barring is less pronounced in the female, which has grey rather than yellow (male) eye. Juvenile resembles Garden Warbler but is larger, stockier, more grey and shows wing-bars, and has dark brown or grey eyes. Keeps well hidden. Call is grating 'tack' resembling that of Garden Warbler, as does song which is given in short song-flight. The characteristic grating call note is included in the song.   P

occupied and pairs formed. In Europe this is the spring, when woods, gardens and fields are filled with the beautiful tones of innumerable birds singing loudly and vigorously. In other seasons one can wander for hours without hearing a single bird-song, although some species, notably the Starling, Serin, Firecrest and Wren, sing almost all year round.

When the pair is formed the male usually sings less, concentrating more on direct sexual behaviour and nest-building. Later, when the female is incubating, he may sing again, but as soon as the eggs are hatched singing gives way to the effort of keeping many hungry stomachs full. Thus singing in most parts of Europe has stopped by late June or July.

Song activity not only varies with the time of year but also with the time of day. Most birds sing first early in the morning and then again at dusk. The time at which they start varies from species to species. Some, like the Reed, Marsh and Sedge Warblers and of course the Nightingale, sing all night. Others, like Willow Warbler, Robin and Blackbird, start about an hour before sunrise. By the time the sun rises above the horizon

Booted Warbler

Barred Warbler

imm.

Orphean Warbler

imm.

Garden Warbler

♂

♀

Biackcap

ORPHEAN WARBLER *Sylvia hortensis* L 6" Common in open woods, groves and parks. Large, with dull black hood, distinctly light-coloured iris, white outer tail-feathers and white underside. Somewhat similarly coloured Sardinian Warbler is much smaller. Juvenile resembles juvenile Barred Warbler but has comparatively shorter tail and bill and less distinct wing-bars. Call is sharp 'tack'. Song is loud, thrush-like in the south-eastern European subspecies *S.h. crassirostris*. In the south-western European subspecies *S.h. hortensis* the song is much more monotonous, consisting of alternating high and low notes. V

GARDEN WARBLER *Sylvia borin* L 5½" Common in gardens, parks and open woods with plentiful undergrowth. Brown upper side and greyish-white underside; legs grey-brown. Has no specific characteristics. Most easily confused with Olivaceous, Booted and juvenile Barred Warbler. Notice the very rounded shape of head distinguishing from most other brown warblers. Stays well hidden in foliage even when singing. Song is musical, mellow and liquid, resembling that of Blackcap but longer and more subdued. Call is sharp 'tack'. SP

BLACKCAP *Sylvia atricapilla* L 5½" Common in parks and woods with rich undergrowth. Small black cap of male and reddish brown cap of female diagnostic. Juveniles resemble female. Has no white on tail. Less secretive in behaviour than Garden Warbler, but often stays well hidden. Sturdy and able to endure quite severe cold. Often eats berries. Sings from well covered perch. Song is a short, mellow musical warble of rising strength, less subdued and uniformly liquid than that of Garden Warbler. Call is short mechanical 'tack'. SW

practically all species have started singing. The weather also influences song activity, especially early in the season when dark or cold days will keep most species silent. But rain and mild weather stimulate song.

So the urge to sing is under the influence both of external stimuli, especially light, and of internal conditions, principally the male hormone. It is thus possible to induce birds to sing outside the regular season by giving them hormone injections.

The way the song is delivered is usually characteristic of each species. Most deliver the song from a special post either in the

SARDINIAN WARBLER *Sylvia melanocephala* L 5½" Very common in shrubs and bushes in open and mountainous country, but also in woods with undergrowth. Solid black cap of male, and easily visible red eye-ring of male and female are characteristic. Orphean Warbler is much larger. Very active. Fans tail in flight. Call consists of loud chattering notes. Song, which is usually given in Whitethroat-like song-flight, is long, hurried and musical, interspersed with chattering notes. V

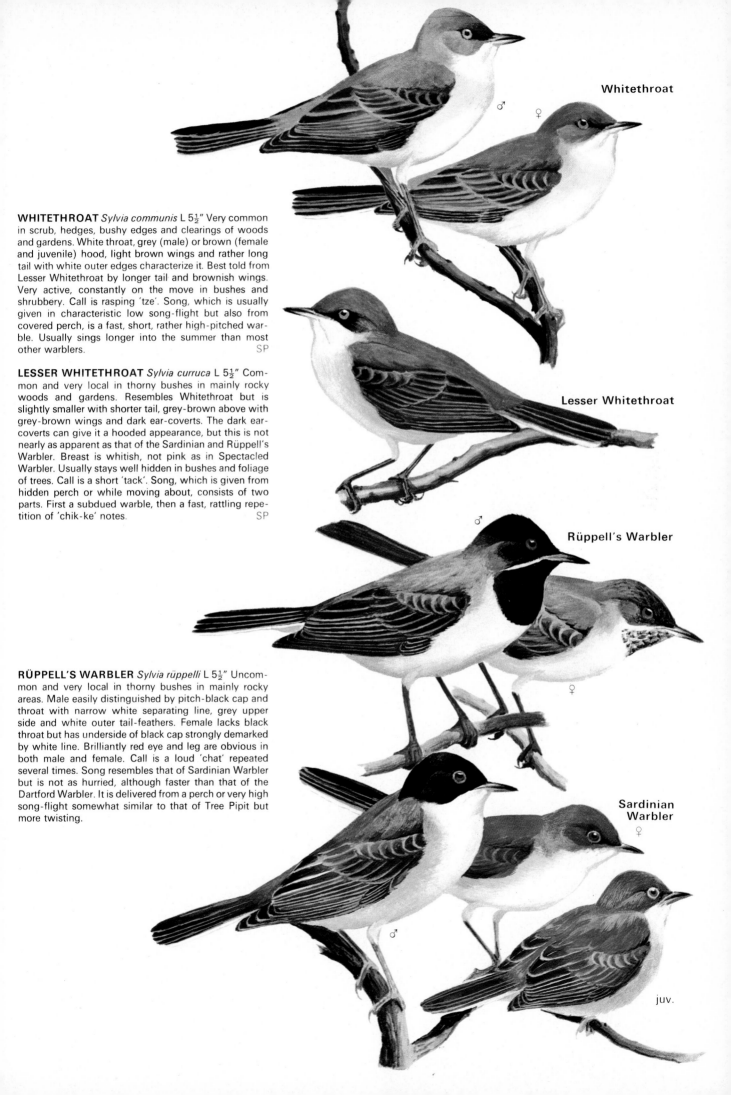

Whitethroat

Lesser Whitethroat

Rüppell's Warbler

Sardinian Warbler

WHITETHROAT *Sylvia communis* L 5½" Very common in scrub, hedges, bushy edges and clearings of woods and gardens. White throat, grey (male) or brown (female and juvenile) hood, light brown wings and rather long tail with white outer edges characterize it. Best told from Lesser Whitethroat by longer tail and brownish wings. Very active, constantly on the move in bushes and shrubbery. Call is rasping 'tze'. Song, which is usually given in characteristic low song-flight but also from covered perch, is a fast, short, rather high-pitched warble. Usually sings longer into the summer than most other warblers.   SP

LESSER WHITETHROAT *Sylvia curruca* L 5½" Common and very local in thorny bushes in mainly rocky woods and gardens. Resembles Whitethroat but is slightly smaller with shorter tail, grey-brown above with grey-brown wings and dark ear-coverts. The dark ear-coverts can give it a hooded appearance, but this is not nearly as apparent as that of the Sardinian and Rüppell's Warbler. Breast is whitish, not pink as in Spectacled Warbler. Usually stays well hidden in bushes and foliage of trees. Call is a short 'tack'. Song, which is given from hidden perch or while moving about, consists of two parts. First a subdued warble, then a fast, rattling repetition of 'chik-ke' notes.   SP

RÜPPELL'S WARBLER *Sylvia rüppelli* L 5½" Uncommon and very local in thorny bushes in mainly rocky areas. Male easily distinguished by pitch-black cap and throat with narrow white separating line, grey upper side and white outer tail-feathers. Female lacks black throat but has underside of black cap strongly demarked by white line. Brilliantly red eye and leg are obvious in both male and female. Call is a loud 'chat' repeated several times. Song resembles that of Sardinian Warbler but is not as hurried, although faster than that of the Dartford Warbler. It is delivered from a perch or very high song-flight somewhat similar to that of Tree Pipit but more twisting.

open (for instance, Blackbird) or well-hidden (Nightingale). Some sing while they move about in the foliage and others have characteristic song-flights like the Whitethroat and Sedge Warbler.

As the song is of importance in species recognition, it is natural to assume that it is inborn. This is true at least to a certain degree. The Chaffinch is the species most studied in this respect and it is found that Chaffinches who have never heard another Chaffinch sing have a very simple song which only vaguely resembles that of a normal Chaffinch. If they are given the opportunity of hearing other Chaffinches sing (as they

MÉNÉTRIES' WARBLER *Sylvia mystacea* L 5½" Common in shrubs (tamarisk), often in rocky areas but also in river valleys. Not recorded in western Europe. Greyish-brown upper side. Male has rather poorly-pronounced black cap. Eye is dark red with yellow eye-ring. Underside whitish with buffish breast and wash on flanks. Tail rounded. Female is more brown on upper parts. Very active, keeping well hidden in bushes. In flight tail is carried high. Call is a sharp repeated 'tart'. Song resembles that of Whitethroat but is more musical and variable.

Ménétries' Warbler

Subalpine Warbler

Desert Warbler

SUBALPINE WARBLER *Sylvia cantillans* L 5" Common in low bushes of dry scrubland, and in wood clearings. Grey above, with orange throat, breast and flanks clearly separated by white moustachial stripe. Throat and breast of female paler and browner. Resembles Spectacled Warbler but underside more orange and wings grey rather than light brown. Juveniles similar to female. Best distinguished from juvenile Sardinian Warbler by paler colours and from juvenile Spectacled Warbler by the lack of the conspicuous brown wing patch characteristic of that species. Skulking in behaviour, keeping well hidden in the bushes. Characteristically raises and spreads tail. Call is short, sharp 'teck'. Song, often given in song-flight, is very musical, resembling that of Whitethroat without the harsh notes. Not as fast as that of Sardinian Warbler. V

DESERT WARBLER *Sylvia nana* L 4½" Common in bushy steppes and deserts. A very rare autumn visitor to western Europe. Resembles Garden Warbler but is much lighter in colour. Sexes similar. Very small, sandy-coloured upper side, whitish underside with no distinguishing marks other than rather prominent, white outer tail-feathers. Stays well hidden in bushes and flies low over the ground from one patch of scrub to the next. Call is short trill. Song is a low series of repeated 'tee' notes.

SPECTACLED WARBLER *Sylvia conspicillata* L 5″
Common in open dry localities with shrubs. Resembles
small Whitethroat but has narrow white eye-ring and
darker, more reddish breast and paler legs. Told from
Subalpine Warbler by conspicuous brown area on wings
and by buffish rather than orange breast. Females told by
conspicuous brown area on wing. Legs are paler than
those of any other *Sylvia* species. Secretive in behaviour.
Call is rattling. Song is a short high-pitched, rather
monotonous and deliberate warble given from exposed
perch or long song-flight.

MARMORA'S WARBLER *Sylvia sarda* L 5″ Fairly
common in dry bushy localities, often in rocky country.
Resembles Dartford Warbler but has grey, not brown-
red underside. Female is browner on upper side with
lighter underside. Juveniles are similar to females
except for even lighter underside. Long tail and dark
colours distinguish it from all other warblers. In habits it
resembles Dartford Warbler. Extremely difficult to catch
sight of as it stays well hidden in the scrub. Call is short
'tick'. Song, which is given in short song-flight, does not
resemble that of Dartford Warbler, being more mellow,
weaker and slurred.

would in nature), their song will develop normally, and it is
obvious that some of the more refined aspects of the song have
to be learned.

Some birds include parts of songs or calls of other birds in
their own songs. This is particularly true of the Marsh Warbler
and Icterine Warbler, both among our most brilliant songsters.
Marsh Warblers have been recorded imitating more than
thirty different songs and calls. This naturally gives an enormous
variability to the song of these species, though they usually
include characteristic phrases of their own songs, making
identification possible.

Spectacled Warbler

Marmora's Warbler

imm.

Dartford Warbler

imm.

DARTFORD WARBLER *Sylvia undata* L 5″ Fairly
common in dry, bushy localities in Mediterranean
region, rarer on heaths with scrub, especially gorse, in
north-western Europe. Long-tailed, very dark brown
above, reddish brown below. Male has richer tints than
female. Keeps well hidden. Darker than any other warbler
except for similar Marmora's Warbler which has a dark
grey, not reddish breast. In winter sometimes found in
small flocks. Usually holds tail cocked upwards and
flicks it frequently. Flight low and weak with characteristic movements of tail. Wing-beats fast. Call consists of
hard and loud 'chir' and 'tuck' notes. Song resembles
that of Whitethroat but is feebler and includes fewer
rasping notes. It consists of short phrases interrupted by
pauses of varying length. Can be heard singing throughout the year. Song is not as rapid as that of Sardinian
Warbler. Often given in short song-flight.   R

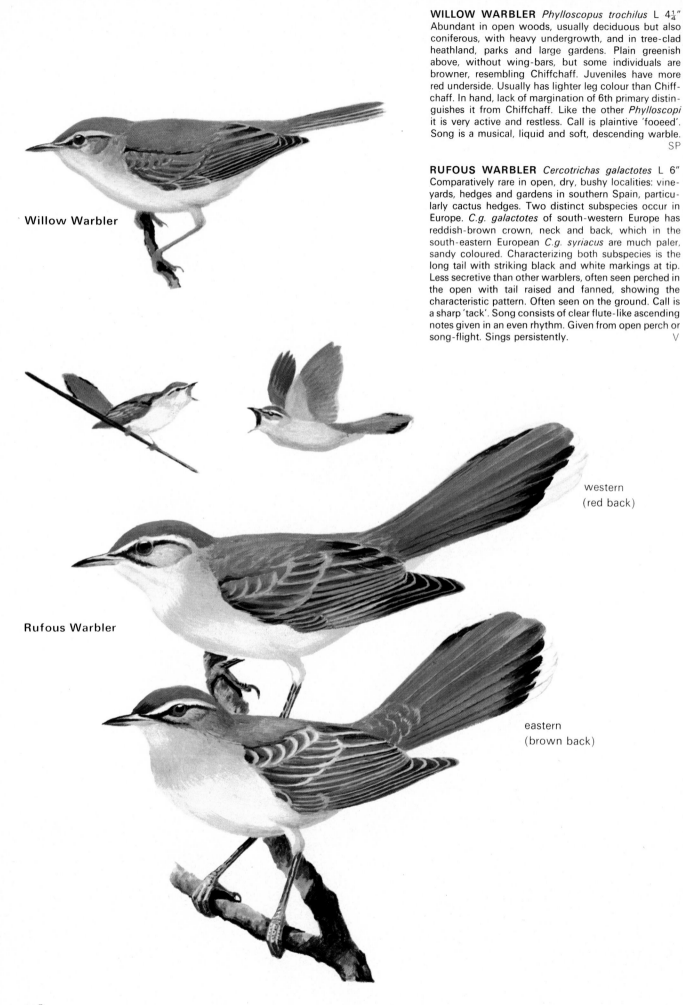

WILLOW WARBLER *Phylloscopus trochilus* L 4¼″
Abundant in open woods, usually deciduous but also coniferous, with heavy undergrowth, and in tree-clad heathland, parks and large gardens. Plain greenish above, without wing-bars, but some individuals are browner, resembling Chiffchaff. Juveniles have more red underside. Usually has lighter leg colour than Chiffchaff. In hand, lack of margination of 6th primary distinguishes it from Chiffchaff. Like the other *Phylloscopi* it is very active and restless. Call is plaintive 'fooeed'. Song is a musical, liquid and soft, descending warble.
SP

RUFOUS WARBLER *Cercotrichas galactotes* L 6″
Comparatively rare in open, dry, bushy localities: vineyards, hedges and gardens in southern Spain, particularly cactus hedges. Two distinct subspecies occur in Europe. *C.g. galactotes* of south-western Europe has reddish-brown crown, neck and back, which in the south-eastern European *C.g. syriacus* are much paler, sandy coloured. Characterizing both subspecies is the long tail with striking black and white markings at tip. Less secretive than other warblers, often seen perched in the open with tail raised and fanned, showing the characteristic pattern. Often seen on the ground. Call is a sharp 'tack'. Song consists of clear flute-like ascending notes given in an even rhythm. Given from open perch or song-flight. Sings persistently.
V

Willow Warbler

Rufous Warbler

western
(red back)

eastern
(brown back)

248

Even before the female warblers have arrived on the breeding grounds, the male may have selected a place for the nest and built a rather flimsy structure. Once the female is within his territory he will lead her to this nest, but the real nest where the eggs are laid is in most cases made by the female alone. The final site of the nest is also chosen by the female. Nest-building among the warblers varies from the rather flimsy open structure of the Garden Warbler to the beautiful deep nest of the Gold-crest. Sedge Warblers build nests suspended from a few reeds or nettles. Spider webs are extensively used in many nests to hold the structure together. The length of time used to construct the nest varies from a few days to a couple of weeks.

The eggs vary in number from two to eight, but about four is the most common clutch-size. As is the case with many birds, clutch-size varies with latitude, the more northern populations laying larger clutches than the southern. This is related to the greater length of the summer day in the north, enabling the parent birds to collect more food for the growing young.

Warblers' eggs vary in ground colour from white to red and blue, with spots, blotches and zones of black and shades of brown. The incubation, in which both male and female usually participate, takes about ten to fourteen days. Incubation does not start until at least two eggs are laid; thus the time of hatching is almost identical in spite of twenty-four hours difference in time of laying.

The chick in the egg is equipped with an 'egg-tooth', a hard,

Below Dartford Warbler

calcified spike at the tip of the upper mandible, with which it picks a hole in the egg. As soon as the young has worked its way out of the egg, the parent bird removes the egg shell. It usually flies quite a long distance from the nest before dropping it so as not to betray the site to predators. The young are naked for the first few days and have to be incubated by the parents, particularly at night. Their eyes do not open until after several days as they are not fully developed at the time of hatching.

Almost immediately after hatching, the young start thrusting their heads upward with wide open gapes to which the parent bird responds by feeding them. The gape and tongue are

Chiffchaff

Wood Warbler

Green Warbler

Dusky Warbler

Radde's Willow Warbler

CHIFFCHAFF *Phylloscopus collybita* L 4¼" Very common in deciduous and coniferous woods with undergrowth, and woodland edges. Prefers higher trees than Willow Warbler. Resembles Willow Warbler closely but is browner, usually has blackish legs (but they can be light) and in the hand notice margination of 6th primary. Call is plaintive 'hooeed'. Song is rather monotonous repeated 'chiff-chaff', combined in various ways, sometimes with grating introductory notes. Very active, often flicking wings. The most sturdy *Phylloscopus*, arriving at breeding grounds before the others. RSP

WOOD WARBLER *Phylloscopus sibilatrix* L 5" Common in mature deciduous and mixed woods. Bright yellow throat and breast and yellow area on wings distinguish it. Underside is white. Very active. Call is liquid 'diu'. Song, often given in song-flight, is characteristic series of 'sip' notes repeated at an accelerating rate. Second song, often combined with the trill, is a series of lengthened call-notes. S

GREEN WARBLER *Phylloscopus nitidus* L 4¼" Common in mountainous woods in the Caucasus. Very rarely observed elsewhere in Europe. Resembles Wood Warbler but has yellow on entire underside. Upper side is more green (less yellow). Song resembles Willow Warbler's. Call is not as mellow as Willow Warbler's.

DUSKY WARBLER *Phylloscopus fuscatus* L 4¼" Very rare Asiatic autumn visitor, resembles Radde's Willow Warbler closely but has more slender bill, darker upper side and more rusty colour at rear end of stripe over eye and on flanks. Usually found in damp areas with rich undergrowth. Skulking in behaviour. V

RADDE'S WILLOW WARBLER *Phylloscopus schwarzi* L 5" Very rare autumn visitor to western Europe from Asiatic breeding grounds. Found in scrub and trees. Olive-brown upper side, yellow-brown flanks, stout bill and prominent stripe over eye. V

BONELLI'S WARBLER *Phylloscopus bonelli* L 4½"
Common in mountainous mixed and coniferous woods, but also sometimes found in similar habitats of lower elevation. A rare autumn visitor to north-western Europe. Pale greenish-brown upper side, with yellowish patch on wings and rump, and white underside are characteristic. Juveniles have less contrast between back and rump than adults. Active, usually keeping well hidden in foliage. Call is a rather plaintive 'hoo-eet'. Song resembles trill of Wood Warbler but is not accelerated. It consists of two different phrases of different pitch and length.   V

YELLOW-BROWED WARBLER *Phylloscopus inornatus* L 4" Rare but regular autumn visitor to north-western Europe from Asiatic range. On migration found in woods as well as bushes. Very small with green upper side, white underside, pale yellow stripe over eye and two distinct wing-bars. Sometimes has faint yellow stripe through crown. Sometimes shows conspicuous yellow patch on primaries. Resembles Willow Warbler in habits, and often associates itself with other migrating *Phylloscopus* species and tits. Call resembles that of Willow Warbler but is more high-pitched and sharp, sometimes consisting of two syllables.   P

ARCTIC WARBLER *Phylloscopus borealis* L 4¾" Common in damp birch and mixed woods and scrub. A very rare autumn visitor to western Europe. Rather large but slim *Phylloscopus* with one wing stripe well-defined, a second hardly visible, well-marked yellowish stripe over eye and pale legs. Juveniles are not as bright green as adults. The bill is long. Arctic can be confused with Greenish Warbler but notice distinct stripe over eye and pale legs. Very active, flicking wings in the manner of Willow Warbler. Usually keeps well hidden in the canopy. Call is a metallic 'zick'. Song is short, high trill.   V

GREENISH WARBLER *Phylloscopus trochiloides* L 4¼" Common in deciduous and mixed woods, particularly near hedges and clearings, parks and gardens. Resembles Willow Warbler and Chiffchaff but has more distinct stripe over eye and a narrow (sometimes invisible) wing-bar. Arctic Warbler also has one wing-bar but has paler legs and more pronounced stripe over eye. Very active, but usually keeps well hidden in the foliage. Call is a high-pitched 'psee'. Song is loud, starting with a few calls, then merging with a trill followed by a short high-pitched warble.   V

vividly coloured, often with special patterns which make the identification of the young possible.

Nest sanitation is an important procedure. The faeces of the young are neatly enclosed in a gelatinous bag. Feeding stimulates defecation and as soon as the young bird has been fed, it will turn its rear end into the air and defecate. The bag is taken by the parent bird which either swallows it or flies away with it to drop it some distance from the nest. The young grow fast and when ten to twelve days old they are ready to leave the nest. For a period after this they are still fed by the parents.

The different warblers vary greatly in abundance. In north-

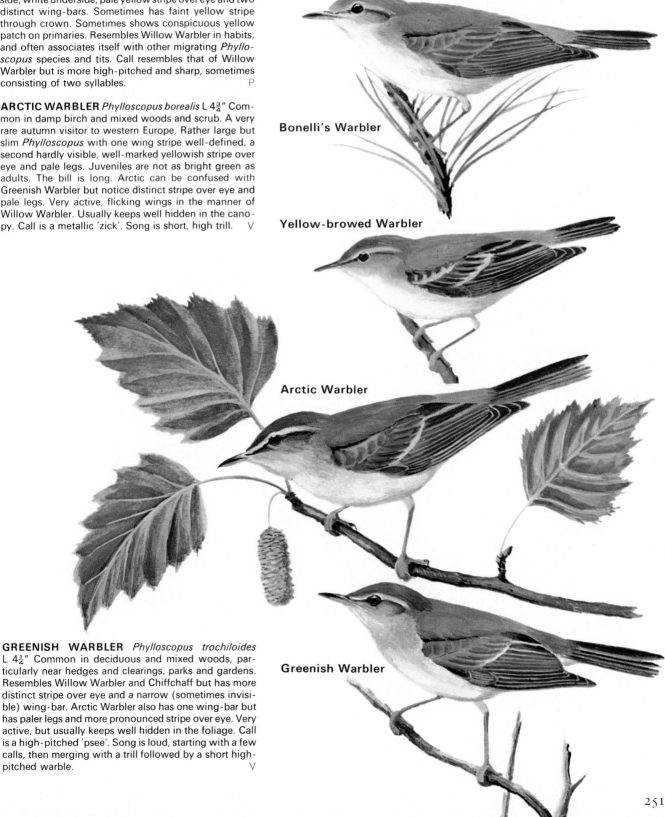

Bonelli's Warbler

Yellow-browed Warbler

Arctic Warbler

Greenish Warbler

Pallas' Warbler

Goldcrest nest

Goldcrest

♂

♀

juv.

♂

Firecrest

♀

juv.

PALLAS' WARBLER *Phylloscopus proregulus* L 3½″
Very rare, late autumn (October and November) visitor to north-western Europe from Asiatic breeding grounds. Mainly found in coniferous and mixed woods, but also in bushes and scrub. Very small, resembling Firecrest, but with more black on head and prominent, bright yellow upper rump (diagnostic). Yellow crown stripe is not always visible but is evident when the bird is seen head on. Yellow rump is particularly prominent in flight, especially when the bird hovers briefly to pick insects off leaves as is its habit. Best told from somewhat similar Yellow-browed Warbler by yellow rump and more prominent yellow crown stripe (a pale stripe is sometimes present on Yellow-browed Warbler). Sometimes associates with foraging flocks of Goldcrests and tits. Habits resemble those of Goldcrest, including fluttering among the foliage for insects. Call is a high-pitched 'tweet', quite unlike any call of Goldcrest or Firecrest.
V

GOLDCREST *Regulus regulus* L 3½″ Very common in coniferous and mixed woods, outside breeding season also in hedges and scrub. Smallest European bird. Generally green colours distinguished it from small tits. Adult has black edge to yellow and orange (male only) crown. Juvenile lacks characteristic crown pattern. In all plumages told from Firecrest by lack of stripes over and through eye. Juvenile told from *Phylloscopus* warblers by small size, rather plump body and very small, thin bill. Very active, usually keeping high in trees and constantly fluttering among the branches. Outside breeding season usually seen in small flocks, sometimes together with tits. Wing action very rapid, flight weak. Call is extremely thin and high-pitched. Song is of similar quality ending in short warble. Basket nest of moss hangs from branch, usually of conifer.
RP

FIRECREST *Regulus ignicapillus* L 3½″ Common in deciduous, coniferous and mixed woods and parks. Resembles Goldcrest but in all plumages told from it by pronounced white stripe over eye and black eye-stripe. Colour generally looks clearer than in Goldcrest. Told from Pallas' Warbler by the lack of the yellow rump. Habits resemble those of Goldcrest. Call is less high-pitched than that of Goldcrest and song is a monotonous, accelerating repetition of 'zis' notes.
RW

western Europe. Willow Warbler, Chiffchaff and Wood Warbler are common in and on the edges of woods; Icterine, Garden Warbler, Blackcap and Lesser Whitethroat occur in small woods, large gardens and parks, whereas the Whitethroat is characteristic of scrub or more open country. Reed, Marsh and Sedge Warblers are typical night singers in swamps and reed-beds.

Eastern Europe has a number of species only rarely found in the west: River, Lanceolated, Aquatic, Barred, Arctic and Greenish Warblers. The largest variety of species is found in southern Europe along the shores of the Mediterranean, but generally these birds do not occur in as large numbers as their northern counterparts. Found in southern wet thickets are Cetti's, Great Reed, Savi's and Moustached Warblers. In thickets and scrubland in various areas of the Mediterranean countries, Sardinian, Spectacled, Subalpine, Dartford (reaching southern England) and Marmora's Warblers are found. In southern gardens, parks and woods other species occur: Orphean, Bonelli's, Melodious, Olive-tree and Olivaceous Warblers.

Many details of the lives of these warblers are unknown, and there is much for an interested observer to do. But there are many difficulties: warblers often live secretive lives, the sexes are not always easy to tell apart, and some of the southern species live in almost inaccessible thickets, and several are far from numerous. This only makes the task the more interesting for the birdwatcher.

Flycatchers

family *Muscicapidae*, subfamily *Muscicapinae*

The flycatchers are specialists in the art of catching flying insects. The flycatcher waits, perched on a branch or wire, until an unsuspecting insect buzzes by, whereupon it throws itself into the air and more often than not grasps the insect in its bill and immediately devours it. It then returns to await another passer-by.

There are some 286 species of flycatchers in the world and of these, four breed within the European continent, and one, the Brown Flycatcher, is a rare visitor from its Asiatic haunts.

The New World flycatchers (family *Tyrannidae*) are completely unrelated to our flycatchers but are so called because they hunt insects in much the same way.

Flycatchers are warbler-sized, short-billed songbirds. Unlike the warblers they tend to have an upright stance and they are much more sedate in their behaviour than are the restless warblers.

In spring, male Pied and Collared Flycatchers are beautifully dressed in black and white whereas their females and the Spotted Flycatcher are a more earthy grey. The male of the Red-breasted Flycatcher has a flashing orange throat and both sexes show two white patches on the tail, which is constantly flicked. This species is eastern in its distribution and differs from the other flycatchers in being more warbler-like in its search for food, although it occasionally behaves more like its namesakes.

As all our flycatchers live almost exclusively on insects, they are highly migratory and none of them venture to stay within the boundaries of our relatively cold continent during the winter.

Although much of their food consists of flying insects, flycatchers also take wingless insects and larvae, particularly during the breeding season when many stomachs have to be filled. Most specialized in taking flying insects is the Spotted Flycatcher. Like the swifts, which also exclusively live on winged invertebrates, Spotted Flycatchers lead an inactive life through the early morning hours when few insects have started flying about. On the other hand they continue the hunt long after most birds have retired in the evening. As all of us have experienced, insects do not stop their activities when the sun goes down, and the Spotted Flycatcher takes advantage of this.

Flycatchers have been studied intensively and the Pied Flycatcher in particular is one of the birds whose breeding behaviour is now fairly well known. There are many reasons for this: male and female are usually easily told apart, and the species readily builds in nest boxes, often near human habitation. Very little is known, however, about the bird's winter life in the forests of central Africa.

The males are usually the first to arrive on the breeding grounds in the spring. They immediately take up territories which are centred around one or more favourable nesting sites, old woodpecker holes, nest boxes, or similar cavities. The male guards these with enthusiasm, and experiments with nest boxes have shown that in many areas the availability of suitable sites rather than the availability of food is the factor limiting the population. The males sing their pleasant little song with energy. More than three thousand songs in a day have been counted. The female attracted to the vicinity will immediately cause the male to demonstrate his nesting holes, which he enters. If the female is favourably inclined, she will follow him into one of the holes. This may be the beginning of pair formation, but on the other hand the female may be dissatisfied with the choice and move into the territory of a neighbour who will show his choice of sites to her.

When the pair is formed, the female starts building the nest and soon afterwards lays the first of her pale blue eggs. The time of this event in a given locality varies from year to year and has been shown to be correlated with the temperature of the early spring, an event which takes place long before the flycatchers arrive and which the bird does not experience itself. The connection is probably the number of insects available when the birds arrive in spring. If they are plentiful, it is possible for the female to collect enough food to be able to produce the six to nine bluish eggs earlier than in leaner years. Clutch-size is again dependent on the time of laying and is larger the earlier this takes place.

Like most passerines the Pied Flycatcher lays one egg a day and as the clutch approaches completion the female starts incubating the eggs. At this point the male sometimes disappears from his old territory and takes up a new one in the neighbourhood. If he is successful in attracting another female, he will attend her until she starts laying eggs and then he may return to his former mate. About ten per cent of Pied Flycatcher males are polygamous, but there are also a number of males (probably young ones) who are unable to find themselves a single mate.

When the male has left his second mate, this is for good (unless they accidentally meet the following year, the chance of which is small); he concentrates all his attention on the first mate. He will feed her while she is incubating and, as soon as the eggs are hatched, start feeding the young together with the female. The incubation time is just under two weeks; it may be up to two and a half weeks after hatching before the young venture away from the nest.

PIED FLYCATCHER *Ficedula hypoleuca* L 5″ Common in open, usually deciduous or mixed, woodland and park-like habitats with little undergrowth. Females have brown and white plumage almost indistinguishable from female Collared Flycatcher but are usually more brown above. Collared males have more white on wing, while black and white Pied male lacks pale collar. Typical flycatcher in habits but does not usually return to same perch after aerial sally. Call a short 'wit', emphasized when alarmed. Song rather unmelodious but variable stream of 'cher' notes.   SP

COLLARED FLYCATCHER *Ficedula albicollis* L 5″ Common in open woods, parks and gardens. Two distinctly different subspecies: *Ficedula albicollis albicollis* of Italy and central Europe, of which male has white neck-band and pale upper rump; and *Ficedula albicollis semitorquata* of Balkans, Crimea and Caucasus, which resembles black male Pied Flycatcher very closely but has more white on wing and tail. Grey-brown females almost indistinguishable from Pied. Song is a repeated 'zoet'. Call is a hard 'teck'.   V

RED-BREASTED FLYCATCHER *Ficedula parva* L 4½″ Common in woods and parks, mainly deciduous. Prominent white patches on tail-feathers of brownish bird distinguish it. Male has bright orange throat throughout the year. Cocks and flicks tail very frequently. Much more warbler- than flycatcher-like in habits. Call is chattering but soft. Song is loud and trilling, reminiscent of Willow Warbler's.   P

SPOTTED FLYCATCHER *Muscicapa striata* L 5¼″ Common in open woods, parks and gardens. Brownish-grey with striped breast. Sexes similar. Typical flycatcher in stance and behaviour. Flicks tail frequently. Call is a sharp 'zit'. Song is a repetition of three or four call notes, mainly heard soon after arrival in spring. SP

BROWN FLYCATCHER *Muscicapa latirostris* L 4¾″ Very rare autumn visitor to north-western Europe from Asia. Typical flycatcher without tail, wing or breast markings and with a narrow white stripe over eye. Sexes similar. Keeps more hidden than other flycatchers.   V

Pied Flycatcher

♂

♀

Collared Flycatcher ♂

♀

Red-breasted Flycatcher

♂

♀

Brown Flycatcher

Spotted
Flycatcher

Opposite Top to bottom: Stonechat, Blue Rock Thrush and Rock Thrush

WHEATEAR *Oenanthe oenanthe* L 5¾" Common in open country, preferring areas with sparse vegetation. The most widespread and numerous of the wheatears. Tail in all plumages has evenly cut black tip with long black central feathers. Male distinguished by a steel-grey back and crown in summer. Females resemble other female wheatears but have characteristic tail pattern and more pronounced white stripe over eye. Juveniles resemble females but are spotted. Greenland subspecies *Oenanthe oenanthe leucorrhoa*, which migrates through western Europe, is slightly larger with brighter colours. Call is a hard 'tack'. Song, given from perch or short song-flight, is a short warble of lark-like quality.   SP

ISABELLINE WHEATEAR *Oenanthe isabellina* L 6¼" Common in open steppes and low hills. Large, uniform sandy colour with less contrasting wings than other wheatears. Tail pattern resembles Wheatear's, but dark parts paler. Facial pattern not pronounced. Rather inactive. Call is loud, metallic, piping 'wheet'. Song contains whistling notes. Often imitates other birds.   V

The Collared Flycatcher resembles the Pied in its breeding behaviour in almost all respects. Unlike the Pied Flycatcher, which prefers park-like landscape but is also found in closed-canopy woods, the Spotted Flycatcher is not found in conifer forests but is generally associated with man and his buildings. It does not use closed nest boxes but builds openly on ledges, in creepers, over doors, even in piles of wood. The Red-breasted Flycatcher also builds in holes in trees and tree stumps, but is much less closely associated with man.

Thrushes and Their Allies
family *Muscicapidae*, subfamily *Turdinae*

About 300 species of this subfamily inhabit the world, representatives being found everywhere except the Antarctic. More than thirty species are found in Europe, among them such familiar birds as the Robin and Blackbird. There are also rare stragglers like the American Robin, the North American

Wheatear

♂

♀

juv.

♀

Isabelline Wheatear

♂

counterpart of our Blackbird, having only the red breast in common with our Robin.

Thrushes are medium-sized to small birds with slender bills, and the young are heavily spotted. For convenience the subfamily is further subdivided into two subgroups, the chats and the thrushes. As the chats contain such diverse species as nightingales and wheatears, even this group is best broken down further into different genera: the wheatears (genus *Oenanthe*), the whinchats *(Saxicola)*, the redstarts *(Phoenicurus)*, Robin *(Erithacus)*, Red-flanked Bluetail *(Tarsiger)*, the nightingales *(Luscinia)*, and Rufous Warbler *(Cercotrichas)*.

Wheatears are small, black, white and earth-coloured ground birds with slender bills. One species, the Wheatear, is found all over Europe whereas the others have a more limited southern distribution. The Black-eared Wheatear (the male of which is dimorphic in plumage with either black or white throat) occurs abundantly in the Mediterranean countries. The Pied Wheatear is limited to the Black Sea coast, the Black Wheatear to the Iberian peninsula and the Isabelline Wheatear, a relatively recent European breeder, to a narrow strip of land from Istanbul westward along the northernmost coast of the Aegean. The Desert Wheatear, which is distinguished by its almost completely black tail, is a rare straggler from Africa and Asia where it is found on dry barren steppes and deserts.

Wheatears are birds of the open country and although the Black-eared may often be seen perched on bushes and trees, they usually stay on the ground, generally among rocks and boulders. The Pied Wheatear shows a great preference for cliffs along seashores.

With the exception of the Black Wheatear, all the European species are highly migratory; they feed on insects which are not available in our inhospitable winter climate. Particularly interesting is the migration of the Greenland subspecies of the Wheatear, which is larger and more brightly coloured than its European ancestors. This population undoubtedly invaded Greenland from Europe, but true to tradition, as is the case with many birds, it retained its old migratory habits. Each year these little birds cross the northern North Atlantic from Greenland to Europe in autumn and vice versa in spring, to follow their old route to the wintering grounds in Africa. Only rarely do Wheatears from Greenland remain on the same side of the Atlantic to winter and in the few cases they have been observed in southern parts of North America, they were probably birds which had been thrown off course, in other words birds which can be regarded as vagrants from Europe. As Wheatears fly at the rate of about 30 mph and they have to cover a distance of at least 600 miles over open sea, it means they have to be on the wing for twenty hours without food and without rest, a truly amazing feat.

Wheatears migrate mainly at night and usually singly. During the day they move slowly in the direction of their goal as they seek food on fields and moors. On coasts where any stretch of water has to be crossed, one can therefore see Wheatears concentrating as they await nightfall or good weather conditions to continue their flight.

Wheatears live exclusively on invertebrates such as insects, worms, snails and spiders, which they find on the ground. Occasionally they can be seen catching flying insects in the manner of flycatchers or catching insects on the ground as shrikes habitually do, from an exposed perch. The Pied Wheatear is particularly likely to feed like this.

PIED WHEATEAR *Oenanthe pleschanka* L 5¾" Common on stony steppes, and along sea and river cliffs. Irregular in occurrence. Black and white pattern of male diagnostic. Black back clearly distinguishes it from Black-eared Wheatear male. Outer part of white on tail is bordered with black. Females resemble Black-eared females closely but are more earth-brown (rather than sandy-brown) on back. Often perches high, dropping to the ground like a shrike to obtain insects. Very lively. Not found as much on flat ground as Wheatear. Call is hard 'tack'. Song is lark-like with whistling notes, given in phrases of varying length, usually given from perch or song-flight. V

BLACK-EARED WHEATEAR *Oenanthe hispanica* L 5¾" Very common in open rocky and sandy habitats. In all plumages it has a little more white on tail than Wheatear. Males have two forms (dimorphic), a black-throated and a white-throated. Black-throated form distinguished from Pied Wheatear by buff, not black, back; from male Desert Wheatear by richer buff colour of back and extent of white along edges of tail. Females also told from Wheatear by darker ear-coverts and paler back with contrasting darker wings. Female of southeastern European subspecies more earth-brown on back and practically indistinguishable from Pied Wheatear female. Call consists of hard 'tack', usually followed by a whistling note. Song, which is given from perch or song-flight and rather more often than Wheatear's, resembles Wheatear's but is louder and higher-pitched. Sometimes imitates the song of other species. V

DESERT WHEATEAR *Oenanthe deserti* L 5¾" Very rare autumn visitor from African and Asiatic breeding grounds. Frequents dry open habitats. Resembles black-throated form of Black-eared Wheatear, but only rump is white and wings are not as solid black. Back is more sandy coloured, not as rich buff. Female resembles female Black-eared and Pied Wheatear but has no white on edge of tail. Call is a hoarse whistle. V

BLACK WHEATEAR *Oenanthe leucura* L 7" Common in dry rocky mountains and seashores. Largest of the wheatears, in all plumages uniformly black or blackish except for white rump and part of outer tail-feathers. Although female is more brownish black, it is much darker than any other European wheatear. Flight is heavy. Call is a high-pitched 'pee-pee-pee-pee'. Song is a rich, short warble resembling that of Blue Rock Thrush but not as loud. Given from perch on rock or in long song-flight. V

Pied Wheatear

♂

♀

Black-eared Wheatear

♀

♂

black-throated form

♂

Desert Wheatear

♀

♂

Black Wheatear

♀

♂

259

Wheatears nest in holes among rocks and stones. The nest is a large, rather disorderly assembly of straw, hair and feathers. The five to eight eggs are light blue; the female does most of the incubation, which lasts for two weeks, and another two weeks pass before the young are ready to leave the nest.

Two other inhabitants of the open country are the chats, Whinchat and Stonechat. Both have a wide distribution in Europe, the Whinchat extending its range further north than the Stonechat, which on the other hand is found in the Mediterranean countries only visited by the Whinchat on migration.

Both prefer open country with scattered bushes and other tall vegetation, but particularly where their ranges overlap, the Stonechat prefers drier localities than the lush meadows favoured by the Whinchat. In closely related species, selection of different habitats in areas of overlapping range is common and serves to lessen competition between species for food and nesting sites.

The male Stonechat is more boldly coloured than the male Whinchat, which has a characteristic stripe over the eye. In all plumages the two can be told apart by the white areas on the tail of the Whinchat which are absent on the Stonechat. The Stonechat looks more plump than the Whinchat. They both have the characteristic habit of perching with an upright stance, well exposed on the top of a bush or other tall plant such as a thistle. The food of both consists of insects, spiders, snails and other animal matter. Occasionally they catch insects in the air but more commonly they take their food on the ground. They both flick their tails frequently. While the Whinchat is

WHINCHAT *Saxicola rubetra* L 5″ Common in open heaths and grassland with bushes, and occasionally in fields. Notice prominent stripe over eye of male. In all plumages told from Stonechat by white base of outer tail-feathers (prominent in flight). This white area is much smaller than that of the Red-breasted Flycatcher, which is quite different in build and habits. Perches upright, usually on top of a low bush, thistle or other exposed perch. Often bobs tail. Call starts with a musical 'due', continuing with hard 'teck, teck'. Song, which is given from perch or song-flight, is a short, high-pitched warble, often with some notes imitating other birds. SP

STONECHAT *Saxicola torquata* L 5″ Common in open heaths and grassland with bushes, usually preferring rougher country than Whinchat. Black hood of male diagnostic. Has no white on tail, distinguishing females and juveniles from generally paler Whinchat. White rump only on male. Stockier-looking and more upright when perched than Whinchat, which it resembles in habits. Head seems large and very rounded. Call consists of sharp 'teck' notes. Song, which is given from perch or in song-flight, consists of short, repeated, rather high-pitched notes. RS

Whinchat

juv.

♀

♂

Stonechat

♀

♂

juv.

migratory, leaving Europe altogether in the cold season, the Stonechat is only migratory in its north-easternmost range, where the winters are more severe. The Whinchat is the better singer, almost always delivering its song from an exposed perch. The song can be quite varied and may contain imitations of the songs of other birds. The Stonechat has a characteristic song-flight: with very fast wing-beats it dances up and down over the same spot as it delivers its short, rapid song.

The female builds the nest on the ground, usually well-hidden in thick vegetation like heather, gorse or tussocky grass. The four to seven eggs of the Stonechat are blue with brownish spots; the eggs of the Whinchat are bright blue. Incubation takes from ten to fourteen days and the young leave the nest at the age of two weeks, but are often fed by their parents for two to three more weeks as they gradually learn the difficult task of securing their own food. Two broods are regularly raised by Stonechats, occasionally by Whinchats.

The two rock thrushes are well named as they are thrush-like in build and song and show a great affinity for rocky or mountainous landscape. The Blue Rock Thrush male is a brilliant dark blue colour whereas the female is a vermiculated dark brown and much less striking. It is a resident, birds living at the higher altitudes moving down into the warmer valleys in winter. The Rock Thrush, on the other hand, is a summer visitor to Europe, spending the winter with the populations inhabiting the African highlands. The male Rock Thrush is one of our most gorgeously coloured birds, with its powder blue, red, white and black pattern. The female is brownish with fine

ROCK THRUSH *Monticola saxatilis* L 7½″ Common in rocky and mountainous areas with or without scattered trees usually at high altitudes but sometimes lower. Male unmistakable with blue, white and red pattern. In all plumages distinguished by orange-red tail. Retiring in habits, often hiding among rocks. Usually seen singly or in pairs. Call is a short 'tack'. Song, which is given from open perch or in song-flight, is a musical, fluting warble, but is very variable.　　　　　　　　　　　　　　V

BLUE ROCK THRUSH *Monticola solitarius* L 8″ Common in sunny, rough mountains with sparse vegetation, more often at lower altitudes than Rock Thrush. Male unmistakable with dark blue plumage. In winter looks blacker. Female barred, resembling female Rock Thrush but with dark brown, not chestnut, tail. Shy and retiring in habits. Like Rock Thrush it typically dives among rocks when approached. Usually seen singly or in pairs. Call is a hard 'tick'. Song is loud, musical and thrush-like. It is usually given from perch on rock or song-flight.　　　　　　　　　　　　V

Rock Thrush

Blue Rock Thrush

vermiculation, like the Blue Rock Thrush female, but easily told from her by the shorter, reddish tail. The Rock Thrush is a shy and wary bird which does not allow a close approach before it dives into hiding among the rocks where it lives. The Blue Rock Thrush is more confident, but shares the same habit and ability to disappear completely among boulders and rocks in spite of its outstanding colours. Both are excellent songsters, their flute-like songs ringing loudly through gorges and ravines.

The Rock Thrush usually breeds at higher altitudes than the Blue Rock Thrush. Both build a nest well-sheltered under boulders or in crevices. The four to six eggs are bluish. Observ-

REDSTART *Phoenicurus phoenicurus* L 5½" Common in parks, gardens and open deciduous and mixed woods, rarely in coniferous. Male unmistakable. In all plumages reddish tail, constantly jerked, distinguishes it from all but much darker Black Redstart. Active, often catches insects in flycatcher fashion. Nests in holes or on ledges. Call is plaintive 'fu-et'. Song is short, melodious, Robin-like warble ending in a short twitter.   SP

Redstart

Black Redstart

ing these two birds is a beautiful experience, but one usually has to go to their summer homes in the mountains to be sure to find them—perhaps this is part of their charm.

Two species of Redstart are widespread in Europe, the Redstart and the Black Redstart, the Redstart in particular. Güldenstädt's Redstart breeds in the Caucasus on the very edge of our area, but its range is chiefly Asia. It is unlikely to extend its range westward.

They are small soft-billed birds, usually sitting upright like flycatchers and often sharing the habit of catching insects on the wing. Most characteristic of them in all ages and plumages is the reddish tail, which is constantly flicked. This draws attention to the bird, and probably serves to announce its presence to

BLACK REDSTART *Phoenicurus ochruros* L 5½" Common in mountains, towns, villages and along rocky coasts. Very dark plumage, with reddish tail, distinguishes male from all other species. Females and immatures resemble Redstart but are much darker. Resembles Redstart in habits. Nests in holes. Call is a series of 'tic' notes. Song, usually given from perch on building or rock, is a short, fast, simple edition of that of Redstart, often ending with a peculiar rattle.   RSWP

other members of the species. It has been shown that red colours are attractive to the Redstart, whereas to the related Robin with its equally bright red breast they induce fear or aggression. The males are much more attractively coloured than the females, which are brownish or grey-brown except for the tail.

The Redstart is a migratory bird which winters in Africa where the warmer winter climate allows a great abundance of insects. The Black Redstart is only a partial migrant, and as is the case with so many others of our birds of a similar distribution, it is the northern and eastern populations which move

BLUETHROAT *Luscinia svecica* L 5½″ Fairly common in scrub along edges of swamps, lakes and streams and on heaths. In all plumages distinguished by reddish patches at base of tail, conspicuously shown by frequent flicking and cocking of tail. Northern subspecies *Luscinia svecica svecica,* nesting in Scandinavia and Russia, has red centre of blue bib whereas southern subspecies *L.s. cyanecula* has white centre. Stays well hidden. Call is a short 'tack'. Song, often given in song-flight, is varied, gentle, musical warbling, rather high-pitched.   P

Bluethroat

♂ red-spotted form

♂ white-spotted form

♀

juv.

juv.

Robin

ROBIN *Erithacus rubecula* L 5½″ Very common in woods with undergrowth, parks and gardens. Adults told by orange breast and brown tail. Told from Red-breasted Flycatcher male by more extensive and well-defined red breast and lack of white on tail. Mottled juvenile told by dark brown tail. Juvenile Nightingale is similarly mottled but has longer tail, slimmer build. Spends much time on the ground. Visits bird feeders. Often flicks wings and tail. Often very tame. Call is series of 'tic' notes. Song, given from low perch, is series of fast, rather high-pitched, warbling notes, usually starting subdued.   RSWP

toward the milder winter climates in the southern and south-western parts of our continent. The nearness of the seas moderates the severity of the winter to such a degree that many species which cannot survive the bitter winters of continental Europe prosper in Britain.

Besides catching insects in flight, a habit most pronounced in the male Redstart, they feed on the ground and among the branches and leaves of low trees and bushes. Whereas the Redstart prefers open woodland and park-like landscapes, including gardens, the Black Redstart prefers a rocky, more open type of landscape and in its northern range shows an affinity for open, industrial or ruinous areas in cities and towns. Thus this species, which is a very local breeding bird in England,

Arthur Singer

Opposite Above, Robin. Below, Redstart.

increased considerably in numbers after the last war, taking up territory in the bombed-out sites in London and other southern cities. As rebuilding has progressed, the Black Redstart has had to give up many of these sites.

Both species nest in cavities, the Black Redstart in cracks in cliffs and rocks, the Redstart in tree cavities and even in holes in the ground under roots or stones. Redstarts are readily attracted to nest boxes, which are also sometimes used by the Black Redstart. Four to eight eggs are laid; the Redstart's are blue, while the Black Redstart's are white. The incubation and fledging times for both species are about two weeks each. The Black Redstart is commonly double brooded, the Redstart only occasionally, the latter sometimes nesting again for the second brood. Both species have rather simple but pleasant songs.

In our gardens the Redstart is a frequent summer visitor, but we can enjoy the company of the Robin throughout the year.

Red-flanked Bluetail

RED-FLANKED BLUETAIL *Tarsiger cyanurus* L 5½″
Fairly common in deep, swampy, coniferous woods and thickets. A very rare autumn visitor to north-western Europe. In all plumages has bluish-grey rump and tail. No other European bird of its size has blue tail. Adults have prominent orange flanks somewhat paler in female than male. Immature heavily spotted but also has blue tail. In habits resembles Redstart but is seen more on the ground. Secretive, keeping well hidden in scrub. Sings from exposed perch. Call is a short 'teck teck'. Song is very loud, musical and thrush-like.   V

The Robin is without doubt the most popular and well known bird in Britain; its trustful behaviour combined with its beauty and elegance easily explain its popularity. But this tameness is not shared by all Robins—Robins from continental Europe are more wary than the British and prefer more secluded habitats in woods and thickets rather than the close proximity to man so characteristic of the British population (but many British Robins do nest in woodland). Winter visitors from continental Europe share the same wariness and only reluctantly approach bird tables and houses. The brown back, light belly and red breast and throat form a perfect harmony of discreet colours, and large dark eyes underline the confidence this bird shows in man. It feeds on the ground usually under bushes and trees, but readily comes into the open when, for instance, the top soil is being turned to expose a wealth of invertebrates for the Robin to devour. It is also easily attracted to bird tables. Its food consists mainly of insects and other invertebrates but some berries and other fruits are also taken; during the winter months when food is scarce, almost any household scrap is devoured with pleasure.

The Robin is, in spite of the impression of placidity, a very aggressive bird towards its fellows. Both male and female occupy separate territories during the winter, and these are fiercely defended against intruders. The beautiful song which can be heard throughout the year, with the exception of a short period during the summer, announces the occupation of a

juv.

Nightingale

Thrush Nightingale

NIGHTINGALE *Luscinia megarhynchos* L 6½" Common in swampy thickets, wet undergrowth of woods and parks. Sometimes in drier thickets and woods. Uniformly brown with more chestnut tail in all plumages, including mottled juvenile. This distinguishes juvenile from similarly mottled juvenile Robin which has shorter, darker tail and is less slim. Rather large and long-tailed. Almost indistinguishable in the field from Thrush Nightingale but has more clean brown back (not greyish), redder tail, and never has barring on breast. In the hand told from Thrush Nightingale by short 1st primary but long 2nd primary. Very secretive, keeping well hidden in bushes. Much more often heard than seen. Call is a liquid 'hu-eet'. Song is very loud and musical with characteristic series of deep 'jug' notes and drawn-out 'pins'. Sings from depth of thickets, often at night, but also during day. S

THRUSH NIGHTINGALE *Luscinia luscinia* L 6½" Common in swampy thickets and wet undergrowth of woods and parks. Resembles Nightingale closely but can sometimes be identified by greyer back and tail and finely barred breast (difficult to see). In the hand told from Nightingale by long 1st primary, but shorter 2nd primary (2nd shorter than 4th in Thrush Nightingale; longer in Nightingale). Song resembles that of Nightingale and is even louder, but less musical. Sings from well-hidden perch, often at night, but also during day. V

territory. If this does not succeed in keeping other Robins away, the owner will display its red breast bodly to its opponent and usually this causes the fast retreat of the intruder. If not, a fierce fight may well develop. Such a fight usually ends with the retreat of the 'morally' inferior intruder. Should the winning bird venture into the loser's territory his chances of repeating his former success are extremely slim.

In early spring the females give up their territories, join a male and the two will now jointly defend the area where they later build their nest. The nest is usually placed on a ledge among ivy or in some other well-protected place. In England five eggs are usually laid, but in Scandinavia the clutch size averages larger, six or seven, whereas in the south it is smaller, around four eggs. The incubation time is usually two weeks and the young spend another two weeks in the nest before leaving. The young are still fed by the parents for some time after leaving. Robins are often double brooded and the male is then left to feed the young of the first clutch while the female incubates the eggs of the next. In Britain and southernmost Europe the Robin is resident, but in the north-eastern part of its range it is migratory.

In swampy woods of north-easternmost Europe, ranging as far as eastern Finland, the gorgeously coloured Red-flanked Bluetail is found. It is a bird of retiring and little-known habits. It seems to be spreading slowly westward and although it moves to south-east Asia in winter, it is occasionally met with in western Europe on migration.

Related to the Robin is the Bluethroat, the male of which in

Siberian Rubythroat

♀

♂

summer has a beautiful blue breast rimmed with red and white and with a red (the northern subspecies) or white (the southern subspecies) central spot. In all plumages the Bluethroat can be told by the red areas towards the base of the tail. The Bluethroat prefers scrub or low trees, usually in mountains Here its characteristic and very beautiful song adds greatly to the charm of such landscapes. The nest is placed on the ground. The six or seven eggs are bluish, and incubation and fledging times are the same as for the Robin. Unlike the Robin, the Bluethroat is migratory, leaving Europe completely in winter. When it rests during its rather rapid migration, the bird keeps to cover and is difficult to see.

Most famous of songsters is the Nightingale. Not one but two different species have inspired European poets through the centuries. The Nightingale has its centre of distribution in southern and western Europe whereas the north-eastern part is inhabited by the Thrush Nightingale, which is very similar in looks as well as in song. During the Ice Age the continuous distribution of the one kind of nightingale was split into two populations by the ice covering northern and central Europe. The two populations evolved in different directions probably because of differences in surroundings. When the ice retreated, the two populations spread again and eventually met, but they differed so much that they were actually two distinct species.

Nightingales are larger than Robins and more thrush-like in appearance with their long tails and brown colours. They live in dense thickets, the Thrush Nightingale with a definite

SIBERIAN RUBYTHROAT *Luscinia calliope* L 5½″
Common in coniferous woods with rich undergrowth. A very rare straggler to south-western Europe. Builds covered nest on the ground. Facial pattern of male unmistakable with bright red throat, white stripe over eye and moustachial stripe. Female told from other brownish soft-billed non-warblers by pronounced whitish stripe over eye and white throat. Juvenile resembles female but is more spotted. In behaviour resembles Robin. Song is loud and musical.

Grey-cheeked Thrush

Olive-backed Thrush

Eye-browed Thrush

Dusky Thrush

Naumann's Thrush

GREY-CHEEKED THRUSH *Catharus minimus* L 7½"
A very rare autumn visitor to western Europe from North America. Small, greyish brown, with grey face and without distinct eye-ring. Call is a rather nasal 'vee-a'. V

OLIVE-BACKED THRUSH *Catharus ustulatus* L 7"
A rare visitor to western Europe from North America. Small, greyish brown, with buffish face and rather distinct buffish eye-ring. Call is a high-pitched 'whit'. V

EYE-BROWED THRUSH *Turdus obscurus* L 7½"
A rare autumn visitor to Europe from Asia. Male has grey head, neck and breast with distinct white stripe over eye, olive-brown back and buff flanks. Female is browner, with spots on flanks. Call resembles that of Song Thrush. V

DUSKY THRUSH *Turdus naumanni eunomus* L 9½"
A rare autumn visitor to Europe from Asia. Very dark with conspicuous stripe over eye, rusty area on wings (both sides) and rump, and boldly barred or spotted breast and flanks. Call resembles that of Fieldfare. V

NAUMANN'S THRUSH *Turdus naumanni naumanni* L 9½" Same species as Dusky Thrush. A rare autumn visitor to Europe from Asia. Grey-brown plumage above, with buffish stripe over eye and reddish breast and tail, distinguishes male. Female is brown with more spotted breast. Call resembles that of Fieldfare.

preference for moist ground, being found almost always close to water; the Nightingale is less particular in its choice of habitat. Though nightingales are often heard, they are difficult to see, as they usually stay well hidden. The beautiful and far-reaching song is uttered from the depths of the thickets, and even though the bird will continue to sing when approached, it is often very hard to pick out in the shadow of the mass of branches. Nightingales may sing throughout the day, but at night their song is heard much more clearly as few other birds sing after darkness has fallen. The nest is as well hidden as the bird and is placed on or close to the ground. The four to six olive-brown eggs are incubated for two weeks and fledging takes the same time. Nightingales are migratory, spending the winter in Africa.

In easternmost Europe the Rubythroat, a Robin-sized brown bird with a scarlet throat, is found in summer. Both in habits and choice of habitat it resembes the Robin but it is not nearly as well-known and, like the Red-flanked Bluetail, is a very rare vagrant to western Europe.

The true thrushes are the largest members of the *Muscicapidae*. They are slender, harmoniously built birds which spend most of their time on the ground. Best known is the Blackbird, distinguished from the other thrushes by having a greater difference in plumage between the sexes. More typical of the group is the almost-as-common Song Thrush with its brown upper parts and spotted underside.

Seven species nest in Europe. The Blackbird, Song Thrush and Mistle Thrush are distributed throughout the continent whereas the Redwing and Fieldfare are found breeding mainly in northern Europe, the Ring Ouzel in mountainous regions and the Black-throated Thrush in easternmost Europe. The Grey-cheeked Thrush, Olive-backed Thrush and the very beautiful American counterpart to our Blackbird, the American Robin, are rare vagrants to western Europe from their North American breeding grounds. From the Siberian forests, Eye-browed Thrush, Dusky Thrush, Naumann's Thrush, Siberian Thrush and White's Thrush visit eatern and central Europe occasionally. They have been known to visit more western countries only very rarely.

Thrushes are birds of open parkland and woods and have shown an amazing adaptability in taking advantage of the increasing urbanization of our countries. Most advanced in this respect is the Blackbird, and in practically all European countries it is now a very common garden bird. This process seems to have started in England long ago but is more recent on the Continent. In Holland, Blackbirds started occurring in towns and gardens in the middle of the last century, whereas they moved into the Scandinavian garden at the turn of the century. In the eastern Baltic countries this occurred even later, in the 1930s. The Blackbird used to be a wary bird of the woods and this is still true of part of the population, but by far the larger population is now found near human habitation, where food is generally much more easily available.

The Song Thrush has also become closely attached to the gardens and parks of many cities. In the north the Fieldfare and the Redwing are also moving into towns. The Mistle Thrush has become a faithful visitor to lawns in many parts of Europe, notably in Britain. This urbanization of the thrushes has coincided with a change in the migratory habits of some of them. This is particularly true of the Blackbird which in Scandinavia, before going to town, was mainly a migrant, spending the winter in the British Isles and the neighbouring parts of the

Continent. Now these Blackbirds stay in Scandinavia through-out the year and only the 'wild' population of the woods is migratory to any degree.

Thrushes, however, are generally migratory and on rainy, foggy nights one can often hear the high-pitched piping of migrating Song Thrushes and Redwings over cities, the lights of which seem to attract them. Redwings and Fieldfares usually occur in rather large flocks in winter, the Mistle Thrush in smaller, more loosely knit groups as is also the case with the Ring Ouzel. Of great interest is the Fieldfare's successful invasion of Greenland, which was a truly accidental phenom-enon. In January 1937 a large flock of Fieldfares, apparently crossing from Norway to Scotland, got caught up in an easterly gale which brought them across the Atlantic to Green-land, where they remained in the south-western part and started breeding in the bushes and scrub found there. Here they have successfully settled and become permanent residents.

Thrushes live on worms, insects, snails and berries, of which they find a wealth in well-kept gardens. In the summer the food is mainly animal matter, whereas it is mainly vegetable during the winter. The Mistle Thrush has earned its name from its affection for mistletoe berries. It swallows them whole and the berries are soon digested; but the seeds are discharged with the slimy faeces, which easily stick to branches and trees where the plant can take root. The Song Thrush has a weakness for snails, the shells of which it breaks on stones, often at a favourite 'anvil', where large numbers of broken shells give away the workshop. Blackbirds often keep winter territories where they find at least part of their food, but this is not the case with the more migratory species, which roam the countryside in flocks. Fieldfares have a greater preference for open country than the other species, which prefer woodland edges and areas with many bushes and scattered trees where they find berries and fruits. In some areas thrushes can be seen feeding on shorelines, where they take advantage of the rich invertebrate life found in washed-up seaweed even in winter.

The song of the Blackbird is delivered from a prominent perch and the mellow, beautiful fluting can be heard a long way off. In towns and villages it is the most prominent bird-song in spring and it is heard particularly often at dusk and dawn. The Song Thrush is its closest rival, its song being more varied than that of the Blackbird. Next on the scale is the Mistle Thrush, and poorest among our thrushes in vocal ability are the Ring Ouzel and Fieldfare. The Redwing, which has a rather simple song, shows great variety in the theme locally, probably more so than any other European bird.

Whereas most thrushes are solitary nesters, the Fieldfare, especially in Scandinavia, nests in colonies which may reach very large numbers. As with most colonially nesting birds, it is probably the added protection against predators which has encouraged this behaviour.

All thrushes build cup-shaped nests which are usually streng-thened by a layer of dried mud, making them very durable. Most line the mud cup with fine grass but the Song Thrush glues the lining together with saliva and lays its eggs directly on the hard surface without using any lining. This makes the nest easy to recognize.

Although a thrush's nest may be found almost anywhere, it is usually placed in the fork of a tree or bush; but Blackbirds also very often nest on ledges. An interesting phenomenon can sometimes be observed when a Blackbird builds on a ledge

RING OUZEL *Turdus torquatus* L 9½" Fairly common in rocky country with bushes or scattered trees. White crescent-shaped breast-band identifies adult. Also notice less pitch-black appearance (scaled with white) than Blackbird, with lighter area on wing. Juvenile more spotted than juvenile Blackbird. On migration mixes with other thrushes. Has clacking call and, when flushed, gives Blackbird-like alarm. Song, given from exposed perch, is usually a ringing 'tew, tew, tew', but sometimes resembles that of Song Thrush, though more mono-tonous and interspersed with short chuckling.   SP

BLACKBIRD *Turdus merula* L 10" Abundant in gardens, parks and woods. Male unmistakable with pitch-black plumage and bright yellow bill. Uniform brownish colour of female and dark spotted appearance of juvenile iden-tify them easily. Juveniles are lighter in colour and more heavily spotted than females. They are not as spotted as juvenile Ring Ouzel, which is also more greyish and has whitish markings on wings. Feeds openly on the ground. In winter may occur in flocks though mainly solitary in behaviour. Call is repeated 'chack'. Song is a musical, fluting warble. Sings from open perch mostly at dusk and dawn.   RW

BLACK-THROATED THRUSH *Turdus ruficollis* L 9½" Common in clearings and edges of coniferous forests; in winter in more open country. Rare visitor to western Europe. Dark breast, grey upper side distinguish male. Female and juvenile brown with closely spotted breasts. Asiatic subspecies Red-throated Thrush *(Turdus rufi-collis ruficollis)* male has reddish breast and reddish tail in all plumages. This subspecies is an even rarer vagrant to western Europe. Both subspecies have rusty under-wing. In behaviour both resemble Fieldfare. Song resembles Song Thrush's.   V

SIBERIAN THRUSH *Turdus sibiricus* L 9" Rare autumn visitor to Europe from Asia. Male very dark with white stripe over eye, characteristic underwing pattern, white spots on tail; female like scaly Song Thrush, but like the male, has white spots on tail and characteristic underwing pattern. Juveniles resemble females but are more heavily spotted. Shy and skulking in behaviour. Call resembles that of Song Thrush.   V

AMERICAN ROBIN *Turdus migratorius* L 10" Rare autumn and winter visitor to western Europe from North America. Unmistakable. Juveniles have spotted, not clear, red breast. Behaviour and voice resemble those of Blackbird.   V

juv.

♂

♀

Ring Ouzel

juv.

♂

♀

Blackbird

♂

♀

♂ red-throated

Black-throated Thrush

♀

♂

Siberian Thrush

American Robin

271

Redwing

Song Thrush

Mistle Thrush

Fieldfare

White's Thrush

REDWING *Turdus iliacus* L 8″ Common in birch woods and parks, sometimes in towns. Outside breeding season in other deciduous woods and fields. Prominent stripe over eye, speckled underside and red flanks diagnostic. Gregarious outside breeding season, often associating with Fieldfares. Icelandic subspecies *T. i. coburni*, visiting Britain in winter, has more heavily streaked breast and is slightly larger than continental subspecies. Call is penetrating, prolonged high-pitched 'zee-up'. Song is short repetition of flute-like notes followed by low, rather unmusical warble, but is very variable.   RW

SONG THRUSH *Turdus philomelos* L 9″ Very common in woods, parks and gardens, though not as numerous as Blackbird. Uniform brown above, spotted below, and buff underwing distinguish it from all other thrushes. Solitary except during migration. 'Workshops' of broken snail shells around stones are often found in woods and gardens. Call is thin, short 'seep'. Song is flute-like and varied, tending to repeat short sections.   RSWP

MISTLE THRUSH *Turdus viscivorus* L 11″ Common in mature woods and the edge of woodlands. Sometimes, usually outside breeding season, found in open country. In some areas also in gardens in towns and villages. Large, heavily spotted below with white underwing and uniformly grey-brown above; pale outer tailfeathers. Occurs in small flocks outside breeding season. Stands more erect on the ground than other thrushes. Flight characteristic with alternating flapping and closing of wings. Call is characteristic chatter with pauses between bursts. Song resembles Blackbird's but is briefer and less flute-like.   RSW

FIELDFARE *Turdus pilaris* L 10″ (variable). Common in open woods. Nests in colonies, sometimes in gardens and parks of towns and villages. Can also nest singly. Outside breeding season found on fields and pastures in large flocks, often accompanied by Redwings. Large, with grey head and rump, darker tail, chestnut-brown back and spotted underside. Varies considerably in size and colour, but general pattern is maintained. Travels in long undulating 'bands'. Flight characteristic with alternating flapping and short closing of wings. Call is loud 'schack, schack'. Song is twittering and often given in flight.   WP

WHITE'S THRUSH *Zoothera dauma* L 11″ Common in woods with undergrowth. Rare winter visitor to western Europe. Large, covered with prominent, black, crescent-shaped spots. Bold black and white underwing. Flight undulating. Wary. Call piping.   V

where there are similar ledges close by, for instance between the rungs of a ladder hanging on a wall. The Blackbird obviously has difficulty in selecting one site and several neighbouring ledges may hold partially built nests. These contain less and less material the further away they are from the nest eventually used. Blackbirds have also been known to place nests in cars which were in use and on several occasions they have successfully raised broods which were driven back and forth daily.

Thrushes lay three to six, usually spotted, bluish eggs, which are incubated by both male and female for two weeks. The young spend twelve to sixteen days in the nest but even after leaving it they will be fed by the parents for some days. Most thrushes are double brooded, and ocasionally Blackbirds rear four broods in the year. But owing to predation, they may lay several clutches without success.

Their close affinity to man makes the thrushes very good subjects for study in bird biology by the amateur and their beautiful song, so characteristic of the spring in our gardens and woods, makes them well worth protecting. The harm they do to fruits and berries must be considered in relation to the large numbers of invertebrate pests they eat.

A danger to the thrushes and to many other species of birds is the use of synthetic pesticides on a large scale. In particular the chlorinated hydrocarbons, for instance DDT, form a threat to our wild life because, unlike many of the older types of pesticide, they persist for a long time and accumulate in the animal to an increasing degree as the food chain is ascended. In many cases directly lethal effects on birds of these popular insecticides have been proved, but even more dangerous may be the decreased fertility of birds which have ingested sublethal amounts of the poison. Due to the accumulation through the food chain it is most obvious among the species at the end of the chain, particularly birds of prey. A decline in the numbers of breeding pairs and particularly in the number of young raised coincides closely with both the place and the time of application of pesticides, and the potential danger to our wild life from these chemicals is at last being realized. Control of the use of pesticides and a shift to less persistent types seem to be the best hope if our wild life is not to be greatly impoverished by our own neglect and ignorance.

Bearded Tit
family *Muscicapidae*, subfamily *Timaliinae*

The Bearded Tit or Reedling resembles the tits in appearance and habits but belongs to the family *Muscicapidae*. It lives in reed-beds in marshes and eats mainly insects. In winter it also takes quantities of seeds of marsh plants. It is mainly sedentary and large numbers may perish in particularly harsh winters.

The nest is a deep cup, woven of grass and reeds, placed low among the reeds, close to the ground. Five to seven white eggs blotched with brown are laid. Both parents incubate for a period of twelve or thirteen days and the fledging period is nine to twelve days.

Weavers
order *Passeriformes*, family *Ploceidae*

When the term 'weaver' or 'weaver finch' is used, most people associate it with African species and their elaborate nests or with cage birds of beautiful colours. Few realize that the family includes one of our most commonly seen birds—the ubiquitous

House Sparrow. Other European members of this large family are the House-Sparrow-like Spanish Sparrow, the Tree Sparrow and the inhabitants of the great European mountains, the Rock Sparrow and the Snow Finch.

Weavers are stocky, small to medium-sized birds with thick heavy bills. The European species are much less brightly coloured than their southern relatives and are mostly grey, brown, black and white.

They are all sedentary in habits but Snow Finches move to a lower altitude during the winter.

All are seed-eaters and only the young are fed on insects. The House Sparrow, as we have all had the opportunity to see, will eat almost anything left from the human table and is particularly fond of bread. Outside the breeding season all weavers are social in habit and roam the open countryside in flocks.

The House Sparrow has associated itself so closely with man that it is rare to find it more than a few hundred yards from his dwellings. So successful has this association been from the point of view of the House Sparrow that it has spread to almost all settled areas. In many places, particularly North America and Australia, the House Sparrow was originally introduced by

BEARDED TIT *Panurus biarmicus* L 6½″ Very local, but numerous where it occurs, in extensive reed-beds, along streams or lakes or in swamps. Brownish colours and very long tail distinguish it. Male has distinctive black moustachial stripe and black under tail-coverts. These features are missing in female and juvenile. Very active, climbing about in reeds with jerky movement. Flight weak, with very rapid wing action and characteristic tail movements, usually low over reeds. Outside breeding season occurs almost exclusively in flocks. Call is a hard 'tink, tink' like stones knocked together. Song twittering.
RW

SNOW FINCH *Montifringilla nivalis* L 7″ Common in high mountains above tree limit and below snow limit, moving to lower altitudes in winter. Often found near human habitations. In all plumages easily told from Snow Bunting by grey head. Note large white wing patches and tail-feathers. Females more brownish with less extensive white areas than males. Juveniles resemble females. Bill colour changes from yellow in winter to black in spring. Less compactly built than buntings. Perches more upright. Often jerks tail. Outside breeding season often found in small flocks. Nests in crevices or under rocks. Call is rather harsh 'zjeeb'. Song, given from rocky perch or song-flight, is twittering.

Bearded Tit

juv.

♀

♂

Snow Finch

♀

♂

HOUSE SPARROW *Passer domesticus* L 5¾" Abundant on farms, in towns and villages. Closely associated with man. Male has grey crown, black bib. Female and juvenile much more uniformly coloured with unstreaked breast, striped back and buffish stripe over eye. Gregarious. Nests under roofs, in holes, nest boxes or builds bulky domed nests in bushes and trees. Calls and song consist of a number of monotonous chirps. Italian Sparrow *Passer domesticus italiae*, in which male distinguished by chestnut crown and clear white cheeks, is found on Italian peninsula, Corsica and Crete. RWP

sentimental Europeans who did not envisage the millions of birds which have resulted from the few individuals brought over to soothe their homesickness. The House Sparrow is now the most widespread of all land birds. The Tree Sparrow has also been introduced in many countries but has generally been less successful, and in Europe its association with man is much looser than that of the House Sparrow. So is the case of the Spanish Sparrow, which prefers open fields, leaving towns and villages for the House Sparrow.

Our sparrows have no real song but make do with rather unmusical chirps.

House Sparrow

Italian Sparrow

Spanish Sparrow

SPANISH SPARROW *Passer hispaniolensis* L 5¾" Common but local near fields. Less closely associated with human habitation than House Sparrow. Male easily distinguished from male House Sparrow by larger black bib, black stripes on flanks and back, and chestnut crown. Extent of black is variable, but always more than on House Sparrow male. Females and juveniles told with difficulty by lighter throat, darker back and faint dark stripes on flanks. Nests colonially in the open, in thickets, nests of large birds or trees. Nest similar to House Sparrow's. Calls and song resemble House Sparrow's but are richer. V

House Sparrows and Tree Sparrows characteristically nest in cavities of many kinds, under eaves, in haystacks and nest boxes, usually in colonies. But in some seasons many nests may be built in trees and bushes, and both the House and Tree Sparrows frequently build in the bottoms of the large nests of herons, storks and birds of prey. The Snow Finch and Rock Sparrow usually place their nests in rock crevices. The Spanish Sparrow usually nests in vegetation.

Our sparrows lay four or five spotted eggs which are incubated for two weeks. The young remain in the nest for another two weeks.

Opposite Above, Bullfinches. Below, Hawfinch.

Tree Sparrow

Rock Sparrow

juv.

Finches

order *Passeriformes*, family *Fringillidae*

Our most colourful garden birds belong to the family of finches. Many species are common in gardens and are easily observed.

They are small to medium-sized, bright-plumaged birds with heavy bills. The heaviest bill of all our finches is that of the Hawfinch, a beautifully coloured bird which unfortunately is not seen as often as some other species because it spends most of its time high in the canopy of deciduous woods. Its bill is huge. It is conical in shape and a perfect tool with which the Hawfinch expertly cracks open even the hardest seeds. In northern Europe its speciality is cherries. The flesh of the cherries, which is relished by Starlings and thrushes, is not eaten but the stone is cracked open with the bill. The preference for this particular fruit is ancient: a fossil of a Hawfinch 100,000 years old was found to have cherry seeds in its stomach. In southern Europe, Hawfinches can manage the even harder olive stones. To crack these open the bird has to apply a pressure of more than a hundred pounds, quite a feat by a bird weighing no more than two ounces.

Our other finches have smaller bills and handle less difficult seeds. The bill of the Goldfinch is rather thin and pointed and this species also lives on very small seeds, often from thistles. Most bizarre of bill shapes is that of the Crossbill, in which the tips of the upper and lower mandible cross completely either to the

TREE SPARROW *Passer montanus* L 5½" Common in cultivated areas with trees. Less closely associated with human habitation than House Sparrow. Smaller, more delicately built than House Sparrow, with which it often mixes. Note chestnut crown, small bib and black spot on white cheek. Sexes similar. Nests in holes, mainly in trees. Uses nest boxes. Calls resemble House Sparrow's but are higher-pitched and sharper.   RWP

ROCK SPARROW *Petronia petronia* L 5½" Common but local in rocky country, uncultivated or cultivated. Very pale with striped crown and prominent white spots on tail. More active than House Sparrow with which it sometimes associates. Sometimes runs. Usually seen in small flocks looser than those of House Sparrows. Many calls resemble House Sparrow's but has characteristic 'dui-ee' call.

winter ♂

♀

♂ summer

Chaffinch

Brambling

♂ winter

♀

♀

♂ summer

♂

♀

right or left of each other. Not only are the bill and jaw joint asymmetrical, but the mandible can be pushed sideways as much as one centimetre. When a Crossbill opens a fir cone to get at the protected seeds, it squeezes its bill in between the scales and, by a combination of twisting and sideways movements of the mandible, loosens or breaks the scale so that it can extract the two seeds with its sticky tongue. Pine cones, the scales of which are much stronger, are usually opened by biting through the scales.

Male finches are brighter coloured than females. This is particularly true of the two members of the subfamily *Fringillinae*, the Chaffinch and the Brambling. These two species also differ from the rest of our finches not only in various anatomical particularities but also in certain behavioural characteristics. They are more territorial in behaviour and feed their young from the bill whereas the *Carduelinae*, the subfamily to which our other finches belong, regurgitate the food to be given to their offspring.

Most finches are arboreal in their habits, but there are exceptions to this rule. The Twite is often found nesting far from the nearest tree and in winter Chaffinches, Bramblings, Twites, Linnets and Greenfinches are more often than not seen feeding in open country, although they nest in trees or bushes.

In spite of their seed-eating habits, many of the finches are migratory at least to some degree. Most do not leave Europe but merely seek slightly more favourable climates. This is particularly true of the species which find their food on the ground as

CHAFFINCH *Fringilla coelebs* L 6″ One of the most common European birds. Nests in woods, deciduous and coniferous, gardens and parks. In winter also found in flocks in more open country. Notice distinct white wing-bars, white on outer tail-feathers, blue and red plumage of male, and greenish plumage of female and juvenile. Outside breeding season often seen in flocks varying in size from a dozen to thousands. Flocks may consist mainly of individuals of the same sex. Often mixes with Bramblings. Seeks food on the ground. Song, given from rather exposed perch, is melodious, short rattling with many geographic variations. Flight call is a short 'juep juep', and usual call a ringing 'pick'.   RWP

BRAMBLING *Fringilla montifringilla* L 6″ Common but variable in numbers. Nests in woods and semi-open country. In winter found in woods, parks, gardens and fields, usually in flocks. Notice distinct white upper rump, black back and white wing-bar. Flocks often mixed with Chaffinches. In years of irruption flocks can number thousands, even millions of birds. Seeks food on the ground. Song is rather monotonous repetition of Greenfinch-like calls, given from an exposed perch. Flight call is nasal 'tjaek, tjaek'.   WP

Bullfinch

Hawfinch

BULLFINCH *Pyrrhula pyrrhula* L 5¾" Rather common, in deciduous and coniferous woods, parks and gardens. Notice white rump, black and grey upper parts, red underside and short heavy bill of male, more subdued brownish colours of female. In winter often seen in small flocks. Movement very slow and deliberate. Feeds mainly in trees and bushes on berries, buds and seeds. Flight slow and undulating. Song, not well developed, is low, piping warble, but will learn to sing in captivity. Call is soft, melancholy 'peu, peu'.　　　　　　　　RWP

HAWFINCH *Coccothraustes coccothraustes* L 7" Uncommon. Often missed as it is wary, spending most of its time among the foliage of the treetops. Almost exclusively found in deciduous woods. Notice extremely large, heavy bill, short tail and characteristic colour pattern; also white pattern on wings, characteristic in flight. Usually seen singly, in pairs or family groups. Song is low and twittering, rarely heard. Call is metallic 'tpik'.　　R

snow cover will make survival very difficult for them.

Several species of finches show irregular movements called eruptions. This phenomenon, the irregular occurrence of a certain species in different areas and at different times, is caused by an imbalance between food supply and food demand. It therefore happens more commonly in areas where the supply of food fluctuates and among bird species which are specialized in their food demands. This condition is particularly pronounced in the northern coniferous forests where the seed production of evergreens fluctuates and many species of bird live on them. The Crossbill, Two-barred Crossbill (which lives on larch) and Pine Grosbeak are examples among the finches, but other birds like Waxwing and Nutcracker are also known for a similar behaviour. To a lesser degree the same fluctuation is found in the seed production of beech, birch and alder, and Brambling, Redpoll and Siskin, which are specialized in these seeds, therefore also show an explosive pattern in their migration. The eruptions usually take place in years when a high production of seeds is followed by a very low production. Because of the success in breeding the preceding year when food was abundant, the birds are numerous but their food supply is unusually low. If they are to survive they have only one alternative which is to move to areas where the food supply may be better. This is exactly what they do and eruptions of Crossbills have been closely related to the seed crops in their normal breeding areas. In these years Crossbills swarm over western Europe, reaching far beyond their normal range. They often settle down to breed in these new places and may even breed successfully for more than one season. But it is almost always a temporary phase, and no permanent settlement results. More often irregularly migrating species either succumb or return to their normal breeding range.

The most impressive invasions are probably performed by Bramblings, which in certain years occur in immense numbers. Usually this is within their normal range and the irregularity is more in numbers than in place. These flocks of Bramblings can number millions of individuals and the trees where they settle look as if they have magically got all their leaves back. Branches

CITRIL FINCH *Serinus citrinella* L 4½" Common in mountains with open coniferous woods. In winter moves to lower altitudes. Unstreaked greenish-yellow underside and rump, yellow wing-bars and grey neck distinguish adult. Juvenile is brownish and heavily striped. It lacks the yellow wing-band of Goldfinch juvenile and is considerably more heavily striped, particularly above, than any other finch. Flight undulating, resembling that of Goldfinch. Usually seen in flocks. Call is a plaintive but characteristic 'sit'. Song, often given in song-flight, resembles that of Serin.   V

Citril Finch

juv.

Serin

may even break under the weight of the multitude of birds. These flocks exhaust the local food supply very quickly and are therefore forced to be constantly on the move.

The eruptions of other finches are usually less impressive and, as with the Brambling, it is more in numbers than in place that irregularity is found. During years of eruption some will occur outside their normal range but usually only in rather small numbers.

The life cycles of some of the finches have, mainly because of their abundance, been studied in great detail, for instance that of the omnipresent Chaffinch. Chaffinches are found breeding in the woods and gardens of every European country with the

SERIN *Serinus serinus* L 4½" Common in open woodland, parks and gardens. Streaked plumage, yellow underside and rump distinguish it. Immatures are less yellow, more streaked. Sociable, usually seen in small flocks. Often feeds on the ground. Flight undulating. Call is a varied twittering 'chirlit'. Song, which is given from high open perch or in song-flight, is a jingling, sibilant twitter. Very vocal.   V

exception of Iceland, where practically no woods are found. The territory occupied by each Chaffinch varies in size. The smallest territories, which might not be much more than a thousand square meters, are found in mixed woods where food is most abundant. In the poorer pine woods, territories may be of areas more than twenty times the area of the smallest. These territories are occupied in the early spring, but even during their winter existence in flocks, Chaffinches show territorial behaviour, each Chaffinch in a flock not tolerating another closer than three or four inches. Fights can sometimes develop if two birds are accidentally too close to each other, but

GREENFINCH *Carduelis chloris* L 5½" Very common in rather open, cultivated country, gardens and parks. Greenish or brownish with distinct yellow spots on tail and wings. Females and juveniles are easily told from other brownish finches by their heavy build and wing and tail pattern. Bill and head large. Usually encountered in pairs or small flocks, in winter sometimes mixing with sparrows and other finches. Flight undulating. Calls include a rapid trilling 'chick, chick, chick', and more nasal 'twee-ee'. Song, which is given from high open perch or in butterfly-like song-flight, is a twittering mixture of calls. RSWP

Greenfinch

Siskin

usually a threatening attitude in which the white wing-bars are displayed is enough.

In the northern part of their range the males arrive a little earlier in spring than the females and the male immediately takes up a territory. He announces his ownership by singing, and intruders are chased away. An intruder is approached and reacts by retreating from the male's threatening posture in which the white wing-bars are displayed and the breast feathers fluffed up to give the impression of greater size. If this is not enough to discourage the opponent, regular fights develop, often starting in the air where the birds engage each other so viciously that they fall to the ground in a confused bundle of

SISKIN *Carduelis spinus* L 4¼" Common. Nests in coniferous and mixed woods. Outside breeding season seen typically in birch and alder, but also in other types of woods. Streaked, greenish with yellow areas on sides of tail, and yellow wing-bars are characteristic. It is much smaller and more streaked than Greenfinch. Outside breeding season in flocks, sometimes with Redpolls. Makes compact flocks in flight. Wheezy call diagnostic. Song, delivered from high perch or in song-flight, is twittering. RW

GOLDFINCH *Carduelis carduelis* L 4¾" Common in all kinds of open country with scattered trees and bushes, in parks and gardens. In winter also open fields. Adult unmistakable. Sexes very similar but female can be told by slightly less extensive red on the face. Juvenile brownish and streaked. In all plumages the wide yellow wing-bar is diagnostic and especially striking in flight. Gregarious outside breeding season, usually occurring in small flocks, sometimes mixed with other finches. Often seeks its food (seeds) in thistles and similar plants, climbing nimbly over them. Usually perches in the open. Flight is markedly undulating. Call is a characteristic, liquid 'deedelit', often repeated. Song, delivered from an exposed perch, is a similarly liquid twittering.　　RS

LINNET *Acanthis cannabina* L 5" Very common on heaths and in open country with hedges and bushes, in parks and gardens. In winter usually found in open country. Male characteristic with greyish head and dark brown back. In summer, red on breast and front, part of which can be retained in winter plumage. Female and juvenile resembles Twite but have much more pronounced white wing and tail patches. Bill is dark, also in winter. In all plumages it has a whitish, streaked throat whereas Twite has a buffish unstriped throat and Redpoll a small black bib. Gregarious outside breeding season, flocks often associated with other finches. Flight undulating but less so than Goldfinch's. Call 'tsweet'; twitters in flight. Song, usually given from open perch, is a pleasant, varied twitter.　　RSW

legs and wings. One will eventually give up and fly back into his own territory, the other still in hot pursuit. But well into the pursued's territory, the roles are suddenly reversed and the pursuer is chased. It seems as though the bird's morale is strongly boosted by the fact that he is on his home field, a phenomenon not unknown among men. Fights of this kind will repeat themselves for long periods in the spring and in this way the boundaries of neighbouring territories are defined. The

Goldfinch

Linnet

Chaffinch is one of the birds most likely to attack its own image in a window or other reflecting surface; females as well as males do this.

As spring progresses, the male sings more strongly and more often. The female attracted to his territory enters it but more often than not she will be chased away; only slowly does this aggressive behaviour towards a member of the opposite sex give way to sexual behaviour. Bullfinches show another

TWITE *Acanthis flavirostris* L 5¼" Common in moorland and cultivated open country with or without low bushes in summer. In winter frequents completely open land, often along seashores like Snow Bunting and Shore Lark. Rather nondescript, brownish, striped plumage. Like Linnet it has white patches on wings and tail, but these are less distinct. Male has pinkish rump. Female has greyish-brown, spotted rump. In winter bill is yellow (Linnet's bill is dark) but in summer it is dark. Upper side generally darker and breast richer yellow-brown than Linnet's. Throat is unstriped buffish (whitish and streaked in Linnet). Gregarious outside breeding season. Flight undulating but less so than Goldfinch. Flocks in flight rather close. Nests in loose colonies. Call is a nasal, metallic 'tweeh'. Song, delivered from perch or in song flight, resembles that of Linnet but is slower and harder.
RW

REDPOLL *Acanthis flammea* L 5" Fairly common in birch and mixed woods. Red forehead and small black chin-spot distinguish it from all other species except Arctic Redpoll. Told from this by more streaked rump and underside and less distinct white areas. Several sub-species of varying sizes and shades of darkness occur. The Lesser Redpoll *(A.f. cabaret),* found in the British Isles and the Alps, is smaller and darker than the Mealy Redpoll *(A.f. flammea)* of Scandinavia. Greater Redpoll *(A.f. rostrata)* from Greenland is dark and the largest. Gregarious, often nesting in colonies. Flocks are compact. Actively searches trees and bushes for food (seeds). Flight undulating. Call is a hoarse 'chi-chi-chit'. Song, given from perch or in song-flight, is a trilling twitter.
RWP

♂ winter

♂ summer

Twite

♂

♀

Redpoll

♂

♂ Mealy Redpoll

♀

interesting phenomenon in their pair formation. The female approaches the desired male in a threatening attitude. If he behaves timidly, he is immediately chased away and the female loses interest in him. If on the other hand he does not let her intimidate him and instead receives her attacks boldly with his beautiful red underside displayed, her attack will subside and instead the two birds will peacefully start playing with each other's bills. Later the male will start feeding the female. The male is the dominant member of the family, but on the other hand, a male will not fight a female regardless of how viciously she may attack him. The whole performance has but the one purpose of insuring the dominance of the male over the female. Unlike the Chaffinch, the Bullfinch and most of the other finches do not have a very well-defined territory.

The true function of territory has not been clarified. It is of importance in dispersing the birds over a large area but it is also to the advantage of the bird to know its area well so that it will have a better chance of avoiding predators. The spacing out of the birds also insures a certain food supply for the family. Tits and other hole-nesters take the nesting site as the primary object of defence. Territory may also be helpful in keeping the spreading of contagious diseases to a minimum.

The songs of our finches, by which they announce the occupation of a territory and attract the females, are usually rather simple but pleasing to the human ear. They are usually delivered from an exposed song post, often used day after day by several species. Greenfinch and Serin have a characteristic song-flight during which the wings are moved very slowly and the bird tilts from side to side, recalling the flight of a butterfly.

Among finches the female alone builds the nest, which in many species is a very beautiful construction. The Chaffinch's nest is covered on the outside with lichen held together by spider webs. This camouflages the nest very effectively and can make it almost impossible to see. Inside this there is a firm layer of moss and grass, then a layer of grass followed by the innermost cup made of very small roots, feathers and hair. It usually takes the females about a week to build it and it takes more than one thousand trips to the nesting site. The Goldfinch is efficient and careful in nest building, like the Chaffinch, but uses a lot of poplar 'cotton' and other plant fibres as material.

Finches lay two to eight eggs, which are usually whitish or bluish and spotted. In most species only the female incubates the eggs. The males of practically all the *Carduelinae* feed their mates in this period, some females receiving all their food in this way. The male regurgitates the food which is to be given to the female. Incubation does not usually start until the last or next to last egg is laid. An exception to this is the Crossbill which starts incubating as soon as her first egg is laid. This is essential as the eggs are often laid when it is still very cold, often well below freezing. Crossbills and several other northern finches, such as the Pine Grosbeak, are very reluctant to leave the nest and will let one approach them closely.

The period of incubation is about two weeks and the young spend ten to twelve days in the nest. Young Crossbills are closely brooded for several days after they have hatched and grow more slowly than other finches. They remain in the nest for fifteen to eighteen days. This is an adaptation to the very early time of breeding which again is an adaptation to the plentiful supply of pine seeds at that time of the year.

Some finches raise two or even three broods a year. As should be evident, they are fascinating birds to watch, and

ARCTIC REDPOLL *Acanthis hornemanni* L 5" Fairly common in more open tundra. In winter as Redpoll, from which it is told by unstreaked white rump, fewer streaks on underside and more clear white areas, particularly on head. This is particularly evident in the Greenland subspecies, Hornemann's Redpoll (*A.h. hornemanni*), whereas the Scandinavian subspecies, Coues's Redpoll (*A.h. exilipes*) resembles the Redpoll more. Often occurs with Redpoll. Habits and voice as those of Redpoll.   V

TRUMPETER FINCH *Rhodopechys githaginea* L 5½" A very rare visitor to Mediterranean countries from north African breeding grounds. Male in summer unmistakable. In winter plumage resembles female and juvenile more. Notice very short bill. Terrestrial in habits. Call is short and nasal.

SCARLET GROSBEAK *Carpodacus erythrinus* L 5¾" Common in damp bushy areas. Rare autumn visitor to western Europe. Male unmistakable. Female and juvenile streaked greyish brown, with distinct wing-bars. Characteristically holds head tucked between shoulders. Call is piping and trilling. Song is piping and trilling. Pallas' Rosefinch (*Carpodacus roseus*), a rare visitor to eastern Europe from Asia, is slightly larger with red areas paler. Great Rosefinch (*Carpodacus rubicilla*), a resident of the Caucasus, is also more pink (entire underside). Bill of both sexes straw-coloured.   V

PINE GROSBEAK *Pinicola enucleator* L 8" Fairly common in coniferous and mixed woods. Very large. Male red, female green, immature more grey, all with two distinct wing-bars. Outside breeding season in flocks. Usually tame. Call consists of three high whistles. Song is a loud warble.   V

Arctic Redpoll

♀

♂

♂ winter

♂ summer

Trumpeter Finch

♀

♀

♂

Scarlet Grosbeak

Pine Grosbeak

♂

♀

PARROT CROSSBILL *Loxia pytyopsittacus* L 6½" Fairly common in coniferous and mixed woods with preference for pine (Crossbill prefers spruce). Resembles Crossbill, but is more plump with larger head and bill. As in Crossbill, male is red, female green and juvenile greenish-grey. Outside breeding season may mix with Crossbills but more usually found in 'clean' flocks. Habits resemble Crossbill's. Irregular in winter occurrence south of its range. Call deeper and louder than Crossbill's. V

CROSSBILL *Loxia curvirostra* L 6½" Common in coniferous forests. Male red or orange-red, female green and juvenile grey-green, all without wing-bars. Crossing of bill not always noticeable. Told from Parrot Crossbill by smaller (not as deep) bill and head, and less stocky appearance; and from Two-barred Crossbill by lack of wing-bars. May nest in almost any season but mostly from January to April. Usually seen in small flocks. Climbs on outer branches of conifers acrobatically, tearing cone scales to get at seeds. Occurs in varying numbers mainly depending on local crop of cones. Sometimes makes large-scale invasions, during which it can reach any part of Europe and often settles to nest for one one or more seasons if conditions are favourable. Call is unmistakable 'kip, kip, kip' given with great emphasis. Song is twittering, with characteristic calls interspersed.

R

because of this their beautiful colours and pleasant songs are highly valued in our woods and gardens. But they are not universally loved. In forestry circles Crossbills are regarded with suspicion because of their seed-eating habits, but the harm they do has been proved to be minimal. A slightly different story is that of the Bullfinch, aesthetically one of our most beautiful birds. Bullfinches eat mainly seeds, especially the fruits of the ash, but in late winter when these become scarce, they start eating the buds of trees and bushes in increasing amounts. On fruit farms a flock of Bullfinches can cause appreciable economic

Parrot Crossbill

Crossbill

juv.

harm. In ordinary gardens they also eat the buds of flowering bushes, but as these are of value only as something beautiful to see, one might argue that the Bullfinch, which is certainly beautiful, serves the same purpose as the flower.

Buntings
order *Passeriformes*, family *Emberizidae*

The buntings are almost as characteristic of open country as the larks. They inhabit both cultivated and uncultivated open

TWO-BARRED CROSSBILL *Loxia leucoptera* L 6″ Uncommon in coniferous woods with preference for larch. Smaller than Crossbill with weaker bill and two distinct, white wing-bars. Habits resemble those of Crossbill but more irregular in occurrence. In some years some birds reach most western European countries, but never in as large numbers as Crossbill. Call consists of three or four Redpoll-like notes, higher and decidely different from call of Crossbill. Song is long and canary-like.   V

CORN BUNTING *Emberiza calandra* L 7″ Very common but often local in open country with only few bushes. Greyish brown, heavily streaked without distinctive features. Sexes similar. Heavy-looking. Some show dark spot in centre of breast. Outside breeding season in flocks, often mixed with other buntings and finches. Flight heavy (easily told from larks even at a long distance), often with legs dangling. Some males are polygamous. Call is short and harsh 'tsrip'. Characteristic song, which is usually given from exposed perch (often from wires), is monotonous, jingling.   R

Two-barred Crossbill

juv.

Corn Bunting

Little Bunting

♀ ♂

♂ winter

Rustic Bunting

♂ summer

♀

LITTLE BUNTING *Emberiza pusilla* L 5¼" Uncommon in wet, fairly open tundra; on passage also found in marshes and on hills. A rare autumn visitor to western Europe. Chestnut and black on head in summer diagnostic. In other plumages, without distinct field characters but combination of small size, streaked and spotted plumage with rusty cheeks distinguishes it. Most easily confused with Reed and Rustic Bunting females and juveniles, but is much smaller with paler colours and finer black streaking of breast and flanks. Call is a sharp 'tick'. Song is short and melodious, of same quality as Robin's.   P

RUSTIC BUNTING *Emberiza rustica* L 5¾" Fairly common on edges of moist woods and thickets. Outside breeding season also in more open situations. A rare spring and autumn visitor to western Europe. Black and white patterned head of summer male diagnostic. In other plumages best told from other buntings by rusty breast-band and flanks and brown pattern on head. Most easily confused with female and juvenile Reed Buntings, but these have blackish spots on breast and flanks, not rusty. Moustachial streak is less conspicuous in Rustic Bunting female and juvenile. Often raises crown feathers. Call is a short, sharp 'tick'. Song varied, but usually rather short with a Dunnock-like quality.   V

country, and some species are also found at woodland edges and clearings but only rarely in true woods. The change of the face of the European continent by man from a well-wooded land mass with only few areas of steppes to a vast, almost woodless field, which ecologically is equivalent to the steppe, has benefited many species of buntings as well as other birds of the open country.

The family has a very wide distribution and ranges from the extreme north where the Snow Buntings, inhabiting the northern shores of Greenland, are the most northerly breeding passerine, to the tropics. They are small to medium-sized, rather heavy birds with conical, typically seed-eater's bills and rather long tails. Their colours are generally subdued although yellow, white and black are found in many species, particularly in the characteristic facial patterns of the males of many of the European species. Females are brownish and striped, most without prominent characteristics. This often causes trouble for the field ornithologist in his attempts to identify the birds.

Rock Bunting
♂

♀

Ortolan Bunting
♂

♀

juv.

Fifteen species breed within the boundaries of our continent and three more are accidental visitors from their Asiatic breeding ground (Chestnut, Red-headed and Black-faced Buntings). One of these, the Red-headed Bunting, has caused some controversy as it is a very common cage bird. Like many cage birds, it often escapes and as the European climate does not differ much from that of its original haunts it is capable of surviving for a long time. Records of the species therefore must be examined carefully to determine whether these birds are really true wanderers or merely escapes. Most often it is impossible to determine with certainty. Many other birds which are often kept in captivity are occasionally observed in the wild but their origin is usually easy to determine. Nobody would, for instance, suggest that the hundreds of budgerigars seen alone or in flocks of sparrows came here all the way from Australia of their own accord.

Other accidental visitors of this family are the various North American sparrows. Few of these seem to have crossed the

ROCK BUNTING *Emberiza cia* L 6¼″ Fairly common in mountains with bushes and scattered trees and vine-yards, in winter moving to lower altitudes. Grey and black head pattern distinguishes male. Female much duller but has grey throat (no other European bunting has this). Immatures resemble immature Yellowhammer in general colours and chestnut-coloured rump but are separated by reddish underside. Also told from immature Cretzschmar's and Ortolan Buntings by chestnut rump and dark bill. White outer tail-feathers displayed as it flicks its tail. Often seen on the ground, but also perches freely in trees. Call is a thin, sharp 'zeet'. Song, which is usually given from high, open perch, is a high-pitched series of 'zee' notes, somewhat varied in sequence.   V

ORTOLAN BUNTING *Emberiza hortulana* L 6½″ Com-mon in rather open, dry country with scattered bushes and trees. Sometimes gardens. Outside breeding season also in more exposed areas and cultivated fields. Adult male told from other buntings except Cretzschmar's by greenish-grey unmarked head and rusty-brown under-side. From Cretzschmar's by yellow (not orange) throat and greenish-grey (rather than grey) head and neck. Female has yellow throat (rusty in Cretzschmar's). Head is greenish-grey with streaks. Juveniles rather indis-tinctly streaked brown, with brown (not chestnut as in Yellowhammer and Rock Bunting) streaked rump. At short range narrow eye-ring and light colour of bill noticeable. Less buffish on underside than juvenile Cretzschmar's. Call is a high-pitched soft 'tsee'. It is a rather secretive bird which is often difficult to catch sight of, keeping well hidden. Song resembles that of Yellow-hammer but is much slower. The last notes are of a lower pitch than the preceding ones.   P

Atlantic unaided. There are several examples of flocks migrating along the coast of North America and alighting on ships on the way to Europe. Sometimes they stay on board, their seed-eating habits insuring their survival, and do not depart until European shores are in sight. As is the case with practically all the other North American stragglers, most of the birds are observed in the British Isles.

In migratory habits the buntings show great variability, ranging from the strictly resident Cirl Bunting to the highly migratory Ortolan Bunting. Others, like the Yellowhammer, Corn and Reed Buntings, are partial migrants, the northern-most populations moving southward to avoid the severe winter climate. Some species show interesting features in their migratory habits. The Black-headed Bunting of south-eastern

CRETZSCHMAR'S BUNTING *Emberiza caesia* L 6½" Common in dry, rocky country with scattered bushes. Resembles Ortolan Bunting in all plumages, but male has grey (not greenish) head and rather orange (not yellow) throat. Females have rusty (not yellow) throat. The head is bluish-grey with some streaks. Juveniles are slightly more buff below but not safely distinguished in the field from juvenile Ortolan. Told from juvenile Rock Bunting by more brown (not chestnut) rump and flesh-coloured (not black) bill. Usually seen on the ground. Call is sharper than Ortolan's. Song is a short twitter resembling that of Ortolan.

REED BUNTING *Emberiza schoeniclus* L 6" Common in and near reed-beds, in winter also resorting to cultivated areas, sometimes in the company of other buntings and finches. Male in summer plumage unmistakable with white collar, black hood and bib. Female has strongly patterned head, and white throat surrounded by dark streaks. White outer tail-feathers show as bird flicks tail. Can be confused with Rustic Bunting female and juvenile but has black streaks on breast and flank, not rusty. Much larger than Little Bunting, which is lighter with finer streaks. Outside breeding season often in small flocks. Call is a loud 'zeek'. Song, which is usually given from open perch, is short and monotonous 'chi-chi-chi-chitty'.   RWP

Cretzschmar's Bunting

Reed Bunting

Europe travels almost due east to its winter quarters in India, one of the very few European migrant passerines not showing a more or less north-south direction. Another species also south-eastern in its distribution, the Rose-coloured Starling, shows a similar pattern.

Snow Buntings, nesting in Greenland, most often migrate to the North American continent in winter, but some undoubtedly cross the Atlantic together with Greenland Wheatears to reach Europe.

The autumn migration of the Ortolan Bunting is sadly reflected on the menus of many French restaurants; the bird is regarded as a great delicacy in several Latin countries. During this period, Ortolans are caught by the hundred. Already well-covered, they nevertheless happily devour the seeds offered

RED-HEADED BUNTING *Emberiza bruniceps* L 6"
Common in rather open, bushy country, often near water, even in reed-beds. A rare visitor to western Europe, usually in cultivated fields. Many of the records are probably escaped cage birds as it is popular as such. Male unmistakable with red head and breast. Female most resembles female Black-headed Bunting, but whereas Black-headed Bunting female has some chestnut on back, this is lacking in the Red-headed Bunting, which is more green. Red-headed also has whitish rather than yellow under tail-coverts. Juveniles not safely separable from juvenile Black-headed Bunting. Habits resemble those of Black-headed Bunting. Call is a series of harsh notes. Song is a short, fast, monotonous warble.   ?V

PINE BUNTING *Emberiza leucocephala* L 6¼" Common in rather open, bushy country and open mixed and coniferous woods. A rare autumn visitor to western Europe, usually occurring in cultivated areas. Male unmistakable with white and brown pattern on head. Female has indistinct brown breast-band, but white crown is diagnostic. Juveniles most closely resemble juvenile Rustic Bunting in having chestnut rump, but have less chestnut on wing. Gregarious outside breeding season. Resembles Yellowhammer in habits. Call resembles that of Yellowhammer, of which it may be a sub-species. Song somewhat similar to that of Chaffinch with an ascending pitch.   V

CINEREOUS BUNTING *Emberiza cineracea* L 6½"
Very rare and local, breeding on island of Mytilene in the Aegean Sea. Present from March to August. Prefers barren, rocky country. Colours greyish, male with unmarked yellow head, female and juvenile with less yellow and more stripes on head and throat. Song is simple, bunting-like.

Red-headed Bunting

Pine Bunting

Cinereous Bunting

YELLOWHAMMER *Emberiza citrinella* L 6½" Very common in rather open country with bushes, edges and clearings of woods, in winter also on open cultivated fields. Streaked yellow head, chestnut-brown rump and white outer tail-feathers. Females and immatures less boldly coloured and generally more heavily streaked, most easily confused with female and juvenile Cirl Bunting, but have chestnut, not brown, rump. Outside breeding season found in flocks, often with other buntings and finches. Feeds on ground. Call is sharp 'tjip'. Song, uttered from exposed perch, is monotonous 'little bit of bread and no——— cheese'.　　　　RW

them in captivity, only to be slaughtered when bulging with fat, thus ending their migration on a plate in the company of four or five other members of the species.

In the Middle East not only the Ortolan but practically any other songbird passing through is caught in large numbers, mainly in nets, and offered for sale. The slaughter is of such magnitude that some of the species cannot sustain the continued loss. The decline of the European population of Ortolans can be attributed to this practice which is regarded with disgust by the people of more northern countries, perhaps because the amount of meat, delicious as it may be, is so small for each life sacrificed.

juv.

♂

♀

Yellowhammer

♀

♂

Yellow-breasted Bunting

YELLOW-BREASTED BUNTING *Emberiza aureola* L 5½" Common in moist thickets and birch woods. In winter also in more open country. Rare autumn visitor to western Europe. Male unmistakable with black head, chestnut breast-band on yellow underside and distinct white wing-bars, which are also present in winter plumage. Female resembles Yellowhammer but is darker above with characteristic striped crown. Juveniles resemble female but are less distinct in pattern. Told from Yellowhammer by yellow-brown rump; from Cirl Bunting by streaked under tail-coverts and paler colours. Gregarious, nests in loose colonies. In winter found in flocks. Call is short 'tick'. Song resembles Ortolan's but is louder and faster.　　　　V

Buntings live mainly on seeds but during the summer a large number of insects are taken and most species feed their young exclusively on animal matter. The food is found on the ground. In winter several species may be seen together in especially good feeding grounds, for instance Yellowhammer, Corn and Reed Buntings near haystacks. These flocks are not very closely knit and generally buntings are far less social than finches. An exception is the Snow Bunting, which in winter is seen almost exclusively in flocks. Their white and dark contrasting patterns and tinkling calls as the flock takes to the wing over a partially snow-covered field are almost as integral a part of the north-western European winter with its lead-coloured sky as is the monotonous song of the omnipresent Yellowhammer in the early summer.

The migration of the Lapland Bunting is puzzling. It is quite numerous on its northern breeding grounds but nowhere in Europe can it truly be called common, even within what are the traditional wintering grounds. Perhaps the cryptic colours and skulking behaviour in winter, in combination with the decreased activity of the ornithologist in this season, account for our poor knowledge of its true distribution and abundance.

In spring the flocks of wintering buntings are soon broken up and one starts hearing their songs. Most buntings are not

CIRL BUNTING *Emberiza cirlus* L 6½″ Common in open country with bushes, trees, hedges. In winter also in more open fields. Facial pattern distinguishes male. Told from Yellowhammer by brown, not chestnut, rump; from Yellow-breasted Bunting by unstreaked under tail-coverts and darker colours; from Ortolan Bunting by more pronounced facial pattern and dark, not flesh-coloured, bill. Outside breeding season in flocks, often with other buntings and finches. Call is repeated 'sip'. Song, given from exposed perch, is vibrating repetition of metallic notes.   R

Cirl Bunting

Black-headed Bunting

BLACK-HEADED BUNTING *Emberiza melano-cephala* L 6½″ Fairly common in rather open country with scattered bushes and trees. Male unmistakable with solid black hood. Adults told from other buntings by unstreaked yellow or white underside and lack of white on tail. Female resembles Red-headed female but has chestnut on back, and yellow (not white) under tail-coverts. Juveniles are not safely separated from juvenile Red-headed. Red-headed may be subspecies of Black-headed. Resembles Yellowhammer in habits. Call is short 'sit'. Song starts with a few similar short notes ending in short, pleasant warble. Usually given from exposed perch.   V

great experts in the art of singing and their utterances are usually simple. But what they lack in quality is made up by an untiring repetition of their simple melodies. Throughout Europe the endlessly repeated 'didi, di, di-dueh' of the Yellowhammer is heard all day, and the dry jingle of the Corn Bunting is delivered with a sometimes irritating consistency.

The Corn Bunting, with its simple looks devoid of any ornament and its uncharming sound, has a very interesting breeding biology. Most birds are monogamous, but in some regions the Corn Bunting male may attract several females—as many as seven have been counted—and while he limits his activities to singing from an exposed post in good view of his

♂ winter

♀

juv.

♂ summer

Lapland Bunting

♂ winter

♂ summer

♀

Snow Bunting

LAPLAND BUNTING *Calcarius lapponicus* L 6" Common in open and fairly open Arctic tundra; in high mountains in southern part of range. In winter rather uncommon in fields and open areas near seashores. Summer male has black head and throat with buffish stripe over eye, and unstreaked chestnut neck-band, distinguishing it from Rustic and Reed Bunting males. Winter male, female and juvenile much less distinct with streaked brown plumage. Usually shows some chestnut on wing (adults also on nape) and has indistinct buffish central stripe on head, distinguishing it from very similar Reed Bunting female. More compact and short-tailed than most buntings. Has long hind claw. Gregarious, often mixing with flocks of other buntings, finches and larks. Terrestrial, running on the ground. Call is short trill. Song, usually given in song-flight, has same quality as Skylark's, but is shorter. WP

SNOW BUNTING *Plectrophenax nivalis* L 6¼" Common in open rocky country reaching high up into mountains, but in the northern part of range also found at sea level. In winter frequents open coastal areas but also found on open high ground inland and on fields. Black and white summer plumage identifies male. Winter male, female and juvenile paler than any other buntings; large white wing patches particularly noticeable in adult birds, less so in immatures. Males have black back, females and juveniles brown back. Gregarious outside breeding season, when usually seen in flocks, occasionally with other buntings, finches and larks. Rarely perches in trees. Sometimes flicks tail. Flight undulating. Call is short descending whistle. Song, given from rocky perch or song-flight, is a loud, short, lark-like warble. RW

territory and the nesting sites of his wives, they faithfully raise his offspring. Polygamous behaviour has not been very much investigated, but a number of European species are polygamous. Penduline Tits may mate with several females, but this is a successive number of wives, not the harem-type relationship the Corn Bunting has with its mates. Wrens and Pied Flycatchers may also have more than one mate and examples have been recorded for a number of normally monogamous species. Others, such as Black Grouse and Ruff, have a lek-display in which female association with the socially displaying male is restricted to the sexual act. The behaviour of the Woodcock, where males seek out females, who accept several different suitors, resembles true promiscuity. Polyandry, in which one female is attended by several males, is very rare. It is probably the case among both Dotterels and Red-necked Phalaropes, where the female, having laid the eggs, leaves the burden of raising the next generation to the male and herself moves on to another male. From a theoretical point of view this mode of rearing young should be more efficient than the normal, because the female, relieved of the burden of incubation and care of the young, can lay many more eggs. In spite of this the fact remains that polyandry is of rare occurrence among birds.

Other buntings are more conventional in their breeding behaviour. The females usually make the nest, a simple open cup built on the ground or not far above it. Although the male may take part in the incubation occasionally, the female carries the heavier load in this respect.

The eggs, four to eight in number, are whitish, often with beautiful patterns of dark lines. They are laid in the mornings at intervals of about twenty-four hours. Incubation lasts for about two weeks and begins after the last egg is laid. The young stay in the nest for two weeks. While in the nest, their delicate bodies, not yet protected by their own feathers, are shielded from direct sun and rain by the partially outstretched wings of the parent birds.

Accidentals
Fewer than five records from this century

Common Name	Scientific Name	Origin	Observed
Wandering Albatross	*Diomedea exulans*	South Seas	France, Belgium, Italy
Yellow-nosed Albatross	*Diomedea chlorohynchos*	South Seas	Iceland
Grey-headed Albatross	*Diomedea chrysostoma*	South Seas	Norway
Light-mantled Sooty Albatross	*Phoebetria palpebrata*	South Seas	France
Capped Petrel	*Pterodroma hasitata*	America	Great Britain, France
Kermadec Petrel	*Pterodroma neglecta*	South Seas	Great Britain
Collared Petrel	*Pterodroma leucoptera*	South Seas	Great Britain
Frigate Petrel	*Pelagodroma marina*	Atlantic	Great Britain, Denmark
Madeiran Petrel	*Oceanodroma castro*	Atlantic	Great Britain, Spain
Magnificent Frigate-bird	*Fregata magnificens*	South Seas	Great Britain, France
Bald Ibis	*Geronticus eremita*	Africa	Spain
Black Duck	*Anas rubripes*	America	Great Britain
Bufflehead	*Bucephala albeola*	America	Great Britain, Iceland
Hooded Merganser	*Mergus cucullatus*	America	Great Britain
Swallow-tailed Kite	*Elanoides ferficatus*	America	Germany
American Kestrel	*Falco sparverius*	America	Denmark
Sora	*Porzana carolina*	America	Great Britain
Green-backed Gallinule	*Porphyrio madagascariensis*	Africa	Italy
American Purple Gallinule	*Porphyrula martinica*	America	Great Britain
White-tailed Plover	*Vanellus leucurus*	Asia	Russia, France, Malta
Western Sandpiper	*Calidris mauri*	America	Great Britain
Eskimo Curlew	*Numenius borealis*	America	Great Britain
Willet	*Catoptrophorus semipalmatus*	America	Sweden? France? Yugoslavia?
Lesser Crested Tern	*Sterna bengalensis*	Africa	Spain, France, Switzerland, Italy
Royal Tern	*Sterna maxima*	America, Africa	Great Britain
Forster's Tern	*Sterna forsteri*	America	Iceland
Bridled Tern	*Sterna anaethetus*	America, Africa	Great Britain
Noddy	*Anous stolidus*	South Seas	Germany
Crested Auklet	*Aethia cristatella*	North Pacific	Iceland
Parakeet Auklet	*Cyclorrhynchus psittacula*	North Pacific	Sweden
Spotted Sandgrouse	*Pterocles senegallus*	Africa, Asia	Italy
Chestnut-bellied Sandgrouse	*Pterocles exustus*	Africa	Hungary
American Nighthawk	*Chordeiles minor*	America	Great Britain, Finland
Belted Kingfisher	*Ceryle alcyon*	America	Iceland, Holland
Little Swift	*Apus affinis*	Africa	Ireland
Needle-tailed Swift	*Chaetura caudacuta*	Asia	Great Britain, Italy, Finland
Yellow-bellied Sapsucker	*Sphyrapicus varius*	America	Iceland
Desert Lark	*Ammomanes deserti*	Africa, Asia	Spain
Bar-tailed Desert Lark	*Ammomanes cincturus*	Africa, Asia	Malta
Hooper Lark	*Alaemon alaudipes*	Africa, Asia	Malta
Indian Sand Lark	*Calandrella raytal*	Asia	Spain
Bimaculated Lark	*Melanocorypha bimaculata*	Asia	Great Britain, Italy, Finland
Common Bulbul	*Pycnonotus parbatus*	Africa, Asia	Spain
Brown Thrasher	*Toxostoma rufum*	America	Great Britain
Isabelline Shrike	*Lanius isabellinus*	Asia	Great Britain, Germany
Daurian Jackdaw	*Corvus dauuricus*	Asia	Finland
Gray's Grasshopper Warbler	*Locustella fasciolata*	Asia	France, Denmark
Thick-billed Reed Warbler	*Acrocephalus aedon*	Asia	Great Britain
White-crowned Black Wheatear	*Oenanthe leucopyga*	Africa, Asia	Malta
Moussier's Redstart	*Phoenicurus moussieri*	Africa	Italy, Malta
Tickell's Thrush	*Turdus unicolor*	Asia	Germany
Narcissus Flycatcher	*Ficedula narcissina*	Asia	France
Red-eyed Vireo	*Vireo olivaceus*	America	Great Britain, Iceland, Germany
Black-and-white Warbler	*Mniotilta varia*	America	Great Britain
Tennessee Warbler	*Vermivora peregrina*	America	Iceland

Common Name	Scientific Name	Origin	Observed
Parula Warbler	*Parula americana*	America	Iceland
Yellow Warbler	*Dendroica petechia*	America	Great Britain
Myrtle Warbler	*Dendroica coronata*	America	Great Britain
Black-throated Green Warbler	*Dendroica virens*	America	Germany
Northern Waterthrush	*Seiurus noveboracensis*	America	Great Britain, France
Yellowthroat	*Geothlypis trichas*	America	Great Britain
American Redstart	*Setophaga ruticilla*	America	France, Great Britain
Bobolink	*Dolichonyx oryzivorus*	America	Great Britain
Yellow-headed Blackbird	*Xanthocephalus xanthocephalus*	America	Denmark, Sweden?
Baltimore Oriole	*Icterus galbula*	America	Great Britain, Iceland
Summer Tanager	*Piranga rubra*	America	Great Britain
Oriental Greenfinch	*Carduelis sinica*	Asia	Denmark
Song Sparrow	*Melospiza melodia*	America	Great Britain
Fox Sparrow	*Passerella iliaca*	America	Great Britain, Iceland, Germany, Italy
White-throated Sparrow	*Zonotrichia albicollis*	America	Great Britain
Slate-coloured Junco	*Junco hyemalis*	America	Great Britain, Italy, Iceland
Rose-breasted Grosbeak	*Pheucticus ludovicianus*	America	Great Britain
Rufous-sided Towhee	*Pipilo erythrophthalmus*	America	Great Britain
Indigo Bunting	*Passerina cyanea*	America	Iceland
Siberian Meadow Bunting	*Emberiza cioides*	Asia	Italy
Yellow-browed Bunting	*Emberiza chrysophrys*	Asia	Belgium, France
Chestnut Bunting	*Emberiza rutila*	Asia	Holland, France
Black-faced Bunting	*Emberiza spodocephala*	Asia	Germany
Pallas' Reed Bunting	*Emberiza pallasi*	Asia	Denmark

Distribution Maps

The distribution maps show the breeding range in red and the wintering range in blue. Purple indicates the areas where the bird occurs all year round. Roman numerals indicate the months of the year when the species occurs in its breeding and wintering areas. Arrows indicate the general direction followed in the course of spring and autumn migrations. Birds which occur irregularly during invasions have the direction of these mass movements indicated with arrows.

Index to the distribution maps

1   Black-throated Diver
    Gavia arctica

2   Red-throated Diver
    Gavia stellata

3   Great Northern Diver
    Gavia immer

4   White-billed Diver
    Gavia adamsii

5   Great Crested Grebe
    Podiceps cristatus

6   Red-necked Grebe
    Podiceps grisegena

7   Horned Grebe
    Podiceps auritus

8   Black-necked Grebe
    Podiceps caspicus

9   Little Grebe
    Podiceps ruficollis

10   Fulmar
     Fulmarus glacialis

11   Manx Shearwater
     Puffinus puffinus

12   Great Shearwater
     Puffinus gravis

13   Cory's Shearwater
     Procellaria diomedea

14   Sooty Shearwater
     Puffinus griseus

15   Wilson's Petrel
     Oceanites oceanicus

16   Leach's Petrel
     Oceanodroma leucorhoa

17   Storm Petrel
     Hydrobates pelagicus

18   Gannet
     Sula bassana

19   White Pelican
     Pelecanus onocrotalus

20   Dalmatian Pelican
     Pelecanus crispus

21   Cormorant
     Phalacrocorax carbo

22   Shag
     Phalacrocorax aristotelis

23   Pygmy Cormorant
     Phalacrocorax pygmaeus

24   Bittern
     Botaurus stellaris

25   Little Bittern
     Ixobrychus minutus

26   Little Egret
     Egretta garzetta

27   Great White Heron
     Egretta alba

28   Squacco Heron
     Ardeola ralloides

29   Cattle Egret
     Ardeola ibis

30   Grey Heron
     Ardea cinerea

31   Purple Heron
     Ardea purpurea

32   Night Heron
     Nycticorax nycticorax

33   Glossy Ibis
     Plegadis falcinellus

34   White Stork
     Ciconia ciconia

35   Black Stork
     Ciconia nigra

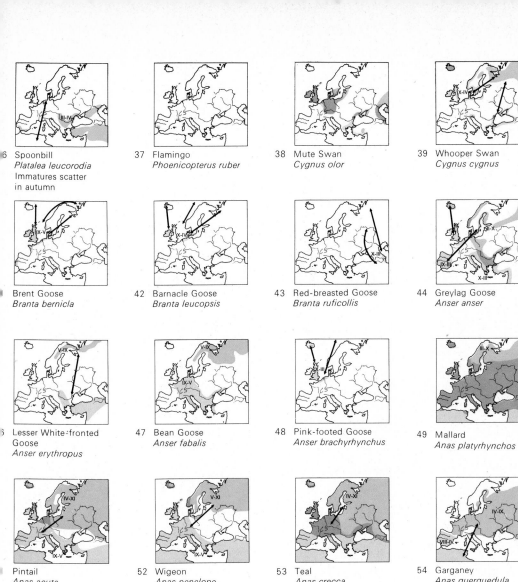
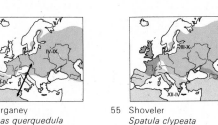
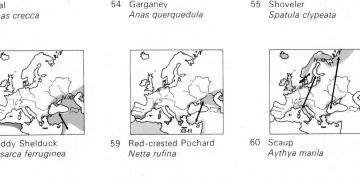
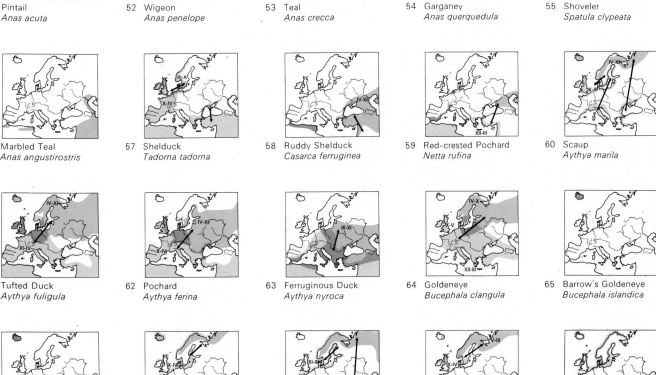

36 Spoonbill
Platalea leucorodia
Immatures scatter
in autumn

37 Flamingo
Phoenicopterus ruber

38 Mute Swan
Cygnus olor

39 Whooper Swan
Cygnus cygnus

40 Bewick's Swan
Cygnus bewickii

41 Brent Goose
Branta bernicla

42 Barnacle Goose
Branta leucopsis

43 Red-breasted Goose
Branta ruficollis

44 Greylag Goose
Anser anser

45 White-fronted Goose
Anser albifrons

46 Lesser White-fronted
Goose
Anser erythropus

47 Bean Goose
Anser fabalis

48 Pink-footed Goose
Anser brachyrhynchus

49 Mallard
Anas platyrhynchos

50 Gadwall
Anas strepera

51 Pintail
Anas acuta

52 Wigeon
Anas penelope

53 Teal
Anas crecca

54 Garganey
Anas querquedula

55 Shoveler
Spatula clypeata

56 Marbled Teal
Anas angustirostris

57 Shelduck
Tadorna tadorna

58 Ruddy Shelduck
Casarca ferruginea

59 Red-crested Pochard
Netta rufina

60 Scaup
Aythya marila

61 Tufted Duck
Aythya fuligula

62 Pochard
Aythya ferina

63 Ferruginous Duck
Aythya nyroca

64 Goldeneye
Bucephala clangula

65 Barrow's Goldeneye
Bucephala islandica

66 Harlequin Duck
Histrionicus histrionicus

67 Long-tailed Duck
Clangula hyemalis

68 Velvet Scoter
Melanitta fusca

69 Common Scoter
Melanitta nigra

70 Eider
Somateria mollissima

71 King Eider
Somateria spectabilis

72 Red-breasted Merganser
Mergus serrator

73 Goosander
Mergus merganser

74 Smew
Mergus albellus

75 White-headed Duck
Oxyura leucocephala

76 Egyptian Vulture
Neophron percnopterus

77 Griffon Vulture
Gyps fulvus

78 Black Vulture
Aegypius monachus

79 Lammergeyer
Gypaëtus barbatus

80 White-tailed Eagle
Haliaeetus albicilla

81 Pallas' Sea Eagle
Haliaeetus leucoryphus

82 Golden Eagle
Aquila chrysaetos

83 Imperial Eagle
Aquila heliaca

84 Steppe Eagle
Aquila rapax

85 Spotted Eagle
Aquila clanga

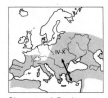

86 Lesser Spotted Eagle
Aquila pomarina

87 Bonelli's Eagle
Hieraaetus fasciatus

88 Booted Eagle
Hieraaetus pennatus

89 Short-toed Eagle
Circaetus gallicus

90 Buzzard
Buteo buteo

91 Rough-legged Buzzard
Buteo lagopus

92 Long-legged Buzzard
Buteo rufinus

93 Honey Buzzard
Pernis apivorus

94 Goshawk
Accipiter gentilis

95 Sparrowhawk
Accipiter nisus

96 Levant Sparrowhawk
Accipiter brevipes

97 Red Kite
Milvus milvus

98 Black Kite
Milvus migrans

99 Black-winged Kite
Elanus caeruleus

100 Osprey
Pandion haliaetus

101 Marsh Harrier
Circus aeruginosus

102 Hen Harrier
Circus cyaneus

103 Pallid Harrier
Circus macrourus

104 Montagu's Harrier
Circus pygargus

105 Gyrfalcon
Falco rusticolus

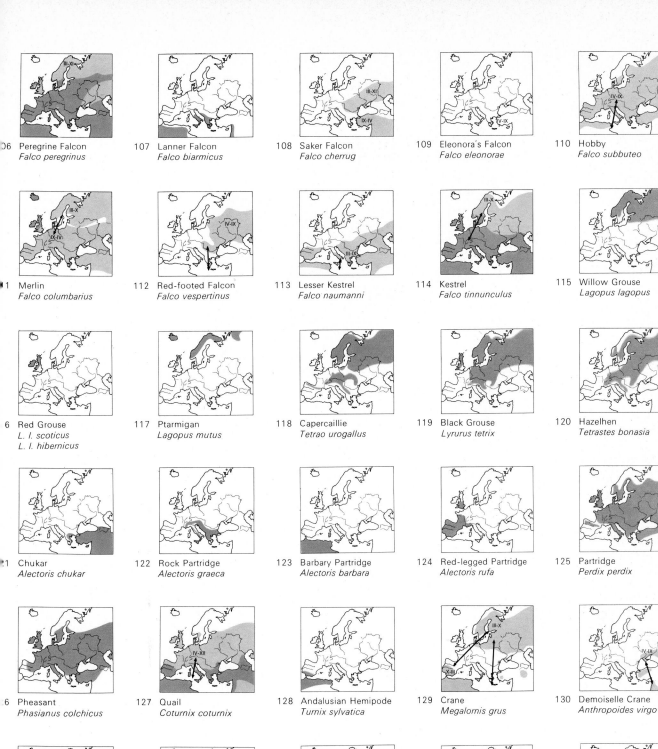

106 Peregrine Falcon
Falco peregrinus

107 Lanner Falcon
Falco biarmicus

108 Saker Falcon
Falco cherrug

109 Eleonora's Falcon
Falco eleonorae

110 Hobby
Falco subbuteo

111 Merlin
Falco columbarius

112 Red-footed Falcon
Falco vespertinus

113 Lesser Kestrel
Falco naumanni

114 Kestrel
Falco tinnunculus

115 Willow Grouse
Lagopus lagopus

116 Red Grouse
L. l. scoticus
L. l. hibernicus

117 Ptarmigan
Lagopus mutus

118 Capercaillie
Tetrao urogallus

119 Black Grouse
Lyrurus tetrix

120 Hazelhen
Tetrastes bonasia

121 Chukar
Alectoris chukar

122 Rock Partridge
Alectoris graeca

123 Barbary Partridge
Alectoris barbara

124 Red-legged Partridge
Alectoris rufa

125 Partridge
Perdix perdix

126 Pheasant
Phasianus colchicus

127 Quail
Coturnix coturnix

128 Andalusian Hemipode
Turnix sylvatica

129 Crane
Megalornis grus

130 Demoiselle Crane
Anthropoides virgo

131 Great Bustard
Otis tarda

132 Little Bustard
Otis tetrax

133 Water Rail
Rallus aquaticus

134 Spotted Crake
Porzana porzana

135 Baillon's Crake
Porzana pusilla

136 Little Crake
Porzana parva

137 Corncrake
Crex crex

138 Purple Gallinule
Porphyrio porphyrio

139 Moorhen
Gallinula chloropus

140 Coot
Fulica atra

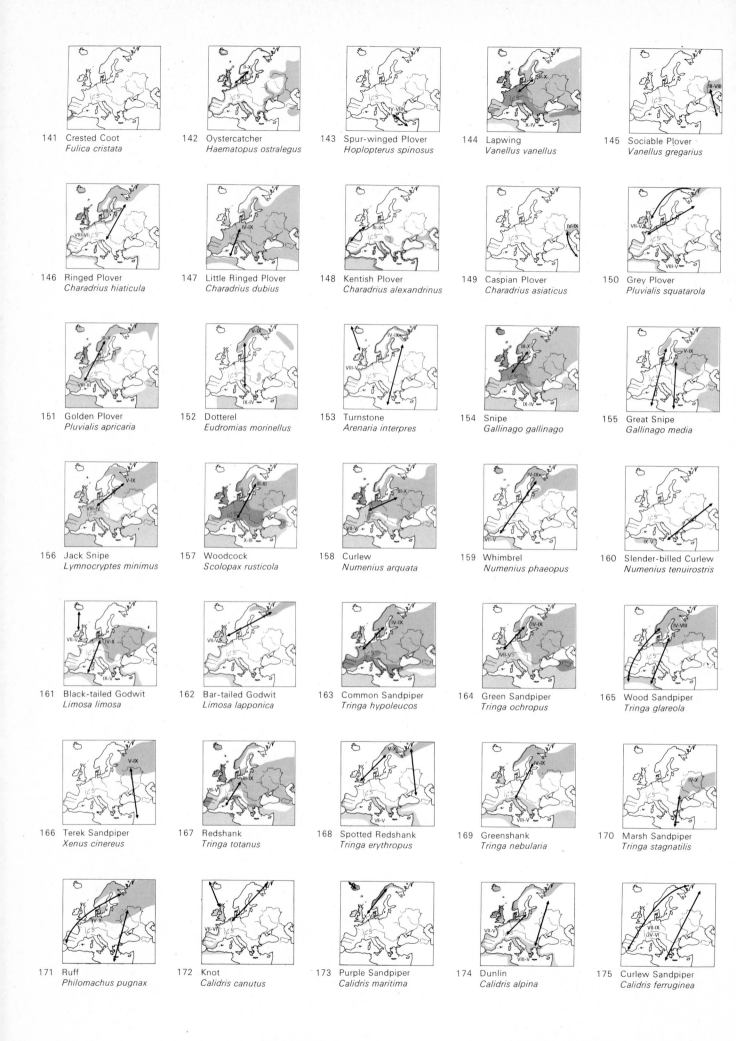

141 Crested Coot
Fulica cristata

142 Oystercatcher
Haematopus ostralegus

143 Spur-winged Plover
Hoplopterus spinosus

144 Lapwing
Vanellus vanellus

145 Sociable Plover
Vanellus gregarius

146 Ringed Plover
Charadrius hiaticula

147 Little Ringed Plover
Charadrius dubius

148 Kentish Plover
Charadrius alexandrinus

149 Caspian Plover
Charadrius asiaticus

150 Grey Plover
Pluvialis squatarola

151 Golden Plover
Pluvialis apricaria

152 Dotterel
Eudromias morinellus

153 Turnstone
Arenaria interpres

154 Snipe
Gallinago gallinago

155 Great Snipe
Gallinago media

156 Jack Snipe
Lymnocryptes minimus

157 Woodcock
Scolopax rusticola

158 Curlew
Numenius arquata

159 Whimbrel
Numenius phaeopus

160 Slender-billed Curlew
Numenius tenuirostris

161 Black-tailed Godwit
Limosa limosa

162 Bar-tailed Godwit
Limosa lapponica

163 Common Sandpiper
Tringa hypoleucos

164 Green Sandpiper
Tringa ochropus

165 Wood Sandpiper
Tringa glareola

166 Terek Sandpiper
Xenus cinereus

167 Redshank
Tringa totanus

168 Spotted Redshank
Tringa erythropus

169 Greenshank
Tringa nebularia

170 Marsh Sandpiper
Tringa stagnatilis

171 Ruff
Philomachus pugnax

172 Knot
Calidris canutus

173 Purple Sandpiper
Calidris maritima

174 Dunlin
Calidris alpina

175 Curlew Sandpiper
Calidris ferruginea

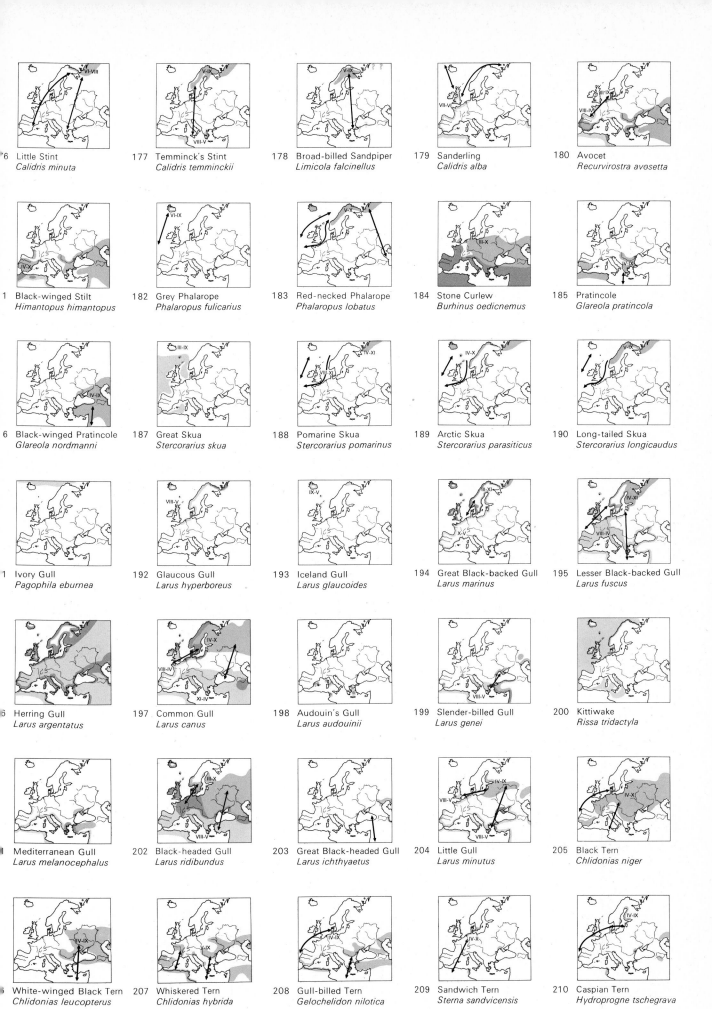

176 Little Stint
Calidris minuta

177 Temminck's Stint
Calidris temminckii

178 Broad-billed Sandpiper
Limicola falcinellus

179 Sanderling
Calidris alba

180 Avocet
Recurvirostra avosetta

181 Black-winged Stilt
Himantopus himantopus

182 Grey Phalarope
Phalaropus fulicarius

183 Red-necked Phalarope
Phalaropus lobatus

184 Stone Curlew
Burhinus oedicnemus

185 Pratincole
Glareola pratincola

186 Black-winged Pratincole
Glareola nordmanni

187 Great Skua
Stercorarius skua

188 Pomarine Skua
Stercorarius pomarinus

189 Arctic Skua
Stercorarius parasiticus

190 Long-tailed Skua
Stercorarius longicaudus

191 Ivory Gull
Pagophila eburnea

192 Glaucous Gull
Larus hyperboreus

193 Iceland Gull
Larus glaucoides

194 Great Black-backed Gull
Larus marinus

195 Lesser Black-backed Gull
Larus fuscus

196 Herring Gull
Larus argentatus

197 Common Gull
Larus canus

198 Audouin's Gull
Larus audouinii

199 Slender-billed Gull
Larus genei

200 Kittiwake
Rissa tridactyla

201 Mediterranean Gull
Larus melanocephalus

202 Black-headed Gull
Larus ridibundus

203 Great Black-headed Gull
Larus ichthyaetus

204 Little Gull
Larus minutus

205 Black Tern
Chlidonias niger

206 White-winged Black Tern
Chlidonias leucopterus

207 Whiskered Tern
Chlidonias hybrida

208 Gull-billed Tern
Gelochelidon nilotica

209 Sandwich Tern
Sterna sandvicensis

210 Caspian Tern
Hydroprogne tschegrava

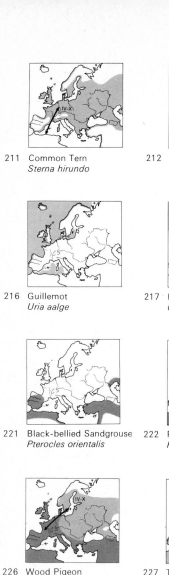
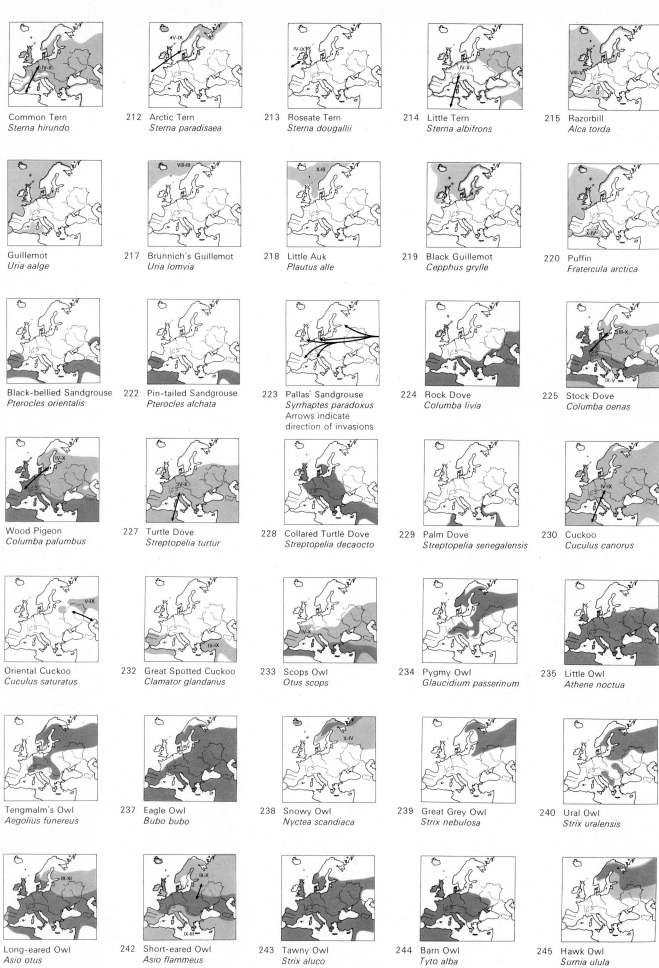

211 Common Tern
Sterna hirundo

212 Arctic Tern
Sterna paradisaea

213 Roseate Tern
Sterna dougallii

214 Little Tern
Sterna albifrons

215 Razorbill
Alca torda

216 Guillemot
Uria aalge

217 Brünnich's Guillemot
Uria lomvia

218 Little Auk
Plautus alle

219 Black Guillemot
Cepphus grylle

220 Puffin
Fratercula arctica

221 Black-bellied Sandgrouse
Pterocles orientalis

222 Pin-tailed Sandgrouse
Pterocles alchata

223 Pallas' Sandgrouse
Syrrhaptes paradoxus
Arrows indicate
direction of invasions

224 Rock Dove
Columba livia

225 Stock Dove
Columba oenas

226 Wood Pigeon
Columba palumbus

227 Turtle Dove
Streptopelia turtur

228 Collared Turtle Dove
Streptopelia decaocto

229 Palm Dove
Streptopelia senegalensis

230 Cuckoo
Cuculus canorus

231 Oriental Cuckoo
Cuculus saturatus

232 Great Spotted Cuckoo
Clamator glandarius

233 Scops Owl
Otus scops

234 Pygmy Owl
Glaucidium passerinum

235 Little Owl
Athene noctua

236 Tengmalm's Owl
Aegolius funereus

237 Eagle Owl
Bubo bubo

238 Snowy Owl
Nyctea scandiaca

239 Great Grey Owl
Strix nebulosa

240 Ural Owl
Strix uralensis

241 Long-eared Owl
Asio otus

242 Short-eared Owl
Asio flammeus

243 Tawny Owl
Strix aluco

244 Barn Owl
Tyto alba

245 Hawk Owl
Surnia ulula

46 Nightjar
Caprimulgus europaeus

247 Red-necked Nightjar
Caprimulgus ruficollis

248 Swift
Apus apus

249 White-rumped Swift
Apus caffer

250 Pallid Swift
Apus pallidus

51 Alpine Swift
Apus melba

252 Kingfisher
Alcedo atthis

253 Bee-eater
Merops apiaster

254 Blue-cheeked Bee-eater
Merops superciliosus

255 Roller
Coracias garrulus

56 Hoopoe
Upupa epops

257 Green Woodpecker
Picus viridis

258 Grey-headed
Woodpecker
Picus canus

259 Great Spotted
Woodpecker
Dendrocopos major

260 Syrian Woodpecker
Dendrocopos syriacus

61 Middle Spotted
Woodpecker
Dendrocopos medius

262 Lesser Spotted
Woodpecker
Dendrocopos minor

263 White-backed
Woodpecker
Dendrocopos leucotos

264 Three-toed Woodpecker
Picoides tridactylus

265 Black Woodpecker
Dryocopus martius

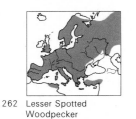   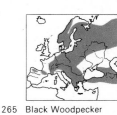 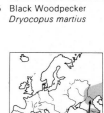

6 Wryneck
Jynx torquilla

267 Short-toed Lark
Calandrella cinerea

268 Lesser Short-toed Lark
Calandrella rufescens

269 Calandra Lark
Melanocorypha calandra

270 White-winged Lark
Melanocorypha leucoptera

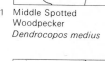   

1 Black Lark
Melanocorypha yeltoniensis

272 Crested Lark
Galerida cristata

273 Thekla Lark
Galerida theklae

274 Skylark
Alauda arvensis

275 Woodlark
Lullula arborea

   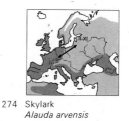 

6 Shore Lark
Eremophila alpestris

277 Sand Martin
Riparia riparia

278 Crag Martin
Hirundo rupestris

279 Swallow
Hirundo rustica

280 Red-rumped Swallow
Hirundo daurica

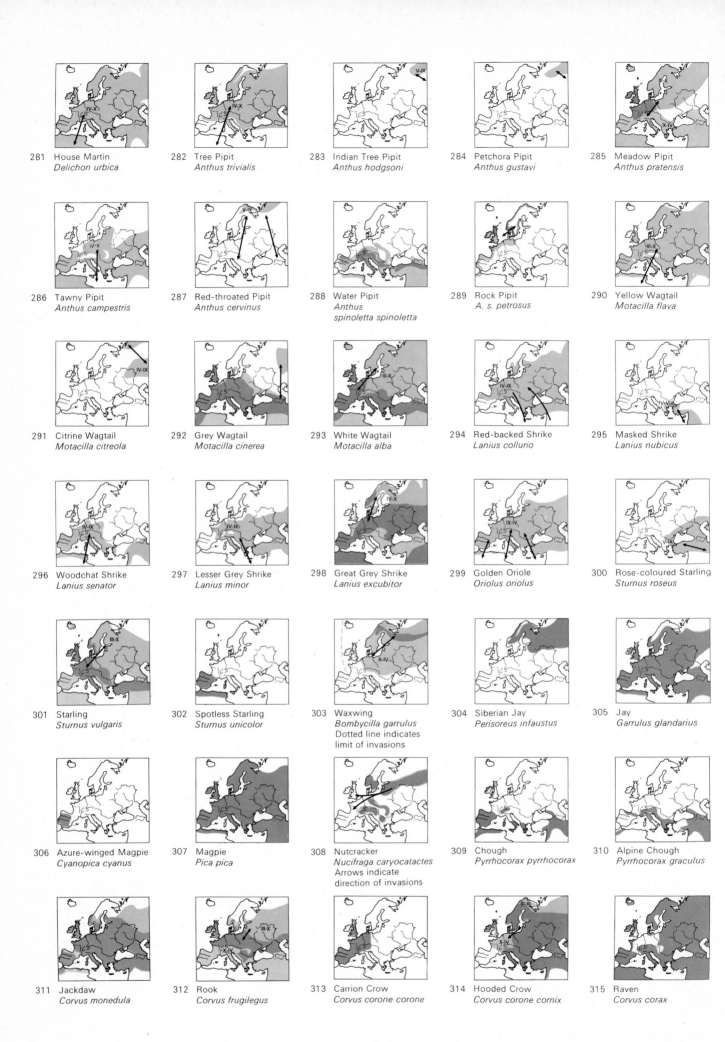

281 House Martin
Delichon urbica

282 Tree Pipit
Anthus trivialis

283 Indian Tree Pipit
Anthus hodgsoni

284 Petchora Pipit
Anthus gustavi

285 Meadow Pipit
Anthus pratensis

286 Tawny Pipit
Anthus campestris

287 Red-throated Pipit
Anthus cervinus

288 Water Pipit
*Anthus
spinoletta spinoletta*

289 Rock Pipit
A. s. petrosus

290 Yellow Wagtail
Motacilla flava

291 Citrine Wagtail
Motacilla citreola

292 Grey Wagtail
Motacilla cinerea

293 White Wagtail
Motacilla alba

294 Red-backed Shrike
Lanius collurio

295 Masked Shrike
Lanius nubicus

296 Woodchat Shrike
Lanius senator

297 Lesser Grey Shrike
Lanius minor

298 Great Grey Shrike
Lanius excubitor

299 Golden Oriole
Oriolus oriolus

300 Rose-coloured Starling
Sturnus roseus

301 Starling
Sturnus vulgaris

302 Spotless Starling
Sturnus unicolor

303 Waxwing
Bombycilla garrulus
Dotted line indicates
limit of invasions

304 Siberian Jay
Perisoreus infaustus

305 Jay
Garrulus glandarius

306 Azure-winged Magpie
Cyanopica cyanus

307 Magpie
Pica pica

308 Nutcracker
Nucifraga caryocatactes
Arrows indicate
direction of invasions

309 Chough
Pyrrhocorax pyrrhocorax

310 Alpine Chough
Pyrrhocorax graculus

311 Jackdaw
Corvus monedula

312 Rook
Corvus frugilegus

313 Carrion Crow
Corvus corone corone

314 Hooded Crow
Corvus corone cornix

315 Raven
Corvus corax

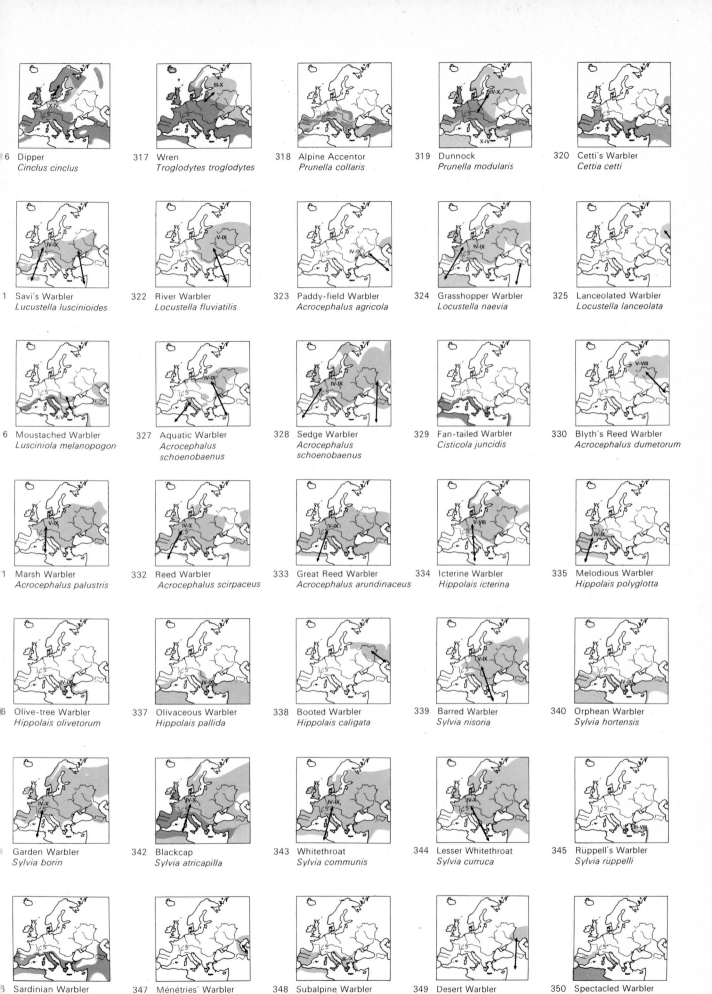

316 Dipper
Cinclus cinclus

317 Wren
Troglodytes troglodytes

318 Alpine Accentor
Prunella collaris

319 Dunnock
Prunella modularis

320 Cetti's Warbler
Cettia cetti

321 Savi's Warbler
Lucustella luscinioides

322 River Warbler
Locustella fluviatilis

323 Paddy-field Warbler
Acrocephalus agricola

324 Grasshopper Warbler
Locustella naevia

325 Lanceolated Warbler
Locustella lanceolata

326 Moustached Warbler
Lusciniola melanopogon

327 Aquatic Warbler
*Acrocephalus
schoenobaenus*

328 Sedge Warbler
*Acrocephalus
schoenobaenus*

329 Fan-tailed Warbler
Cisticola juncidis

330 Blyth's Reed Warbler
Acrocephalus dumetorum

331 Marsh Warbler
Acrocephalus palustris

332 Reed Warbler
Acrocephalus scirpaceus

333 Great Reed Warbler
Acrocephalus arundinaceus

334 Icterine Warbler
Hippolais icterina

335 Melodious Warbler
Hippolais polyglotta

336 Olive-tree Warbler
Hippolais olivetorum

337 Olivaceous Warbler
Hippolais pallida

338 Booted Warbler
Hippolais caligata

339 Barred Warbler
Sylvia nisoria

340 Orphean Warbler
Sylvia hortensis

341 Garden Warbler
Sylvia borin

342 Blackcap
Sylvia atricapilla

343 Whitethroat
Sylvia communis

344 Lesser Whitethroat
Sylvia curruca

345 Rüppell's Warbler
Sylvia rüppelli

346 Sardinian Warbler
Sylvia melanocephala

347 Ménétries' Warbler
Sylvia mystacea

348 Subalpine Warbler
Sylvia cantillans

349 Desert Warbler
Sylvia nana

350 Spectacled Warbler
Sylvia conspicillata

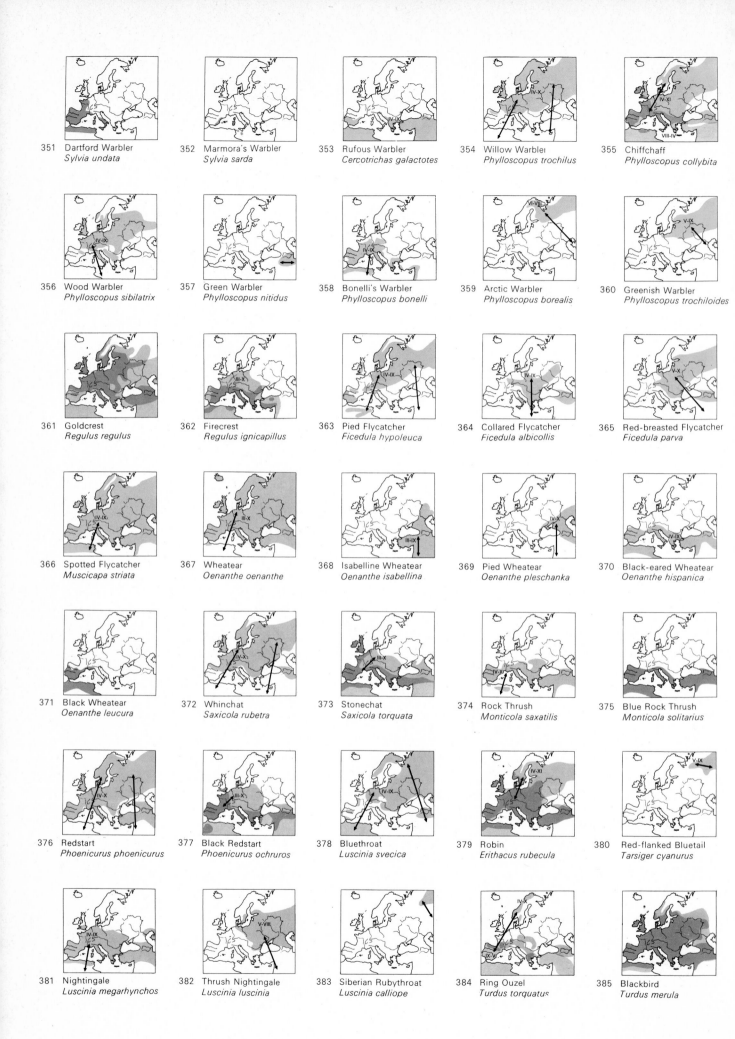

351 Dartford Warbler
Sylvia undata

352 Marmora's Warbler
Sylvia sarda

353 Rufous Warbler
Cercotrichas galactotes

354 Willow Warbler
Phylloscopus trochilus

355 Chiffchaff
Phylloscopus collybita

356 Wood Warbler
Phylloscopus sibilatrix

357 Green Warbler
Phylloscopus nitidus

358 Bonelli's Warbler
Phylloscopus bonelli

359 Arctic Warbler
Phylloscopus borealis

360 Greenish Warbler
Phylloscopus trochiloides

361 Goldcrest
Regulus regulus

362 Firecrest
Regulus ignicapillus

363 Pied Flycatcher
Ficedula hypoleuca

364 Collared Flycatcher
Ficedula albicollis

365 Red-breasted Flycatcher
Ficedula parva

366 Spotted Flycatcher
Muscicapa striata

367 Wheatear
Oenanthe oenanthe

368 Isabelline Wheatear
Oenanthe isabellina

369 Pied Wheatear
Oenanthe pleschanka

370 Black-eared Wheatear
Oenanthe hispanica

371 Black Wheatear
Oenanthe leucura

372 Whinchat
Saxicola rubetra

373 Stonechat
Saxicola torquata

374 Rock Thrush
Monticola saxatilis

375 Blue Rock Thrush
Monticola solitarius

376 Redstart
Phoenicurus phoenicurus

377 Black Redstart
Phoenicurus ochruros

378 Bluethroat
Luscinia svecica

379 Robin
Erithacus rubecula

380 Red-flanked Bluetail
Tarsiger cyanurus

381 Nightingale
Luscinia megarhynchos

382 Thrush Nightingale
Luscinia luscinia

383 Siberian Rubythroat
Luscinia calliope

384 Ring Ouzel
Turdus torquatus

385 Blackbird
Turdus merula

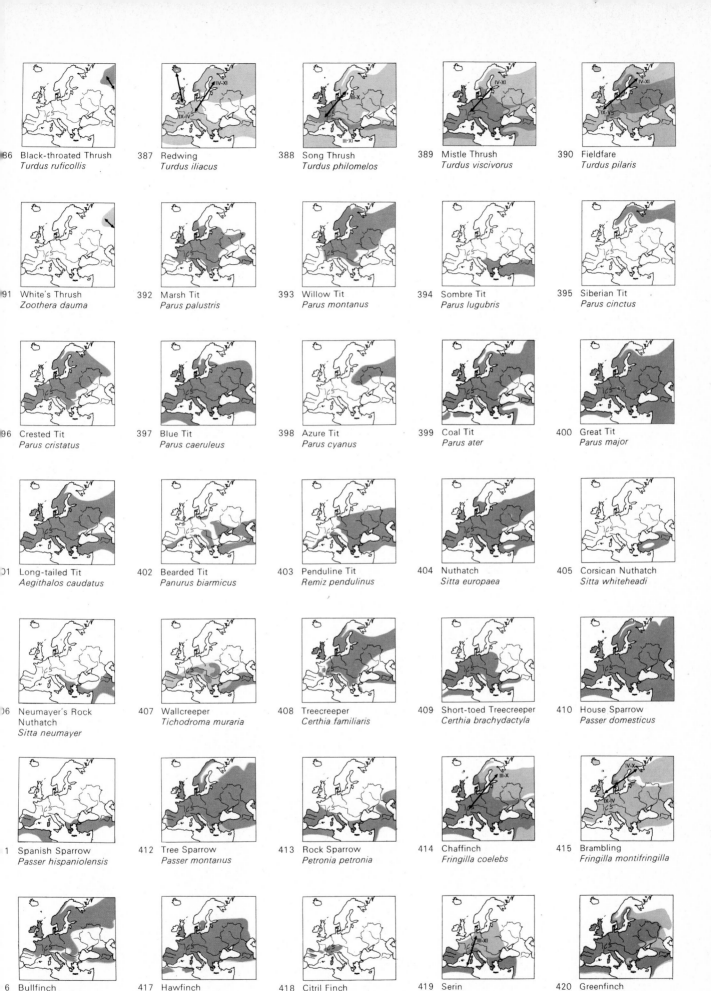

386 Black-throated Thrush
Turdus ruficollis

387 Redwing
Turdus iliacus

388 Song Thrush
Turdus philomelos

389 Mistle Thrush
Turdus viscivorus

390 Fieldfare
Turdus pilaris

391 White's Thrush
Zoothera dauma

392 Marsh Tit
Parus palustris

393 Willow Tit
Parus montanus

394 Sombre Tit
Parus lugubris

395 Siberian Tit
Parus cinctus

396 Crested Tit
Parus cristatus

397 Blue Tit
Parus caeruleus

398 Azure Tit
Parus cyanus

399 Coal Tit
Parus ater

400 Great Tit
Parus major

401 Long-tailed Tit
Aegithalos caudatus

402 Bearded Tit
Panurus biarmicus

403 Penduline Tit
Remiz pendulinus

404 Nuthatch
Sitta europaea

405 Corsican Nuthatch
Sitta whiteheadi

406 Neumayer's Rock Nuthatch
Sitta neumayer

407 Wallcreeper
Tichodroma muraria

408 Treecreeper
Certhia familiaris

409 Short-toed Treecreeper
Certhia brachydactyla

410 House Sparrow
Passer domesticus

411 Spanish Sparrow
Passer hispaniolensis

412 Tree Sparrow
Passer montanus

413 Rock Sparrow
Petronia petronia

414 Chaffinch
Fringilla coelebs

415 Brambling
Fringilla montifringilla

416 Bullfinch
Pyrrhula pyrrhula

417 Hawfinch
Coccothraustes coccothraustes

418 Citril Finch
Serinus citrinella

419 Serin
Serinus serinus

420 Greenfinch
Carduelis chloris

421 Siskin
Carduelis spinus

422 Goldfinch
Carduelis carduelis

423 Linnet
Acanthis cannabina

424 Twite
Acanthis flavirostris

425 Redpoll
Acanthis flammea

426 Arctic Redpoll
Acanthis hornemanni

427 Scarlet Grosbeak
Carpodacus erythrinus

428 Pine Grosbeak
Pinicola enucleator

429 Crossbill
Loxia curvirostra
Arrows indicate
direction of invasions

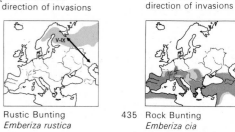

430 Parrot Crossbill
Loxia pytyopsittacus
Arrows indicate
direction of invasions

431 Two-barred Crossbill
Loxia leucoptera
Arrow indicates
direction of invasions

432 Corn Bunting
Emberiza calandra

433 Little Bunting
Emberiza pusilla

434 Rustic Bunting
Emberiza rustica

435 Rock Bunting
Emberiza cia

436 Ortolan Bunting
Emberiza hortulana

437 Cretzschmar's Bunting
Emberiza caesia

438 Red-headed Bunting
Emberiza bruniceps

439 Pine Bunting
Emberiza leucocephala

440 Cinereous Bunting
Emberiza cineracea

441 Reed Bunting
Emberiza schoeniclus

442 Yellowhammer
Emberiza citrinella

443 Yellow-breasted Bunting
Emberiza aureola

444 Cirl Bunting
Emberiza cirlus

445 Black-headed Bunting
Emberiza melanocephala

446 Lapland Bunting
Calcarius lapponicus

447 Snow Bunting
Plectrophenax nivalis

448 Snow Finch
Montifringilla nivalis

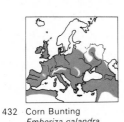

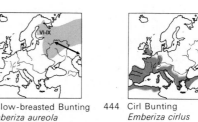

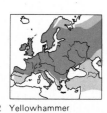

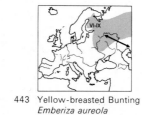

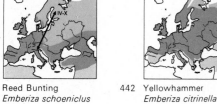

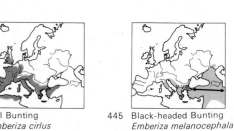
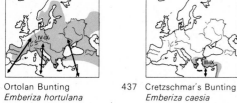

Bibliography

Hundreds of books on birds are published every year. Each country has its own extensive literature and a complete listing of books on European birds alone would take up more space than this entire volume. But some books are of special interest and below you will find a short list of the most important works on European birds. Besides the books on birds of a certain geographical region, many monographs treat individual birds or groups of birds, and the largest series of this kind are Collins' *New Naturalist* and Ziemsen's *Die Neue Brehm-bucherei*.

Bannerman, D.A. and Lodge, G.E. *The Birds of the British Isles*. 12 vols. London, 1953-63.

Bauer, K. and Rokitansky, G. *Die Vögel Österreichs, Kritische Übersicht der Bisher für Österreich nachgewiesenen Vogelarten und -Rassen*. Neusiedl, 1951

Bernis Madrazo, F. *Prontuario de la Avifauna Española (Incluyendo Aves de Portugal, Baleares y Canarias)*. Madrid, 1954.

British Ornithologists' Union. *Check-list of the Birds of Great Britain and Ireland*. London, 1952.

Cerny, W. et al. *Fauna CSSR—Ptaci (Vögel)*. Prague.

Curry-Lindahl, K. *Våra Fåglar i Norden*. 4 vols. Stockholm, 1959-63.

Dementiev, G.P. and Gladkov, N.A. *Birds of the USSR*. 6 vols. Moscow, 1951-54.

Etchécopar, R.D. and Hüe, F. (trans. by P. A. D. Hollom). *The Birds of North Africa from the Canary Islands to the Red Sea*. Edinburgh, 1967.

Eykman, C. *De Nederlandsche Vogels*. 3 vols. Wageningen, 1937-49.

Frieling, H. *Was fliegt den da?* Stuttgart, 1958.

Geroudet, P. *La Vie des Oiseaux*. 6 vols. Neuchatel and Paris, 1947-56.

Haller, W. *Unsere Vögel, Artenliste der Schwiezerischen Avifauna*. Aarau, 1954.

Hollom. P.A.D. *The Popular Handbook of British Birds*. London, 1962.

Hollom, P.A.D. *The Popular Handbook of Rarer British Birds*. London, 1960.

Hulten, M. and Wassenich, V. *Die Vogelfauna*. Luxembourg, 1960-61.

Ivanov, A.I., Portenko, L.A. et al. *Ptitsy SSSR Akademii Nauk*. Moscow, 1951-60.

Kennedy, P.G. et al. *The Birds of Ireland*. Edinburgh and London, 1954.

Keve, A. *Magyarorszag Madarainak Nevjegyzrke*. Budapest, 1960.

Lövenskiold, H.L. *Håndbok över Norges Fugler*. Oslo, 1947.

Lövenskiold, H.L. *Avifauna Svalbardensis*. Oslo, 1964.

Makatsch, W. *Die Vögel Europas*. Leipzig, 1966.

Makatsch, W. *Die Vogelwelt Macedoniens*. Leipzig, 1950.

Makatsch, W. *Verzeichnis der Vögel Deutschlands*. Radebeul and Berlin, 1957.

Matvejev, S.D. *Ornithogeographia Serbia (La Distribution et la Vie des Oiseaux en Serbie)*. Belgrade, 1950.

Mayaud, N. et al. *Inventaire des Oiseaux de France*. Paris, 1936.

Merikallio, E. *Finnish Birds*. Helsinki, 1958.

Niethammer, G. *Handbuch der Deutschen Vogelkunde*. 3 vols. Leipzig, 1937-42.

Niethammer, G. *Handbuch der Vögel Mitteleuropas*. Vol. 1. Frankfurt am Main, 1966.

Niethammer, G. et al. *Die Vögel Deutschlands: Artenliste*. Frankfurt am Main, 1964.

Pateff, P. *The Birds of Bulgaria*. Sofia, 1950.

Peterson, R.T. et al. *A Field Guide to the Birds of Britain and Europe*. London, 1966.

Salomonsen, F. *Oversigt over Danmarks Fugle*. Copenhagen, 1963.

Sokolowski, J. *Ptaki ziem Polskich*. 2 vols. Warsaw, 1958.

Sveriges Ornitologiska Förening. *Förteckning över Sveriges Fåglar*. Stockholm, 1951.

Tait, W.C. *Birds of Portugal*. London, 1924.

Thomson, A.L. (ed). *A New Dictionary of Birds*. London, 1964.

Timmermann, G. *Die Vögel Islands*. Reykjavik, 1938-49.

Vaurie, C. *The Birds of the Palearctic Fauna*. 2 vols. London, 1959-65.

Verheyen, R. *La Vie des Oiseaux*. Brussels, 1943-51.

Voous, K.H. *Atlas of European Birds*. London, 1960.

Witherby, H.F. et al. *The Handbook of British Birds*. 5 vols. London, 1949.

Ornithological Magazines

Magazines treating the various aspects of bird life are published in hundreds every year. Almost every country in the world and certainly most countries in Europe have several magazines of varying content and importance. Most are published by ornithological societies, some are published by museums and universities, and some are private publishing ventures. The most important European publications on ornithological subjects are listed below together with the society or institute publishing them. Where no such society or institute is mentioned, the publishing is commercial.

Austria	*Egretta. Vogelkundliche Nachrichten aus Österreich*	
Belgium	*Gerfaut*	Société Ornithologique de la Belgique
Denmark	*Dansk Ornithologisk Forenings Tidskrift*	Dansk Ornithologisk Forening
France	*L'Oiseau*	Société Ornithologique de France
	Alauda	
Finland	*Ornis Fennica*	Ornitologiska Föreningen i Finland
Germany	*Journal für Ornithologie*	Deutsche Ornithologische Gesellschaft
	Anzeiger für Ornithologie	Ornithologische Gesellschaft in Bayern
Great Britain and Ireland	*British Birds*	
	Ibis	British Ornithologists' Union
	Bird Study	British Trust for Ornithology
	Irish Bird Report	Irish Ornithologists' Club
	Annual Report	The Wildfowl Trust
	Birds	The Royal Society for the Protection of Birds
	Scottish Birds	Scottish Ornithologists' Club
	Zoological Record: Aves	Zoological Society of London
Hungary	*Aquila*	Institutus Ornithologicus Hungaricus
Italy	*Rivista Italiana di Ornitologia*	
	Avocetta	Associazione Ornitologica Italiana
Netherlands	*Ardea*	Nederlandsche Ornithologische Vereeniging
	Limosa	Club van Nederlandsche Vogelkundigen
Norway	*Sterna*	Norsk Ornitologisk Forening
Poland	*Acta Ornithologica*	Musei Zoologici Polonici
Spain	*Ardeola*	Sociedad Española de Ornitologia
Switzerland	*Nos Oiseaux*	Société Romande pour l'Etude et la Protection des Oiseaux
Sweden	*Vår Fågelvärld*	Sveriges Ornitologiska Förening
Yugoslavia	*Larus*	Institute of Biology. University of Zagreb

Recordings

Records of bird-songs and of calls are becoming increasingly popular. They are extremely useful as an aid in identification besides being a pleasure to listen to. The most important European series are listed below. Many other valuable records are available, but the ones listed cover a large number of species in a more or less systematic order.

Fentaloff, C., Thielcke, G. and Tretzel, E. *Stimmen Einheimischer Vögel*. Kosmos. Stuttgart.

Kirby, J. *Listen . . . the Birds*. European Phono Club. Amsterdam.

North, M.E.W. and Simms, E. *Witherby's Sound Guide to British Birds*. London.

Palmer, S. *Radions Fågel Skivor*. Sveriges Radio. Stockholm.

Roche, J.-C. *Oiseaux en Camargue*. Pacific. Neuilly.

Roche, J.-C. *Oiseaux en Bretagne*. Pacific. Neuilly.

Roche, J.-C. *Oiseaux en Soleil*. Pacific. Neuilly.

Roche, J.-C. *Guide Sonore des Oiseaux d'Europe*. Jean-Claude Roche. Collobrières.

Veprintsev, B. *The Voices of Birds in Wild Nature*. Union Studio of Disc Recording. Moscow.

Wahlstrøm, S. *Våra Svenska Fåglar i Ton*. AB Svensk Litteratur. Stockholm.

Index
Asterisks refer to illustrations